# The Professional Counselor

## A Process Guide to Helping
### Third Edition

**Harold L. Hackney**
*Fairfield University*

**L. Sherilyn Cormier**
*West Virginia University*

**Allyn and Bacon**
*Boston • London • Toronto • Sydney • Tokyo • Singapore*

*Vice President, Education:* Nancy Forsyth
*Series Editor:* Ray Short
*Marketing Manager:* Kathy Hunter
*Senior Production Administrator:* Marjorie Payne
*Editorial Assistant:* Christine Shaw
*Cover Administrator:* Linda Knowles
*Composition/Prepress Buyer:* Linda Cox
*Manufacturing Buyer:* Megan Cochran
*Editorial-Production Service:* Chestnut Hill Enterprises, Inc.

**Library of Congress Cataloging-in-Publication Data**

Hackney, Harold
    The professional counselor : a process guide to helping / Harold
Hackney, L. Sherilyn Cormier. — 3rd ed.
      p.  cm.
    Cormier's name appears first on previous ed.
    Includes bibliographical references and index.
    ISBN 0-205-19192-4 (alk. paper)
    1. Mental health counseling.  2. Counseling.  I. Cormier, L.
Sherilyn (Louise Sherilyn)  II. Title.
RC466.C67  1995
616.89—dc20                         95-23597
                                          CIP

Printed in the United States of America

10  9  8  7  6  5  4  3  2  1      00  99  98  97  96  95

# Contents

# *Preface*

This is a book about the counseling process. When asked what they do in counseling, counselors tend to identify with counseling theories. "I am behavioral," or "I am systemic," etc. However, theory is the cognitive map one uses when working with a client. Theory points to the ways one thinks about problems, about how human beings change their behavior, their attitudes, or their ways of experiencing life. Process, on the other hand, is the means by which one implements a counseling theory—what one *does* when one is practicing that theory.

Counseling process had its roots in Freud's psychoanalysis. His "talking cure" approach, in which the therapist was a dispassionate listener and interpreter, came to be called the psychoanalytic *method*. That method, or process, was a broad, macroscopic approach to the patient's internal world. As behaviorism began to impact the counseling movement, and particularly, as the work of Robert Carkhuff and Allen E. Ivey began to influence counseling, the counseling process became much more of a microscopic approach. In fact, Ivey described his method as *microcounseling*.

Counseling process has taken yet another turn in the past five years. We have come to realize that what works with one client of a particular ethno-cultural background may prove ineffective with a client of a different ethno-cultural background. Consequently, counselors must have some expertise in multicultural processes. This awareness has led counselors back to a *macro-method* approach to counseling process, which calls upon the counselor to view the client's world through the client's cultural *lens*, gender *lens*, and racial *lens*. The term, *multicultural counseling*, has come to be identified with this approach.

We have attempted to reflect this movement in this third edition of *The Professional Counselor: A Process Guide to Helping*. Each chapter attempts to reveal the counseling process as it is influenced by multicultural thinking. While we continue to incorporate the five stages of counseling and the various theory-based interventions that are used in the process, we also modify both the approach to and impact of those counselor activities to reflect the more complex world of multicultural counseling.

The reader will find familiar chapter titles with one notable exception. We have infused material contained in Chapter 12 of the previous edition into the first eleven chapters. And we have added a new Chapter 12 which examines three auxiliary practices of the professional counselor: crisis intervention, consultation, and conflict resolution. Each of these practices has grown in its importance in the past decade. crisis intervention reflects the growing demand by our society for immediate intervention services when crises occur. This service can range from the telephone crisis hotline to the local elementary school's Student Assistance Team or the community crisis response team. Conflict resolution and management have experienced similar growing demand as our society has grown more conflictual in the neighborhood, workplace, and school. Finally, because counselors are trained in human relations and are accessible to the public, the demand for their consultation by community and school groups has grown in recent years.

Each chapter is an attempt to reflect current thinking of counselors, psychologists, and educators. Where lack of consensus exists on a topic, we have attempted to reflect the divergent views so the reader can make informed decisions. We have not attempted to project where the counseling process will be ten years hence, although we are reasonably sure that, by then, the practice of counseling will have changed once again.

Some of the modifications in this edition came about from the helpful comments of our colleagues. We particularly thank the following reviewers: Elizabeth Iglesias, West Virginia University; John L. Garcia, Southwest Texas State University; and Stephen M. Klein, University of Minnesota.

Finally, we have suggested classroom exercises, discussion questions, and current professional resources at the end of each chapter. These are an invitation to the reader to become more involved in the subject matter so as to develop deeper insights into the process and practice of professional counseling.

Chapter *1*

# The Context for Counseling

## Purpose of This Chapter—

In this chapter, we introduce a number of concepts and conditions that are fundamental to the process of helping. In so doing, we seek to provide a structure for the content of the remainder of the book. Counseling must be viewed within a context. The factors that contribute to that context include philosophy, current theoretical premises, culture—in other words, the social milieu. That milieu changes over the years within a specific society. And of course it changes when one moves from one society to another—for example, from an American setting to a Caribbean setting. In addition, we address helper qualities that are universal, crossing cultures and time. Our ultimate objective in this chapter is to have you, the reader, begin to identify yourself within these parameters, and possibly to do some introspection regarding how your personal qualities match those of the professional counselor.

## Considerations as You Read This Chapter—

- As you read about the different theoretical approaches to client problems and change, which ones do you find most comfortable?
- How do you view life? Do you believe that most things that happen to people are unplanned and coincidental, or do you believe that life events tend to fit a "larger plan"?
- Is life's challenge a matter of analyzing situations and developing successful responses to those situations? Or is life's challenge to become the best person one can be, given the cards life deals us.
- How do you describe *your culture*? From whom did you get that culture? Your parents? Your community? Your nation?

1

This is a book about the counseling process and how it enhances lives of persons who are seeking change, developing self-understanding, or learning how to anticipate and meet new life challenges. We approach this chapter, and this book, from the perspective of the beginning counselor. Perhaps we should restate that as the *various perspectives* of beginning counselors because some of you will view counseling as an exciting, perhaps glamorous profession; others will sense that counseling is a demanding, often frustrating, emotion- laden experience; a few may not have any expectations until you have seen your first clients. While it is virtually impossible to describe precisely what the counseling experience will be like for you, there are some general parameters of the counseling process that certainly will be part of your experience. How you choose to fit counseling into your personal life view, how you relate to other people, and how you value process and outcome—these are the touchstones of beginning counselors. In addition, there are specific skills and learning experiences that make initial contacts with clients less awkward, more comfortable, and most of all, more productive.

## *What Is Counseling?*

Surprisingly, counseling is not an easy concept to define. For one thing, it is a much overused term. We have financial counselors and employment counselors, camp counselors, retirement counselors, legal counselors, and nutrition counselors. If there are as many types of counselors as there are adjectives, then it becomes apparent that we must somehow differentiate the practice of interpersonal/intrapersonal counseling from this myriad of other activities. Thus, we identify the process and the person in the title of this book as the *professional counselor.*

*Professional* counseling involves an interpersonal relationship with someone who is actively seeking help with personal issues that interfere with or detract from a satisfactory life. The second person, the professional counselor, is willing to give help and is personally capable of and trained to help in a setting that permits help to be given and received. This definition does not totally satisfy the need to differentiate counseling from other processes. For example, it does not address the issue of whether or not counseling is the same as or different from advising or consulting. So we must add that the process of counseling is directed toward people who experience difficulties as they live through the normal stages of lifespan development. Thus counseling is a process that "insist(s) upon the necessity of viewing clients as basically healthy individuals whose problems are essentially developmental in nature" (Brooks & Gerstein, 1990, p. 477). Counseling helps us to stay on track as we grow up, accept new life challenges, mature in wisdom, and prepare for our lives to end.

## Why Counseling?

It may be necessary to remind some aspiring counselors that the problems of life can be solved in many ways, counseling being only one of those ways. The vast majority of the human race have never experienced professional counseling. Does that mean that they are functioning at some sublevel of life? Of course not. Many people adapt to life's challenges, using personal resources, friends and family, or religious faith. But even with these resources, challenges can sometimes accumulate to the point that an unencumbered, skilled helper can facilitate the process of growth and adaptation to these challenges.

Viewed in this way, counseling can assume the function of change, prevention, or life enhancement. As change, we are concerned with situations that, for whatever reason, have become disruptive and we are unable to continue through the normal passage of life without excess stress, dissatisfaction, or unhappiness. As prevention, counseling is able to take into account those predictable life events that produce stress, cause us to draw on our psychological resources, and ultimately, demand adaptation to changing life forces. Finally, there is a third form of counseling, enhancement counseling, that goes beyond life's challenges and predictabilities. As a counseling goal, enhancement attempts to open our experience to new and deeper levels of understanding, appreciation, and wisdom about life's many potentialities.

## The Parameters of Counseling

As we consider remedial, preventive, and enhancement counseling, it may become apparent that there are many ways to describe what happens. We can talk about counseling as change or growth. Or we can talk about counseling as a process or product. If we go very deeply into an examination of these alternatives, it becomes apparent that we are beginning to talk about philosophical and cultural issues as well as psychological or interpersonal concerns. How we view these issues and concerns will determine what we do in the interview. If I happen to hold an optimistic view of human beings and how they adapt to life's ups and downs, my view of what should happen in counseling will be quite different from that of the person who holds a cautious, or even pessimistic, view of human beings and how they adapt. If I have only experienced life in a sheltered or monolithic culture, then I may view counseling as not involving cultural dimensions. If I solve my problems by careful examination and analysis of issues, decisions to be made, appropriateness of outcomes, and so on, then I might naturally assume that others should approach life problems in a similar fashion. Or, if I see life as a multifaceted *gestalt*, then I might feel less urgency to identify, prescribe, and thus, control the outcomes of counseling. These are just a part of the *counselor's* context on entering counseling.

Occurring simultaneously with these issues, counseling addresses the personal concerns of the client. These concerns may have strong basis in reality, or they may be self-generated by the client's discomfort. And it is also obvious that clients come as optimists or pessimists, bold or cautious. Whatever the case, the counselor must have a healthy appreciation for the very broad range of behaviors, attitudes, self-concepts, cultural agendas, and feelings that emerge as people develop. In other words, *normal* behavior, *normal* functioning, or *normal* feelings can include occasional flirtations with abnormal, a kind of testing the limits of one's self. It is best observed in the lives of adolescents, but it is found in people of all ages and stages of development. On the other hand, *normal* does not mean the same as *functional*. Functional behavior is that which *facilitates* growth, problem-solving, and coping. People can behave in ways that are within the range of normal but still not be behaving functionally. When we listen to the personal concerns of clients, we must seek to understand both life as they see it and the reasons they see life as they do. Only then can we begin to participate as helpers in the counseling relationship. Only then can clients begin to move toward more functional behavior. In a similar way, dysfunctional does not necessarily mean *abnormal*, which is why many people now refer to their families of origin as dysfunctional.

Finally, there is no way to understand human existence if we separate it from the setting or environment in which existence occurs. Children cannot be fully understood separate from their families of origin, their neighborhoods, or their peer groups; adults cannot be understood separate from their families, career, or ethnicity; and individuals cannot be dissected into intellectual selves, occupational selves, affective selves, or whatever. Each of us is an ecological existence within a cultural context, living with others in an ecological system. Our intrapersonal dimensions are interdependent with others who share our life space. A keen understanding and appreciation of this interdependence will facilitate our understanding of ourselves as counselors, and of our clients as people seeking to recover, to grow, or to enhance their lives.

### Counseling and Theory

Counseling is also understood in terms of the theory that is used to describe it. Currently there are over one hundred such theoretical approaches or orientations to counseling, most of which were developed from the experiences and life views of practitioners. These theories have been described within a context of *forces* (Ivey, Ivey, & Simek-Morgan, 1993). The first force or collection of counseling theories includes Freud's psychodynamic approach and those approaches that might be called neo-Freudian or counter-Freudian. The second force includes the cognitive-behavioral theorists, people such as B.F. Skinner, Albert Ellis, William Glasser, Aaron Beck, Donald Meichenbaum, Eric Berne, Joseph Wolpe, E.G. Williamson, D. Biggs, and many of the systemic theorists. The third force of counseling theory embodies the existential-humanistic therapists, Carl Rogers, Frederick Perls, Viktor Frankl, and Rollo May. Finally, Ivey et al. (1993) and Pederson (1991) have identified a fourth force which they call multicultural counseling and therapy. These most commonly practiced theories of counseling are summarized in *Table 1-1*.

Counseling theories can serve a number of functions. They serve as a set of guidelines to explain how human beings learn, change, and develop; they also propose a model for normal human functioning (and ways in which human dysfunction may be manifested); and they suggest what should transpire in the counseling process and what the outcomes of counseling *could* be. In short, a counseling theory offers a "map" of the counseling process and the route its participants should take to achieve certain goals. Rarely does a counseling theory prescribe what the *specific* goals of counseling should be. Since there is much room for alternative viewpoints on such matters as normal human functioning, how people change, and what is a desirable outcome, different theories have emerged to reflect these various viewpoints. On a more practical level, counselors use theories to organize information and observations, to explain or conceptualize client problems, and to order and implement particular interventions with clients.

One might think, or even believe, that some theories are more valid than others, but that does not seem to be the case. Using a meta-analysis approach for analyzing the effects of over four hundred psychotherapy outcome studies, Smith and Glass (1977) concluded that the

> *results of research demonstrate the beneficial effects of counseling and psychotherapy. Despite volumes devoted to the theoretical differences among different schools of psychotherapy, the results of research demonstrated negligible differences in the effects produced by different therapy types. . . . (p. 760)*

Probably what makes a *believer* in a particular counseling theory is the degree to which that approach is a good fit with the counselor's personality, life experiences, interpersonal skills, and philosophy.

**TABLE 1-1  Synopsis of Theoretical Approaches to Counseling and Psychotherapy**

| Theoretical System | Founder or Major Contributors | Theory Base | Key Philosophic, Conceptual Process, and Relationship Identifiers |
|---|---|---|---|
| *First Force: Psychodynamic Theories* | | | |
| Psychoanalytic Therapy | Sigmund Freud | Psychoanalysis | Deterministic, topographic, dynamic, genetic, analytic, developmental, historical, insightful, unconscious, motivational |
| Adlerian Therapy | Alfred Adler | Individual Psychology | Holistic, phenomenological, socially oriented teleological |
| Jungian Therapy | Carl Jung | Analytical | Teleological, transpersonal, individuational persona, animus, anima |
| Object Relations | James Framo Ronald Fairbairn Gerald Zuk | Psychoanalysis | Transfer of impulses of other family members, family of origin, past-oriented |
| Family Systems | Murray Bowen | Analytical | Triangles, fusion, differentiation of self, nuclear family emotional system, family projection process, emotional cut-off, sibling position |
| *Second Force: Cognitive-Behavioral Theories* | | | |
| Behavioral Counseling, Therapy, and Modification | B.F. Skinner J. Wolpe | Behaviorism | Behavior-based, pragmatic, scientific, learning-theoretical, experimental, goal-oriented, environmental and contactual |
| Cognitive-Behavioral | A. Beck D. Meichenbaum | Cognition Behaviorism | Cognitive-based, thought and behavioral behavior oriented, goal-oriented, environmental and contractual |
| Transactional Analysis (TA) | Eric Berne | Transactional Analysis | Cognitive, analytic, redecisional contractual, interpretational confrontational, social-interactive, awareness-evocative |
| Rational-Emotive Therapy (RET) | Albert Ellis | Behaviorism Cognition | Cognitive, thought pattern analytic, didactic, decisional, contractual, here-and-now |

| Therapy | Theorist(s) | Theoretical Base | Descriptors |
|---|---|---|---|
| Reality Therapy | William Glasser | Reality Theory | Reality-based, rational, antideterministic, responsibility-oriented, contractual, nonpunitive, here-and-now, pragmatic |
| Structural Family Therapy | S. Minuchin, J. Haley | Ecological Systems | Family rules, roles, interactional patterns, alignments, splits, enmeshed, disengaged |
| Strategic Family Therapy | M. Selvini-Palazzzoli, Jay Haley, Don Jackson | Ecological Systems | Family boundaries, second-order change, *hubris*, circular causality, systemic |

*Third Force: Existential-Humanistic Theories*

| Therapy | Theorist(s) | Theoretical Base | Descriptors |
|---|---|---|---|
| Person-Centered Therapy | Carl Rogers | Person-Centered Theory | Phenomenological, existential, here-and-now, self-responsible, self-healing, client-focused |
| Gestalt Therapy | Frederick (Fritz) Perls | Gestalt, Psychoanalytic, Behavioral | Phenomenological, existential, here-and-now, awareness-evocative, confrontive, client-focused |
| Logotherapy | Viktor Frankl | Existentialism Psychoanalytic | Phenomenological, existential, here-and-now, meaning of life, supportive, client-focused |
| Existential Psychotherapy | Rollo May | Existentialism | Phenomenological, existential, here-and-now, responsibility for self, meaning of life, supportive, client-focused |

*Fourth Force: Multicultural Counseling*

| Therapy | Theorist(s) | Theoretical Base | Descriptors |
|---|---|---|---|
| Multicultural Counseling and Therapy (MCT) | A.E. Ivey, H.E. Cheatham, D.W. Sue, P.B. Pederson, J.G. Ponterotto, C.E. Vontress, P. Arredondo, F.A. Ibraham | Behaviorism, Phenomonology Anthropology, Liberation Pedagogy Feminist Theory | Meta-theoretical, culturally-based, emic and etic, orientation, locus of control, awareness-evocative, oppression sensitive, liberation of consciousness (*Conscientização*), world-view |

Adapted from Gurl Gilliland, Richard James, and James Bowman, *Theories and Strategies in Counseling and Psychotherapy*, pp. 2–3. © 1994. Reprinted by permission of Allyn & Bacon.

In recent years, the counseling profession has witnessed an increasing convergence among theorists and a growing realization that no single theory can explain or fit all client challenges. The result is an emerging view that theory is meant to serve the user, and when no single theory totally fits the counselor's needs, then a blending of compatible theories is an acceptable practice. The result is referred to as an *eclectic* or *integrative* approach.

The following list represents certain elements about counseling that are operative, for all of the major theoretical approaches.

**1.** Counseling involves responding to the feelings, thoughts, and actions of the client. Thinking of this in another way, the counselor deals with both attitudes and behaviors of the client. Existing theoretical approaches differ with respect to their emphasis and order of responsiveness to feelings and behavior. Some approaches (person-centered, existential) favor an emphasis on feelings; others (rational-emotive, reality therapy, cognitive behavioral) emphasize the importance of behaviors and actions; an eclectic approach would acknowledge the importance of being able to identify and respond appropriately to feeling states, behavior patterns, and relationship patterns.

**2.** Counseling involves a basic acceptance of the client's perceptions and feelings, regardless of outside evaluative standards. In other words, you must first accept who the client is before you can begin to consider who the client might become. Clients need your understanding of their current situations and concerns before they can anticipate growth and change in a new direction.

**3.** Confidentiality and privacy constitute essential ingredients in the counseling setting. Physical facilities that preserve this quality are important.

**4.** Counseling is voluntary. Ordinarily, it is not effective when it is something that the client is required to do. Regardless of how the client is referred, the counselor never uses coercion as a means of obtaining or continuing with a client.

**5.** Generally speaking, the counselor operates with a conservative bias against communicating to the client detailed information about his or her own life. Although there are times when counselor self-disclosure is appropriate, counselors generally do not complicate the interview by focusing attention on their personal life.

**6.** One skill underlying all systems of counseling is that of communication. Counselors and clients alike continually transmit and receive verbal and nonverbal messages during the interview process. Therefore, awareness of and sensitivity to the kinds of messages being communicated is an important prerequisite for counselor effectiveness.

**7.** Counseling is, at minimum, a cross-cultural experience, and probably a multicultural experience.

## Counseling and Philosophy

Few of us consider ourselves to be philosophers. And yet, we all have a philosophical outlook on life. Some people see life as a sequence of events and experiences over which we have little or no control. Others view life as a challenge to be analyzed, controlled and directed. Some of us see the purpose of life to be achievement and self-improvement. Others view life as a process to be experienced. Who is right? Everyone. Philosophical outlooks on life are varied, allowing us to choose or to identify with that outlook that seems to fit each person best.

Philosophy also is reflected in the practice of counseling. George and Cristiani (1981) have related counseling to three philosophical positions that have carried down through the ages. The first of these, *essentialism*, assumes that humans are rational beings by nature, that reason is the natural goal of education, and that the classical thinkers are the chief repository of reason (Blocher, 1966, p. 17). From this orientation come the problem-solvers, the analyzers, those who search for patterns in life.

The second philosophical position, *progressivism*, is concerned with the fundamental question, "What will work?" Knowledge is based on experimental results, truth is identified through consequences, and values are relative rather than absolute. From this orientation come the persons who rely on data and research for their truths, believe that pragmatic solutions do exist for human problems, and are committed to the pursuit of logical and lawful relationships in life.

The third philosophical position, *existentialism*, holds that life's meaning is to be found in the individual, not in the environment or the event. Lawfulness (progressivism) or rational thinking (essentialism) are meaningless unless the individual gives them meaning. People who align with this view of life believe that values are real and individually determined, and that experiences are subjective rather than lawful or predictable. Individual responsibility is emphasized; human reactions are the result of choice or potential choice.

Obviously, all counselors enter their profession with some variation of these viewpoints. Each counselor's philosophical view will be reflected in how he or she reacts to client problems and how those problems may be addressed. Similarly, clients enter counseling with some variation of these viewpoints, which will be reflected in how they view their problems and what they may consider to be viable solutions.

## Counseling and Culture

Increasingly, our society is becoming aware of the complex role that culture plays in interpersonal relationships. Pederson (1991) has observed that:

> *Before we were born, cultural patterns of thought and action were already prepared to guide our ideas, influence our decisions, and*

*help us take control of our lives. We inherited these cultural patterns from our parents and teachers who taught us the "rules of the game." Only later and sometimes never, did we learn that our culture was one of the many possible patterns of thinking and acting from which we could choose. By that time, most of us had already come to believe that "our" culture was the best of all possible worlds.* (p. 6)

By culture, Pederson includes demographic variables (e.g., age, sex, place of residence), status variables (e.g., social, educational, economic), and affiliations (formal and informal), as well as ethnographic variables such as race, nationality, ethnicity, language, and religion. This definition is broader than that used by some authors who would limit cultural concepts to ethnic or racial criteria. Even a narrower definition of culture demands that we understand the context from which a person of another culture functions, the assumptions about relationships, about authority, power, and privilege, about right and wrong, about success and failure, about values worth fighting to preserve.

In Pederson's view of culture, the construct "multicultural" becomes generic to all counseling relationships. If *multicultural* embraces such variables as gender, ethnicity, race, religion, and sexual orientation, then it is almost certain that every counseling relationship will cross at least one of these dimensions and probably several dimensions. Thus, all counseling is multicultural.

Even if both counselor and client are Caucasian, one may be gay and the other heterosexual, or one may be male and the other female, one may be older and the other younger, one may be privileged and the other poor. Crossing such multiple boundaries becomes a multicultural relationship with all the complexities inherent in multiple interactions of social variables.

The implications for counseling and for the counselor are quite clear. If understanding and acceptance of the client are to occur, then the counselor must understand those cultural factors that have shaped and continue to influence the client's worldview. Even before that can happen, the counselor must understand his or her own worldview and how it is shaped in ways similar to the client's experience even when the two worldviews are substantially different from one another. To do less is to flirt with what Wrenn (1962) termed *cultural encapsulation* many years ago. Cultural encapsulation involves defining reality according to one set of cultural assumptions and stereotypes, becoming insensitive to cultural variations among individuals and assuming that our view is the only real or legitimate one, embracing unreasoned assumptions that we accept without proof. Clearly, successful counseling cannot go forward when the counselor is handicapped by cultural encapsulation.

## Counseling Conditions and Their Effects

Many clients find it to be a major move to seek counseling. Apart from the fact that our society associates problems with weakness or inadequacy, the process of finding a person who is trustworthy, confidence-inspiring, and competent is a daunting challenge. For the most part, clients are ill-informed on entering counseling. If the experience is new, they may lack the knowledge about counseling to be able to appraise the situation, determine the counselor's personal qualities, and make the judgment to commit to the process. The counselor must also make an initial assessment of the situation, determine that his/her skills are appropriate to the client's presenting concerns, and that the interaction of personalities and personal values are a good match for counseling success. What conditions or events provide signals both to clients and counselors that the prospective relationship holds promise for success?

Clients feel encouraged by such things as feeling support and understanding from another person, beginning to see a different and more hopeful perspective, or experiencing a more desirable level of relating to others. Similarly counselors feel reinforced as they are able to establish those conditions that lead to successful counseling outcomes. Although different theoretical orientations emphasize somewhat different counseling outcomes, most practitioners agree on some rather basic outcomes. When counseling has been successful, clients often experience the following types of outcomes:

**1.** *They begin to perceive their problems and issues from quite different contexts.* Many times clients have formulated a set of explanations for their problems. Such explanations may reflect cultural factors, societal factors, or familial factors. In the Eurocentric context (reflecting a Northern European cultural heritage), the issue might be one of helping clients to "own" their problems. Owning means that clients begin to accept responsibility for themselves, *their problems*, and *solutions*. However, there is another way of viewing the source of many client problems. It is generally agreed that many problems that are experienced by people of color can be traced to active or passive forms of racial discrimination. Similarly, for people with physical disabilities, many of the problems they face may be associated with societal insensitivities involving access, employment skills, or misinformation. Thus, many clients enter counseling blaming their problems inappropriately on others, while other clients may enter counseling blaming their problems inappropriately on themselves.

**Example:** Julius, a nineteen-year-old black male, seeks counseling for a recent bout with depression. Raised in an upper-middle class home in an integrated suburban neighborhood, he has been a college student for about eighteen months. During this time, he has found himself pulled between the majority white culture of his college and the sizeable body of minority students. He has started to question some of his earlier views about race and opportunity, particularly as he has come to know an increasing number of other black students—many more, in his words, than he ever knew in high school. He is beginning to address what Helms (1994) has described as moving from the conformity stage to the integrative awareness stage of racial identity. Thus, it would be important for the counselor to determine whether Julius' depression was related to racial identity development or to pathological factors, or both.

**2.** *Clients develop a more useful understanding of problems and issues.* Once clients begin to view the sources of their problems more appropriately, they frequently develop greater understanding or insight into the problem. There are four aspects of problem awareness that understanding brings into client awareness: feelings and somatic reactions (affect) associated with the problem; thoughts (cognitions) related to how they perceive or explain their problems; behavior patterns that may be associated or attributed to experiencing the problem; and interpersonal relationships that affect or are affected by the problem occurrence. Understanding these different dimensions of a problem helps clients to perceive their reality more clearly and to gain or experience more control over their reactions to an issue.

**Example:** Jim, a white college student, complains of being depressed since his girlfriend ended their relationship. He describes his situation as feeling down, hurt, lonely, and unloveable. He shows no clinical signs of depression (e.g., sleeplessness, weight loss, or isolation). Rather, he has taken on a "mopey" demeanor, looking for all the world like someone who needs to be taken care of. Through counseling, Jim begins to realize that his reaction is similar to how he would respond as a child when his mother would get on his case. Then, he reports, she would start to feel sorry for her effect on him and would try to repair the obviously damaged relationship. In other words, Jim began to understand that his style of dealing with stressful relationships was to manipulate the other person into repairing the damage. In so doing, Jim never had to assume any responsibility either for the initial issue or for the solution to the relationship problem. Thus, his reaction involved feelings, how he explained the problem to himself (as someone else's doing), his mopey appearance, and how he would manipulate relationships. Through counseling Jim also began to understand the relationship between his problem resolution style and his resulting behaviors that reflected passivity and inertia. Finally, Jim came to understand that his interactional patterns with his mother were intruding and controlling his relationships with women.

**3.** *Clients acquire new responses to old issues.* Many counseling theorists now agree that, for most clients, insight or understanding of problems is not a sufficient counseling outcome. In addition to developing greater understanding of issues, clients also need to acquire more effective ways of responding, verbally and/or behaviorally, to problematic situations. Otherwise, they tend to repeat their ineffective interactional style and fail to make any connection between how they understand their problem and what they do when experiencing their problem.

> **Example:** Mary and John see a counselor because of "poor communication" in their marriage. Gradually, they realize that part of the problem is that John is at work all day in a very intense environment and wants to come home to relax, to sit down with the TV or paper, and to be left alone. Mary, on the other hand, has been at home alone all day with a young child. She seeks out John for some adult conversation until he pushes her away. Mary retreats in tears. While an understanding of the dynamics of this scenario may be useful to both Mary (she might be able to understand that it was not she, personally, whom John was rejecting) and to John (he, in turn, might realize that Mary had reasonable and understandable needs), it is unlikely that they will be able to alter or interrupt their re-entry behavior patterns through understanding, alone. They must also develop new behavioral patterns or interactions that would meet each person's unique end-of-the-day needs.

**4.** *Clients learn how to develop effective relationships.* For a great number of people who end up in a counselor's office, adults and young people alike, effective and satisfying interpersonal interactions are nonexistent or rare. Since change is often created and enhanced by a network of social support, it is essential for clients to begin to develop more adequate relationships with other people. Often the counseling relationship is the initial vehicle by which this occurs.

> **Example:** Renee comes to see a counselor because she wants to lose a significant amount of weight. In talking to her, the counselor realizes that her obesity has also shielded her from having significant relationships with other people, particularly males

(Renee may have perceived this as having *prevented* her from having significant relationships). It is unlikely that Renee will have much success in losing weight unless she also learns to feel more comfortable in initiating and developing a greater social support network.

To summarize, counseling usually results in more than one single, all-inclusive outcome for clients. Effective change is multifaceted and comprehensive and includes keener understanding of the dynamics of problem sources and maintenance, new insights, different and more facilitative behavioral responses, and more effective interpersonal relationships.

## Case Illustration of Possible Counseling Outcomes

### The Case of Margaret

Margaret is a thirty-year-old woman who has been married for ten years, and has two school-aged daughters. She is employed as a mail clerk in a large business office. She describes her job as satisfying and her relationship with her children as adequate. Her presenting (initial) complaint is about her marital relationship, although she states that her husband has refused to come to counseling with her. She reports that she feels dependent on her husband or on acquaintances because she never learned to drive a car and has never really developed any interests or friendships on her own. At the same time, she feels increasingly angry and upset about the way he "orders her around" and tries to keep her "under his thumb." Recently her emotions have become so frayed that she cries easily at home and at work and has developed a pre-ulcerous condition.

Given an effective counseling experience, Margaret might realistically expect to see some of the following kinds of changes:

1. Development of more positive perceptions of herself
2. Greater awareness and understanding of her conflict between being dependent on and independent of her husband
3. Improved family and marital relationships
4. Less digestive upset
5. Greater awareness of and ability to think, feel, and act as an individual, using her own internal resources
6. Recognizing how to respond to what may be an emotionally abusive relationship

## *Characteristics of Effective Helpers*

In order to help clients achieve desired outcomes, counseling must offer clients a new or fresh experience, one somewhat different from the normal range of experience in their lives. Counseling is a reciprocal interaction in which both the counselor and client create and shape the process. Being the trained helper, the counselor has the greater responsibility for ensuring that the counseling process is beneficial and therapeutic for the client. To a large extent, the degree of helpfulness found in the relationship is related to the person of the counselor. Much research evidence amassed over the years indicates that a helper's personal qualities can enhance or detract from the helping process and are as essential (or even more essential) as specific skills or knowledge (Bergin & Lambert, 1978; Jevne, 1981).

In this section, we discuss eight qualities associated with effective counselors. Some are based on results of research (Corrigan, Dell, Lewis, & Schmidt, 1980; Loesch, Crane, & Tucker, 1978; Rowe, Murphy, & DeCsipkes, 1975). Others are based on our clinical and supervisory observations of both good and poor counselors. These eight qualities include:

Self-awareness and understanding

Good psychological health

Sensitivity to and understanding of racial, ethnic, and cultural factors in self and others

Open-mindedness

Objectivity

Competence

Trustworthiness

Interpersonal attractiveness

### *Self-Awareness and Understanding*

On the road to becoming an effective counselor, a good starting place for most counselors is a healthy degree of introspection and self-exploration. Specific areas we suggest you might examine and seek to understand include:

**1.** Awareness of your needs (for example, need to give or to nurture, need to be critical, need to be loved, need to be respected, need to be liked, need to please others, need to receive approval of others, need to be right, need for control).

**2.** Awareness of your motivation for helping (for example, what do you get or take from helping others? How does helping make you feel good?)

**3.** Awareness of your feelings (for example, happiness, satisfaction, hurt, anger, sadness, disappointment, confusion, fear).

**4.** Awareness of your personal strengths, limitations, and coping skills (for example, things about yourself you do well or like, things about yourself you need to work on, how you handle difficulties and stress).

Self-awareness and understanding are important in counseling for a variety of reasons. First, they help you see things more objectively and avoid "blind spots," that is, difficulties that may arise because you do not understand some aspects of yourself, particularly in interpersonal interactions. One such difficulty is *projection*. Counselors who do not understand their needs and feelings may be more likely to *project* their feelings onto the client and not recognize their real source (for example, "I had a very angry client today," instead of "I felt angry today with my client"). Projection is one example of a process we discuss later in this chapter called *countertransference*, or the emotional reactions of the counselor to the client.

Self-awareness and understanding also contribute to greater security and safety for both counselor and client. Lack of self-awareness and understanding may cause some counselors to personalize or overreact to client messages and respond with *defensiveness*. For example, a client questions whether counseling "will do her any good." The counselor's need to be respected and approved are jeopardized or threatened, but the counselor is not aware of this. Instead of responding to the *client's* feelings of uncertainty, the counselor is likely to respond to personal feelings of insecurity and portray defensiveness in his or her voice, or other nonverbal behavior.

### Good Psychological Health

While no one expects counselors to be perfect, it stands to reason that counselors will be more helpful to clients when they are psychologically intact and not distracted by their own overwhelming problems. White and Franzoni (1990) report that studies of the psychological health of psychiatrists, psychologists, and psychotherapists in general reveal higher rates of depression, anxiety, and relationship problems than the general population. Even master's degree level counselors-in-training "show evidence of higher levels of psychological disturbance than does the general populace" (White & Franzoni, 1990, p. 262).

Unfortunately, some persons either do not recognize when their own psychological health is marginal, or else realize it but continue to counsel anyway, often using counseling as a defense mechanism to reduce the anxiety they feel about their own issues. At selected times in their lives, counselors may need to refer clients with similar life problems to other counselors and/or seek out the services of a competent counselor for themselves.

## *Sensitivity to and Understanding of Racial, Ethnic, and Cultural Factors in Self and Others*

Many clients live in two worlds, the world of their cultural and racial-ethnic heritage and the world of their reality. Only in recent years has the counseling profession begun to act on this awareness and reflect its implications for clients, counselors and the counseling process. As our society has become more multicultural, we have begun to understand the oversimplification of earlier worldviews. Where culture and ethnicity once were defined in terms of race, we now can understand that ethnic variations within race, and other cultural variations within ethnicity are constantly tugging at and shaping our reality. We have already stated that good psychological health allows the counselor to be more helpful to clients. It is just as true that awareness of ones' own ethnic and cultural heritage and how that heritage shapes one's worldview either contributes to or detracts from one's effectiveness as a counselor.

There are two views of how counselors should be aware of their own and their clients' cultural and ethnic contexts. These are referred to as *etic* and *emic* approaches to multiculturalism. The etic approach is culture-specific, that is, it holds that all cultures are unique and must be understood for their uniqueness. The emic approach argues for a more subjective or inclusive understanding of how culture affects the counseling process. Concerns have been raised (Lee, 1991; Locke, 1990) that the inclusivity of the emic approach (taking into account such variables as gender, sexual orientation, physical disabilities, etc.) could make the concept of multiculturalism less clear or even meaningless. Proponents of the emic or general approach believe that culture is defined by more than racial or ethnic factors alone. Others (Ivey et al., 1993; Pederson, 1991) believe that both etic and emic approaches to multiculturalism are needed and that "The basic problem facing counselors is how to [understand] behavior in terms that are true to a particular culture while at the same time comparing those behaviors with a similar pattern in one or more other cultures" (Pederson, 1991, p. 7).

## *Open-Mindedness*

Open-mindedness suggests freedom from fixed or preconceived ideas that, if allowed expression, could affect clients and counseling outcomes. Open-mindedness must include enlightenment, knowledge of the world *outside* the counselor's world. It must also include an acute understanding of one's inner world and how those internal standards, values, assumptions, perceptions, and myths can be projected upon clients if the counselor is not vigilant.

Open-mindedness serves a number of significant functions in counseling. First, it allows counselors to accommodate client feelings, attitudes, and behaviors that may be different from their own. Second, it allows counselors to interact effectively with a wide range of clients, even those regarded by society at large as unacceptable or offensive. Finally, open-mindedness is a prerequisite for honest communication. In their study of communication, Anderson, Lepper, and Ross (1980) found that people who are not open-minded continue to believe incorrect things about clients, even in light of new and different information.

## *Objectivity*

Objectivity refers to the ability to be involved with a client and, at the same time, stand back and see accurately what is happening with the client and in the relationship. It has also been described as a component of *empathy*—the ability to see the client's problem *as if* it were your own without losing the "as if" condition (Rogers, 1957, p. 99). It is extremely important to maintain objectivity for the client's benefit. Most clients are bombarded with views and advice from many well-meaning persons, such as friends and family, who are also part of the problem and thus are not objective. Counselor objectivity gives the client an additional set of eyes and ears that are needed in order to develop a greater understanding or a new perception (or reframe) of the issue.

Objectivity also helps the counselor avoid getting caught up in certain client behaviors or dysfunctional communication patterns. For example, clients sometimes try to manipulate the counselor to "rescue" them, using a variety of well-learned and sophisticated ploys. Counselors who remain objective are more likely to recognize client manipulation for what it is and respond with therapeutic appropriateness. It must sound like a contradiction to ask you to be both empathic and involved with your clients and at the same time, be objective. Clearly, we are asking for an involved and caring objectivity.

Objectivity also acts as a safeguard against developing inappropriate or even dysfunctional emotional feelings *about* or *toward* a client. Counselors must learn to recognize when *countertransference* develops in the relationship. As we mentioned earlier, countertransference involves either a counterproductive emotional reaction to a client (often based on projection) or the entanglement of the counselor's needs in the therapeutic relationship. Some of the more common ways in which countertransference may manifest itself include the need to please one's clients, overidentification with certain client problems, development of romantic or sexual feelings toward clients, need to give constant advice, and a desire to form friendships with clients (Corey, Corey, & Callanan, 1992). Astute counselors gradually learn to identify certain kinds of clients who consistently elicit strong positive or negative feelings on their part and also certain kinds of communication patterns that entice the counselor into giving a less objective and nonhelpful response.

## *Competence*

Ethical standards of all mental health professions call for maintaining high standards of competence. According to Egan (1994), competence refers to whether the counselor has the necessary *information*, *knowledge*, and *skills* to be of help, and is determined not by behaviors but by outcomes. Kleinke (1994) describes competency as including *knowledge* in such areas as psychological processes, assessment, ethics, and other areas relevant to professional work, *clinical skills*, *technical skills*, *judgment*, and *personal effectiveness* (pp. 149–151). And, of course, competence also includes multicultural competence that we have already discussed.

Counselor competence is necessary to transmit and build confidence and hope in clients. Clients need to develop positive expectations about the potential usefulness to them of the counseling experience. Competent counselors are able to work with a greater variety of clients and a wider range of problems. They are more likely to be of benefit to their clients and to make inroads more quickly and efficiently.

Sometimes referred to as expertness, competence is often associated with a model of counseling known as the *social influence model* (Strong, 1968; Strong & Schmidt, 1970; Strong & Claiborn, 1982). The two basic assumptions of this model are:

1. The helper must establish a power or a base of influence with the client through a relationship comprising three characteristics or relationship enhancers: competence (expertness), trustworthiness (credibility), and attractiveness (liking).
2. The helper must actively use this base of influence to effect opinion and behavior changes in the client.

An increasing amount of evidence on this model suggests that clients' respect for the counselor increases in direct proportion to their perception of the counselor's expertness or competence (Goldstein, 1980).

### *Trustworthiness*

Counselor trustworthiness includes such qualities as reliability, responsibility, ethical standards, and predictability. Trust can be hard to establish, and it can be destroyed by a single action and in a brief moment. Counselors who are trustworthy safeguard their clients' communications, respond with energy and dynamism to client concerns, and "never make a person regret having made a revelation" (Cavanaugh, 1982, p. 79). The essence of trustworthiness can be summarized in one sentence: *Do not promise more than you can do, and be sure you do exactly as you have promised.* Trustworthiness is essential, not only in establishing a base of influence with clients, but also in encouraging clients to self-disclose and reveal often very private parts of their lives. The counselor cannot act trustworthy. The counselor must *be* trustworthy.

### *Interpersonal Attractiveness*

Clients perceive counselors as interpersonally attractive when they see them as *similar to* or *compatible with* themselves. Clients often make this assessment intuitively, although probably based on selected dimensions of the counselor's demeanor and attitude, particularly their likability and friendliness. In other words, it is helpful to be down to earth, friendly, and warm, rather than formal, stuffy, aloof, or reserved. Interpersonal attractiveness can be influenced by race and gender factors as well. However, the counselor's *worldview* is probably of greater importance than either race or gender. Counselors who are perceived as attractive become an important source of influence for clients and may also inspire greater confidence and trust in the counseling process.

Perhaps the most important point we should make about the qualities of effective helpers involves awareness and growth. Few beginning helpers will feel prepared, either technically or personally, to begin working with clients. In part, this is a matter of developing self-confidence in the new skills that have been learned. But, it is also associated with their personal growth as human beings. Experienced counselors find that they learn much about themselves and about the process of living through their work with clients. We have certainly found that to be true in our own experience. Each new client introduces us to ourselves in another way. Very often, that experience reveals aspects of our own life adjustment which merit attention and exploration. When this happens, we become increasingly aware of both our strengths and our limitations. It is around those personal strengths that effective counselors build their approach to helping. And it is around those personal limitations that we attempt to structure growth experiences, with the expectation that we will either reduce the limitations or we will attempt to circumscribe their effect on our clients and our counseling practices.

## *The Developmental Nature of Learning to Counsel*

Over the years, counselor educators have participated in a recurring debate regarding the experience of learning to counsel. The two poles of this debate are that: (a) potential counselors already possess the "skills" of counseling but must learn how to differentiate these skills and use them selectively with clients; or (b) that the skills of counseling have been rather specifically defined and can be taught to potential counselors with a reasonably high degree of success, whether or not they possessed the skills initially. Obviously, most counselor preparation programs fall somewhere between these two poles. But regardless of the source of those skills, whether they are inherent in the candidate's personhood, or are imbedded in the curriculum of the preparation program (or both), the process of bringing them into dominance is worthy of our attention.

We have all known someone who was untrained, but yet was a natural counselor. In getting to know such people, we often find that they assumed the helper role as children. They may even have been identified by their families as the peacemaker, the facilitator, the understanding one, the one to whom other family members could turn. Such a role emerges both from temperament and from expectations. Such helpers evolve into the role as their sensitivities, skills, and confidence grow over time. Similarly, students entering counselor preparation programs find that the process is a developmental experience. That is to say, early in the training, the focus tends to be on professional issues external to the person, and like this chapter, the context for helping. Gradually, the focus of preparation turns to the personal qualities of helpers and the process becomes more personal. From this, attention turns to the skills of counseling—what effective counselors are doing and thinking as they work with clients. Finally, preparation begins to integrate these skills with the practical experience of counseling clients in professionally supervised settings.

## Summary

In this chapter, our aim has been to describe the various parameters of the counseling process, to relate the process to counseling theory, philosophy and culture, to illustrate the purposes of effective counseling, and to highlight the major personal characteristics of effective counselors. The counseling relationship has certain features that set it apart from other professional or social relationships or even friendships. One of the most significant features of the counseling relationship is that the counselor is a trained professional capable of providing assistance in a competent and trustworthy manner.

In Chapter 2, we take a more focused look at the landscape of the counseling process. Following chapters examine portions of this landscape in greater detail. The larger intent of this book is to provide the skills dimension of the learning process, and to offer some structure for the implicit and explicit interactional nature of these skills. Each chapter will conclude with suggested exercises to assist your integration of the content and a list of suggested readings that would allow you to explore certain topics in greater depth.

## Exercises

**I.** *Purposes and Goals of Counseling*
Two client case descriptions are presented in this activity. Based on the case description for each client, identify possible counseling outcomes that also appear feasible and realistic. You may wish to share your responses with your instructor or another student.

1. Ben is a middle-aged (early fifties) man. He has been fairly happily married for twenty-five years and has two grown children. Ben also has been mostly satisfied with his job as a business owner. During the last year, however, he has begun to question just about everything in his life. His work seems boring and unchallenging, and his marriage and relationship have become very routine. About the only thing he still feels very good about is his relationship with his children. Lately he has also been feeling very attracted to one of the younger female secretaries in his company. He is very nervous about sexual harassment issues, the stability of his marriage, and how his children might react if they knew what was going on in his mind. He is starting to wonder if he has crossed over a line and is beginning to lose it.

2. Margaret is an older woman (in her late seventies). Her hearing has begun to deteriorate and she finds that often she must ask people to repeat themselves when they speak to her. She has also had a couple of bad falls in the past year, one of which resulted in a severe back sprain. She lives alone in a two-room apartment and receives only a social security check. She has no means of transportation other

than public transportation. She often complains of loneliness and boredom.

**II.** *Qualities of Effective Counselors*

Listed below are the eight qualities of effective counselors described in this chapter. With a partner or in a small group, discuss what you believe is your present status with respect to each quality. For example, how open-minded are you? What makes it easy (or difficult) for you to be open-minded and relatively tolerant of different values and ideas? Then identify several areas which you may need to work on during your development as a counselor. In the second example, which factors do you believe would have the greatest impact on Margaret's psychological health?

1. Self-awareness and understanding
2. Good psychological health
3. Sensitivity to and understanding of racial, ethnic, and cultural factors in self and others
4. Open-mindedness
5. Objectivity
6. Competence
7. Trustworthiness
8. Interpersonal attractiveness

## Discussion Questions

1. Counseling has been described by some as a "purchase of friendship." Do you agree with this statement? How do you believe counseling differs from a close friendship?

2. Whom do you know that possesses the qualities to be an effective counselor? What are some of this person's qualities? How do you suppose these qualities were acquired?

3. Considering your age, background, racial/ethnic heritage, and life experiences, what do you think you have to offer to clients that is different from what they would receive from their friends or family members?

4. What are the most important reasons why you want to be a counselor? How might a typical client react to your *reasons* for choosing counseling as a career?

5. How likely are you to see a counselor yourself? In what ways do you think counseling could help you in your own development as a person and as a counselor? For which reasons might you resist getting involved in this experience?

## *Recommended Readings*

Cavanaugh, M.E. (1990). *The Counseling Experience*, Prospect Heights, IL: Waveland Press. Chapter 4, The person of the counselor.

Coombs, A.W. and Gonzalez, D.M. (1994). *Helping Relationships: Basic Concepts for the Helping Profession*, 4th ed. Boston, MA: Allyn & Bacon. Chapter 2. What makes a good helper?

Corey, M.S. and Corey, G. (1993). *Becoming a Helper*, 2nd ed. Pacific Grove, CA: Brooks/Cole. Chapter 1, Are the helping professions for you?

Fox, R. (1993). *Elements of the Helping Process: A Guide for Clinicians*. Binghamton, NY: Haworth Press. Chapter 1, To do our work.

Gladding, S.T. (1988). *Counseling: A Comprehensive Profession*. Columbus, OH: Merrill Publishing Co. Chapter 2, The effective counselor: Personal, theoretical, and educational factors.

Hackney, H. and Cormier, S. (1994). *Counseling Strategies and Interventions*. Boston, MA: Allyn & Bacon. Chapter 1, The helping profession.

Hill, C. and Corbett, M. (1993). A perspective on the history of process and outcome research in counseling psychology, *Journal of Counseling Psychology, 40*, 3–24.

Hoare, Carol H. (1991). Psychosocial identity development and cultural others, *Journal of Counseling and Development, 70*, 45–53.

Kottler, J.A. and Brown, R.W. (1992). *Introduction to Therapeutic Counseling*, 2nd ed. Pacific Grove, CA: Brooks/Cole. Chapter 1, Therapeutic counseling. What it is and how it works.

# Chapter *2*

## *Stages and Skills of Counseling*

### *Purpose of This Chapter—*

Structure is the overall objective of this chapter, the structure of the counseling process and how that structure helps you determine what the counselor should be doing. The beginning point of counseling is a time when you and your client must decide, both independently and mutually, whether this particular pairing of persons and personalities offers the potential for help, for change, and for growth. Beyond that decision, you must reach agreement on what the problem is, how counseling might assist in changing problematic circumstances, what counseling activities would help produce that change, and finally, when the helping effort should conclude. Then the chapter examines this process from the client's perspective, which will be different from your own.

### *Considerations as You Read This Chapter—*

- How do you approach new relationships? Do they make you nervous? Offer excitement?
- What do you suppose other people observe in you when you are beginning a new relationship?
- What do you think it would be like if you were a minority seeking help from someone of a majority culture (or vice versa). What kinds of thoughts would go through your mind? How do you think you might view the other (helping) person?
- How much structure do you prefer in most situations? What kind

of structure do you need in relationships? What kinds of structure would make you comfortable in the counseling relationship?
How would you accommodate your client's needs for structure if
they were different from your own?

For many years counseling was viewed as a process that did not lend
itself to concrete behavioral analysis. For this reason, some people began to think of counseling as having indefinable, almost mystical,
qualities. In the 1970s, through the work of people such as Robert
Carkhuff, Allen Ivey, and Stanley Strong, this mystical character began to disintegrate and be replaced by more specific definitions. Gradually, counseling has taken on a much more defined character.

In this chapter we shall examine the helping process from the
counselor's vantage point and from the client's experience. We shall
consider how two strangers meet and begin to establish understandings that gradually evolve into a meaningful and productive relationship. These instrumental stages and the counseling skills indige-
nous to them are presented as a conceptual base for the chapters to
follow.

## Stages of Counseling

Counseling is often described as a process. The implicit meaning of
this label is a progressive movement toward an ultimate conclusion,
that conclusion being the resolution of whatever precipitated the need
for help. This progressive movement may be described as a series of
stages through which the counselor and client move. These stages include:

1. Rapport and relationship building
2. Assessment or definition of the problem
3. Goal-setting
4. Initiating interventions
5. Termination and follow-up

Rapport and relationship building is an all-inclusive stage. It operates
from the first moment of contact with the client to the final moments
of termination. Thus, it is an encompassing stage. The remaining stages
overlap in such a way that assessment begins while the relationship is
still developing, or early goal-setting begins even while assessment is
continuing (see *Figure 2-1*). Just as these five stages collectively describe
the process of helping, each stage can be described in terms of progressive movement.

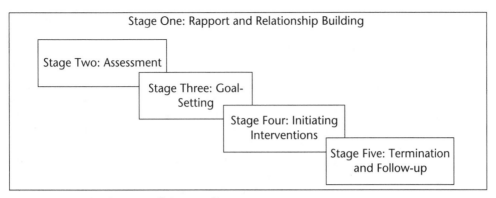

**FIGURE 2-1  Stages of Counseling**

## *Establishing the Relationship*

The term *relationship* has many inferential meanings, including the ties between two people in love, kinship within the family, the bond between close friends, and the understanding that can develop between humans and animals. In the counseling setting, *relationship* takes on a more specific meaning. When the counselor establishes rapport with a client, the relationship includes such factors as respect, trust, and a sense of relative psychological comfort. In other words, rapport refers to the psychological climate that emerges from the interpersonal contact between you and your client. Consequently, good rapport sets the stage for positive psychological growth, while poor rapport leads to undesirable or even counterproductive outcomes.

Obviously, this psychological climate will be affected by a number of factors, including your personal and professional qualifications and the client's interpersonal history and anxiety state. In other words, even the best-trained, best-adjusted counselor still faces a variety of challenges when meeting a new client. Many of these preexisting conditions can be anticipated. For example, few of us like the prospect of asking others for assistance. Thus, when we are forced to admit to ourselves that we need help, we approach it with two sets of feelings: (1) "I know I need help and will feel better when I get it"; and (2) "I wish I weren't here." This conflict is quite common in the early stages of counseling and is particularly evident in the rapport-building stage.

Other preexisting client conditions relate to the client's previous experience with sharing personal information, interaction with authority figures, with older persons, and with the opposite sex or with a person of a different cultural background. Some of these conditions are affected by the client's ethnic/cultural background as well. In Chapter 1 we referred to some of these factors within the context of interpersonal attraction, trustworthiness, competence, and sensitivity to and understanding of cultural factors in oneself and others. The culturally sensitive client will read your nonverbal and verbal messages and make inferences about these qualities. These first impressions influence rapport-building and may need to be reexamined later when you and your client have reached a more comfortable level with each other.

These interpersonal reactions can assume overriding importance in the situation and begin to influence or even control the process of counseling. When this happens, we refer to the psychological dynamic as *transference* or *countertransference*. Transference occurs when the client associates certain qualities with the counselor. For example, if the counselor's demeanor reminds the client of his/her nurturing mother, demanding boss, or prejudiced colleague, the client may decide that the counselor is *like* this person, or in extreme cases of transference, *is* this person. Transference can be either positive (favorable comparison) or negative (unfavorable comparison). Countertransference, which we referred to in Chapter 1, describes the same psychological condition, except it is the counselor who is associating imagined qualities with the client. While this might seem less likely, in fact it is not uncommon.

Although we have suggested that relationship building is a critical stage in the counseling process, we do not mean to imply that once the counselor has established a relationship with the client, he or she must live with the product. On the contrary, the relationship is a living, evolving condition. Impressions made in the early stages of counseling often change and mature as the counselor and client work together. Often the early impressions are revisited and reexamined and each person grows in understanding. The critical determinant in this maturing process is the counselor's ability to recognize psychological dynamics, interpersonal assumptions, and the subterranean emotions that are part of the relationship.

Skillful counselors develop a self-congruent style for meeting clients, a style that reflects both the counselor's personal qualities and counseling experience. Even though there is no set formula for establishing rapport, some guidelines and skills are associated with this stage of counseling.

The process begins with adequate social skills. Introduce yourself. Hear the client's name and remember it. Invite the client to sit down and see to it that he or she is reasonably comfortable. Address the client by name. If he or she appears highly anxious, initiate some social conversation and watch to see if the anxiety begins to dissipate. Notice nonverbal behavior and use it to try to understand the client's emotional state. Invite the client to describe his or her reason for coming to talk to you. Allow the client *time* to respond. This behavior is often described as *attending* or *active listening*. It communicates to the client that you are interested in the person, what she or he has to say, and that you will try to understand both the spoken and the unspoken message in the communication.

The relationship is not established in a single contact. Several sessions may be required before the client becomes comfortable with you and begins to admit you into his or her inner world. During these several sessions, consistency is an important quality. Your behaviors, your attitudes and opinions, your promptness and attention to detail, your acknowledgement of the client's personal and cultural integrity, all will be observed by the client. If you vary from session to session in these details, the client will find you less predictable and will find it more difficult to become comfortable with you. Equally important is your sensitivity to cultural similarities and dissimilarities in this rapport-building stage. Consider what you already know about persons who are of Latino or German or Vietnamese backgrounds in these initial sessions.

While it is not the same as friendship, rapport in counseling shares some qualities with good friendships, and this often proves confusing. As clients begin to know a little about you and your patterns, they will allow a relationship bond to develop. On the other hand, *you* must also relate to your clients for rapport to develop. If you assume a *role* or a *posture* that doesn't fit what you feel about yourself or about the client, then you will find the relationship to be insincere or shallow. It may seem quite uncomfortable to be so authentic with clients, but the alternative—to pretend to be someone you are not—is a self-defeating and ultimately nonhelpful approach to establishing a therapeutic relationship.

### Assessing the Problem

Even as you and your client are in the process of establishing a relationship, a second process is under way. That process involves the collection and classification of information related to the client's personhood and reasons for seeking counseling. We have labeled this the *assessment stage*, though it might also be thought of as the problem-identification process. In this context, we can think of assessment in three ways. First, assessment depends on the counselor's theoretical and philosophical view of human problems. Second, assessment depends on the conditions present in the client's situation and the counselor's understanding of those conditions. And third, assessment depends on the client's cultural frame of reference and the conditions that frame of reference imposes on the client's worldview.

Client problems may be conceptualized as *needs* (something is missing in my life and its absence is disturbing the natural flow of life forces); *stressors* (something unpleasant has entered my life and its presence is producing distress and distraction); *life conditions* (conditions outside my control are limiting my potential happiness and success in life); *misinterpretations* (the way I am thinking about my life limits my alternatives); *dysfunctional social patterns* (I am a worse person with some people than I am with others and that is a source of distress and unhappiness); or more likely, a combination of these factors. Counseling theories tend to classify these client conditions as either *affective, behavioral, cognitive,* or *systemic* in origin (Corsini & Wedding, 1989). In other words, the client's problems emerge from emotional sources, undesirable behavioral contingencies, cognitive misrepresentations of reality, or systemic/contextual contingencies.

For many years, mental health providers debated among themselves which was the most accurate representation of human problems. That debate has subsided but remains an issue even today. Perhaps the most viable resolution of the debate is to suggest that the view that makes the most sense to you is the approach you will follow. Prochaska and Norcross (1994, p. 4) report research on theoretical preferences of 818 American psychologists, counselors, psychiatrists, and social workers, which indicates a decided preference (34 percent) for an eclectic or integrative approach to conceptualizing human problems.

In actual practice, it is more important to attempt to assess problems in more than one way to avoid the constraints of personal bias or theoretical encapsulation. This also includes thinking of the problem in the client's social context as well as in a theoretical context. While the "source" of a problem may be conceptualized as emotion-based (affective), behavior-based (behavioral), thought-based (cognitive), relationship-based (systems), or milieu-based (cultural), the impact or consequences of the problem may be felt as feelings, worries, undesirable consequences, missing or unsatisfactory interpersonal relationships or unfair discrimination (see Chapter 4).

The assessment stage is, first, a data-collecting time. You will want to open all of your communication channels to receive information that the client is communicating. At first you may sense no patterns, no meaning to the information. As you continue to work with the client, however, patterns will emerge, and you will begin to understand how the client perceives and tries to affect reality. You will also begin to see your client in the larger context of his/her environment, social setting, or world of relationships. And as the subtleties become increasingly obvious, either by their repetition or by their inconsistencies, you will begin to recognize how you can help your client.

Many views exist as to how assessment should be conducted. Our view is that you should have some blueprint to follow. Otherwise, the amount of detail will begin to overwhelm the process, and you will either overlook important information to solicit and consider or you will become distracted from your purpose, which is to determine just what the problem is before you begin to provide solutions. In Chapter 4, we offer an approach to problem assessment that is widely used in clinical settings.

The process of clinical assessment involves several specific skills, including observation, inquiry, making associations among facts, recording information, and forming hypotheses or clinical "hunches." *Observation* includes:

1. Taking notice of the client's general state of anxiety or discomfort
2. Establishing some sense of the client's cultural context
3. Noting gestures or movements that suggest either emotional or physical dysfunctions
4. Hearing the manner in which the client frames or alludes to his or her problems (for example, some tend to diminish while others inflate aspects of a problem)
5. Noting verbal and nonverbal patterns

What may appear to be an insignificant detail at the moment can prove to be part of a significant pattern over time. Thus, observation, mental attentiveness to the persona of the client, is a significant component of the assessment process.

*Inquiry* is equally important. Beginning counselors have a tendency to ask a lot of initial questions but few follow-up questions, while experienced counselors pursue *certain* topics in great detail. Issues related to health, medication, feelings of despair or depression, self-destructive thoughts, and even interpersonal conflicts are examples of such topics. Inquiry is the skill of asking for the finer points, the details behind the event, the information that provides the meaning to an event or condition. Open-ended questions explore processes; closed questions provide specifics. Both are important inquiry tools.

Collected information must somehow be organized and recorded. Some counselors take notes as they acquire information. Others record sessions on audio- or videotape. Some do neither but allow time immediately following the session to write down observations and impressions. The recording of information is a disciplined process. If not done systematically and promptly, it is lost and therefore useless. It is a common counselor lament that information previously given is unavailable because it was not recorded promptly.

When the counselor utilizes observation and inquiry to collect information related to the client's presenting problem, the result is a huge quantity of material. The more observant the counselor, the greater the amount of data. Somehow this information must be synthesized so as to make it usable. This synthesis is conducted within a context. The context may be a counseling theory, or it may simply be the counselor's view of life. Whatever the case, the process involves associating facts and events, constructing possible explanations for events, and making educated (or intuitive) guesses. This assimilation process condenses a large quantity of information into a more usable form. These hypotheses, hunches, and educated guesses become the foundation stones for the next stage, identifying and setting counseling goals. At this time, it is vital that you incorporate multicultural perspectives into your assessment. Pederson (1991, p. 9) cautions, that "Behavior [or feelings, or cognitions, or social systems are] not data until and unless [they are] understood in the context of the person's culturally learned expectations." Finally, you might ask the client what he or she thinks the problem is. This simple question often elicits the most important information, the most accurate insights of the entire process. It is surprising that counselors often fail to ask this straightforward question.

## Goal-Setting

Setting goals is very important to the success of counseling. And yet, some clients and even some counselors resist setting goals. The act of setting a goal involves making a commitment to a set of conditions, a course of action, or an outcome. Sometimes the highly stressed client or the disoriented client may find goal-setting difficult to do. Even in this situation, the goal ultimately becomes one of setting goals.

Why are goals so important? The best answer is a simple one. We set goals in order to know how well counseling is working and when counseling should be concluded. Isn't it enough to let the client decide these questions? Yes and no. The client is an important source of information and reaction to counseling. However, because counseling can generate dependent relationships, the immediate desire to hold on to a rewarding relationship may overshadow the more appropriate objectives of counseling. Furthermore, as will be evident later, the kinds of things that are done in counseling, the interventions, are often determined by the counseling goal.

The process of setting goals is mutually defined by the counselor and client. The counselor has the advantage of greater objectivity, training in normal and abnormal behavior, and experience in the process. The client has the advantages of intensive experience with the problem and its history, potential insights, and awareness of personal investment in change. Thus, the client needs to be involved in the thinking as well as the decisions about what should happen.

The skills involved in goal-setting may be divided into three classes. First are the counselor's inferential skills. A counselor must be able to listen to a client's vague descriptions of existing and desired conditions and read between the lines of those messages. Rarely are clients able to describe crisply and concisely what they would like to accomplish through counseling. On the contrary, most clients describe their reasons for seeking help in generalities. The typical client is more likely to conceptualize concerns as "I don't want to feel this way any longer," rather than "I want to start feeling that way." So, given this condition, the counselor must be able to think of alternative behaviors and attitudes even as he or she listens to clients describe their concerns.

The second skill involves differentiation between ultimate goals, intermediate goals, and immediate goals. Most of us think in terms of ultimate goals: for example, when I grow up; when I graduate from college; when I get that promotion; when my boat comes in. But if we are to accomplish ultimate goals, we must be able to think in terms of intermediate goals (in the next six months I plan to . . .) and immediate goals (I will do the following things tomorrow). Intermediate and immediate goals provide the strategies necessary to accomplish ultimate goals and are the real vehicle for change in counseling.

The third skill of the goal-setting process involves teaching clients how to think realistically in intermediate and immediate terms. In other words, the counselor may need to teach clients how to set goals that are attainable. In Chapter 5, we discuss ways in which you can use these three sets of skills to help clients set realistic goals for counseling.

Finally, it should be emphasized that counseling goals are never chiseled in stone. Goals can be altered when new information or new insights into the problem call for change. Sometimes a goal is identified inappropriately and must be dropped. It is important to remember that the major function of goals is to provide direction to the counselor and the client.

### Initiating Interventions

There are different points of view concerning what a good counselor should do with clients. These viewpoints are, by and large, related to different counseling theories. As you are aware from Chapter 1, a variety of counseling theories exist, each of which can be used by counselors to organize information, define problems, and select intervention strategies. For example, a person-centered orientation would suggest that the counselor involves rather than intervenes by placing emphasis on the relationship. The existential counselor would view intervention as encouraging clients to recognize and assume personal responsibility for their choices. The behavioral counselor seeks to initiate activities that help clients alter and manage personal contingencies, both in the counseling session and in the clients' real world.

The cognitive counselor intervenes by introducing conditions that invite cognitive dissonance or disrupt static cognitive states. The systemic counselor intervenes by challenging interpersonal "rules" or interrupting systemic sequences. The multicultural counselor (as Ivey et al, 1993) imply, uses the total spectrum of approaches *and* intervenes by understanding the client's cultural milieu and helping the client take charge of his/her life within that milieu. In short, all counselors, regardless of theoretical orientation, have a therapeutic plan that they follow, a plan that is related to the assessment of the presenting problem, to their view of human nature and change processes, and to the resulting goals that have been agreed upon.

The real issue in talking about interventions is change and how it occurs. The whole object of counseling is to *initiate and facilitate desirable change*. Thus, when you and your client are able to identify desirable goals or outcomes, the next logical question is "How shall we accomplish these goals?" In Chapters 7–10 we shall discuss specific types of interventions used in counseling. For the moment, let us consider briefly the process a counselor goes through in identifying counseling interventions based on the assessment process.

Having defined the "problem," the first thing you should do is ask clients what solutions or remedies they have already tried. Most of the time, clients will be able to describe one or more things they have done which were to no avail or only minimally successful in alleviating the problem. This information not only saves you from suggesting alternatives that will be rejected; it also gives you a sense of the client's past efforts to remedy difficulties and the client's resourcefulness as a problem solver. Occasionally clients will report that something they attempted did work but for one reason or another, they discontinued the remedy. Client-induced interventions that were temporarily effective can sometimes be modified and made more effective. Such answers might also broaden your definition of the problem to include the client's inability to stay with a solution until it succeeded.

Assuming all client-induced interventions were ineffective, the next step is to relate problems to interventions, depending on the character of the problem. That is to say, problems that appear to be a result of how the client is viewing a life situation may be defined as cognitively determined problems. This would suggest that interventions that are directed toward cognitive change should be considered. If the problem appears to be related to the client's social environment (family, work, friends, community), then interventions that are designed to alter interdependent social systems should be considered. If the problem appears to be couched in terms like "hurt," "sadness," or "anger," then it may be affectively based, in which case interventions that facilitate affective disclosure and exploration should be included. Or if the problem's character appears related to the client's actions or efforts to affect others, the problem may be behaviorally based. Then the most effective interventions may be designed to help the client achieve more successful behaviors. The intervention strategies described in Chapters 7, 8, 9, and 10 are grouped around these dimensions of client problems. Chapter 7 examines affective strategies; Chapter 8 presents cognitive strategies; Chapter 9 addresses strategies for behavioral change; and Chapter 10 explores strategies and interventions designed to bring about system change.

Choosing the right intervention is often a process of adaptation. Not all interventions work with all clients, or as well as one might predict. Sometimes the "perfect" intervention turns out to be perfectly awful. It is important that you approach selection of interventions judiciously, prepared to change strategies when the intervention of choice is not working. This process is similar to the treatment of medical problems. When one treatment does not produce the desired response, the practitioner should have an alternative treatment in reserve or reevaluate how the problem is defined.

The skills related to initiating interventions are: (1) competency in using a specific intervention; (2) knowledge of appropriate uses of a specific intervention; (3) knowledge of typical responses to that type of intervention; and (4) observational skills related to the client's response to the intervention. Developing the skills necessary to use different interventions requires that the counselor be able to practice in safe surroundings under expert supervision. Typically, this kind of practice occurs in a counseling practice or supervised clinical field practice. Counselors who try interventions on clients without the benefit of supervised practice are fooling themselves about their potential harmful effect on clients or about their ability to recover from destructive situations.

The counselor also needs to know how clients normally react to a specific intervention. Usually this is expressed in terms of a range of typical reactions. The object is to recognize the abnormal reaction, the unpredictable response, the result of which might intensify the problem rather than alleviate it. For example, the "empty chair" (discussed in Chapter 7) is a gestalt technique often used to help clients recognize and expand their awareness of alternative feelings or reactions. It is a powerful technique, one that sometimes provides access to hidden and possibly frightening feelings. Occasionally this technique will unlock an overwhelming amount of emotion for the client. In such a case, the counselor must be able to recognize that the client's reaction is more than the typical response to this treatment. Related to this awareness of potential effects are the counselor's observational skills. It matters little that the counselor knows the warning signs if he or she does not see them flashing. These three characteristics—

skill with a specific intervention, knowledge of its effects, and ability to "read" client reactions—constitute the skills inherent in effective counseling interventions.

## Termination and Follow-Up

It is difficult to get beginning counselors to think of termination. They are so much more concerned with how to begin counseling, that ending the process seems a distant problem. However, all counseling has as its ultimate criterion the successful termination of the client. With this in mind, let us consider the significance and subtleties of the termination process.

Counseling, and especially good counseling, becomes a very significant event for most clients. The relationship to the counselor may be the most important relationship in the client's life at that moment. Thus, it is imperative that the counselor acknowledge how important he or she is to most clients and how much his or her actions affect them. Some counselors will find this flattering. Others may find it uncomfortable. Some will find it incomprehensible that they could become so important to a stranger in so short a time. However, the fact that the relationship is important does not negate the fact that the relationship must eventually end.

How does a counselor terminate a counseling relationship without destroying the gains that have been accomplished? It must be done with sensitivity, with intentionality and forethought, and by degree. As the client begins to accomplish the goals that had been set, it becomes apparent that a void is being created. The temptation is to set new goals, create new activity, and continue the counseling process. However, even this may not succeed in filling the void. Eventually, the client begins to realize that the original purpose for seeking counseling no longer supports the process. At this point a creative crisis occurs for the client.

Long before the client reaches this awareness, the counselor should be recognizing the signs, anticipating the creative crisis, and laying the groundwork for a successful termination. As a general rule, the counselor should devote as many sessions to the active terminating process as were devoted to the rapport-building process. This is what is meant by termination by degree. When it is apparent that the counseling relationship may not last more than four to six more sessions, it is time for the counselor to acknowledge that the relationship will eventually end. This can be done simply by saying, "I think we are soon going to be finished with our work."

It is not uncommon for this early acknowledgment to provoke a denial or even a temporary crisis. Up to this point, the client may not have been thinking about facing his or her problems alone. If the client denies, allow it. The denial is part of the recovery process and will dissipate. On the other hand, if the counselor resists the denial by assuring the client that he or she is much stronger, it may only intensify the crisis. It is important to remember that the client must get used to this new thought. In succeeding sessions, the opportunity may arise to introduce the thought again. Gradually, the client will come around, will begin to let self-resourcefulness fill the void, and ultimately will "decide" that counseling can end soon.

Occasionally, clients need a bit of security to take with them, even though they feel ready to terminate. This can be accomplished by making a follow-up appointment six weeks, three months, or even six months in advance. It may be a good idea to ask clients to decide whether they feel the need to keep the appointment as the date approaches. If they do not, they can call and cancel and let the counselor know that they are doing well. On the other hand, it is also important to communicate to clients that if new counseling needs arise, they should feel free to call before the appointment date. In Chapter 11 we discuss in greater depth the skills and concepts associated with termination and follow-up.

## Using the Stages to Plan for Counseling

Counseling begins with building a relationship and then moves to assessment, and from assessment to goal-setting, and so on. The fact that one begins assessment before completing the rapport-building stage does not negate this progression. Perhaps the best use of stages is to provide a blueprint for the beginning counselor. For example, as you begin working with a client, you may expect to devote the early sessions to developing a helping relationship. This is very important time. When the client begins accepting and trusting the counseling experience (and thus, you), this may be a signal to move fully into the assessment stage. However, you will soon realize that relationship- and rapport-building continue to be issues to be addressed even as you move into the subsequent stages. As you and your client study the problem, comments will be made, wishes visualized, that point directly toward potential counseling outcomes. The process begins to seem like a natural flow. With experience, this blueprint becomes second nature, until it is no longer necessary to think in terms of stages. However, even experienced counselors find occasionally that cases are not progressing well. It is not uncommon for a case to stall or for a sense of lack of movement to take over. When that happens, it is a good idea to return to the blueprint, analyze the progress of the case in terms of stages, and redirect the counseling process where appropriate.

## The Client's Experience in Counseling

Very early in the development of his person-centered approach to counseling, Carl Rogers described how the client experiences positive change in psychotherapy. This description became formalized as the Process Scale (Rogers & Rablen, 1958) and was used for many years to study client change. The scale describes seven kinds of client reaction as change occurs. Typically, the client begins counseling by talking about externals (work, relatives, etc.) rather than self. This gradually changes to include references to feelings, albeit past feelings or those that are external to the client. In the third stage, the client elaborates on feelings, but these are historical rather than current. At the fourth level, the client begins to talk about present feelings and acknowledges ownership of these feelings. The fifth stage is one in which the client allows him/herself to experience current feelings in the presence of the counselor. In the final two stages the client begins (1) to experience previously denied feelings and (2) to be accepting and comfortable with those feelings. Rogers never forced this development. Rather, he allowed the client to move at whatever speed was comfortable through this developmental progression.

The client's experience can be similarly described within the context of the five stages of counseling. As we noted earlier, most clients approach counseling with mixed feelings. While they want to improve their life situation, they are reluctant to become involved in the counseling process. This is the first obstacle for many clients to overcome. In the following sections, we discuss some typical responses clients have during these five stages of counseling.

### Rapport and the Client's Experience

Inexperienced clients enter counseling without knowing exactly what to expect or what will be expected of them. Because of this information deficit, they may feel uncertain, vulnerable, or guarded and doubtful. When the counseling relationship crosses cultural boundaries, this sense of vulnerability is even more emphasized. In addition to an information deficit, the client who is culturally different from the counselor may have concerns that are directly related to the person of the counselor. Will he/she understand how life is for me? Will he/she be sympathetic to the special problems I may face in life? Or will the counselor expect me to conform to the values and standards of his/her own cultural background? Will we be able to negotiate our differences and find a common ground of understanding and acceptance?

There are a number of things that the counselor can do to ease this client anxiety. A helpful word of direction—whether it be a suggestion of where to sit, how long the session will be, or a description of what takes place when people are counseled—will be welcomed. When the relationship involves multicultural dimensions, it is appropriate to acknowledge those factors, and communicate your respect and acceptance for your client's worldview. If you don't know the client's worldview, it is appropriate to learn what it is. Sue (1992, p. 6) has argued that traditional counseling which fails to acknowledge cultural worldviews can actually harm minorities and women because it may transmit a set of individualistic cultural values that maintain the status quo and as such, represent a political statement. His identification of *traditional* counseling includes those approaches that fail to acknowledge multicultural factors in the counseling process.

Not all clients will react tentatively to the newness of the situation or with reservations that are culturally determined. Some task-oriented clients begin as though it were already the third session and give little indication that they are anxious or uncertain. This, too, does not mean that rapport has been established. The issues of trust, respect, and safety have been suspended temporarily as the client rushes into the process. Those issues may arise later as the client begins to look to the counselor for reactions.

By the end of the first session, many clients have begun to relax and take in the environment of the counseling setting. They may notice and comment on such things as furniture, pictures, and room arrangement. The client is taking mental pictures and forming first impressions. Between the first and second session, these mental pictures have a significant role. They are the bridge between sessions. If the mental pictures are inaccurate, as is often the case, the client will enter the second counseling session with erroneous perceptions that will lead, once again, to heightened anxiety.

Usually the second session begins on a somewhat better footing than did the first. At the least, the client understands some of the conditions surrounding the counseling process (e.g., time limits, responsibility, and so on). But the client must also check out the impressions recalled from the first session and, of course, discover what direction the second session will take. As a result, the second session might be another nervous experience. If you are still attending to relationship issues, the client will become reassured once again, and the focus of the session will gradually shift to substantive issues. This same development will be repeated for several sessions. But as the client and counselor become better acquainted and more comfortable with one another, the progression from relationship to substantive issues takes less and less time.

### *Assessment and the Client's Experience*

Most clients expect assessment to take place, but their expectations are often quite different from what actually happens. It is not uncommon for clients to ask for some form of verification of the nature and intensity of their problem(s). This expectation probably is fostered by the medical model. One goes to the family physician with a fever, swollen glands, and aching joints, and expects to leave with a prescription for medication and some advice on how to treat the symptoms. A more analogous situation would be one in which the patient undergoes lab tests to determine the source as well as the appropriate treatment. In fact, neither analogy adequately describes the assessment process in counseling. For that reason, it is a good idea to explain the process early in counseling, thereby informing the client as well as soliciting the client's assistance.

Clients also have a strong interest in determining what or who "caused" their problems. Very often this question is pursued with such vigor that one would expect the answer to be the solution. In fact, the cause of most human concerns is rarely the solution to the problem. There are exceptions to this, of course. An example would be the feminist therapist's view that "it is not sufficient to help a woman work through a depressive episode. It is critical to help this woman develop consciousness of how society's expectations of her gender relate to her depression," thus achieving a balance of self and environment (Cheatham et al., 1993, p. 113). Similar perspectives are appropriate with people of color who suffer from societal oppression, or with physically challenged clients whose struggle with the environment is a major part of their problems.

Knowing why a set of conditions exists will not make them go away. But this knowledge may have implications for some of the goals of counseling. We cannot assume that *all* human problems are internal, that is, determined by how the client thinks, feels, or behaves. Some problems include an *external* dimension. Family therapy has helped us recognize this fact. It is also true that society and culture factors can be part of the problem for women, for the gay community, for the physically challenged, and for the culturally different. When this is recognized, the assessment process must account for these external factors as well as the more traditional internal factors.

For whatever reason, clients tend to approach assessment with mixed feelings. While the solution to their problem may be found in the process, so might the cause and that may prove to be intractable. What if the problem is unsolvable? This process of assessment leads the counselor and client to the next stage, setting goals to deal with the client's unique situation.

## Goal-Setting and the Client's Experience

As counseling progresses, both client and counselor grow in their understanding of one another and of the dynamics and interrelationships that are part of the client's problems. And as this happens, appropriate solutions or outcomes often begin to appear which may seem unreachable without the counselor's help. Thus, the client will look to the counselor for assistance in identifying interventions or strategies that will lead to the desirable outcome. Although this involves a certain amount of trust in the counselor's ability to assist, it may also be accompanied by some suspicion. The client probably does not intend to be suspicious of the counselor. Rather, the suspicion grows from the fear that the problem cannot be solved, the situation cannot or will not change, or the prospect of change is too threatening to contemplate. This latter resistance is described in Chapter 10 as homeostasis, a tendency to maintain the status quo. Thus, some clients will resist setting goals. It is as though their mantra is "Nothing ventured, nothing lost." Only as they experience some success in counseling will these reservations begin to dissipate, but that takes both time and wise direction by the counselor.

Will the client accept your assistance and direction? One criterion clients use in determining this is the extent to which you appear to understand the client or the problem. The client may express this condition as, "She understands my problem in the same way I understand it," or "He really understands what makes me tick." Thus, goal-setting is intimately connected to the process of assessment. And, of course, goal-setting is intimately connected to action.

### *Interventions and the Client's Experience*

Many clients enter counseling vacillating between hope and doubt. Having already failed at solving their problems, they find it difficult to imagine that someone else could find the magic key. On the other hand, the need to find relief demands that they continue their search. In this context, the counselor begins to suggest, to assign, to challenge, to encourage, to empathize, and to monitor. Many clients have an early rush of hopefulness as positive rapport is established and assessment begins. Soon, however, they begin to look for change and may become discouraged if none is apparent. There are many ways to help clients through this period. Some counselors begin by cautioning their clients that a lull sometimes occurs before change. Other counselors handle this phenomenon by carefully planning goals and objectives so as to assure some level of early success. Another approach would view this as a natural crisis in the counseling process, one in which the client is beginning to address the issues of personal responsibility for change.

Change is a vulnerable process. We do not let go of old ways until we have new ways to put in their place. When the new is forced on us, we often resist or retreat until we can make the necessary personal adaptations. It is not uncommon for clients to react enthusiastically to interventions, to make major strides, and then to regress to old patterns. Typically, the regression is less than the original progress and is temporary. Nevertheless, as clients observe first their progress and then their regression, they can begin to doubt the process, or more accurately, their prospects for change through counseling.

As they recover from these temporary setbacks, clients regain their confidence and new patterns become more stable. By this time, some clients can begin to anticipate a new kind of crisis, the crisis of termination. They are feeling better about themselves, about their ability to handle problems, and about the counseling process. A cognitive dissonance emerges which may be conceptualized as

*Through counseling I am stronger, more satisfied, more in control. Thus, I soon may need to end that which has proven so helpful. But I'm not sure I would be as strong, as satisfied, as in control without counseling. On the other hand, I will never know if counseling is propping me up or if I have really changed unless I leave counseling.*

The resolution of this conflict is critical to the success of the counseling process. **Only when the client decides to take the risk of ending counseling can it ever be established that counseling helped.** It is critical at two levels. First, counseling gains must be supported and maintained in the client's real environment. And second, the client must be able to view himself or herself as a changed person.

## Termination and the Client's Experience

Counseling is no more permanent than any other life condition. When termination occurs as a result of successful counseling, the process is one of both accomplishment and regret. Feeling self-confident, more integrated, and forward-looking, the client experiences a sense of optimism about the future. At the same time, the client is saying good-bye to a significant relationship, unique in that it allowed the client to be the center of attention, concern, and effort. One does not give up such relationships easily. Thus, there is also a sense of loss blended into the termination. These two emotional undercurrents will surface as the client and counselor discuss the ramifications of terminating. Some clients may even be confused by these seemingly contradictory feelings. Under these circumstances, they probably are misinterpreting the loss reaction as weakness or nonreadiness to terminate.

When termination occurs as a result of unsuccessful counseling, the critical factor is who initiated the termination. If the counselor initiates it, either because he or she lacked the requisite skills or because the relationship between counselor and client was counterproductive, then ethical and personal issues must be acknowledged. The ethical issues relate to professional responsibility for the client's well-being. Usually this is handled by making an appropriate and successful referral. Personal issues are those which deal with client interpretations of why referral is necessary. As was noted earlier, clients are quite vulnerable when they seek counseling. If the experience turns out unsuccessfully, some are likely to turn on themselves as having failed again. Others may conclude that counseling will not work, just as they had feared. The counselor must acknowledge and help the client work through these reactions as part of the termination process.

On the other hand, if the client initiates termination, a different set of dynamics arises. In this situation, both the client and counselor are vulnerable. The counselor's responsibilities are no less real, however, and include referral considerations, and if possible, personal considerations.

Perhaps the most difficult of termination situations is that in which counseling has been partially successful but cannot be continued. This might occur as a result of the counselor or client changing residence, as a result of client decisions to discontinue or postpone counseling, or as a result of the counselor's conviction that the client should begin working with another counselor. In this case, the client experiences loss even more intensely than when counseling was successful. That loss may be justifiable. The anger is a means of adapting to the new circumstances. But the fear is a potentially debilitating condition and must be addressed for successful termination to occur.

Whatever the reason for termination, you are professionally obliged to extend a helping relationship to the client until you are replaced by another helping professional. This may take the form of providing an opportunity to make future appointments, calling the client at a future date to check in, finding a mental health professional who would be an appropriate reference and who would be willing to accept the referral, or collaborating with the professional to whom the client has been referred.

## Dependence and Growth

Throughout the counseling process, psychological dynamics are present and are affecting the development of the relationship, the progress toward goals, and ultimately, the outcome. We have already discussed such issues and trust, respect, and psychological comfort in this context. Another dynamic should be addressed: client dependence.

As you and your client begin to understand one another and the counseling relationship unfolds, a state of client dependence often develops quite appropriately. It is at this time that some obstacles to the relationship will become factors. If cultural differences between you and your client have not been accommodated, client dependence is far less likely to occur.

Typically, client dependency begins at a low level, while the client is deciding whether to become involved in the counseling relationship. As confidence in you grows, so does the dependency on both you and the process. Through the relationship-building and assessment stages this dynamic is particularly noticeable. Even in the goal-setting stage, many clients will lean as much as possible on the counselor to make the decisions, to point out the direction counseling will take. However, an important transition occurs during this stage as clients begin to realize that the decisions they are making, the goals they are setting, are very important personal commitments. It is at this time that dependency begins to shift from the counselor toward self-responsibility. This transition becomes increasingly obvious in the intervention stage as the client assumes more and more responsibility for changes in behavior, attitudes, and emotions. The final accomplishment in this evolution from dependence to independence is reflected in the client's decision to terminate. Even as the client wrestles with the conflicting desires to keep the relationship and let it go, there is an underlying awareness that success means termination, cutting the bonds, and becoming self-managing.

## Summary

All relationships have structure. That structure may take the form of roles that the participants play, rules that they follow as they interact with one another, or concepts about what different types of relationship are like. Until we understand the structure of a relationship, we find it difficult to understand how to be part of that relationship. In this chapter, we have provided a structure for viewing the counseling relationship. Beginning with building the helping relationship, the counselor then moves on to assessment, goal-setting, planning and initiating interventions, and finally termination and follow-up. These stages are never accomplished without the participation of the client. Within each stage, there is much to be considered. Often two stages will overlap. Occasionally, the counselor and client will need to take stock and move back to an earlier stage. Throughout these stages, evaluation is an important activity, whether it be considering how well the relationship seems to be developing, whether the problem has been correctly identified, whether the goals that have been identified are appropriate (or achievable), how well the interventions seem to be working, and of course, what needs are part of the process of ending the relationship.

Finally, we considered the client's part in this experience. How does the typical client react to this passage from initiation to termination? What are *normal* expectations? These many facets of the counseling experience are important but often intangible. Thus, while you attend to the progress of counseling, it is also important that you attend to the client's experience, listening for the intangible, the unique, the nonconforming aspects of each client's passage.

## Exercises

1. Select a partner and role-play a counseling relationship. Determine in advance which of the five stages you will illustrate in the role-play (building a relationship; assessment; goal-setting; interventions; termination). Have other class members observe and then identify the stage. Continue this exercise until you have illustrated all five stages. Then discuss the following question:

    Are the counselor's verbal behaviors the same across all stages or do they change? Describe any changes you would expect to see.

2. Using the same partner, develop a role-play in which the relationship stage is enacted. One of you should assume the identity of a person of a distinctly different culture than the other. After the enactment, discuss what dynamics you experienced in the role play. What insights did you gain? What problems did each of you experience? What implications for learning did you discover? Share your experience with minority members of your class and ask them if they could offer additional insights.

3. Select a partner and determine who will be the counselor and who will be the client. Then enact the following role-play.

    You and your client have been working for five months and have reached a plateau. Most of the client's presenting problems at the outset of counseling have been resolved. In your judgment, based on the client's report, the client is functioning well and could really terminate counseling at this time. The client both agrees and disagrees with this assessment. He or she has no new problems to address, but really regrets (and perhaps fears) to see counseling end. You have no desire to terminate prematurely, but your concern is that the client realize and accept that he/she is functioning well and is not in need of further counseling.

    Following the role-play, discuss among yourselves the dynamics that seemed to arise during the session. What were your feelings? The client's feelings? Were you able to stay on task? Could you see the client's ambivalence? Could you help the client with that ambivalence? Where do you think the relationship was heading?

## Discussion Questions

1. How is assessment different from goal-setting? What counseling activities are part of assessment but not part of goal-setting? What activities are common to both?

2. Discuss the ramifications of the relationship-building stage. How does it affect the assessment stage? The goal-setting stage? The intervention stage? Termination?

3. If counseling interventions do not seem to be working, what might be the problem? How would you know?

4. What do you think is the most important stage in the counseling relationship? Why do you choose this stage? How does your choice reflect your theoretical biases? Your own cultural-ethnic background and values? Your gender? Would you consider yourself more attuned to what people do, to what people think, or to how people feel? How much of people's reactions can be attributed to their personal qualities? How much to their environment?

5. How does one *know* when counseling should terminate? Is there more than one way of knowing?

## Recommended Readings

Axelson, J.A. (1993). *Counseling and Development in a Multicultural Society*, 2nd ed. Pacific Grove, CA: Brooks/Cole. Chapter 1, Culture and counseling.

Hackney, H. and Cormier, S. (1994). *Counseling Strategies and Interventions*, 4th ed. Boston, MA: Allyn & Bacon. Chapter 9, Conceptualizing problems and setting goals.

Hansen, J.C., Rossberg, R.H., and Cramer, S.H. (1994). *Counseling Theory and Process*, 5th ed. Chapter 13, Stages in the counseling process.

Lee, C.C. and Richardson, B.L. (1991). *Multicultural Issues in Counseling: New Approaches to Diversity*. Alexandria, VA: ACA Press. Chapter 2, Cultural dynamics: Their importance in multicultural counseling.

Waehler, C.A. and Lenox, R.A. (1994). A concurrent (vs. stage) model for conceptualizing and representing the counseling process, *Journal of Counseling and Development, 73*, 17–22.

# Chapter 3

# *Rapport and Relationship*

### *Purpose of This Chapter—*

This chapter examines the first of the five stages, establishing rapport and a positive therapeutic relationship. Counselor qualities and behaviors and client qualities and input that are associated with therapeutic relationships are discussed. The increased likelihood that counseling will be a multicultural experience is recognized as an important factor in forming the relationship. The chapter seeks to address relationship issues that would be part of that multicultural counseling experience, including the counselor's responsibility for both the client's cultural identity and sensitivity as well as his/her own.

### *Considerations as You Read This Chapter—*

- You have known many relationships. What have your relationship experiences been like? Which ones were supportive, helpful, or meaningful to you? What personal needs did they satisfy in you?
  - Which of your relationships have had the same effect on the other person? What is it about you, or the things you do in a relatioship, that would prove supportive, helpful or meaningful to another person?
- How well do you know yourself as a person? Where did you get your eccentricities? Your values? Your ways of viewing yourself and others?
  - What were the values of your family? Did your family value closeness or separateness? Organization or disorganization?

Confronting or avoiding? Touching or distance? Inclusiveness or exclusiveness?

• With what social, cultural or ethnic group did your family identify?

The relationship you establish with your client is the beginning point, foundation, for all that will follow in the counseling process. Clients "need to feel cared for, attended to, understood, and genuinely worked with if successful therapy is to continue" (Deffenbacher, 1985, p. 262). People who choose to become mental health providers must be able to offer a rather unique kind of relationship to their clients. It incorporates many elements of a social relationship, a friendship relationship, and an intimate relationship, and yet it is none of these. It is a relationship created and maintained by both parties, yet it develops and continues primarily to serve the needs of only one of the participants. It is built on many of the qualities found in the best and most intimate friendships—trust, safety, openness, and sharing—yet to protect the welfare of the client, distinct boundaries exist.

Being able to establish such relationship qualities with people may have been one of the major reasons you have chosen to study counseling. But therein lies a danger. If establishing relationships has been one of your interpersonal strengths, you may be taking that part of your skills for granted. Counseling relationships are far more complicated than social relationships or even friendships. In addition to the assumed relationship qualities, they involve ethical behaviors, professional competence, the personal mental health of the helper, the unidirectional purposes of the encounter, and the integrity of the client. If you take interpersonal skills for granted, you will miss many of the clues clients give that shape the unique demands of the counseling relationship.

Meeting the unique demands of the counseling relationship calls for the counselor to seek to build rapport, to bring interpersonal anxiety in the relationship to a functional level, to provide the genuineness and self-confidence that engenders client trust. The goal is to create a counseling atmosphere that communicates respect for the client, a warmth and accepting disposition, and a willingness to commit to a serious effort to be of help.

It is important to note that counseling skills are only part of the construction of this relationship. An important portion of the structure draws on your personal qualities which include your self-comfort, your liking of other people, your sense of what constitutes personal failure in life, your willingness to get involved in other peoples' lives without being able to control the outcome. A third dimension of the counseling relationship is the client's personal qualities and how they interact with your own. It is possible for you to bring major personal strengths and yet the interaction between you and your client produces a chemistry that is not therapeutically facilitative. Thus, relationship is a composite of counselor personal qualities, client personal qualities and therapeutic skills. In the remainder of this chapter, we shall consider each of these contributions.

## Characteristics of an Effective Therapeutic Relationship

One of the giants of the counseling profession was Dr. Carl Rogers. Early in his career he proposed that there are six counseling conditions that are both necessary and sufficient to produce constructive client personality change (Rogers, 1957). Although the notion that any *conditions* may be sufficient to bring about change is arguable today, it is beyond argument that certain conditions do facilitate a beneficial relationship and others do not. It follows that clients are more likely to achieve their goals when a good and positive relationship exists.

Conditions that have been identified as important in the establishment of an effective counselor-client relationship include *accurate empathy, counselor genuineness, and an unconditional caring or positive regard for the client.* These variables are derived from person-centered therapy (Rogers, 1957; Holdstock & Rogers, 1977; Meador & Rogers, 1984; Raskin & Rogers, 1989). Proponents of diverse theoretical orientations join on this one issue, that effective counselors are personally integrated and self-aware, value the client as a unique person, and are able to understand how and what the client is experiencing.

A constructive counselor-client relationship serves not only to increase the opportunity for clients to achieve their goals, but also serves as a potential model of a healthy interpersonal relationship, one that clients can use to improve the quality of their other relationships outside the counseling setting.

### Empathy

Accurate empathy calls for the counselor to "understand what the other person (the client) is experiencing, thinking, and feeling, and how the other perceives his or her behavior" (Holdstock & Rogers, 1977, p. 139). If you think about the conditions in this definition, you realize that it is quite a tall order to be empathic. This definition, and the person-centered approach to counseling, carries some limitations as well. It is individualistic in its focus, by accounting for the client's world primarily through intrapersonal qualities and perceptions, while calling less for an accounting of the client's environment and how that impacts the client (Usher, 1989).

There is some question as to whether empathy is a "learned" counseling response, a personal quality, or some combination of the two (Hackney, 1978). Quite possibly, all human beings are born with a capacity to relate to others and their tribulations. If that is so, it is also possible that our early life experiences either bring out that capacity or leave it dormant. Whether or not this is the explanation, it is a fact that not all would-be counselors are able to listen with the empathic ear, to project themselves into their clients' experiences in such a way as to experience, vicariously, the client's world. Curiously, actors tend to be highly empathic. They are able to project themselves into the role and bring it to life. Perhaps it is the creative imagination, paired with a sensitivity to feelings and nuances that allow this to happen for the actor. Certainly, it is a product of experience as well. For these reasons, we believe that counseling students can develop strong and effective empathic skills through their preparation and experience.

Cheatham et al. (1993) believe that counselors must include in their preparation a cultural awareness or *conscientização* that involves learning how to discuss their clients' issues in a cultural context. Knowing the cultural values of your clients is essential if accurate communication is to occur (Carter, 1991). Seeing the world through the client's eyes includes understanding how different cultural groups view their world. This *worldview*, according to Ibraham (1991, p. 15) includes the client's perspectives on ethnicity, culture, gender, age, lifestage, socioeconomic status, education, religion, philosophy of life, beliefs, values, and assumptions. Many of these perspectives are communal in nature, with the client's individual interpretations added on. They have been learned, beginning at an early age, from family, community, and cultural/ethnic affiliations. Ridley, Mendoza, & Kanitz (1994) describes this quality as *cultural empathy*.

---

What does it mean to be a woman? What does it mean in the Muslim context to be a woman? What does it mean in the Detroit Arab-American context to be a woman? What does it mean in the Irish context to be a woman? What does it mean in the Boston Irish context to be a woman? Does the Boston Irish woman see her world any differently than does the Detroit Arab American woman? Do their views of the role of *woman* affect their views of themselves? Of their values? Of their world?

---

The next step is taking action on that empathic experience. How do you know when the client senses that you have understood? Clients often give you the answer through their responses. It isn't unusual for a client to react with some surprise or relief. Expressions like

"Yes, that's exactly how I feel" or "Yes, that's it" indicate recognition of the level of your understanding. When clients say something like that after one of your responses, you are assured that they sense your strong identification with them and their feelings or their problem. The matter of a strong identification can also pose problems in multicultural counseling. Not only is it very difficult to know enough about multiple cultures to be able to identify strongly with each client; it may also be beyond your client's imagination that you *could* identify strongly with him or her. Vontress (1988, p. 349) has observed that minority clients have experienced such a history "of wrongs and hardships at the hands of white Americans that they tend to view whites in general with varying degrees of suspicion." If this occurs, it is important that you recognize the issue as rapport-related rather than personalizing the client's reaction and taking offense. In addition to recognizing this negative transference, it is very important that the client's mistrust is not fed by being insensitive to cultural differences or denying that such differences exist.

Strong empathic relationships are such that one person may begin a thought and the other person complete it with accuracy, sensitivity, and emotion. Learning to understand is not an easy process if it does not come naturally. It involves the capacity to switch from your set of experiences to that of the other person, as though you actually viewed the world through that person's eyes. It involves accurately sensing that person's feelings, as opposed to feelings you had or might have had in a similar situation. It involves skillful listening, so you can hear not only the obvious but also the subtle shadings of which perhaps even the client is not yet aware. Counselor empathy contributes to the establishment of rapport, the conveying of support and acceptance, and the demonstration of respect and civility. It helps the counselor and client clarify issues and contributes immensely to the collection of client information (Egan, 1994).

### *Genuineness*

Genuineness refers to the counselor's state of mind. It means that the counselor can respond to the client "as a full human person and not just in terms of the role of therapist" (Holdstock & Rogers, 1977, p. 140). Egan (1994) describes genuine people as being "at home with themselves and therefore (being comfortable as) themselves in all their interactions." It includes being congruent, spontaneous, nondefensive, open to the experience, consistent, and comfortable with those behaviors that help clients (pp. 55–56). In short, it is being who you really are, without pretenses, fictions, roles, or veiled images. It suggests a large amount of comfort with self; thus it is a quality that we acquire through life experiences.

If you are uncomfortable with who you are as a person, you will find it to be very challenging to be genuine with your clients. Your first task is to find ways to become more comfortable with yourself. Many aspiring counselors accomplish this by entering into a counseling relationship as client.

This quality is often referred to as *congruence*, which means that your words, actions, and feelings are consistent—that what you say corresponds to how you feel, look, and act. Helpers who attempt to mask significant feelings or who send simultaneous and conflicting messages are behaving incongruently. For example, if I say that I am comfortable helping a client explore his or her sexual orientation issues, but show signs of my discomfort with the topic, then I am in a state of incongruence. Such incongruence can contribute to client confusion or even mistrust. Ridley (1994, p. 260) adds to this the notion of cultural self-awareness. He believes that

> *The effectiveness of counselors in processing cultural information depends greatly on their ability to be self-analytical. They must distinguish their cultural assumptions from those of their clients. Then they must strive to overcome their prejudices, stereotypes and biases. In short, they must become culturally self-aware.*

The word *spontaneous* is also used in reference to genuineness. This is the ability to express oneself easily and with tactful honesty without having to screen your response through some social filter. It does not mean that you will verbalize every passing thought to your client; nor does it give you license to blurt out whatever is on your mind. Spontaneity communicates your "realness" to the client and provides the client with a basis for understanding you and establishing a meaningful relationship with you.

Helpers who are genuine are often perceived by clients as more human. Clients are more likely to discuss private views of themselves when the counselor possesses a degree of nonthreatening self-comfort. Counselor genuineness also reduces unnecessary emotional distance between the counselor and the client. This is why it is referred to as a *facilitative condition*.

### Positive Regard

Unconditional positive regard was one of the original conditions identified by Rogers (1957) as necessary and sufficient for positive personality change to occur. He defined it as prizing the client as a person with inherent warmth and dignity, regardless of such external factors as the client's behavior, demeanor, and appearance. In a contemporary context, we think of it as a positive affirmation for the client *as a human being*. The counselor who experiences a positive regard for clients reflects not only his or her *view* of who that client is, but also embraces the *client's worldview*. This incorporates the client's ethnic and cultural sense of self, as well as other aspects of the client's life experience that have shaped the client's worldview, and the client's wish to change.

## Behaviors Associated with Empathy

Empathy is a *communication state* reflecting the listener's success in perceiving the client's world *as if* the listener were the client, but without losing awareness of the "as if" condition. However, many writers have noted that empathy has no impact on the counseling process if the client does not recognize that you are being empathic. Therefore, there are *two* types of skills associated with empathy: (a) skills associated with accurate perception of another person's worldview; and (b) skills associated with the communication of one's empathic perceptions to another person. The primary skills associated with the communication of empathy include:

1. Nonverbal and verbal attending
2. Paraphrasing content of client communications
3. Reflecting client feelings and implicit client messages
4. Pacing or synchrony of client experience

### Nonverbal Attentiveness

Clients often determine whether a helper is attentive by observing the helper's nonverbal behavior. In fact, even if a helper *states* "Go head and talk—I'm listening to you," the client may not believe this verbal message if the counselor is looking away, leaning back in the chair, or generally appearing disinterested. Whereas verbal communication is intermittent, nonverbal communication is continuous. When verbal and nonverbal messages contradict one another, the client will usually believe the nonverbal message (Gazda, Asbury, Balzer, Childers, & Walters, 1984). This is due, in part, because so much of the communication that occurs between people is expressed nonverbally rather than verbally. Effective nonverbal attentiveness includes the use of appropriate eye contact, head nods, facial animation, body posture, and distance between speaker and listener.

Ivey et al. (1993) have studied the differential effects of nonverbal behavior for different cultural groups. They have found that the skills normally associated with "therapy" tend to include nonverbal gestures that are more typical of a Eurocentric orientation. That makes sense, of course, since most of our current theories of psychotherapy originated either in Europe or the United States. Moreover, Ivey's research points to a significant problem when Eurocentric approaches to nonverbal communication are used with non-Eurocentric clients.

**TABLE 3-1  Nonverbal Attending Patterns in European North American Culture Compared with Patterns of Other Cultures**

| Nonverbal Dimension | European North American Pattern | Contrasting Example from Another Culture |
| --- | --- | --- |
| Eye contact | When listening to a person, direct eye contact is appropriate. When talking, eye contact is often less frequent. | Some African-Americans may have patterns directly opposite and demonstrate more eye contact when listening. |
| Body language | Slight forward trunk lean facing the person. Handshake a general sign of welcome. | Certain Eskimo and Inuit groups in the Arctic sit side by side when working on personal issues. A male giving a female a firm handshake may be seen as giving a sexual invitation. |
| Vocal tone and speech rate | A varied vocal tone is favored, with some emotionality shown. Speech rate is moderate. | Many Latina/o groups have a more extensive and expressive vocal tone and may consider European North American styles "flat." |
| Physical space | Conversation distance is ordinarily "arms length" or more for comfort. | Common in Arab and Middle-Eastern cultures is a six-to twelve-inch conversational distance, a point at which the European North American becomes uncomfortable. |
| Time | Highly structured, linear view of time. Generally "on time" for appointments. | Several South American countries operate on a more casual view of time and do not plan that specified, previously agreed-upon times for meetings will necessarily hold. |

Note: It is critical to remember that individuals within a single cultural group vary extensively. Adapted from A.E. Ivey, M.B. Ivey, and L. Simek-Morgan (1993). *Counseling and Psychotherapy: A Multicultural Perspective.* Boston, MA: Allyn & Bacon. Reprinted with permission.

*Table 3-1* presents a comparison of normally practiced nonverbal communication behaviors for European North Americans and persons of other cultures. [Note: European North Americans generally refers to persons of Germanic, Scandinavian, French, and English cultures or their decendents, persons often referred to erroneously as white Anglo-Saxon protestants (WASPS).]

Can you find yourself in *Table 3-1*? If not, what cultural group's description does fit you? How would you interpret the nonverbal communication of a person of the opposite sex whose pattern was obviously different from yours?

One of the problems many Americans have with discussions about multicultural differences is that they believe in the melting pot philosophy of American culture. That line of thinking is that as immigrants to America become *enculturated*, they replace their culture-of-origin with a homogenized American culture. It is true that over several generations, many Americans have *modified* their cultural expressions in the direction of a generic cultural norm. But if you scratch beneath the surface, you will find evidence of your culture-of-origin.

How might one know what behaviors would be understood and which might be misinterpreted by a client of different cultural origins from your own? The most obvious answer is to study cultures and become aware of their patterns of communication. But this could be a life's study in itself. The next best thing is to become very sensitive to cultural variations among people, attempt to identify with their patterns of communication, and in so doing, acknowledge or respect their uniqueness. Sometimes this effort becomes the subject of a respectful verbal discussion between you and your client.

### *Verbal Attentiveness*

Nonverbal attentiveness is supported by verbal attentiveness—that which is said to clients that demonstrates an interest in them. There are different ways of expressing verbal attentiveness. One way to show verbal attentiveness is to allow clients to complete sentences. Cutting off a client's communication by interrupting will discourage full expression, unless of course, the client is rambling or telling stories, in which case an interruption may be useful. Gordon (1969) observed that interruptions are not always verbal expressions; they include any behavior that distracts the client or interferes with the client's ability to continue with the interview at a particular pace.

The most common way to communicate verbal attentiveness is through the occasional use of short *verbal encouragers*, such as "Mm-hmm," "I see," "Go on," and so forth. When used selectively, these short phrases can have a powerful effect in communicating your interest and encouraging expression. Overuse of these responses, on the other hand, can induce a monotonous effect in the session and can be irritating or frustrating to clients.

Another aspect of verbal attentiveness is verbal following, also referred to as *tracking* (Minuchin, 1974) or *attending* (Ivey et al., 1993). A person engages in tracking by following the content and actions expressed in the client's communication. Minuchin likens the therapist's use of tracking to "a needle tracking grooves in a record" (1974, p. 127). The counselor is nonintrusive and leads by following, accepting, and encouraging the client's communication rather than initiating or changing topics.

Tracking can be used in a variety of ways. It is not restricted to just one type of response. It may be a statement or a question, and it may take the form of any number of different verbal responses, such as clarification, paraphrase, reflection of feeling, and open-ended question (a question that disallows a yes or no response). The critical element in tracking is to support the direction your client's communication is taking.

The voice can also be a very powerful tool in communicating with clients. It is important to learn to use your voice effectively and to adapt the pitch, volume, rate of speech, and voice emphasis to the client and to the situation. As Ivey (1994) observes, "(s)ome people will find one voice interesting, whereas others find that same voice boring, and still others may consider it warm and caring" (p. 30). An important concept to consider in the use of the voice is that of *verbal underlining*—the manipulation of volume and emphasis (Ivey, 1994). Verbal underlining is a way of using the voice to match the *intensity* of your nonverbal behaviors with those of the client. For example, if the client is speaking loudly about a situation that caused anger, you can also add intensity and emphasize key words in your response with your voice.

Finally, Ivey et al. (1993) introduce *focus* as an aspect of verbal attentiveness. Focusing is better described as *selective attending*, in that the counselor is making a choice of what aspects of a communication to which to respond. This is illustrated with a specific client statement to which the counselor might respond by focusing on the client, the client's spouse, the client's family background, the "problem," the counselor's reaction, a *we* focus that communicates communal effort on the part of the client and counselor, or a cultural/environmental context (pp. 60–61). Ivey et al. (1993) believe that when the counselor is working from multicultural counseling theory, focus should reflect a balance between the individual, family, and multicultural issues.

### *Paraphrasing and Reflecting Client Messages*

Sometimes the best way to communicate one's attentiveness is to give back to the client what you heard. This can be a brief restatement of the client's communication; or it may be your paraphrasing of the client's message. Generally speaking, your response will not be as complex as the client's message. Client messages may contain an objective or cognitive component and a subjective or affective component. The *cognitive* component includes thoughts and ideas about situations, events, people, or things; it answers the question "What happened?" The *affective* component refers to the client's emotions or feelings which accompany the cognitive component. Affective messages answer the question "How does the client feel about what happened?" Notice the cognitive and affective portions of the following client message:

> *I really care for and respect my husband. He gives me just about all I need in the way of security, comforts, and so on. If only he could let himself give me affection too. Sometimes even when I'm with him, I feel lonely.*

The cognitive part of this message—What happened?—is fairly obvious. The client thinks her husband is a good provider. The affective component—How is she feeling about the situation—refers to her emotional experience of loneliness.

Not all client messages contain easily recognized cognitive and affective components. Some messages have only a cognitive component, as when a client says "I think my professors here are just average." Other messages may contain only the affective portion; for example, a client may state "I feel lousy about this situation." In both of these examples, the other component was omitted from the message and must be discovered through indirect inquiry or inference.

### *Paraphrasing Client Communication*

Another way to convey empathy is through the use of verbal responses that rephrase to clients the essential part of their communication. The response used to rephrase cognitive client messages is the *paraphrase.* (The response used to rephrase affective client messages is the *affective reflection.*)

Paraphrasing involves selective attending (focusing) on the *cognitive* part of a message—with the client's key words and ideas rephrased into other words in a shortened and clarified form. An effective paraphrase thus does more than simply restate or parrot what the client has said. Jessop (1979) points out that the goal is to rephrase the client's message in such a way that it will lead to further discussion or to increased understanding of the message.

In this example, the counselor has offered a *tentative* ("It sounds like") response, which softens the paraphrase. The helper has also rephrased the client's "I can't seem to stop" to "you aren't able to con-

*The Paraphrase*

*Client:* I know I shouldn't be so hard on myself. But I can't seem to stop second-guessing everything I do.

*Helper:* It sounds like you'd like to be easier on yourself, but you aren't able to control your reactions.

trol" which may invite the client to think more critically of his/her re-action. When a paraphrase is on target, the client is likely to say something to the effect of "Yes, that's exactly how it is." Well-targeted paraphrases often draw clients into exploring the topic in greater depth, in addition to feeling successful in communicating their message.

There are four steps in formulating an effective paraphrase: recall; identification of content; rephrasing key words and constructs; and perception check. First, listen to and recall the entire client message. This process helps to ensure that you have heard the message in its entirety and that you do not omit any significant parts. Second, identify the content part of the message; that is, decide what event, situation, idea, or person the client is talking about. Third, rephrase the key word(s) and construct(s) the client has used to describe this concern in fresh or different words. Be as concise as possible in your paraphrase. Long paraphrases border on summarizations—a skill we describe in a later chapter. Finally, include a perception check that allows the client to agree or disagree with the accuracy of your paraphrase, i.e. "It sounds like." The perception check often takes the form of a brief question. However, helpers also check their perceptions of client messages by phrasing their statements in a tentative manner and by identifying client nonverbal reactions to their paraphrases.

Some helpers are hesitant to paraphrase for fear they might be wrong. Yet, as Gilmore (1973) observed, "(w)ithin limits, it is better to risk giving an inaccurate paraphrase and stopping for clarification than to sit there with an all-knowing look, nodding your head as if you understand" just to avoid being wrong (p. 242). Moreover, clients are not likely to lose respect for you if you are occasionally wrong, particularly when they are given an opportunity to correct your misperceptions.

## *Reflecting Client Feelings*

The *affective reflection* response acknowledges the "other half" of a client's message. It acknowledges affect that the client is communicating verbally or nonverbally. It can be affect that happened in the past, affect that is experienced in the present moment, or anticipated future affect.

*The Affective Reflection*

*Client:* I have been working on this project for six months now. It seems like each time I get close to the solution, something comes up that takes me away from it. I can't tell you how sick I am getting with it.

*Helper:* It must be really frustrating to get right up to the solution and then have everything fall apart.

Learning to reflect client feelings involves three steps. The first is to recognize the client's feelings or affect tone. The second step involves choosing the words to describe those feelings. The third step is to give your perception back to the client in a manner that is reflective rather than prescriptive.

In order to identify the client's feelings accurately, you must become sensitive to certain *verbal* and *nonverbal* cues that are elements of the client's communication. Some of these cues are referred to as *leakage*, since they communicate messages the client did not deliberately intend to have communicated (Ekman & Friesen, 1969; Ekman, 1993). Other cues primarily verbal, are more deliberately intended and are more easily recognized and identified.

In the case of affective leakage, it is important to account for the inferences you may draw. When you say "The client seems happy," that is an inference. If you say, instead, "The client is smiling and that may mean that he is happy," then you have accounted for your inference.

The total impact of a client's message includes verbal and nonverbal elements. The verbal element refers to certain nouns, adjectives, adverbs, and verbs that identify and modify the client's feeling state. In addition, there is the *paralanguage* element, the emphases placed on certain words or phrases. For example, how many ways can the following phrase be stated?

"I'm really worried about finding the time to write."
(a) I'm really *worried* about finding the time to write.
(b) I'm really worried about *finding the time* to write.
(c) *I'm* really worried about finding the time *to write*?

The affect word in this phrase is *worried*. However, the emphasis can change the meaning, and thus the affect. Statement (c) does not communicate the same affect as (a) or (b).

Nonverbal cues can be seen from such elements of the client's communication as head and facial movement, position of body, quick movements and gestures, and voice quality. Although no single nonverbal cue can be interpreted accurately alone, each does have meaning as part of a larger pattern. Thus, relationships exist between nonverbal and verbal aspects of speech. In addition to the relationship between nonverbal and verbal parts of the message, nonverbal cues may also communicate specific information about the relationship of the persons involved in the communicative process, in this case the client and counselor. Nonverbal cues differentially convey information about the *nature* and *intensity* of emotions, sometimes more accurately than verbal cues (Ekman, 1993). Interestingly, facial expressions do not appear to be culture-specific. Ekman (1993, p. 384) reports that "no one to date has obtained strong evidence of cross-cultural disagreement about the interpretation of fear, anger, disgust, sadness, or enjoyment expressions."

After the counselor has identified the client's feelings from the kinds of verbal and nonverbal leakage, the next step involves communicating those feelings back to the client, using different words that convey the same or similar emotional tone. The choice of words used is critical to this skill because words can reflect either the same or different levels of intensity of feelings by the client. Ekman's (1993) research suggests that affect states may incorporate "emotion families." For example, "The anger family would include variations in intensity stretching from annoyance to rage" (Ekman, 1993, p. 386). Because of this varying intensity of affect words and expressions, the *affective reflection* response can occur at two different levels. At the most obvious level, the counselor may reflect only the surface feeling of the client. At a deeper level, the counselor may reflect an *implied* client feeling with the same or greater intensity than that expressed by the client.

The more obvious level occurs when the counselor reflects an affect message that is *overtly* present in the client's message by using a different affect word that captures the same feeling and intensity expressed by the client.

*Client:* I don't like it when you interrupt me like that.

*Helper:* You're angry with me now. *(reflection of overt message)*

The second kind of reflection occurs at a deeper level. This one reflects an affect message that is only *covertly* expressed or implied in the client's statement. Consider, for example, the implied affect message:

*Client:* I don't know why you just sit there and let me stew.

*Helper:* It makes you mad when I don't take better care of you. *(reflection of covert message)*

Notice that the reflection that occurs at a deeper level not only mirrors the covert feeling but also reflects greater intensity of feelings. Furthermore, the most effective reflection is one that emphasizes what the client is concealing in his/her message.

The third step in reflecting client feelings involves a perception check. You can check out the accuracy of the reflection by asking the client a brief question or by recognizing client nonverbal reactions to the reflection. As with the paraphrase response, clients will usually express confirmation and/or relief once their feelings have been identified accurately and understood. Occasionally, however, clients may respond by denying their feelings. In this case, you must decide whether the reflection was inaccurate or simply ill-timed. As Ivey (1994, p. 130) concludes, "(t)hough noting feelings in the interview is essential, acting on your observations may not always be in the best interest of the client. Timing is particularly important with this skill."

## Conditions That Convey Genuineness

Genuineness is also communicated through the counselor's verbal and nonverbal behaviors.

Three classes of behavior, in particular, communicate genuineness or the lack thereof:

Congruence
Openness and discrete self-disclosure
Immediacy

### Congruence

Congruence means that your words, actions, and feelings all match or are consistent with one another. For example, when counselors become aware that they find a client's rambling to be directionless, they acknowledge this—at least to themselves—and do not try to feign interest when it does not really exist. Otherwise, they must conceal their reactions, producing the condition that leads to leakage of nonverbal deceptive behaviors referred to earlier (Ekman & Friesen, 1969).

The sensitive client will find counselor incongruence to be confusing or distracting and may view the incongruence as an indicator of the counselor's lack of competence or sincerity. Thus, counselor incongruence impedes development of the therapeutic relationship. In contrast, counselor congruence is related to both client and counselor perceptions of therapeutic facilitativeness (Hill, Seigelman, Gronsky, Sturniolo, & Fretz, 1981).

Counselors need to be good observers of their own internal reactions and resulting behaviors; otherwise, they will send incongruent or mixed messages to clients. For example, if a helper says disingenuously, "Sure, I want to hear what you have to say about this," his or her true reactions may be revealed through body language, attention span, or lack of attending behaviors. Most clients are sensitive to incongruent counselor behaviors, though they may not know how to interpret them. If the incongruence persists, the client must attach some meaning to it and the real danger is that it will be interpreted negatively.

Awareness of your words, feelings, and responses will help you convey your own meanings more clearly and will lead to cleaner interventions on your part. Moursund notes that: "As you notice contradictions between the words you are saying and the way your body is responding, you can clarify your emotional reactions to the client and to the process that is unfolding between the two of you" (1985, p. 17). You can become more congruent by sharpening your observation of your own experience and by noticing signals that may indicate that you are experiencing conflicting reactions to the client. Physical responses often prove to be more accurate guides to discrepancy and incongruence than do words.

### Openness and Self-Disclosure

Awareness of your thoughts, ideas, and feelings necessarily precedes *openness* and *self-disclosure*. Openness relates to what Rogers (Meador & Rogers, 1984) originally referred to as *transparency*, a condition he described as a willingness to let the client see through his intentions, motives, and agendas. Self-disclosure is more intentional, since it involves a *decision* to reveal information to the client. Thus, openness is a frame of mind, while self-disclosure is a professional decision.

The nature and degree of self-disclosure have ethical and professional implications. Your role of professional counselor carries with it the responsibility to make decisions that serve the best interests of your clients. Self-disclosure can be detrimental to the therapeutic relationship and must be measured for its intent and effect when used. It can serve to help the client gain a different perspective of his/her problems or it can bring attention to the counselor's issues rather than the client's issues. Thus, self-disclosure is a mixed bag. In their study of the effects of self-disclosure, Donley, Horan, and DeShong (1990) concluded that "our data do not support the supposition that counselor self-disclosures have a favorable impact on either counseling process or outcome [and that] counselors ought to be quite circumspect about its use" (p. 412). Kleinke (1994, p. 99) observes that

> [counselors] have the option of disclosing information about themselves (content) or of disclosing their feelings or perceptions about

*what is currently taking place in the therapy session (process) [and that] disclosure about content is necessary to the degree that it is important . . . to be cordial and socially responsive. This entails sharing at least some personal information.*

Counselor openness is related to counselor genuineness. For example, clients sometimes ask questions about the counselor. "Are you married?" "Why did you decide to become a counselor?" "Are you a student?" Such direct questions are best handled with a direct, brief, and honest answer. You may then return to the discussion that preceded the questions. The point is that clients do have some need to know about their counselor. Not all of what they may wish to know is appropriate information for them to have. But, some information is or may be necessary to help the therapeutic relationship grow.

If the request for personal information seems to be excessive, then there are some better ways to respond to the client's queries. For example, it may be more helpful for you to speak to the obvious by saying something like:

1. "You seem anxious about talking about yourself today."

   *Reflecting on the client's feelings of anxiety.*

2. "You've been asking a lot of questions about me."

   *Reflecting on the process.*

3. "Does it feel good to get off the 'hot seat' for a moment?"

   *Focusing on the reversal of roles.*

The verbal skills associated with empathic understanding that were described earlier maintain a primary focus on the client. In contrast, self-disclosure shifts the focus to the helper. Limited use of it actually relieves pressures that the client sometimes feels. Just "as blinking one's eyes helps one to see more clearly, so this brief shift gives the client a chance to come back to his own reactions with a better focus . . . (and) the contrast of the therapist's response with that of the client allows the client to hear his own comments more clearly" (Moursund, 1985, p. 22).

The most effective self-disclosing responses are those that are similar in content and mood to the client's messages. Ivey and Gluckstern (1976, p. 86) refer to this similarity as *parallelism,* meaning that the helper's self-disclosure is closely linked to the client's preceding thematic response. For example:

*Client:* I just wish my father was more understanding and less critical of me. He always seems to want me to do better than I can or to be someone I'm not.

*Helper:* (Parallel response) I do know what it's like to feel like you don't measure up to your parents' expectations. I can remember feeling that way sometimes when I was your age.

*Helper:* (Nonparallel response) I don't like it either when people disapprove of me or my actions. Sometimes I wish people would try to be kinder.

## *Immediacy*

*Immediacy* can be thought of as a special case of openness and self-disclosure involving a particular kind of sharing with clients. It involves sharing a thought or feeling, *as it occurs in the helping session.* Cormier and Cormier (1991, p. 31) write that

> *when persons avoid being immediate with each other over the course of a developing relationship, distance sets in and coldness can quickly evaporate any warmth formerly established.*

Counselor immediacy brings covert, implicit feelings into the open and provides discussion of or feedback about aspects of the helping relationship. This kind of sharing aids not only in the development of the relationship, but can also be a highly effective kind of therapeutic intervention:

> *Rather than hide his own reactions from the client, the therapist's reactions should be used as relevant data. If the therapist tells the client about reactions to him, the client is better able to understand others' reactions to his communications and may better monitor his behavior. Acceptance of all of a client's behavior without comment is neither realistic in terms of generalization to the extra-therapy world nor respectful of the client.* (Gottman & Leiblum, 1974, p. 126)

Instances in the helping relationship where immediacy is particularly useful include:

1. *Hesitancy or carefulness in speech or behavior:* "Kareem, I'm aware that you [or I] seem to be choosing words very carefully right now, as if you [or I] might be in danger of saying something wrong."
2. *Hostility, anger, resentment, irritation:* "Debby, I'm feeling imposed on now because you're indicating you want me to keep this time slot open for you but you may not be able to make it next week. Since this has happened the last two weeks, I'm concerned about what might be happening in our relationship."

3. *Attraction:* "At first, it seemed great that we were so comfortable with each other. Now I'm wondering if we're so comfortable that we may be holding back a little and not sharing what's really on our minds."
4. *Feeling stuck, lack of focus or direction:* "Right now I feel like our sessions are repeating themselves like a scratched record."
5. *Tension:* "I'm aware there's some discomfort and tension we're both feeling now—about who we are as people and where this is going and what is going to happen." (Cormier & Cormier, 1991, p. 32)

Immediacy is often expressed through sharing and feedback statements—statements that convey to the client your sense of what is happening and your reactions to it. Sharing and feedback communicate to the client that you have observed something going on, and that you have certain thoughts or feelings about it that you believe are relevant to the therapeutic relationship. Sometimes you will want to say not only what you feel or think about a specific situation, but also how you feel about the client. This will be more effective if your feelings are expressed as immediate ones; that is, expressed in the *present* rather than in the past or future tense. This is the meaning of keeping the process of relationship in the "here and now."

There is some evidence that helpers tend to avoid immediacy issues even when raised directly by clients (Turock, 1980). This may be especially true for beginning helpers, who are unaccustomed to talking about relationship qualities as they are occurring. Unfortunately, helpers who avoid using this response are likely to contribute to the development of a more cautious relationship.

## Conditions That Convey Positive Regard

Although unconditional positive regard involves an expression of caring and nurturance as well as acceptance, this condition can be conveyed to clients through the appropriate use of certain behaviors, including supporting nonverbal behaviors and enhancing verbal responses. Both of these may convey *a sense of relationship warmth* to clients. According to Goldstein (1980, p. 39), without warmth, some interventions "may be technically correct but therapeutically impotent."

### Nonverbal Behaviors Associated with Positive Regard

When one person has a warm and caring regard for another, the clearest communication of that is through the person's nonverbals. Johnson (1993, p. 163) describes some nonverbals that are associated with the expression of positive regard and warmth in a Eurocentric context:

*Tone of voice: soft, soothing*
*Facial expression: smiling, interested*
*Posture: relaxed, leaning toward the other person*
*Eye contact: looking directly into the other person's eyes*
*Touching: touching the other person softly and discreetly*
*Gestures: open, welcoming*
*Physical proximity: close*

As we have already discussed, other cultures may communicate through quite different nonverbal patterns. For example, Native Americans "accept periods of silence, especially in unfamiliar circumstances such as counseling or psychotherapy. Speaking and silence should be allowed to come naturally and as part of a process" (Sage, 1991, p. 31). Similarly, "harmonious interpersonal relationships among Japanese Americans are maintained by avoiding direct confrontation. Therefore, much of the communication style . . . is indirect and is characterized by talking around the point" (Tomine, 1991, p. 93). And in the Vietnamese culture, "touching a young person on the head is offensive to them . . . [and] social touching of the opposite sex is usually not done . . . except [with] family members" (Tran, 1981, p. 7). Obviously, when a client is of a markedly different culture, the Eurocentric means for conveying a nonverbal message may lead to a misconstrued message or no communication at all. Under such conditions the counselor is unable to convey an affirming respect or other intended messages. Thus, it is important to recognize the unique qualities of the client's cultural patterns to enhance all communication and, specifically, to communicate an affirming respect for the client.

### Enhancing Responses

There is one thing that all clients need from the helper, particularly in the initial stages of helping: *acceptance*. Helpers convey acceptance by responding to client messages with nonjudgmental or noncritical verbal and nonverbal reactions. Thus, when a client states, "I know I'm pregnant again. It will be my fifth abortion. But I don't know who the father is, and I can't stand to use contraceptives," the normal reaction might be disapproval. But if you hope to establish a relationship with your client that allows you to be a positive influence through counseling, such a response would be self-defeating. You do not have to agree with or condone the client's behavior.

A verbal skill related to the communication of affirming respect and acceptance is the use of *enhancing statements*. Enhancing statements are those that comment on some positive aspect or attitude about the client and provide encouragement or support to the client in some fashion.

---

*The Enhancing Response*

The enhancing response provides positive feedback to the client, usually on process rather than outcome criteria; for example,

*"I can see you've really worked hard on this issue."*

*"You're allowing yourself to get close to your feelings now."*

*"You're able to take the risk now, even if it means finding out something uncomfortable or painful."*

---

Enhancing responses can have a strong effect on the client and on the relationship. They are most effective when used *selectively* and *sincerely*. You know the feeling you have about someone who *always* is saying nice things about you—these statements lose their effect when used consistently.

## Functions of a Therapeutic Relationship

The core conditions and associated skills we describe in this chapter are derived from the person-centered approach to helping. Most other helping approaches or theoretical orientations also stress the importance of a sound therapeutic relationship in effective helping, even though some approaches differ in the nature and degree of importance they attach to the role of relationships in counseling. Adlerian psychotherapy, for example, emphasizes the necessity of establishing a democratic and egalitarian relationship with the client. Behavioral approaches identify the importance of a good relationship as a potential reinforcing stimulus to the client.

One of the key ingredients of reality therapy, that of *involvement*, is based on the concept of the helper's ability to relate to clients effectively. The family therapy approaches have placed less emphasis on relationship as a therapeutic condition but speak of *joining with the client or family* as a prerequisite to therapeutic work.

There are at least four primary functions associated with a strong relationship bond between counselor and client. First, the therapeutic relationship creates an atmosphere of trust and safety for the client. This reduces client cautiousness, suspicion, or hesitancy to take risks, thus facilitating the client's disclosure of very personal and sensitive material without the fear of aversive or punitive consequences. Without such disclosure, counseling is likely to have little impact on clients because pertinent issues are not being explored.

Second, the relationship provides a medium or vehicle for intense affect. It permits and protects the client who needs to express strong feelings. Often, expression of such feelings is the initial step in diminishing their intensity and developing a greater sense of self-control.

Third, an effective therapeutic relationship allows the client to experience a healthy interpersonal relationship. Such an experience can assist clients in identifying and enhancing the quality of their relationships with others in their world. For example, clients may learn that it is all right to say how one feels, ask for what one needs, and share thoughts and feelings with others within the context of cultural restraints. They develop more effective forms of communication that are consistent with their worldview.

Finally, the relationship serves an important motivational function for clients. Active involvement with the helper instills confidence and gives hope to the discouraged client who needs some additional impetus to continue the change process. Doherty and Cook (1993, p. 17) note that "relationships are such an integral part of women's selves that it is inaccurate to define women's selves as somehow autonomous and separate from others."

## Effects of Therapeutic Relationships on Clients

Clients' reactions to the helper's level of involvement can range over a number of dimensions. Some clients will feel pleased and satisfied initially with the quality of this interpersonal relationship. They may experience relief that someone finally seems to understand, giving them the opportunity to get burdensome or painful memories out in the open. They also may feel hopeful that someone seems to care enough to become involved in their lives.

Not all initial client reactions will be this positive, however. Some clients, unaccustomed to the informality or intimacy of the setting, may feel threatened, intimidated, or claustrophobic by the therapeutic relationship. They are uncomfortable with so much attention directed at them, with the helper's expression of caring and concern, and with what they perceive as an insufficient amount of role distance.

Still a few other clients may question the counselor's motives or sincerity and view the counselor and the relationship with a degree of skepticism. They may have trouble believing that the helper's intentions are good. They may wonder how committed the helper really is to them and to working on their behalf. These clients are often looking for assurance that counseling will not exploit in any way their vulnerability (Johnson, 1993). Often such clients express their concerns with indirect or mixed messages designed to collect data about the helper's trustworthiness. If counselors fail to respond to the underlying issue of trust and skepticism, the relationship may deteriorate or even terminate, with the counselor still unaware that the real issue was lack of trust (Fong & Cox, 1983).

Counselors may want to be careful about assuming that the conditions and quality of the therapeutic relationship always produce favorable client reactions. Current interpretations of empathy, for example, view it as a multistage process consisting of multiple elements (Barrett-Leonard, 1981; Gladstein, 1983). As such, empathy may be more useful for some clients and less impactful with others. As Gladstein (1983) writes, in the counseling process empathy "will be helpful in certain stages, with certain clients, and for certain goals." However at other times, it "can interfere with positive outcomes" (p. 178).

When clients respond to therapeutic involvement with apprehension or skepticism, it does not mean that the helper stops reacting therapeutically or that the helper denies involvement with the client or withdraws from the relationship. It does mean that the counselor makes a concerted effort to pay close attention to the client's feelings and attempts to relate to the client in a way that matches or tracks the client's feelings and frame of reference. Initially, this might mean moving a little more slowly, not pushing as much, or not conveying implicit or explicit demands for client progress and change. Your understanding of the skills and concepts of the therapeutic relationship may be enhanced by reading the following case. (Case examples will be provided throughout the book to illustrate the major stages and strategies of the helping process. The case examples should help you in the application of the material you read.)

## The Relationship Stage

*The Case of Lenore*

Lenore is a forty-five-year-old woman referred to you by her physician after he failed to find any organic basis for her frequent headaches, which the physical attributed to "stress—particularly in her family life."

In the initial interview, Lenore admits that her constant headaches have been a source of frustration for her. At the same time, she expresses skepticism about how counseling can help her. She hesitantly reveals that she experiences a great deal of stress in her family because of her husband's verbally abusive behavior toward her and toward her two daughters. Yet she feels powerless to do anything to change the situation, particularly because her husband has refused to come for counseling. She also feels helpless about whether counseling will be helpful. Throughout most of the initial interview, she is somewhat passive and reticent, as though she is holding back a barrage of unexpressed ideas, concerns, and emotions.

Your response to her behavior during this initial interview is not to push her or persuade her to see how helpful counseling might be, but simply to try to pace or match her experience and understand her frame of reference. This means that you acknowledge and reflect her skeptical feelings directly. "Lenore, I do understand that you feel doubtful about how talking like this can really help you in your situation." It also means that you attempt to pace or match her nonverbal behavior—her body language, her low-key voice tone, her eye contact.

At the same time, without pressuring her to be more self-revealing, you are somewhat self-disclosing and try to use immediacy to convey to her how difficult it can be to discuss painful feelings with a stranger: "Lenore, sometimes I'm in a situation where I really want things to work but can't imagine how it would be helpful. Sometimes its very difficult to know where or how to start."

Lenore returns for a second session and, although she still expresses reservations, appears more relaxed than before and speaks more freely and with greater animation and energy. You continue to track her body language and voice tone, making sure your nonverbal behavior also reflects increased energy.

Lenore returns a third time. This time, she begins to reveal some of the pain in her family, particularly in her relationship with her husband. You continue to attempt to communicate understanding of her feelings and circumstances by your nonverbal behavior and by reflecting her feelings: "Lenore, it sounds to me like you're feeling disappointed not only with your

husband, but also with yourself." At this point, Lenore begins to sob softly, as though a reservoir of pent-up emotions has finally been tapped.

During this time, you respect her need to cry by offering permission and protection: "Go ahead and cry—don't rush this—take some time to let these feelings and tears come out." You attempt to respond with both warmth and spontaneity to her and to let her know that you are not uncomfortable with the intensity of her feelings, even though she might be uncomfortable: "Sometimes these feelings can be pretty overwhelming, especially if you have been holding them for a long time. It may be helpful to try to express them in any way that you can."

At the end of the third session, Lenore has revealed many feelings and has disclosed a lot of specific material regarding her family situation. She indicates that the opportunity to talk to someone who understands has been very helpful. Although she still feels somewhat discouraged about her ability to effect change in her marital situation, she wants to continue with counseling. She is also starting to be aware of some issues she wants to work on that are independent of the marital situation, such as discovering more about herself and being less dependent on her role as a wife and mother in determining her own identity. The two of you agree to work together for the next ten weeks and then assess the situation and decide where Lenore wants to go from there. In addition, you provide an opportunity for her two daughters to become involved in counseling.

## *Children and the Counseling Relationship*

Thus far, we have discussed rapport and relationship from an adult context. Much of what we have observed may also apply to the adolescent, although the issue of trust is inherently more complex with adolescents who are actively seeking to differentiate themselves from parents. However, the matter of relationship is more variable for younger children. With them, the issue is more likely to be whether or not to trust a stranger. Thompson and Rudolph (1992) observe that "Making friends with children you counsel may be the key to the entire process" (p. 34). They go on to say that

> *Counseling seems to work better if children can control the distance between themselves and the counselor. Adults are often too aggressive in trying to initiate conversations with children. Children prefer to talk with adults at the same eye level, so some care needs to be given to seating arrangements that allow for eye-to-eye contact and feet on the floor. A thick carpet, comfortable chairs, floor pillows, puppets, dollhouses, and other toys to facilitate communication are also recommended for the counseling room.* (p. 33)

There are other developmental issues to take into account. The younger child has not learned many of the subtleties of adult communication. But at a less subtle level, younger children also lack the vocabulary of the adult world. It is important that you modify your adult behavior and vocabulary to match that of the child. A second concern is the physical domain. To young children, adults look like giants. Their appearance serves as a reminder of the child's powerlessness and vulnerability. Finally, it is important to remember that the child's attention span is briefer than that of adults. This has two implications. First, younger children will not be topic-bound for more than a couple of minutes at a time (they may return to a topic several times during a session). Second, the counseling session will not be as long as an adult or adolescent session. You may want to think in terms of twenty-minute counseling sessions for the younger child unless you are using play therapy. In play therapy, the session can be somewhat longer but there will be more play than therapy. Beyond these immediate concerns, the establishment of rapport and relationship with younger children also involves understanding, acceptance, a *liking* of children, and genuineness. Genuineness is especially critical. If young children sense that you are being disingenuous or not taking them seriously, their basis for trusting you will be destroyed and rapport will not occur.

## Summary

A number of conditions and ingredients contribute to the initial stage of building a therapeutic relationship with clients. Accurate *empathy*, counselor *genuineness*, and *supportive respect* are three counselor qualities that form the foundation of therapeutic relationships. While these qualities are conveyed through the helper's attitudes, they are also expressed by certain helping skills, which include facilitative non-verbal behaviors and verbal skills such as paraphrasing, reflecting, self-disclosure, immediacy, sharing, and enhancing responses.

The greatest obstacle in this initial phase of helping is the counselor's tendency to move too quickly. This tendency may be precipitated by clients who want relief from pain and by helpers, particularly inexperienced counselors, who may need to prove something to clients and to themselves.

With all of this as background, it is important to be sensitive and responsive to each client's *worldview*, composed of ethnic/racial, cultural, gender, lifestyle, physical, and age parameters. These uniquenesses alter and shape the nature of helpful counseling relationships.

## Exercises

**I.** *Attentiveness and Empathy*

This exercise involves you and a partner in two interactions. Each interaction will last about five minutes. After both have been completed, assess the impact of each interaction. Ask for your partner's reactions to each situation. In which one did he/she feel most comfortable? In which did he/she feel like stopping or leaving?

**1.** You are to listen carefully to what your partner is saying, but you will send your partner nonverbal signals that indicate boredom: look away, doodle, appear distracted, and so on. If your partner accuses you of being uninterested, insist that you are interested—you may even review what has been said—but continue to send nonverbal signs of boredom. Do not discuss or share these instructions at this time.

**2.** In the second exercise, listen carefully to what your partner is saying and send nonverbal signals that indicate your interest and attentiveness—eye contact, head nodding, facial animation, and so on. Make some attempt to ensure some synchrony between your partner's nonverbal behavior and your own.

**II.** *Identifying Nonverbal and Verbal Affect Cues*

To give you practice in identifying nonverbal and verbal affect cues, complete the following exercises:

**1.** Pick a partner. One of you will be the speaker; the other will be the respondent. After you complete the exercise, reverse roles and repeat it again. The speaker should select a feeling from the following:

contented, happy
puzzled, confused
angry, hostile
discouraged, depressed

Do not tell the respondent which feeling you have selected. Portray the feeling through nonverbal expressions only. The respondent must try to identify the feeling you are communicating as well as the behaviors you use to express the feeling. After he/she has done so, choose another feeling and repeat the process.

**2.** The speaker should select a feeling from the following list:

surprise
elation or thrill
anxiety or tension
sadness or discouragement
seriousness or intensity
irritation or annoyance

Do not inform the respondent which feeling you have selected. Verbally express the feeling in one or two sentences. Be certain to include the affect word itself. The respondent should try to identify the feeling in two ways:

**a.** Restate the feeling using the same affect word as the speaker.
**b.** Restate the feeling using a different affect word but one that reflects the same feeling, for example:

*Speaker:* I feel *good* about being here.
*Respondent:* a. You feel *good*?
b. You're *glad* to be here.

**3.** Choose another feeling and complete the same process.

### III. *Paraphrasing and Reflecting*

Respond in writing to each of the following three client messages. (Feedback follows the chapter exercises.)

**1.** Client: "I'm tired of sitting at home alone, but I feel so uncomfortable going out by myself."

Cognitive part of message: _____

Affective part of message: _____

Paraphrase of cognitive part: _____

_____

Affective reflection: _____

_____

**2.** Client: "I don't know why we got married in the first place."

Cognitive part of message: _____

Affective part of message: _____

Paraphrase of cognitive part: _____

_____

Affective reflection: _____

_____

**3.** Client: "The pressure from my job is a lot to contend with, but I expected it." (said with strained voice, furrowed brow, twisting of hands):

Cognitive part of message: _____

Affective part of message: _____

Paraphrase of cognitive part: _____

_____

Affective reflection: _____

_____

## IV. *Self-Disclosure and Immediacy*

Listed below are four client situations. For the first two, develop and write an example of a *self-disclosure response* you might make to this client. For the second two, develop and write an example of an *immediacy response* you could use with this client. Share your responses with other students, colleagues, or your instructor or supervisor.

**1.** The client hints that he wants to tell you something but is reluctant to do so because it is something he feels very ashamed of.

**2.** The client believes he or she is the only person who has ever felt guilty about a particular issue.

**3.** You experience a great deal of tension and caution between yourself and the client. You both seem to be treating each other with "kid gloves." You are aware of physical sensations of tension in your body, which are also apparent in the client.

**4.** You and your client like each other a great deal and have a lot in common. Lately, you have been spending more time swapping life stories than focusing on or dealing with the client's presented concern of career indecision.

## V. *Positive Regard and Enhancing Responses*

Take a few minutes to think of a person with whom you are currently in a relationship and toward whom you feel affirming respect.

**1.** What kinds of positive feelings do you have for this person? Jot them down.

**2.** What does this person do that you like and value? Jot these things down.

**3.** Based on your positive feelings for the person and on things he or she does that you like, develop some enhancing statements you could use to convey your feelings to this other person. Make a list of them.

**4.** How would you feel making these statements to the person? What might be the effect on the other person?

## *Feedback for Exercises*

**III.** *Paraphrasing and Reflecting*
### Client Message 1

1. The cognitive part of the message is "sitting at home alone." This is the event or situation.
2. The affective part of the message is "I feel so uncomfortable going out by myself."
3. Examples of paraphrase responses:
   a. "Sitting at home alone isn't a very good choice."
   b. "It's hard when neither choice is a good one."
4. Examples of affective reflection responses follow: Note the first two are at the surface level; the second two reflect the implied meaning as well as the obvious message.
   a. "You feel uneasy about venturing out alone."
   b. "You're feeling apprehensive about going out on your own."
   c. "You're really feeling unsure about yourself. It would feel so good to have someone to go out with."
   d. "It's really difficult being alone."

### Client Message 2

1. The cognitive part of the message is "we got married [but] we're incompatible."
2. The affective part of the message is "don't know why." Don't know reflects uncertainty, confusion, or in this case, disbelief.
3. Examples of paraphrase responses:
   a. "It's hard to understand how two incompatible people ended up getting married."
   b. "Even with all of your differences, you still got married."
4. In the following examples of affective reflection responses, the first two are at the surface level; the second two reflect implied omission or what the client would like to have happen.
   a. "You're amazed that the two of you got married."
   b. "Given the basic differences that exist between the two of you, it's puzzling that you ended up together."
   c. "It sounds like you'd feel more comfortable if you weren't so different and shared more of the same interests."
   d. "And perhaps you are looking at yourself and questioning why you would make such a choice?"

### Client Message 3

1. The cognitive part of the message is "There's a lot of pressure."

2. The affective part of the message is implied from the client's nonverbal behavior—strained voice, furrowed brow, twisting of hands—all of which suggest tension.

3. Examples of paraphrase responses:
    a. "You're finding out just how much there is in your job that you have to cope with."
    b. "It's a very demanding job."

4. In the examples of affective reflection responses, the first two are at the surface level and the second two are at a deeper level.
    a. "You expected some pressure from your job, but this is starting to get very heavy."
    b. "The job is becoming a heavy burden."
    c. "From your nonverbals, you're really reacting to the job."
    d. "Even though you expected pressure, you're feeling pretty overwhelmed by the job's demands."

## Discussion Questions

1. How do you approach a new relationship? What conditions do you require to be met before you open yourself to a closer relationship?

2. What are the "unwritten rules" in your family about interactions with nonfamily members? How do you think these unwritten rules will affect the way you relate to clients?

3. If you were a client, what kind of relationship would you expect and value?

4. What do you think is the greatest problem faced by cross-cultural counseling relationships?

5. Is it *always* useful to be genuine with clients? Can you think of any instances in which an expression of genuineness might be inappropriate?

6. What do you suppose it would be like for two persons from different minority cultures to form a counseling relationship? What would their advantages be? What would their disadvantages be?

## Recommended Readings

Axelson, J.A. (1993). *Counseling and Development in a Multicultural Society*. Pacific Grove, CA: Brooks/Cole. Chapter 2: The culture of the counselor.

Cook, E.P. (1993). *Women, Relationships, and Power: Implications for Counseling.* Alexandria, VA: ACA Press.

Donley, R.J., Horan, J.J., and DeShong, R.L. (1990). The effects of several self-disclosure permutations on counseling process and outcome, *Journal of Counseling and Development, 69,* 408–412.

Frederick, S.L. (1988). Learning to empathize with resistance, *Journal of Counseling and Development, 67,* 128.

Ivey, A.E., Ivey, M.B., and Simek-Morgan, L. (1993). *Counseling and Psychotherapy: A Multicultural Perspective,* 3d ed. Boston, MA: Allyn & Bacon. Chapter 2: The empathic attitude: Individual, family and culture.

Josselson, R. (1992). *The Space Between Us: Exploring the Dimensions of Human Relationships.* San Francisco: Jossey-Bass.

Lee, C.C. and Richardson, B.L. (1991). *Multicultural Issues in Counseling: New Approaches to Diversity.* Alexandria, VA: ACA Press. Chapter 2: Cultural dynamics: Their importance in multicultural counseling.

Maurer, R.E. and Tindall, J.H. (1983). Effect of postural congruence on the client's perception of counselor empathy, *Journal of Counseling Psychology, 30,* 158–163.

# *Chapter* *4*

Assessing Client Problems

### *Purpose of This Chapter—*

In this chapter, we examine the process by which counselors can assess the client's presenting problems. That process involves the collection of information relevant to problem definition, conceptualization of that information into a cogent picture of the client in his or her world, and consideration of client resources. Cultural factors that affect client perceptions of their world and counselor perceptions of client problems are introduced.

### *Considerations as You Read This Chapter—*

- Defining a "problem" is a very difficult process. We see our problems differently. How does a professional counselor view problems?
- How does the professional counselor separate his or her worldview from that of the client to permit the objective definition of problems?
- What kinds of information are useful in the understanding of a stranger's problems?
- These questions are at the root of the clinical assessment process. They affect the counselor and client alike. For this reason, it is useful to have some sort of guideline or outline to follow as one collects information and then assimilates that information into a definition of the client's presenting problem, the context in which that problem exists, and the alternatives available to the client in problem resolution.

In most instances, clients see a counselor (or are "encouraged" to see one) because of concerns or problems that are interfering with their daily functioning or are making them feel discouraged, or even desperate. Clients hope that, as a result of counseling, they will feel better and/or their life situation will improve. This expectation has both positive and negative implications for counselors. On the positive side, it behooves the counselor to start moving the sessions in some focused and intentional direction and to do something in addition to sitting and listening. On the negative side, it can create a trap for both counselor and client, who may feel that counseling is not successful unless the counselor is *always* doing something—usually *for* or *to* rather than *with* the client.

In spite of this potential trap, it is important to remember that the reason most clients seek a helper's services is for relief of symptoms or resolution of problems. Counselors who forget this are likely to have clients who feel that their reasons for seeking help are being ignored or overlooked. It is important to take client complaints seriously. One way to do this is to utilize some portion of the counseling process for assessing client concerns. Assessment of client concerns not only gives clients the feeling that the counselor views their problems with a healthy degree of respect, but also provides valuable information to the counselor about conceptualization of client problems and corresponding treatment or intervention approaches.

## Purposes of Assessment

Biggs and Blocher (1987, p. 89) have observed that "To the degree that counselors try to understand their clients, some sort of assessment activity is almost certainly a part of any helping process." Assessment has two primary purposes. First, it is a systematic way to obtain information about the client's presenting problems and concerns. Second, it is useful for identifying the significant variables that contribute to the problems. For example, two clients may come in and present the same initial concern: "I'm depressed." Depression, however, is a construct that has different meanings. Although both clients may feel depressed, assessment of this problem for each is likely to reveal somewhat different descriptions of the problem and different contributing conditions.

It is also important to note that assessment can be *reactive*; that is, the process of obtaining specific information about problems may also effect some change in the problem. For example, a male client who reports that he is self-conscious around women may find that some of his self-consciousness dissipates as he begins to explore his behavior with the counselor and to monitor it more closely outside the counseling sessions. Thus, assessment can also contribute to desired client changes or outcomes.

## Components of Assessment

Assessment refers to anything counselors do to gather information and draw conclusions about client concerns. Although most of the major components of assessment occur early in the counseling process, some degree of assessment goes on continuously during counseling, in that counselors are always seeking missing parts of the puzzle and attempting to place them where they fit.

### Intake or History Interviews

The first identifiable component of assessment is usually referred to as the *intake* or history interview. During this session, counselors are interested primarily in obtaining information about the range or scope of the client's problems and about aspects of the client's background and present situation that may relate to these problems.

An assumption behind the intake interview is that the client is coming to counseling for more than one interview and intends to address problems or concerns that involve other people, other settings, and the future as well as the present. Most counselors try to limit intake interviews to one hour. In order to do this, the counselor must assume responsibility and control over the interview. No attempt is made to make it a "therapeutic session" for the client. The second session can begin to meet those needs. (In other words, the intake interview is like an appendage that precedes the process of establishing a relationship with the client.)

Because the intake session is different from a regular counseling session, it is helpful if the counselor gives the client an explanation about the purpose and nature of the initial session. You might say something like: "José, before counseling begins, I would like to get some preliminary background information about you. So today, I will spend the hour getting to know you and asking you some questions about your school, your work, your family, and so on. Then, next week, we will start focusing and working on the specific concerns that brought you to counseling. Do you have any questions about this?" If the client is in crisis during this first interview, the intake is not conducted and the counselor will address issues related to the crisis instead.

When writing up the intake interview, there are a few cautions to be observed. First, avoid psychological jargon. It is not as understandable as you might think. Avoid elaborate inferences. Remember, an inference is a guess, *sometimes* an educated guess. An inference can also be wrong. Try and prevent your own biases from entering the report. Report writing is affected by ethical issues as well as professional issues. Biggs and Blocher (1987) describe ethical practices related to client assessment:

*1. Counselors must respect the right of the individual being assessed to have a full and accurate explanation of the nature and purposes of the assessment procedure.*

*2. [Where tests and other assessment instruments are used], counselors are responsible for including in the report all of the limitations or reservations that exist regarding validity or reliability, circumstances around the assessment situation or other relevant factors. The person being assessed has a right to know the results, the interpretations made, and the basis for the conclusions and recommendations made as a result of the assessment. (pp. 92–93)*

### The Intake Interview

*I. Identifying data.*

**A.** Client's name, address, and telephone number at which the client can be reached. This information is important in the event you need to contact the client between sessions. The client's address also gives some hint about the conditions under which the client lives (large apartment complex, student dormitory, private home, inner city project, etc.)

**B.** Age, sex, marital status, occupation (or school class and year). Again, this is information that can be important. It lets you know if the client is still legally a minor, and provides a basis for understanding information that will come out in later sessions.

*II. Presenting problems, both primary and secondary.*

It is best that these be presented in exactly the way the way the client reports them. If the problem has behavioral components, they should be recorded as well. Questions that help reveal this type of information include:

**A.** How much does the problem interfere with the client's everyday functioning?

**B.** How does the problem manifest itself? What are the thoughts, feelings, and so on, that are associated with it? What observable behavior is associated with it?

**C.** How often does the problem arise and how long has the problem existed? When did it first appear?

**D.** Can the client identify a pattern of events that surround the problem? When does it occur? With whom? What happens before and following its occurrence? Can the client anticipate the onset of the problem?

**E.** What caused the client to decide to enter counseling at this time?

*III. Client's current life setting.*

What is the background or context for the client's daily functioning?

**A.** How does the client spend a typical day or week?

**B.** What social and religious activities, recreational activities are present?

**C.** What is the nature of the client's vocational and/or educational situation?

**D.** What special characteristics about the client, cultural, ethnic, religious, lifestyle, age, and physical or other challenges must the client address in an ongoing manner?

**IV.** *Family history.*

**A.** Father's and mother's ages, occupations, descriptions of their personalities, family roles, relationships of each to the other and each to the client and other siblings.

**B.** Names and ages of brothers and sisters; their present life situations; relationship between client and siblings.

**C.** Is there any history of mental illness in the family?

**D.** Descriptions of family stability, including number of jobs held, number of family moves (and reasons), and so on. This information provides insights during later sessions when issues related to client stability and/or relationships emerge.

**V.** *Personal history.*

**A.** Medical history: include any unusual or relevant illness or injury from prenatal period to present.

**B.** Educational history: academic progress through high school and any post-high school preparation. This includes extracurricular interests and relationships with peers.

**C.** Military service history.

**D.** Vocational history: Where has the client worked, at what types of jobs, for what duration, and what were the relationships with fellow workers?

**E.** Sexual and marital history: Where did the client receive sexual information? What was the client's dating history? Any engagements and/or marriages? Other serious emotional involvements prior to the present? Reasons that previous relationships terminated? What was the courtship like with present spouse? What were the reasons (spouse's characteristics, personal thoughts) that led to marriage? Are there any children?

**F.** What experience has the client had with counseling, and what were the client's reactions?

**G.** Alcohol and drug use: Does the client currently use, or has the client in the past used alcohol or drugs, and to what extent?

**H.** What are the client's personal goals in life?

**VI.** *Description of the client during the interview.*

Here you might want to indicate the client's physical appearance, including dress, posture, gestures, facial expressions, voice quality, tensions; how the client seemed to relate to you in the session; client's readiness of response, motivation, warmth, distance, passivity, etc. Did you observe any perceptual or sensory functions that intruded on the interaction? What was the general level of information, vocabulary, judgment, abstraction abilities displayed by the client? What was the stream of thought and rate of talking? Were the client's remarks logical? Connected to one another?

**VII.** *Summary and recommendations.*

In this section you will want to acknowledge any connections that appear to exist between the client's statement of a problem and other information collected in this session. What type of counselor do you think would best fit this client (presuming you are only responsible for the intake.) How realistic are the client's goals for counseling? How long to you think counseling might require?

## *Problem Definition*

The second dimension of clinical assessment involves a more extensive definition of the problem. This may begin as part of the intake interview but will continue into the next one to two sessions. Problem definition differs from intake information in that specific details regarding the nature and context of the presenting problem(s) are explored. These details may include not only the one(s) presented initially by the client (referred to as the *presenting problem*), but also may include any others that may have been mentioned during the intake or during subsequent sessions.

Frequently, clients will identify a presenting problem as their reason for seeking help and then, during the subsequent sessions, reveal something else that is the real object of their concern. In these instances, the client has been "testing" the counselor or the counseling process to determine whether or not this is a safe or appropriate environment in which to explore such issues. For this reason—and also because a sound therapeutic relationship is an important prerequisite to the proper identification of goals—it is usually a good idea to have one or more counseling sessions with the client before attempting to define the problem too specifically. The following are areas to explore in reaching a useful understanding of the client's problem(s):

**I. *Components of problem*** (ways in which the problem manifests itself primarily and secondarily).

**A.** Feelings associated with problem (major feeling or affect categories to assess include confusion, depression, fear, anger).
**B.** Cognitions associated with problem (including thoughts, beliefs, perceptions, and internal dialogue, ruminations, or self-talk).
**C.** Behaviors associated with problem (specific actions observable not only by the client but also to others, including counselor).
**D.** Physical or somatic complaints associated with problem.
**E.** Interpersonal aspects of problem (effects on significant others and on the client's relationships with others, including family, friends, relatives, colleagues, peers; also effects significant others may have on client or problem).

**II. *Pattern of contributing events*** (Can the client identify a pattern or sequence of events that seems to lead up to problem and also maintains it?)

**A.** When does problem occur? Where? With whom?
**B.** What is happening at the onset of the problem?
**C.** What is happening just prior to occurrence of problem?
**D.** What typically happens just after its occurrence?

**E.** What makes the problem better? Disappear?

**F.** What makes the problem worse?

***III. Duration of problem*** (extent to which the concern disturbs the client and/or interferes with client's everyday functioning).

**A.** How long has problem existed?

**B.** How often does problem occur?

**C.** How long does problem last when it does occur?

**D.** What led the client to seek counseling *at this time* regarding the problem?

**E.** In what ways does the problem interfere with client's daily functioning?

***IV. Client coping skills, strengths, resources.***

**A.** How has client coped with problem? What has worked? What has not worked?

**B.** How has client successfully coped with other problems?

**C.** What resources, strengths, and support systems does client have to help with change efforts?

**D.** What is the client's cultural *worldview*? Sociopolitical histories of the groups the client identifies with? Language(s) spoken? Impact of gender? Neighborhood client grew up in? Religion client practices? (Ibraham, 1991, p. 15).

In addition to this kind of information collected from problem definition interviews, counselors also can obtain additional assessment information about clients and their problems by using *adjunctive data*, such as psychological tests, self-ratings, and so on.

Finally, problem definition can be approached in numerous ways, as determined by one's theoretical orientation, the use of the *Diagnostic and Statistical Manual*, 4th Edition (*DSM IV*), and/or by contextual realities. This latter context is an attempt to recognize that not all human problems *originate within the individual*, but rather, are imposed by the environment in ways that impel the client's reactions. For example, the Americans with Disabilities Act recognizes the environment as the source, thus target for change, of persons who experience problems related to physical disabilities. Similarly, many minorities experience degrees of discrimination which, if remedied, would have a major impact on the client's "problem." And, young children also experience problems imposed by environmental or contextual conditions. In these cases, the environment may be the source, thus the target for intervention, as well as the client.

## Clinical Assessment with Children

Children pose a unique assessment challenge to the counselor. On the one hand, children are less inhibited than adults in talking about their concerns to a trusted counselor. On the other hand, children, especially young children, lack the cognitive development to describe problems with causal or contextual clarity. As a consequence, you must phrase questions in such a way as to draw out the kinds of information that will allow you to conceptualize the child's world. Children's problems tend to fall into three areas: (a) environmental factors affecting healthy growth and development; (b) self-concept issues; and (c) relationship issues.

Once you have established a safe and trusting relationship with a child, you can begin the intake/problem definition process. This will differ from the adult intake interview described earlier. Depending on the child's emotional state, intake information may be drawn from other significant sources as well as the child (e.g., parents, teachers, siblings, peers). Thus, the first contact with the child may find you already involved in problem definition questions that draw out the child's emotional state, environmental factors contributing to the child's problem, self-views, and significant relationships with others. The highly verbal child will be able to respond to open-ended questions about self, family, friends, and environment. However, the less verbal child may need structured questions (Who? What? Where? How? When?) in order to respond to the counselor. Some child counselors prefer to avoid these types of questions since they also restrict the child's response, and thus the range of information that is gained.

The most important factors are: (a) that you know in advance what type(s) of information you wish to gain from the session; (b) that questions are asked at the child's vocabulary and conceptualization level; and (c) that information obtained is specific rather than general. Laing (1988) points out that this type of assessment is limited by four factors: the extent to which (1) the client understands what information is being requested; (2) the client possesses the information that is requested; (3) the client is willing to provide the information; and (4) the counselor accurately interprets the client's response. Osberg (1989) has added to this list an important fifth factor, that the client possess a minimal amount of introspectiveness to be able to respond to the questions. These factors are particularly appropriate to child counseling.

The intake process has also been used with group guidance activities in elementary schools. Morse and Bockoven (1989) describe the use of an intake interview as a precursor to guidance curriculum projects using the DUSO–R.* They suggest questions such as "What goes well between you and your mom (dad, friends)?" "What do you do that helps it go well between you and your mom (dad, friends)?" Such questions address both relationship issues and personal involvement issues and "provide a sense of the children's goals or desired outcomes for participating in the DUSO-R program" (p. 106).

## *Issues Related to Child Clinical Assessment*

A number of concerns have been raised by state legislatures, social service agencies, and the helping profession regarding the welfare of children. Many of these concerns are revealed in the child counseling process, including child abuse, the effect of divorce on children, the single-parent home, and poverty and childhood. The counselor will be faced with a very fundamental question as he or she works with the young child: *"What is normal?"* What is normal physical, emotional, social, or moral development? What is normal child behavior? What is normal parent behavior? How wide a range of alternatives does the concept "normal" include?

Defining normal, or more particularly, defining abnormal child behavior, is the general domain of the American Psychiatric Association's *Diagnostic and Statistical Manual*, 4th Edition. This source is used by all service providers who conform to guidelines for repayment for psychological/psychiatric services by health insurance companies. It addresses wide-ranging behaviors, such as fighting, verbal and physical abusiveness, cruelty to peers, animals, etc., destructive behaviors, temper tantrums, lying, disobedience and resistant behavior, stealing, hyperactivity, inattentiveness, and failure to learn. It also includes behavioral descriptions for what must be observable by the counselor in order to classify a child as needing professional assistance for a specific problem.

For the child who falls outside the range of normal, the counselor's role will include involvement with others: physicians, psychologists, psychiatrists, social workers, marriage and family therapists, the court system, or the state child welfare system. Oftentimes, the counselor will be the person to initiate these other services. When this happens, it is rarely the case that the counselor's role ends. The more likely outcome is that the counselor will remain involved, ei-

---

* The DUSO-R is a guidance curriculum developed by Dinkmeyer and Dinkmeyer (1982) containing teachers manuals, discussion pictures, and objects, audio cassettes of songs and stories, other activity suggestions such as role-playing, career activities, puppetry, and discussion topics.

ther as a primary or secondary service provider to the child and family. As primary provider, the counselor will continue the counseling relationship with the child, using the other resources as consultant or adjunct services. When the counselor becomes the secondary provider, his/her role is likely to be that of coordinating the school's participation in the larger therapeutic plan.

## Clinical Assessment with Couples and Families

Most professional literature on marital and family therapy emphasizes a systemic approach to working with couples and families (see Chapter 10). With this approach, Sluzko (1978) has observed that:

> *The qualitative shift in the conceptual framework that character-*
> *izes the interpersonal systems approach to the couple requires that*
> *one utilize the* transactions between individuals, *rather than the*
> *characteristics of each given individual, as primary data. Even*
> *when, for one reason or another, attention is zeroed in on one per-*
> *son, his/her behavior is analyzed in terms of its power to affect and*
> *shape the behavior of other members of the system and in terms of*
> *the variables of the ecosystem that may have affected it.* (p. 366)

Given this "qualitative shift in conceptual framework," the types of questions that would characterize the intake and problem definition interview address verbal and nonverbal interaction patterns between members of the identified system (family, couple, peer group, etc.). While it would still be important to obtain demographic information and medical information about the couple or family, the counselor would quickly refocus to factors reflecting effects rather than intentions, the effects of "behaviors upon behaviors [and] the way interpersonal sequences are organized" (Sluzko, 1978, p. 367). Questions that would reflect this orientation might include:

> *"Whenever Antonio does this, how are you likely to respond,*
> *Maria?"*
> *"When Maria reacts, what is the next thing you are likely to say,*
> *Antonio?"*

Note that the counselor does not ask "Why do you respond this way?" The reason or "intention (for a particular act) is considered irrelevant to the understanding of interpersonal processes" (Sluzko, 1978, p. 367).

## Using Assessment Information

Counselors develop different approaches to using the information collected from intake and problem-definition sessions. Some counselors look primarily for patterns of behavior. For example, one counselor noted that his client had a pattern of incompletions in life: he received a general discharge from the Army prior to completing his enlistment, dropped out of college twice, and had a long history of broken relationships. This observation provides food for thought. What happens to this person as he becomes involved in a commitment? What has this client come to think of himself as a result of his history? How does he anticipate future commitments? Another counselor uses the assessment information to look for "signals" that suggest how she might enter the counseling relationship. Is there anything current in the client's life that common sense would suggest is a potential area for counseling attention? For example, is the client in the midst of a divorce; is the client at a critical developmental stage?

The information counselors collect during assessment is also invaluable in planning relevant counseling strategies and approaches to use with problems. For example, a client who reports depression describes the problem primarily in cognitive terms: "I'm a failure, I'm not good at anything, I can't stand it when people don't approve of me. When something goes wrong, it is all my fault." This client has internalized a self-defeating set of beliefs and self-perceptions that are erroneous and not likely to be based on data or facts. The counselor would probably decide to use an approach or strategy with this client that deals directly with cognitions, beliefs, and internal dialogue. (See Chapter 8 for a discussion of cognitive change strategies.)

In contrast, suppose another client who complains of depression is depressed because of a perceived inability to make friends, to form new relationships, and to maintain existing ones. In this instance, the counselor might look at the client's behavior in interpersonal relationships and use behavioral strategies (see Chapter 9) that emphasize acquisition of social skills and interpersonal or systemic strategies (see Chapter 10) that deal with relationships between people.

Counselors who fail to conduct assessment interviews are more likely to formulate erroneous conclusions about client problems and irrelevant or nonworkable counseling approaches and strategies. As a result, not only is more time spent on "hit or miss" counseling, but ultimately clients may leave with the same set of problems they brought to the first session.

To help you tie together the information revealed from assessment of a client with corresponding counseling strategies, we have organized the strategy chapters (Chapters 7 through 10) around the four components of a problem (feelings, behavior, cognitions, relationships). For example, strategies that deal primarily with feelings or have an affective focus are presented in Chapter 7. Cognitive-based strategies are described in Chapter 8, while Chapter 9 presents behavioral strategies. Strategies with an interpersonal or systemic focus are found in Chapter 10.

## Skills Associated with Assessment

In assessing client concerns, the counselor relies on all the skills described in Chapter 3 that are used to build rapport and to establish a good therapeutic relationship. Some of the skills most frequently used during intake and problem-definition interviews include *verbal and nonverbal attending, paraphrasing content,* and use of *questions* to facilitate the assessment process. In this section, we describe and provide examples of three specific kinds of questions useful in assessment: clarifying questions; open-ended questions; and closed questions.

### Clarifying Questions

Sometimes client responses sound cryptic or confused and the counselor is left wondering just what the client was trying to say. It can be very important to seek clarification in these moments rather than guessing or assuming that the communication was unimportant. The clarifying question *asks the client to rephrase the communication, and can be stated in several ways.*

Clarifying questions are self-explanatory. The important point is that they can be overused or underused. When overused, they become distractors. Sometimes the counselor is reluctant to seek clarification lest it impede or distract the client from the topic. If you are simply unable to follow the client's train of thought, it is more important to seek clarification than it is to allow the client to proceed. Otherwise, you run the risk of drawing inaccurate conclusions.

### Open-Ended Questions

Open-ended questions require more than a minimal one-word answer by the client. They are introduced with *what, where, when, who,* or *how. What* questions solicit facts and information; *how* questions are used to inquire about emotions or sequences of events; *where* and *when* elicit information about time and context; *who* yields information about people. It is important to vary the words used to start open-ended questions depending on the type of material you want to focus on and solicit from the client.

Shainberg (1993) observes that a good open-ended question of-

*The Clarifying Question*

"Could you try to describe that feeling in another way? I'm not sure I am following what you mean."

"When you say 'fuzzy,' what's that feeling like?"

"I think I got lost in that. Could you go through the sequence of events again for me?"

"Could you go over that again for me?"

"Is there another way you could describe that feeling?"

"What did you mean when you said your parents were pretty indifferent?"

---

*The Open-Ended Question*

"*What* is there in all of this that you have not seen?"

"*How* do you plan to find employment?"

"*When* are you most likely to feel that way?"

"*What* is keeping you from asking her?"

"*What* is the piece that would unlock the puzzle?"

---

*The Closed Question*

"How old were you when your parents died?"

"Are you an only child, or do you have brothers and sisters?"

"Are you taking any medications now?"

"Have you ever received counseling or therapy?"

---

fers new energy to clients and helps to open them up in a different way, yet she also is aware that many counselors close down clients' energy by the use of "stock" questions such as "How does this make you feel?" Over the years as a therapist, she has amassed examples of creatively worded open-ended questions that help engage the client. Some examples of these (pp. 96–196) are given in the box above.

Specific times when open-ended questions are very useful during counseling sessions include:

1. *Beginning an interview*

   "What would you like to talk about?"
   "What brings you to counseling?"
   "How have things been this week?"
   "Where do you want to begin today?"

2. *Encouraging client elaboration*

"What happens when you lose control?"
"Who else is invested in this problem?"
"When do you notice that reaction?"
"How could things be better for you?"

3. *Eliciting specific examples*

"What do you do when this happens?"
"Exactly how do you feel about it?"
"Where are you when you feel depressed?"

## Closed Questions

A closed question narrows the area or focus of discussion. Thus, when you need a specific piece of information, it is best obtained by a closed question. Closed questions may be answered with a "yes" or "no" or a specific piece of information.

## Effects of Assessment on Clients

The assessment stage of counseling is likely to have a number of possible effects on clients. Although each client's reaction to an intake or problem-definition interview is unique, it is also possible to describe some fairly predictable client patterns of reaction. Some of these are positive; some are negative. On the positive side, assessing client concerns helps clients to feel:

*Understood:* "I believe someone finally understands how terrible these last few months have been for me."

*Relieved:* "Well, it does feel good to get that off my chest."

*Hopeful:* "Now maybe something can be done to help me feel better or get a handle on things."

*Motivated:* "Now that I have someone to talk to, I have some energy to do something about this."

On the negative side, assessment can result in client reactions and feelings such as:

*Anxious:* "Am I really that bad off? I guess so. This is a lot to deal with all at once."

*Interrogated:* "Boy, do I feel on the spot. There are so many questions being thrown at me. Some of them are so personal too."

*Vulnerable:* "How do I know if I can trust him with this? Can he handle it and not share it with anyone else?"

*Evaluated:* "I wonder if she thinks I'm really messed up? Crazy? Stupid? Maybe something really is wrong with me?"

Given these possible reactions, it is important to assess client concerns carefully and with much sensitivity. The ideal outcome is when the client's positive reactions to assessment outweigh the negative reactions. When this occurs, assessment has become a very useful and productive part of counseling without jeopardizing the rapport and relationship the counselor and client have worked so hard to establish prior to this time. Client reactions to assessment are likely to be more positive when the counselor uses questions that are directly relevant to the client's concerns and also used in proportion to other skills and responses.

Nothing can make a client feel defensive and interrogated more quickly than asking too many questions. Sometimes the same information can be gleaned by nonverbal attending behaviors, verbal following, or statements that paraphrase content or reflect affect. Inexperienced counselors seem to have a natural tendency to use questions more frequently than any other response (Spooner & Stone, 1977) and must be especially careful during assessment not to let this skill take over while their other newly learned skills go by the wayside.

## The Intake Interview

### The Case of Angela

Angela appears to be a middle-aged female who works full-time as a teacher. She reports that she is divorced and has not remarried, although she maintains custody of two teenage children. She states that the reason she is seeking counseling at this time is to learn to have better control of her moods. She indicates that she often "flies off the handle" for no reason, with her own children or with her students in the classroom. She also reports that she cries easily and "feels blue" much of the time.

*The Intake Interview*

The intake-history interview with Angela revealed the following information:

*I. Identifying data:*

Angela is forty years old. She lives with her two children (ages twelve and fifteen) in a mobile home outside a small town. She has been divorced for six years. She teaches English to high school juniors.

*II. Range of problems:*

In addition to the problems first presented (feeling out of control and blue), Angela also feels she is a failure as a wife and mother, primarily because of her divorce and her mood swings. Her self-description is predominantly negative.

## III. *Current life setting:*

Angela's typical day consists of getting up, going to work, coming home, doing something with her children, and then grading papers or watching TV. On weekends, she stays at home a great deal. She has few neighbors, only one or two close friends, and does not participate in any recreational, religious, or social activities on a regular basis. She reports a great deal of difficulty in carrying out her regular routine on days when she feels down. Occasionally, she calls in sick and stays home and sleeps all day.

## IV. *Family history:*

Angela is the youngest of three children. She was raised Roman Catholic in a second generation, Italian American family. She describes her relationship to her two older brothers and to her mother as very close. She is not as close to her father, although she reports that he was always very good to her. The family remains close and gathers whenever there is an occasion, a birthday, or a celebration. Angela also reports that as the youngest child and the only girl, she was protected and pampered a great deal by her parents and her brothers while growing up. Currently, she lives a day's drive away from both her parents and her brothers and looks forward to seeing them on family occasions. To her knowledge, none of her immediate family members have had any significant mental health problems, although she thinks that one of her aunts is chronically depressed.

## V. *Personal history:*

**A.** Medical
Angela reports that in the last year she has undergone major surgery twice—once for the removal of a benign lump in her breast and once for the repair of a disc. She also indicates she has been diagnosed as having Addison's disease and is on medication for it, prescribed by a general practitioner, but she frequently forgets to take the medication as prescribed.

Angela reports some sleeping problems, primarily when she is distressed. At these times, she has difficulty falling asleep until 2:00 or 3:00 A.M. Her weight fluctuates by five or six pounds during a given month. When she is upset, she often eats little or nothing for a day or two.

**B.** Educational
Angela has a bachelor's degree in English and a master's degree in Education. She appears to be of above-average intelligence and describes herself as a conscientious student to the point of worrying excessively about grades and performance. As a teacher, she occasionally takes graduate courses to renew her certification.

**C.** Military
Angela has never served in the military.

**D.** Vocational
Angela has been a high school English teacher ever since graduating from college, although she reports that she "dropped out" of her teaching after her first child was born fourteen years ago. She resumed teaching again when she was divorced six years ago. Her children were then six and eight years old. She describes her present job as marginally adequate although not very challenging and not very financially rewarding. She stays with it primarily because of job security and because of the hours (summers off). She reports satisfactory relationships

with other teachers, although she has no good friends at work.

**E.** Sexual and marital

Angela's first sexual experiences were with her former husband, although she reports she received a good bit of sex education from her parents and her older brothers. She asserts that this is a difficult subject for her to discuss. She states that while she felt her sexual relationship with her husband was adequate, he became sexually involved with another woman prior to their divorce. She indicates that before her marriage, she had only two other love relationships with men, both of which were terminated mutually because of differences in values. She describes her marital relationship as good until the time she discovered through a friend about her husband's affair. She has very little contact with her ex-husband, although her two children see him every other weekend. She reports that the children have a good relationship with their father and that he has been helpful to her by taking the children for periods of time when she is feeling depressed and overwhelmed by her life situation. She repeatedly indicates that she blames herself for the failure of the marriage.

**F.** Counseling

Angela reports that she saw a counselor for depression during her divorce (about twelve sessions). She terminated because she thought she had things under control. Now she is concerned about her ability to manage her feelings and wants help to learn how to deal better with her moods, especially feeling upset, irritable, and blue.

***VI.*** *Counselor's observations of Angela.*

During the intake interview, you observe that Angela generally seems to have little energy and is rather passive, as evidenced by her slouched body position, soft voice tone, and lack of animation in facial expressions and body movements. Angela appears to be in control of her feelings, although she cried much of the time while describing her marital and sexual history.

## *Integration of Material from Intake*

Following an initial interview, it is important to tie together the information obtained from the client in some meaningful fashion. In Angela's case, we know that she is a fortyish female who, although she has been divorced for six years, has not ever really resolved the divorce issue in her mind. Furthermore, her concern with mood fluctuations and feeling so blue appears to be substantiated not only by her nonverbal demeanor but also by her verbal reports of symptoms and behaviors typically associated with mild depression:

- She perceives herself as a failure, particularly in her role as a wife and mother.
- She blames herself for the divorce.
- She describes herself negatively.
- She experiences a reduced level of energy and rate of activity when distressed.

- She has very few close relationships with others.
- She experiences some sleeping difficulties and loss of appetite when distressed.
- She does not appear to have any concrete goals and plans for the future apart from her role as mother.

This picture is complicated by her health. She has undergone two operations in the last year and suffers from a fairly complex endocrinological problem which, because of her lack of compliance in taking prescribed medication, probably makes her mood fluctuations and depression more intense and more frequent.

Angela's family is a strength. She is on good terms with her family and enjoys those occasions when they get together. Knowing that strong family ties are characteristic of the Italian American family, this is likely to be a source of significant support. On the other hand, the distance between her home and that of her family does pose a problem.

Continuing beyond the intake interview, it is important for the counselor to continue developing an understanding of the presenting problem. This involves assessment of the components of the problem, intensity, and possible controlling variables associated with Angela's feelings of dysphoria. Some of the information she gave during the intake session will serve as suggestions on which to build during the problem-definition process.

## Problem Definition Analysis

### I. Components of the problem.

*Feelings:* Angela describes her predominant feelings as irritable, upset, and "down" or "blue." Primary somatic reactions during times of stress include loss of appetite and insomnia.

*Cognitions:* When you ask Angela to describe specific things she thinks about or focuses on during the times she feels depressed, she responds with statements such as "I just think about what a failure I am" or "I wish I were a better wife (or mother)" or "I should have been able to keep my marriage together, and because I didn't, I'm a failure." Her cognitions represent two areas or trouble spots often associated with feelings of depression—shouldism and perfectionism. She does not report any thoughts or ideas about suicide.

*Behaviors:* Angela has some trouble specifying things she does or does not do while depressed. She finally says that she often withdraws and retreats to her room, or becomes irritable, usually to her students or children. She also cries easily at these times.

*Interpersonal relationships:* Angela notes that once she feels down, no one around her can really pull her out of it. But she also says that she does not really have close friends to share her feelings or problems with. She believes her depressed feelings interfere with her relationship with her children because they tend to avoid her when she gets into a period of depression. However, she also acknowledges that she can use her feelings to get her children to do things "her way."

### II. Pattern of contributing events.

When Angela describes what seems to lead up to these feelings, she notes the following:

1. Seems to be worst a week before her menstrual period.
2. Failure to take her medication.
3. Being reminded or reminding herself about her divorce.
4. Hassles with her children and/or ex-husband.

In describing what seems to stop the feelings or makes them better or worse, she observes:

1. Having her period over with.
2. Taking her medication
3. Doing something with her children
4. Having to go to work.
5. Having telephone or other contact initiated by her brothers or parents.

### III. Intensity of the problem.

With depression, it is important to assess whether it is a long-term, chronic condition or a short-term response to a situation or event. Angela reports that she has felt more depressed for the last six years since the divorce. However, she acknowledges that as a child and even during her marriage, she was frequently able to use tears to get her way. Thus, her crying at least had value for her in the past, and even currently, she can use it to manipulate her children. She states that, on average, she gets quite depressed for one week out of every month. She rates the intensity of her feelings at about 8 on a 1 (low) to 10 (high) scale. When she feels down, she usually does so for several days. This is the time when she is most apt to call in sick or to become irritable with her students and her children.

### VI. Client coping skills, strengths, resources.

Angela is not readily aware of anything she does to cope effectively with her depressed feelings. She seems to believe that the onset and termination of these feelings are mostly out of her control. She does describe herself as a good student and a good teacher. Her strengths are her reliability and dependability. She does indicate that she has a lot of perseverance and tenacity when she decides she wants something to work out. Angela's family-of-origin is a resource to be explored.

## Integration of Problem-Definition Information with Treatment Planning

The information obtained from this problem-definition session and initial session are of direct value in selecting and planning relevant counseling strategies to help Angela. In her case, the depression seems partially maintained by two potential physiological sources—Addison's disease and premenstrual syndrome (PMS). Therefore, part of your planning would involve having her health assessed and monitored by a physician. Additionally, it is evident that the cognitive and interpersonal spheres are major components and contributing causes of these feelings. It would thus be important to select counseling strategies that focus on the cognitive and interpersonal modalities. Strategies such as cognitive restructuring, reframing, irrational thought analysis, systemic analysis, social skills training, and family counseling are all useful possibilities. (These strategies are described in Chapters 8 and 10.) It is also possible that some of Angela's difficulties stem from dissonance she feels with the cultural values of her childhood and family.

## Summary

Assessment is invaluable for seeking pertinent information about clients and their presenting problems. In addition to the value of information garnered, assessment can also be reactive; that is, it can initiate the process of change for clients. Assessment is usually started by intake sessions that gather information about the client's background and history. Assessment is very important in the early stages of counseling to help counselors formulate hypotheses, but it is also an ongoing process during counseling, as presenting problems and accompanying conceptualizations of issues often change. Specific assessment interviews obtain information about components of the problem, pattern of contributing events, intensity of the problem, and client coping skills. Skills used to obtain such information frequently include paraphrasing content, reflecting affect, summarizing, and a variety of questions.

## Exercises

**I.** *Intake and History Interviews*

**A.** Identify a current or existing problem in the life of a member of your family. It might be a family or relationship conflict, a love or sex issue, a financial problem, or a work or school-related concern. Select someone with whom you feel comfortable discussing this problem. Your task is to discuss how your relative's background and history have affected the development and maintenance of this concern. You may want to refer to the intake and history outline in this chapter to guide your discussion.

**B.** Using triads, identify one person as the client, another as counselor, and one as observer. The assigned tasks are as follows:

*Client*—Describe a present or ongoing concern or issue in your life.

*Counselor*—Conduct an intake or history-taking session with this client following the outline given in the chapter. If possible, audio-record the session.

*Observer*—Be prepared to give feedback to the counselor following the role-play and/or to intervene and cue the counselor during the role-play if he/she has difficulty and gets stuck. Rotate the initial roles two more times so that each person has an opportunity to be in each role once. Time requirement: 1 hour.

## II. *Problem Definition*

**A.** Using the same problem you identified for Exercise IA, identify:

1. The various components of the problem
2. Contributing conditions
3. Intensity of the problem
4. Client's resources, strengths, and coping skills

You may wish to do this alone or in conjunction with a partner, colleague, instructor, or supervisor. It may be helpful to refer to the outline in this chapter to jot down some key words as you go through this process.

**B.** Read Chapter 16, "Italian Families," (Marie Rotunno and Monica McGoldrick) in *Ethnicity and Family Therapy*, M. McGoldrick, J.K. Pearce, and J. Giordano (Eds.), Guilford Press, 1982. Then do an analysis of Angela's intake interview within the context of her family-of-origin. What insights into Angela may be gained through an understanding of her cultural background? How might her background and her family be utilized as part of her counseling?

## III. *Questions*

**A.** In this activity, identify whether each of the questions listed is a clarifying, open-ended, or closed question. Use the key below to record your answers in the blanks provided. Feedback follows the exercises.

C = Clarifying
O–E = Open-ended
Cl = Closed

_____ **1.** "What is it like for you when you get depressed?"
_____ **2.** "Have you had a physical exam in the last two years?"
_____ **3.** "Are you saying you don't give up easily?"
_____ **4.** "How does this job affect your moods?"
_____ **5.** "Do you mean to say that you have difficulty letting go?"
_____ **6.** "Do you have many children?"

**B.** In this activity, you are given five client statements. Practice formulating a question for each client statement. Share your questions in your class or with your instructor or a colleague.

**1.** *Client (a teenager):* "I've got to graduate with my class. If I don't, everyone will think I'm a real screw-up."

**2.** *Client (an elderly man):* "It's just so hard to make a living on a fixed income like I do. If I had it to do over, I'd do it a lot different."

**3.** *Client (a young girl):* "I hate my dad. He's always picking on me."

**4.** *Clients (a couple married for four years):* "It's just not turning out the way we thought. We wanted our marriage to really work. But it's not."

**5.** *Client (a middle-aged person):* "There are just so many pressures on me right now—from all sides. Family, work, friends, you name it."

## *Feedback for Exercises*

**III.** *Questions*

| | |
|---|---|
| **1.** O–E | **4.** O–E |
| **2.** Cl | **5.** C |
| **3.** C | **6.** Cl |

## *Discussion Questions*

**1.** Intake interviews and the problem-definition process are time-consuming and may seem to delay the counseling process. Assume you are the clinical director for a private mental health agency; how would you justify the use of these assessment interviews to the administrative director or to the agency's board of directors?

**2.** Suppose you are seeing a client who presents a crisis situation (e.g., recent rape, decision over abortion, spouse-child abuse). You probably will not have the luxury of devoting a session or more to conduct a complete intake/problem-definition process. What information about the problem and about the client's background and history would be most important to obtain in a fifteen-minute period of time? Discuss with other class members.

**3.** Assessment with young children (ages 6–10) calls for a different type of interaction. How would you modify your approach to this age group? What kinds of information would you solicit? What do you know about yourself that would either facilitate the assessment process or provide obstacles to your success with this age group?

**4.** How do you think the assessment process may be viewed differently by women and by men? Can you also think of instances in which the impact of assessment may vary with the cultural-ethnic background of the client?

## Recommended Readings

Bellack, A. and Hersen, M. (1988). *Behavioral Assessment*, 3d Ed. Elmsford, NY: Pergamon Press.

Egan, G. (1994). *The Skilled Helper*, 5th Ed. Pacific Grove, CA: Brooks/Cole. Chapter 7: Helping clients tell their stories.

Hackney, H. and Cormier, S. (1994). *Counseling Strategies and Interventions*, 4th Ed. Boston, MA: Allyn & Bacon. Chapter 9, Conceptualizing problems and setting goals.

Laing. J. (1988). Self-report: Can it be of value as an assessment technique? *Journal of Counseling and Development, 67,* 60–61.

Lee, C.C. and Richardson, B.L. (1991). *Multicultural Issues in Counseling: New Approaches to Diversity*. Alexandria, VA: ACA Press.

McGoldrick, M., Pearce, J.K., and Giordano, J., Eds. (1982). *Ethnicity and Family Therapy*, New York: Guilford Press.

Miller, M.J. (1990). The power of the "OCEAN": Another way to diagnose clients, *Counselor Education and Supervision, 29,* 283–290.

Sue, D.W. and Sue, D. (1990). *Counseling the Culturally Different, Theory and Practice*, 2d. Ed. New York: Wiley. Chapter 1: The politics of counseling.

West, J.D. (1988). Marriage and family therapy assessment, *Counselor Education and Supervision, 28,* 169–180.

# Chapter 5

# *Developing Counseling Goals*

### *Purpose of This Chapter—*

Counseling, like any activity, must have a focus. For the client, that focus is the problem or concern. The counselor's focus is also on the client's problems, but more importantly, the counselor's focus is on a variety of factors: the client, the counseling process, the problems, and of course, a desirable outcome. This chapter examines the process by which the counselor and client, collaboratively, can work to define what that desirable outcome might be or will be. We first engaged the issue of the client's *worldview* and how that directs the counselor's effort in the chapter on rapport and relationship. Now, in choosing the goals of counseling, those values, beliefs, and practices that compose the client's *worldview* really come into play. This chapter also attempts to identify some of those factors.

### *Considerations as You Read This Chapter—*

• There is a saying "Lord, save me from my wants." The wisdom of this saying is that we may not be very good at choosing the things we would have happen to us. In the context of counseling, what are wise wants or goals?

• Who is best able to judge? The counselor? The client?

• How do we make these decisions?

• What is the impact of our choice of goals on the counseling process?

Often counselors (or sometimes clients) will complain, "The session didn't go anywhere" or "I felt like we were talking in circles." As part of the assessment process, it is important to translate general client concerns into specific desired goals. Goals give direction to the therapeutic process and help both counselor and client to move in a focused direction with a specific route in mind. They represent the results or outcomes the client wants to achieve at the end of counseling. Without goals, it is all too easy to get sidetracked or lost. Goals help both the counselor and client to specify exactly what can and cannot be accomplished through counseling. In this respect, goal-setting is an impoartant extension of the assessment process in counseling. Recall that during assessment, clients focus on specific concerns and issues that are difficult, problematic, or are not going very well for them. In goal-setting, clients identify, with the counselor's help, specific ways in which they want to resolve these issues and specific courses of action they can take for problem resolution.

## Functions of Counseling Goals

Goals serve three important functions in the counseling process. First, goals can have a *motivational* effect in counseling. When clients are encouraged to specify desired changes, they are more likely to work toward accomplishing those outcomes. This is particularly true when clients actively participate in the goal-setting process. Clients are much more likely to support and work toward changes that *they* selected.

Goals also have an *educational* function in counseling in that they can help clients acquire new responses. Goals provide clients with information and standards by which they can encode and rehearse desired actions and responses. Dixon and Glover (1984) explain that

> Once a goal is formulated and selected by a problem solver, it is likely to be rehearsed in the working memory and stored in long-term memory. A goal encoded in this way, then, becomes a major heuristic for the problem solver as he or she interacts with the environment. (pp. 128–129)

This is quite evident in the performance of highly successful performers or athletes who set goals for themselves and then use the goal to rehearse their performance over and over again in their heads. Concert pianists, for example will cognitively rehearse the way they want a particular passage to sound; champion divers will visualize themselves performing a particular dive in a desired fashion both on the platform and before the competition.

Finally, goals provide an *evaluative* function in counseling. The type of outcomes or change represented by the client's goals helps the counselor to select and evaluate various counseling interventions that are likely to be successful for a particular client pursuing a specific goal or set of outcomes. Goals also contribute to the evaluative function in counseling because a goal represents a *desired outcome*, a point at which counseling would be deemed successful. Thus, when outcome goals are established, both the counselor and client can evaluate client progress toward the goals in order to determine when they are being attained and when the goals or the counseling intervention may need revision. Bandura (1969) notes that

> *When desired outcomes are designated in observable and measurable terms, it becomes readily apparent when the methods have succeeded, when they have failed, and when they need further development to increase their potency. This self-corrective feature is a safeguard against perpetuation of ineffective approaches. . . .* (p. 74)

## Parameters of Goal-Setting: Process and Outcome Goals

The counseling process involves two types of goals: *process goals* and *outcome goals*. Process goals are related to the establishment of therapeutic conditions necessary for client change. These are general goals, such as establishing rapport, providing a nonthreatening setting, and possessing and communicating accurate empathy and positive regard. They can be generalized to all client relationships and can be considered universal goals. Process goals are the counselor's primary responsibility; you cannot expect your clients to share the responsibility for these goals. Most of what was discussed in Chapters 3 and 4 are process goals.

Unlike process goals, *outcome goals* will be different for each client. They are the goals directly related to those life changes your clients would hope to accomplish through counseling. As you are able to help your clients understand their concerns, you will want to help them understand how counseling can be useful in responding to those concerns. The two of you will begin to formulate tentative outcome goals together. As counseling continues, the original goals may be modified through better understanding of the problems and through the development of new attitudes and behaviors that will eliminate or reduce problems. Goal-setting should be viewed as a flexible process, always subject to modification and refinement. Most important, outcome goals are *shared* goals, goals that both you and your clients agree to work toward achieving.

Outcome goals that are visible or observable are more useful, because it is easier to determine when they have been achieved. Yet not all outcome goals are stated as visible goals. For example, consider these two outcome goals:

1. To help your client develop his/her self-esteem
2. To increase the number of positive self-statements at home and at work by 50 percent over the next six weeks

Both of these could be considered outcome goals. They might even be so closely related as to be the same in terms of outcomes. (That is, the person who is saying more positive things about himself may be well on the way to developing self-esteem.) Your clients may be more attracted to less explicit goals (e.g., better self-esteem). You may want to view the development of self-esteem as a composite of many smaller and more specific changes. To state it a little differently, self-esteem is a *quality* that is reflected in many behaviors. It is inferred through those observed behaviors. Using enhanced self-esteem as your goal, you have no way of knowing the types of activity that your clients will enter into while proceeding toward the goal. As a result, you and your clients may spend a lot of time talking about self-esteem and how much they have or don't have, but things that can be done to enhance self-esteem are not addressed. Consequently, the first goal (#1 above) does not provide as much information about how counseling should proceed as does the second goal.

When outcome goals are stated precisely, both you and your clients have a better understanding of what is to be accomplished. This better understanding permits you to work more directly with your client's problems or concerns and reduces tangential efforts. Equally important are the benefits you are able to realize in working with specific behavioral goals. You are able to enlist the client's cooperation more directly, since your client is more likely to understand what is to be done. In addition, you are in a better position to select appropriate interventions and strategies when your clients have specific objectives. Finally, both you and your clients are in a better position to recognize progress when it happens, a rewarding experience in its own right.

## *Three Elements of Good Outcome Goals*

Perhaps you have noticed from our previous examples that outcome goals are different from process goals in several respects. A well-stated outcome goal includes the behavior to be changed, the conditions under which the changed behavior will occur, and the level or amount of change. One client may want to modify eating patterns; another may wish to reduce negative self-appraisals; and a third may wish to increase assertive requests or refusals.

The second element of an outcome goal indicates the conditions under which the desired behavior(s) (clients might say desired outcomes) will occur. It is important to weigh carefully the situations or settings in which the client will attempt a new behavior. You wouldn't want to set your client up to fail by identifying settings in which there was little hope for success. The client might agree to modify eating habits at home during the evening, but not to attempt to modify those eating habits at the company picnic on Saturday.

The third element of outcome goals involves the choice of a suitable and realistic level or amount of change. That is to say, *how much* of the new behavior will the client attempt? Some clients enter diets with the expectation that they will reduce their consumption from 3000 calories per day to 900 calories per day. A more realistic and attainable goal might be 1500 to 1800 calories. This brings us to another thought about goals. As we modify goals, we come increasingly closer to the ultimate goals of the client. Each time we set a goal, it is a closer approximation of the client's ultimate objective. Successive approximations are very important. They allow the client to set more attainable goals, experience success more freqently, and make what might be dramatic changes in their lifestyle.

## Obstacles in Developing Specific Goals

Krumboltz and Thoresen (1969) noted that rarely does a client begin by requesting assistance in achieving specific behavioral changes. Instead of saying "I want to be able to talk to teachers without getting nervous," the client is likely to say "I am shy." In other words, a personal characteristic has been described rather than the ways in which the characteristic is expressed. It then becomes the counselor's job to help the client describe those ways in which the characteristic *is expressed* and consequently, *could be expressed differently.*

Taking nonspecific concerns and translating them into specific goal statements is no easy task for the counselor, who must understand the nature of the client's problem and the conditions under which it occurs before the translation can begin.

What can you expect of yourself and your clients in terms of setting specific goals? First, the goals that are set can never be more specific than your understanding, and your client's understanding, of the problem. This means that at the outset of counseling, goals are likely to be nonspecific and nonbehavioral. *But nonspecific goals are better than no goals at all.*

Krumboltz (1966) described these nonspecific or general goals as *intermediate* mental states, but he emphasized that one cannot assume that such goals will free up clients to change their overt behavior. The point is that intermediate mental states are temporary, a first step along the way. At the earliest possible time, the counselor must strive to help the client identify more concrete objectives.

As you and your client explore the nature of a particular problem, the type of goal(s) appropriate to the problem should become increasingly apparent. This clarification will permit both of you to move in the direction of identifying specific behaviors that, if changed, would alter the problem in a positive way. These specific behaviors can then be formulated into goal statements; as you discuss the client's problems in more detail, gradually you can add the circumstances in which to perform the behaviors and how much or how often the target behaviors might be altered.

The GOAL-SETTING MAP (*Figure 5-1*) is a useful tool to help clients learn to set goals. The map provides a visual representation of the goal-setting process and requires that the client focus on the steps that lead to change. The first step is to help your client establish a desired outcome (*Main Goal*). Then encourage your client to identify three to five changes necessary for this desired outcome to occur (*Subgoals*), and finally, the client must identify two to three behaviors that he/she must do for each of the subgoals to happen (*Immediate Tasks*).

When several subgoals are identified, they usually are arranged in a sequence or hierarchy, from easiest to attain to most difficult to attain. Similarly, the immediate tasks related to each subgoal are arranged in a logical sequence and are accomplished in that order. The client completes one subgoal before moving on to another. By gradually completing the activities represented by subgoals and immediate tasks in a successful manner, the client's motivation and energy to change are reinforced and maintained. Successful completion of subgoals also may reduce potential failure experiences. Subgoals always represent actions that move clients in the direction of the desired goal. The most effective counseling subgoals are:

1. Built on existing client resources and assets
2. Based on client selection and commitment
3. Congruent with the counselor's and client's values
4. Identified with immediate tasks the client could reasonably be expected to accomplish

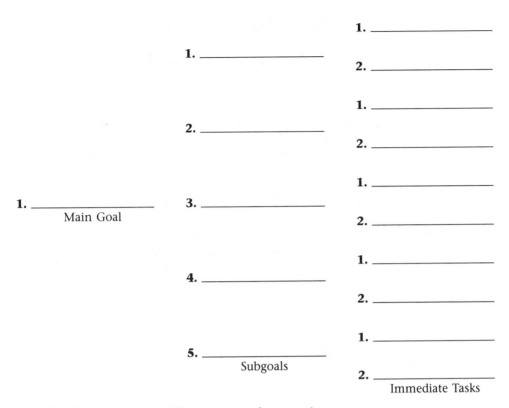

Step #1: Choose a *main goal* (long-term or short-term)
Step #2: Write five steps you must take toward achieving this main goal. These are your *subgoals*
Step #3: For each subgoal, write down two specific things you must do to achieve the subgoal. These are your *immediate tasks.*

**FIGURE 5–1   The Goal-Setting Map**

## Skills Associated with Goal-Setting

Goal-setting involves all of the skills presented in prior chapters. The skills and conditions associated with an effective relationship are necessary in order to establish process goals with clients. The obvious starting point in goal-setting is the relationship and client rapport. Beyond that, you must be able to listen with a skilled ear, hearing the client's wishes and hopes. You must be able to reflect your understandings back to the client, and help the client hear his or her thoughts and feelings as another person hears them. You must be able to summarize the client's message, thus allowing the client to experience the composite of his or her present experience.

Questions are also an integral part of goal-setting. They provide the structure that allows the client to verbalize those goals that may not have been stated or hoped before. Consider the following questions:

1. "How do you want things to change for you?"
2. "What would you like to be doing (thinking or feeling) differently?"
3. "How much do you think you can change your world?"
4. "What are some things that need to happen before you can feel satisfied?"
5. "How will you know when you have succeeded?"

In addition to relationship skills, listening, and questioning, there are two other responses that can be useful during the goal-setting process: *confrontation* and the *ability-potential* response.

## Confrontation

One of the most useful counselor responses is the confrontation. The word itself has acquired some excess emotional meanings. It is sometimes misconstrued to mean lecturing, judging, or punishing. It is more accurate to view the confrontation as a response that enables the client to face that which is being avoided, be it a thought, a feeling, or a behavior. Avoidance is usually expressed as one part of a discrepancy present in the client's message. Thus, the confrontation helps the client to identify a contradiction, a rationalization or excuse, or a misinterpretation.

The discrepancy or contradiction is usually one of the following types:

1. A discrepancy between what clients say and how they behave (for example, the client who says he is a quiet type, but in the interview, he talks freely).
2. A contradiction between how clients *say they feel* and how their behaviors *suggest* they are feeling (for example, the client who says she is comfortable but continues to fidget).
3. A discrepancy between two verbal messages of the client (for example, the client who says he wants to change his behavior, but in the next breath places all blame for his behavior on his parents or on others).

Operationally, the confrontation is a compound sentence. The statement establishes a "you said/but look" condition. In other words, the first part of the compound sentence is the "you said" (a paraphrase or affective reflection). It repeats a message of the client. The second part of the compound sentence presents the contradiction or discrepancy, the "but look" of the client message.

Sometimes, the "you said" part of the message can be implied rather than said, particularly if the discrepant part of the message has just occurred. For example,

*Client:* I just can't talk to people I don't know.

*Counselor:* (You say, etc. [*implied part*]) But you don't know me all that well.

---

*Confrontation Response*

"You say school isn't very satisfying, *but* your grades are excellent." (Discrepancy between stated condition and behavior.)

"You say you have resolved that conflict *but* are you aware of the emotion in your voice?" (Discrepancy between stated feeling and communicated affect.)

"A while ago you said you never want to see Bob again, *and now* you say he's your best friend." (Discrepancy between two verbal messages.)

---

The confrontation *describes* client messages, *observes* client behavior, and *presents* evidence. However, the confrontation is not meant to accuse, evaluate, or solve problems. Use of the confrontation serves several important purposes:

1. It assists in the client's effort to become more congruent, by helping the client recognize when discrepancies exist.
2. It establishes the counselor as a role model for direct and open communication; if the counselor is comfortable acknowledging contradictions, perhaps the client can become more comfortable challenging them too.
3. It is an action-oriented response. Unlike the reflection that mirrors the client's *feelings*, the confrontation mirrors the client's *behavior*. It is useful in initiating action plans and behavior change.
4. It is useful for exploring conflict associated with change and goal-setting.

## Ability-Potential Response

The ability-potential response allows the counselor to suggest that the client has the ability or potential to engage in a specified form of activity. It communicates the counselor's support or confidence in the client's ability to act. It also communicates that the client can assume some power or control over his/her environment. The ability-potential can be used to suggest a course of action that the client may not have considered. As such, it is particularly helpful as a goal-setting response, particularly when the client is unable to identify subgoals or immediate tasks. When used this way, it is best used to give the client an idea of how to identify subgoals and immediate tasks, rather than identifying them for the client.

If your client were to say: "I don't know where I'm going to get the money to pay that bill," an ability-potential response might be: "One possibility is that you could work for a semester and earn the money."

---

*Ability-Potential Response*

*Client:* "I'd like to be able to tell him what I really feel, but if I do, I believe he'll get upset."

*Counselor:* "Perhaps *you could find some positive ways* to tell him if you think about it."

---

Typically, the ability-potential response begins with "you could," "you can," or "you might." As with other types of counselor responses that you have been learning, it can be overused. When that happens, it begins to sound unreal, hollow, and meaningless. Although the ability-potential may sound like advice, it is used effectively as a means of identifying alternatives available to the client. It is misused when, in oversimplification, the counselor attempts to suggest or prescribe a solution; the effect is to negate or ignore the client's concerns.

## Effects of Goal-Setting on Clients

The process of setting goals can have important effects on clients. Most are positive or helpful, although an occasional client may resist the goal-setting process. The advantages of establishing concrete goals are several. Clients feel less confused, clearer about themselves and their wants and needs. Goal-setting helps clients sort out the important from the unimportant, the relevant from the trivial of their lives. Goal-setting encourages clients to make decisions and choices that represent their most significant values and priorities. As a consequence, clients often feel more enlightened and clearer about what they really want for themselves.

Clients also feel a sense of accomplishment. Goal-setting is often the first time during counseling that clients begin to take specific action in response to a problem or issue. Sometimes the problem has been one of longstanding. Through goal-setting, clients can feel better about themselves by overcoming a sense of inertia, by mobilizing their forces, and by starting to set in place a chain of events and behaviors that will lead to problem resolution. As a result, clients often feel a great sense of accomplishment during and after the goal-setting process.

Goal-setting allows clients a different view of their problems and concerns. The process of establishing specific goals can be reactive; that is, the *act* of selecting and defining results can contribute to desired changes in itself. This is particularly true when clients are heavily invested in the goal-setting process. Lloyd (1983) noted that:

> *Clients who are aware of their own specific objectives may do better in therapy than those who are not. The more involved both therapists and clients are in the details of goal attainment procedures, the more likely is the system to be reactive.* (p. 60)

When goal-setting is reactive, clients are likely to feel better about themselves and encouraged about the directions they are choosing to pursue.

Recent research into client perceptions of various aspects of the counseling relationship supports the importance of goal-setting (Halstead, Brooks, Goldberg, & Fish, 1990). In the results of their research, they observed

> *. . . that clients perceived the goal portion of the alliance as being stronger than their counselors did. A possible explanation for this finding, again, may be associated with the nature of the client's personal investment. One would expect the counselor and client to have a comon understanding of the explicit goals that help to guide the counseling process. These goals, from the counselor's frame of reference, serve as a beacon by which to set a course to help the client. To the client, however, the goals of counseling, especially in early sessions, may be associated directly with a way to relieve emotional pain. The goals in counseling may represent a real sense of hope for the client. Therefore, it is likely that clients form stronger personal attachments to their goals in that goals can serve to create solutions to what may look like overwhelming situations.* (p. 216)

## Goal-Setting and Multicultural Issues

Within the multicultural counseling context, the effect of goal-setting is less well understood by counselors. Although there has been only limited research in this area, Taussig (1987) proposes that clients with varying racial-ethnic backgrounds respond positively to the goal-setting process. However, a note of caution is needed. We have already observed how important it is that the counselor have a realistic and accurate understanding of the client's worldview *and the client's world.*

Sue and Sue (1990) state that "counseling culturally different clients may require a different combination of skills (process) and goals" (p. 160) and observe further that:

> *Rather than introspection and self-analysis, which many Third World people may find unappealing, the concrete tangible approach of behavioral counseling is extremely attractive. The Rogerian conditions of paraphrasing, reflecting feelings, and summarizing can be incompatible with cultural patterns. Blacks, for example, may find the patient, waiting, and reflective type of a nondirective technique to be antagonistic to their values.* (Sue & Sue, 1990, p. 163–164)

Helping clients to identify goals that would address conditions in their environment might be as important as goals that involve a change in their perceptions of their environment. Steenbarger (1993, p. 10) illustrates this point:

> *Multicultural approaches . . . are derived from contextualist models of development that posit problems as a function of poor person-environment fit. Thus, client problems are not intrapsychic in this view, but instead are derived from a fundamental tension between the demands and resources of the environment and the needs of the individual.* (Herr, 1991)

Another multicultural issue that impacts goal-setting is racial/cultural identity development. Numerous authorities have described the personal adjustment issues that are related to identity development (Atkinson et al., 1989; Cross, 1971; Hall et al., 1972; Helms, 1990; Jackson, 1975; Sue & Sue, 1990). This work originally focused on Black identity development but has been adapted to other minority groups and to White majority identity development as well. The developmental stages begin with Conformity (Stage I) and continue with Dissonance (Stage II); Resistance and Immersion (Stage III); Introspection (Stage IV); and conclude with Integrative Awareness (Stage V) (Atkinson, Morten, & Sue, 1989). Each of these stages manifests developmental issues that are related to one's attitude toward self, attitude toward others of the same minority, attitude toward others of different minorities, and attitude toward the dominant group. While the literature has not applied this developmental model to other groups (e.g., lesbian/gay clients or persons with disabilities) there would appear to be some appropriateness of fit to other multi-cultural groups as well.

This range of issues related to multicultural development and personal adjustment have obvious goal-setting implications when you are working with a minority client. Your client is experiencing not only those problems which he/she is able to report to you, but also racial/cultural identity developmental issues of which he/she is not even aware. Sue and Sue (1990) note that "therapists may often respond to the culturally different client in a very stereotypic manner and fail to recognize within-group or individual differences" that could be explained by racial/cultural identity development (p. 93). Consequently, it is important that counselors be aware not only of skills related to working with minority clients but also of those identity issues that might make these clients different from clients of the majority culture.

## Client Participation in Goal-Setting

Some counselors may construe goal-setting to mean that you listen to the client, make a mental assessment of the problem, and then prescribe a solution or goal. In fact, such a procedure is likely to be unsuccessful. The nature of counseling is such that the *client must be involved* in the establishment of goals. Otherwise, the client's participation is directionless, or worse, counterproductive. An example will illustrate this point.

A beginning counselor was seeing a client who was overweight, self-conscious about her appearance, reluctant to enter into social relationships with others because of this self-consciousness, and very lonely. Realizing that the problem of being overweight was an important factor, the counselor informed the client that one goal would be for her (the client) to lose one to three pounds per week, under a doctor's supervision, of course. With this, the client became highly defensive and rejected the counselor's goal, saying, "You sound just like my mother."

Goal-setting is highly personal. It requires a great deal of effort and commitment on the client's part. Therefore, the client must select goals that are important enough to make sacrifices to achieve. In the above example, the client's resistance could have been prevented if the counselor had moved more slowly, permitting the client to identify for herself the significance of her being overweight and the importance of potential weight loss. At this point, both the counselor and client could then work together to determine the specific goals and subgoals that, when achieved, might alleviate the client's concerns. As with other aspects of the counseling relationship, goal-setting should be an interactive process for which both counselor and client assume responsibility.

## *Resistance to Goal-Setting*

Occasionally a client may be reluctant to goal-setting or making a commitment to change. While it doesn't happen frequently, there are times when clients simply can't or won't participate in goal-setting discussions. When this happens, the counselor must deal with the questions: "Why is the client not participating?" "Is it a lack of skill or is it resistance?" Skills that might be missing include an inability to conceptualize the *void* between where one is now, today, and where one would wish to be two months from now. We mentioned the concept of *successive approximation* in an earlier chapter. Successive approximation is a way to define change by breaking down the process into a logical sequence of easily achievable steps. It is how we first learned to walk, to talk, to read, to play, to socialize, to work, etc. Even though we have all had these experiences, many adults cannot analyze goal-attainment in terms of steps or stages. They may need to be taught the concept and helped to define the steps that are inherent in a particular goal. One way this lesson may be presented is with a schematic drawing of the process (see *Figure 5-2*). Using such a figure often helps the client visualize the process more easily. By asking the client to help you fill in the blanks for each step in the process, the client becomes involved in the goal-setting procedure.

On the other hand, it may be that the client's reluctance to participate in goal-setting is related to resistance issues. In working with client resistance to goals, it is helpful to realize that such behavior is purposeful; that is, what the client does or avoids doing achieves some desirable result for the client (whether he or she realizes it or not).

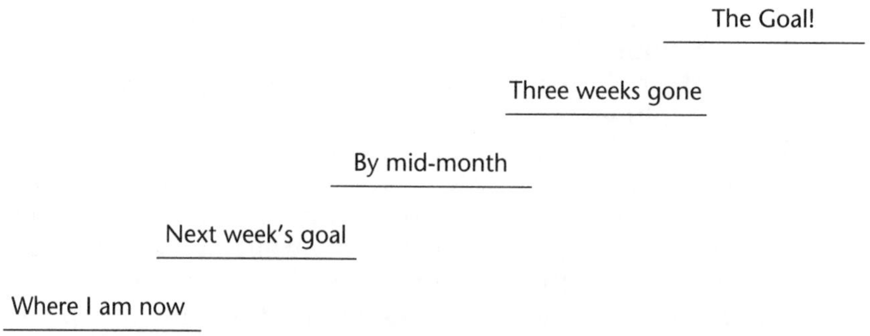

The Goal!
_____

Three weeks gone
_____

By mid-month
_____

Next week's goal
_____

Where I am now
_____

**FIGURE 5–2   Successive Approximation**

We may find that the client who resists setting goals may be protecting the very behavior that is in need of modification because that behavior is also serving some desirable purpose. An example is the chronic smoker. Although an individual may recognize the negative consequences of smoking, including its addictive properties, he/she also clings to the habit, believing that it helps one through the stressful moments, that it helps one relax, or that it increases the enjoyment of a good meal.

It becomes your task to get clients to identify what they gain from their current behavior. In so doing, you may help clients determine whether that gain or outcome can be achieved in more desirable ways. For example, a young student may reject the teacher's authority in order to gain attention from peers. Gaining attention may be a desirable outcome; it is the method that is the problem. Therefore, finding more appropriate ways of gaining increased attention would be a functional goal for counseling.

Sometimes clients resist attempts to establish goals because they feel that the counselor (either overtly or subtly) is pushing them in a certain direction. Unless clients can determine some *personal* goals for counseling, the probability of any change is minimal. You can avoid creating client resistance to goals by encouraging active participation by clients in the goal-setting process.

Finally, some clients resist goal-setting because they are genuinely confused about their desired priorities, needs, and wants. They know what is wrong in their lives, but they cannot visualize a better life. These clients may resist goal-setting because it puts them in touch with their confusion, and also because there is an implicit demand for them to sort things out and look beyond their reality. With such clients, it is often very helpful to acknowledge their confusion directly.

> *Lawanda, I can see you trying and I do know that it's really difficult to imagine a different or an improved situation.*

If you give clients permission to move at their own pace, the *pressure* to set goals does not compound their already building sense of frustration and powerlessness. Indeed, the process of identifying desired priorities, needs, and wants is a goal in itself.

Other possible strategies to help clients set goals include:

**1.** *Language work:* Ask the client to complete open-ended sentences such as, "I want . . .", "I do not want . . .", "I need . . .", "I do not need . . .", "I choose to . . ."

**2.** *Imagery and visualization:* Ask the client to imagine him/herself in an ideal situation and describe it—or to visualize someone else who embodies the qualities and behaviors the client desires. What are those qualities?

**3.** *Role-play and enactment:* Ask the client to attempt to reenact the problem through a role-play.

Some clients may be very conflicted about competing priorities and needs. They may identify several possible directions or options, but still be in conflict and thus unable to choose which course of action is the best one to pursue. These clients resist goal-setting because it exposes the conflict, which often feels uncomfortable or painful. It looks easier to mask or avoid than to deal with the issue head-on. With such clients, it is often helpful to use the *confrontation* (described earlier in this chapter) to point out the apparent conflict:

> *Lucy, on the one hand, you're saying that you want to have some stability in your life. At the same time, you're saying you are considering a job offer in which you will be required to move every two years.*

Confrontation is particularly useful for *identifying* and *describing* the conflict. For actual *working through* the conflict, additional counseling strategies, such as *Gestalt dialoguing* (see Chapter 7), transactional analysis redecision work (Chapter 8), and *reframing* (Chapter 10) are helpful. It would be important to use such strategies with these clients at this point in counseling, since very little progress is likely to be made until this initial conflict is resolved.

## Case Illustration of Goal-Setting

In this example, we illustrate how the counselor could help Angela (from Chapter 4) identify desired outcome goals for counseling. Recall that Angela described her problem as a depressed state in which she perceives herself as a failure, engages in few meaningful activities or relationships, and in general, lacks a purpose in life apart from her role as parent. Also, recall that part of Angela's depressed moods seem to be precipitated and/or maintained by a physiological condition—premenstrual syndrome (PMS).

After you and Angela probe the facets of her concerns, you can consider the specific changes Angela would like to make. Gradually, these changes can be translated into an outline of desired goals (see *Figure 5-1*). Angela and the counselor discussed goals and identified the following:

*Continuation of the Case of Angela*

**I.** *Outcome Goal #1:* Angela wishes to become significantly more positive about herself over the next three months.

    **A.** Angela must learn to recognize when she is involved in negative and self-defeating thoughts or self-talk about herself each day.

        **1.** Angela will start noting the number of times each day that she says or thinks something negative about herself.

        **2.** Angela will begin to keep a list of general topics she tends to use in putting herself down.

        **3.** Angela will start noting what time of day she finds herself involved in negative and/or self-defeating behavior to determine if she is more vulnerable at certain parts of the day or night.

    **B.** Angela must develop a list of positive or self-enhancing statements about herself.

        **1.** Angela will begin focusing on her positive qualities with the counselor's help.

        **2.** Angela will write each positive quality statement she identifies on a $3 \times 5$ card and keep these cards handy during those parts of the day that seem to be her most vulnerable times.

        **3.** When Angela gets negative, she will faithfully read a positive quality card and focus on it until she has overcome the negative surge.

    **C.** Angela will examine the setting(s) in which she is most likely to become self-defeating or negative to determine the effect of setting on her moods.

        **1.** With the counselor's help, Angela will look for a time-of-day pattern to her tendency to become negative or self-defeating.

        **2.** With the counselor's help, Angela will look for other conditions that might be associated with her moods (e.g., being alone, having a lot of tasks, etc.).

        **3.** With the counselor's help, Angela will identify settings to avoid and develop a list of alternative activities when she finds herself in a self-defeating setting.

**II.** *Outcome Goal #2:* Angela wishes to control any negative effects from PMS that might contribute to her moods.

    **A.** Angela will make an appointment with her gynecologist for an examination and consultation on the possible effects of her PMS.

        **1.** She will call within three days and will make the appointment within two weeks.

        **2.** Between now and the appointment, Angela will keep a record of her bouts with the blues, including day, time, situation, and duration of the feelings. She will take this record when she goes for the gynecological appointment.

    **B.** With the physician's help, Angela must determine what changes of behavior, use of

*Continued*

medication, etc., would counteract any effects of PMS on her moods.

   1. With the counselor's help, Angela will use this information to identify how her daily habits must change.

   2. Angela will begin a preventive program, based on the plan she and her counselor develop.

   3. Angela will keep a daily record of her new activities until they become part of her normal routine.

   4. Angela will monitor the intensity of her moods on a 1 to 10 scale in at least three different time periods on a daily basis over the next three months.

**III.** *Outcome Goal #3:* Angela wishes to be more aware of those daily activities and relationships and their meaningfulness or value to her.

  **A.** Angela will determine the relative importance of her work and leisure activities and relationships.

   1. Angela will monitor and log all daily work and leisure activities for a week and with the counselor's help, will categorize these activities into "pleasant" or "unpleasant" categories.

   2. Angela will determine which of the "unpleasant" activities are within her control to change or reschedule.

   3. With the counselor's help, Angela will attempt to reframe the meaning of those "unpleasant" activities so they become at least neutral, perhaps pleasant.

   4. Angela will do the same analysis with her relationships.

  **B.** Angela will establish a more positive balance between negative and positive work/leisure activities and relationships.

   1. With the counselor's help, Angela will analyze her typical weekly schedule to determine whether it is overbalanced by negative activities and relationships.

   2. With the counselor's help, Angela will identify new sources of positive activity and relationships associated with her work and leisure time.

   3. With the counselor's help, Angela will seek to establish and maintain a positive balance in her weekly work/leisure activities and relationships.

**IV.** *Outcome Goal #4:* Angela would like to have a sense of meaning for her life and some sort of a "plan" for the next five to fifteen years, and she would like to feel like she is working toward fulfilling that plan.

  **A.** Angela knows that she must have a better understanding of her values, and determine what kinds of goals and accomplishments are really important to her.

   1. With the counselor's help, Angela will do some values clarification activities to get a better sense of her life priorities.

   2. Angela will begin to look at her present activities and priorities to see if they match her life priorities.

   3. With the counselor's help, Angela will consider how her family background relates to her situation (how well or poorly would her family function if they

*Continued*

were in her present circumstances).

4. With the counselor's help, Angela will consider what "family solutions" would be prescribed for her present circumstances.

5. With the counselor's help, Angela will look for any values conflicts between her present worldview and the worldview she was taught as a child by her family.

6. With the counselor's help, Angela will attempt to resolve any values conflicts she discovers.

B. Angela would like to feel more independent of her ex-husband.

1. She will attempt to be more resourceful about taking responsibility for the children during times when she is feeling blue.

2. She will try to view the children's relationship with their father as a positive factor in her life rather than as a potentially threatening factor.

Notice the process by which these outcome goals are established. First, they begin as overall goals that are directly related to the client's specific or general complaints (Roman numerals). Then specific and observable changes (subgoals) are identified which must occur if Angela is to succeed in accomplishing each overall goal (Capital letter items). Finally, specific tasks are identified that will allow Angela to accomplish each of the subgoals (numbered items). In this way, goal-setting moves from general goals (which are related to the presenting problem) to specific goals to specific tasks.

## Summary

Goal-setting is such a central part of the change process that people often take it for granted. And yet, many people (including many helpers) are not very skilled at setting their own goals or helping others to identify and set goals. In this chapter we have differentiated two types of goals that are part of the counseling process; *process goals* and *outcome goals*. Process goals affect the therapeutic relationship. Outcome goals affect the results of counseling and determine the specific counselor interventions that will be used in counseling. Goals can help motivate clients to make desired changes and can also prove useful as the counselor attempts to evaluate therapeutic progress. Parameters of effective goal-setting include identification of what broad changes the client would wish to accomplish, specific situations that would have to change if this broad goal is to be achieved, and specific tasks the client would have to undertake if the intermediate objectives are to be realized. Goals are also affected by the circumstances surrounding the client's functioning. Clients from different cultural backgrounds than the counselor pose a challenge to be understood and aided in ways that might be different from the counselor's solutions. A keen sensitivity to multicultural forces is essential when helping clients of different backgrounds to set counseling goals.

## Exercises

**I.** *Identification of Client Goals*

Tom is a junior in college. He is bright and personable, but a bit shy. He came to counseling with the problem of relating to the opposite sex. Specifically, he is concerned that there may be some flaw in his personality that turns girls off. His reasons for thinking this grow out of his experience with dating. He reports that girls go out with him once or maybe twice, and then do not accept any more dates. He admits to getting discouraged when he calls a girl for a date and she says she already has a commitment. If this happens twice, he never calls the girl again, assuming that she does not want to date him, and wishing to spare himself further embarrassment.

**1.** Put yourself in Tom's position. Identify a few goals that you think might be appropriate objectives in the counseling process, using the suggested goal outline in *Figure 5-1.*

Main Goal            Subgoals            Immediate Tasks

**2.** Are your goals specific or vague? How would Tom know when he had achieved these goals? How would achieving them affect Tom's dating problem?

**3.** As Tom's counselor, what *process* goals would you set for yourself? How would these process goals relate to Tom's presenting problem?

**II.** *Multicultural Issues and Goal-Setting*

Jimmy Huang is a young (late twenties) Asian American who lives in a large urban environment. He was referred to you by a friend who knows you as an acquaintance. His friend thought you could help Jimmy because he has had difficulty both in seeking and obtaining employment that pays enough to support his family (wife and child), which he feels a strong obligation to provide. In the first session, Jimmy is somewhat reluctant to talk about his situation. He appears to be reserved, polite, but not trusting. He is willing to talk about the mutual acquaintance who referred him, and to some extent, he is willing to talk about his employment history and skills.

**1.** As Jimmy's counselor, what *process goals* would you set for yourself? How would these process goals be affected by Jimmy's cultural background?

**2.** Put yourself in Jimmy's position. Identify a goal which Jimmy might think appropriate in the counseling process, using the suggested goal outline in *Figure 5.1.*

Main Goal            Subgoals            Immediate Tasks

**3.** Is your goal statement in Question 2 specific or vague? How would Jimmy know when he had achieved this goal? How would achieving this goal help Jimmy?

## *Feedback for Exercises*

### *I. Identification of Client Goals*

There are two ways to approach Tom's situation. You could key in on the problems as he verbalized them (possible shyness; his style of giving a girl only two chances to date him; his assumption that the problem is him). Or you could look at possible factors that might be producing the problem (Tom's self-esteem; his social skills). If Tom agreed to the second set of factors, it would be easier to develop a set of goals, subgoals, and tasks than if he pursued the first set of factors.

### *II. Multicultural Goals*

Clearly the first step in working with Jimmy Huang is to get to know him and the cultural heritage that drives his behavior, his values, family obligations, etc. Without an accurate sense of his *worldview*, you could not participate in a goal-setting process with Jimmy Huang that he would find meaningful. In fact, there might be aspects of your *worldview* that would be in direct conflict with Jimmy Huang's values and beliefs. Therefore, the first *process goal* would be to attempt to relate to Jimmy Huang within the context of his cultural background. This could mean that you are in the role of learner and Jimmy Huang is the teacher. While this is a reversal of power structure from the traditional counselor-client relationship, it is more likely to be perceived by Jimmy Huang as a sign that he is being shown respect.

## *Discussion Questions*

**1.** In this chapter we discussed possible reasons for client resistance to goal-setting. Identify some reasons why counselors might also resist developing outcome goals with clients.

**2.** In what ways do outcome goals help the counselor to assess client progress? Describe what you think it would be like to assess counseling progress when no goals had been formulated.

**3.** Identify a recent problematic situation that you or a close friend experienced. What kinds of solutions came to mind for the person? Was goal-setting a part of the process? What are the pros and cons if goal-setting had been part of the process?

**4.** Based on your multicultural counseling knowledge, what precautions or advice would you give a counselor who is helping a client of a different culture to identify goals, subgoals, and immediate tasks?

## Recommended Readings

Axelson, J.A. (1993). *Counseling and Development in a Multicultural Society*, Pacific Grove, CA: Brooks/Cole. Chapter 11: The interaction of counselor and client.

Cook, E.P. (1993). *Women, Relationships, and Power: Implications for Counseling*, Alexandria, VA: ACA Press.

Cormier, W.H. and Cormier, L.S. (1991). *Interviewing Strategies for Helpers: Fundamental Skills and Cognitive-Behavioral Interventions*, 3d ed. Pacific Grove, CA: Brooks/Cole.

Davenport, D.S. and Yurich, J.M. (1991). Multicultural gender issues, *Journal of Counseling and Development, 70*, 64–71.

Hackney, H. and Cormier, S. (1994). *Counseling Strategies and Interventions*, 4th ed. Boston, MA: Allyn & Bacon. Chapter 9: Conceptualizing problems and setting goals.

Priest, R. (1991). Racism and prejudice as negative impacts on African American clients in therapy, *Journal of Counseling and Development, 70*, 213–215.

Richardson, B.L. (1991). Utilizing the resources of the African American church: Strategies for counseling professionals. Chapter 6 in C.C. Lee and B.L. Richardson, Eds., *Multicultural Issues in Counseling: New Approaches to Diversity*, Alexandria, VA: ACA Press.

Sue, D.W. and Sue, D. (1992). *Counseling the Culturally Different, Theory and Practice*, 2d ed. New York: Wiley. Chapter 4: Sociopolitical considerations of mistrust in cross-cultural counseling; Chapter 10: Counseling Asian Americans.

Taussig, I.M. (1987). Comparative responses of Mexican Americans and Anglo Americans to early goal-setting in public mental health clinics, *Journal of Counseling Psychology, 34*, 214–217.

Chapter *6*

Defining Strategies and
Selecting Interventions

*Purpose of This Chapter—*

In this chapter, we shall examine how the counselor develops a therapeutic plan for working with a specific client. The process involves identification of a case strategy (with the accompanying rationale for the choice) and identification of counseling interventions that would serve the strategy and address the therapeutic issues present in the case. This therapeutic or working alliance between counselor and client involves more than the two persons. It includes environmental contexts of both the counselor and client. How those contexts affect each person is critical information to be incorporated into the strategic plan if the counseling process is to be effective.

*Considerations as You Read This Chapter—*

- Planning is a major part of every complex activity. What are you like as a planner?
- When you become involved in a complex activity without a plan, what are you like?
- When you form new relationships with friends and colleagues, what do you find yourself focusing *mainly* on? What they talk about? How they think? What activities they are involved in? Or who they seem to be in their social environment?
- Are the people you get to know best, more like you or very different from you?
- How might these questions relate to you as a counselor?

Thus far, we have described a process in which the counselor and client meet, a therapeutic relationship begins to take form, an assessment of the parameters of the problem occurs, and from this, goals to be accomplished in the counseling relationship begin to emerge. In this chapter we shall examine the therapeutic or working alliance. This working alliance is characterized by the choice of strategies and interventions intended to address the client's problems and identified goals of counseling. The *strategies* that are identified reflect the counselor's "game plan" or counseling plan. The *interventions* that are selected reflect the nature of the problem and the unique qualities and characteristics of the client.

Defining a counseling plan is an interactive process. It reflects the counselor's theoretical preferences, the *worldviews* of both client and counselor, the definition and character of the client's presenting problem(s), the time orientation, and identified goals or outcomes. The challenge is to identify strategies that are most likely to be successful with a particular client. This is an important decision since it shapes the direction counseling will take. The counseling plan actually becomes part of the relationship, in that it reflects what you and your client are focusing on, how you relate to one another in that process, and what potential outcomes will be realized as you work together.

## Theory and the Working Alliance

In Chapter 1 we discussed the range of theories that represent the counseling profession. While numerous, these theories reflect a finite number of philosophical viewpoints, personality development patterns, change processes, and relationship alternatives. They may be crystallized into four broad categories: theories that emphasize *feelings* and *affective states*; theories that emphasize *thoughts* and *conceptual processes*; theories that emphasize *behavior* and *how it shapes our reality*; and theories that emphasize *relationship interactions* and *how they manifest and support feelings, thoughts and behaviors*.

Most students enter counseling programs with a predisposition toward one form of counseling or another. In Chapter 1 we described those "forms" as *forces*: psychodynamic, cognitive-behavioral, existential-humanistic, or interactional. Our predisposition comes from our own life experiences, how we were taught by family and community to interpret those experiences, and our evolving preferences for viewing the human condition. Thus, the psychodynamic view reflects an explanation of the human condition in which internal forces and drives actively shape our contact with the real world. The cognitive-behavioral force reflects a human condition in which we can use thought and behavior to act on our environment and shape it to our preferences. The existential-humanistic view is one in which we strive to define and understand our existence in the context of an ever-changing world of challenge. Finally, the interactional view reflects a human condition in which we are continuously affecting and being affected by an environment that includes other human beings, nature, social contexts, and cultural values.

One could argue that all human beings embrace all four of these forces, and that would be accurate for the most part. But also, each person tends to be more represented in one of the four areas, relying on the other three when human understanding calls for it. That one area is our "starting point," our natural domain, all other things being equal. Thus, one person prepares an organized (thought-out) grocery list, while another prefers to walk the aisles and be inspired (experiential). Yet a third person observes what is on sale, what others have in their shopping carts, what menus are promoted at the produce and seafood counters (interactional).

Finding one's theory is partly determined by finding oneself in the context of theory choices. It is also determined by the nature of one's professional training and the orientation of one's coaches.

## Worldview and the Working Alliance

In addition, the counselor's theoretical orientation will be modified by his/her *worldview*. In an earlier chapter we described worldview as the total perception one has of self, others, environment, and relationships. One's view of others includes a very wide range of culturally based differences. Speight, Myers, Cox, and Highland (1991, p. 31) have argued that "all counseling is multicultural in nature," if we are to take into account the many shades of difference that racial, ethnic, religious, gender, sexual orientation, physical limitations, and other human conditions around which humanity is organized. This multicultural perspective can be approached from culture-specific orientations in which the counselor is aware of and responding to unique cultural qualities of the client. Or it can be approached from a cultural-general perspective that emphasizes similarities across cultures. Which is the better direction to take remains an issue of discussion in the profession. Vontress (1985) fears that the culture-specific approach may lead to overlooking the personal characteristics and humanness of the client. Others argue as forcefully that only a culture-specific approach can fully reflect the nature and qualities of a person's ethnicity, although it is not clear how any one counselor can master the variety of cultures reflected in "the three so-called races (Caucasoid, Negroid, and Mongoloid)" (Betancourt & López, 1993, p. 631).

One way to negotiate this issue is to examine client orientations that are shared among cultures. Sue and Sue (1990) offer, as an example, how the U.S. culture and society tend to be individual-centered, while many cultures are more focused on the family or the community and the individual emphasis is greatly diminished. They illustrate this, citing how traditional Asian societies and many Hispanics focus on the family for identity while, in the Eurocentric view, one develops an individual identity. Ivey, Ivey, and Simek-Morgan (1993) compare the Eurocentric and Afrocentric orientations, again pointing to the Afrocentric emphasis on family and tribe. Drawing on work by Nwachuku (1989; 1990; Nwachuku & Ivey, 1991), they describe the situation where an African Igbo student seeks counseling to help resolve the question of whether he should return home from graduate school to assume family responsibilities. They observe that:

> *In the Eurocentric model, the helper focused immediately on the problem, and, using an "I" focus, encouraged the client to make an independent autonomous decision. The Afrocentric Igbo model of helping was quite different. More time was spent at the beginning of the session, as the counselor helped the client feel comfortable. The client's story was drawn out by the Igbo helper through questioning. After briefly probing the client's personal thoughts about the issue, the interview then focused on the extended family and asked questions about the client's uncle (paternal uncles are important figures in Igbo culture). It soon was apparent that a broader network of decision-makers was involved. The client had been influenced by North American individualism and needed a reminder from the counselor that more people than just himself were involved in this important life decision.* (pp. 67–68)

This example illustrates a guideline of multicultural counseling:

---

When working with clients of different cultures, it is important to determine where the client's identity emphasis lies: within the individual or within the family/community.

---

A similar example can be drawn from the domain of verbal, emotional, and behavioral expressiveness. The western (United States and Eurocentric) orientation to counseling involves heavy dependence on verbal expressiveness, emotional disclosure, and examination of behavior patterns. Other cultures may differ on one or more of these conditions. Sue and Sue (1990) point out that in traditional Japanese culture, "children have been taught not to speak until spoken to," a value that will also have been transmitted in many Japanese American families. They also observe that traditional Hispanic and Asian cultures "emphasize that maturity and wisdom are associated with one's ability to control emotions and feelings, [which] includes public expressions of anger and frustration [as well as] expressions of love and affection" (p. 37). This offers us a second guideline for multicultural counseling:

> When working with clients of different cultures, it is important to determine the client's cultural orientation toward verbal expressiveness and cultural values regarding emotional expression and disclosure.

Finally, it has been noted that many psychotherapies rely heavily on client insight as one of the goals of counseling. Sue and Sue (1990) again note that the traditional Asian advice for handling such feelings as anger, frustration, or depression is "to keep busy and don't think about it," an orientation that goes the opposite direction from insight (p. 38). This leads to a third guideline for multicultural counseling:

> When working with clients of different cultures, it is important to determine the client's orientation toward introspection and insight as opposed to taking action on the external problem.

## Presenting Problems and the Working Alliance

Successful interventions are related to the nature or character of the client's presenting problem. Best results are achieved when selected interventions match the components of the problem (Ost, Jerramalm, & Johannson, 1981). Thus, if the client's presenting problem appears to be predominantly affective or emotional in nature, interventions would be targeted to the affective complaints. Similarly, if a client seems to be using his thought processes to sabotage himself, then the counselor would want to select interventions that addressed the cognitive sources. On the other hand, it is important to realize that most client problems are multidimensional. A problem with negative *self-talk* ("I'm constantly telling myself I'm no good") is not just cognitive, but would also reflect an affective dimension ("I feel lousy about myself"), a behavioral dimension ("I choose to stay home and watch a lot of TV"), and a systemic or interactional dimension ("When I do go out, I avoid contact with others because they find me strange, *or I behave strangely and others react to me accordingly*").

Although problems tend to have multidimensional aspects, the counselor does not have to address all aspects. Frequently a behavioral aspect, if altered, will lead to different social consequences which will, in turn, alter the client's interactional aspect as well. Or, if I am able to *think* more kindly about myself or my problem, I may find that I *worry* less and *behave* less self-consciously. Thus, if the counselor chooses to intervene at the affective door to the problem, changes in the client's affective state will have concomitant effects on the cognitive, behavioral, and interactional aspects of the client's world. This ecological interconnectedness suggests that positive change can occur, regardless of how the problem is *experienced* by the client. However, it may prove less efficient and less effective if you choose to intervene behaviorally, when the client is experiencing the problem affectively (or if the client is culturally disposed toward one aspect and you use an intervention reflecting a different aspect). *Figure 6-1* illustrates how a problem can be explored from different perspectives. Even though these several perspectives will yield different information about the problem, the larger context of the problem is the same.

How does one plan a strategy for counseling intervention if multiple choices exist and "all roads lead to Rome?"

A general guideline for selecting counseling strategies is that clients are more receptive when the choice of strategy matches their experiencing of the problem.

If the client experiences the problem as an emotional trauma, then an affective intervention strategy might seem more plausible to the client. Inconsistency between client experiencing of the problem and counseling strategy can lead clients to conclude that the counselor has failed to understand. This is not to suggest that the counselor's interventions would be exclusively affective in this case. As counseling proceeds, and as the multiple dimensions of the problem become apparent to the client, counseling can begin to address these other dimensions. For example, affective reactions are often reinforced by the client's self-talk. An affective strategy would focus on the client's affective reactions but might include cognitive interventions that addressed the negative self-talk. In this example, the base for this working alliance would be the affective domain. In a different counseling case, the client's experiencing of the problem might be behavioral (for

1. How does the problem make your client feel? How do her feelings affect her effort to change the problem? How might her feelings maintain the problem? What different feelings might change the problem? What is your client's cultural perspective toward feelings associated with the problem?

2. What kinds of things does she do when the problem is "in charge?" How do these behaviors support or maintain the problem? What behaviors could she change and thereby reduce the effects of the problem? What are her cultural predispositions toward *doing* as opposed to *feeling*?

Your client has been experiencing repeated failures in her college courses. She is starting to feel hopeless, thinking about dropping out of college, doesn't know what she might do, wonders if she might try to revive an old high school love and perhaps marry.

3. What kinds of things is your client saying to herself? How might her messages be part of her problem? What cultural messages are part of her self-talk? What role does her cultural values play in the self-statements that she makes, and what alternative self-statements are available?

4. What are her relationships with other students like? With men? How do her professors fit into the picture? How have her parents functioned in her absence? In what ways do relationships support the problem? What are the cultural expectations on her to marry?

**FIGURE 6–1   The Various Ways to Approach a Client's Problem**

example, excessive drinking), thus suggesting that the counseling plan should be behaviorally based. This would involve behavioral interventions, with cognitive, affective, and systemic/interactional excursions from the behavioral component as appropriate.

Sometimes the client's experiencing of a problem fails to produce the best understanding of how that problem should be confronted and the counselor chooses a strategy that yields only qualified success. When this occurs, you should reexamine your rationale for selecting a particular strategy. For example, if a woman presents a problem of poor self-concept, the counseling strategy may be to address her cognitive self. However, as she begins to feel and become more competent, her new self may lead to a crisis in her marriage, causing her to back off her recent gains. It may be that her husband's expectations are for her to remain less competent, thus maintaining a relationship in which he is superior. In this situation, the problem may have been experienced as a cognitive and/or affective issue, while the underlying issues really represent a systemic/interactional problem.

## Time and the Working Alliance

Time is a very important part of the working alliance. It includes the amount of time devoted to each session, the amount of time devoted to the process, how long the problem has been experienced by the client, and the amount of time required to fully address the problem. If the client comes to counseling in crisis, time may be seen as a critical aspect of the problem. Time also has its cultural dimensions. In some cultures, time is a friend; in others, time is a factor to be controlled.

Time also enters into the equation when goals of counseling are considered. Some goals have short-time duration while others may have lifespan implications. Client tolerance for ambiguity and process is a direct reflection of the client's view of time. Generally speaking, clients choose goals that represent either *choice* or *change*, or a combination of the two. Clients who commit themselves to *choices* usually have the prerequisite skills and opportunities to take a particular course of action, but have not yet committed themselves to do so. Clients who commit themselves to *changes* may very well lack necessary skills, opportunities, or behaviors needed to achieve those changes. Thus the fundamental alternative between *choice* goals and *change* goals will have time ramifications, since *change* will likely require more time than *choice*.

The question of how long counseling should take is probably on the mind of most clients as they enter the process. "What is a reasonable amount of time for me to solve my problems?" "Will a 'good' counselor speed up that process for me?" "How patient must I be in waiting for the good feelings to return?" "How long should I wait before deciding that counseling isn't the right solution to my pain?" Such questions are rarely verbalized but often thought.

Counselors think of time issues as well. How much time should I devote to building rapport? To assessment? To the process of goal-setting? How long will the client commit to counseling? What is a reasonable amount of time to wait before seeing some evidence of progress? How long should most counseling take? These are important questions. They reflect the counselor's theoretical underpinnings, tolerance for ambiguity, belief in the process, and understanding of client differences.

## Identified Goals and the Working Alliance

Goals are directly related to the counselor's choice of strategy and interventions. Goals may be classified as immediate, intermediate, or long-term (Hackney & Cormier, 1994). Generally a combination of these goals will be reflected in the working alliance. There are exceptions, of course. When working with a client in crisis, most goals must be short-term. Immediate results are necessary to relieve the crisis. After the crisis, other goals may be considered if the client remains in counseling. Other examples of strategies found in the working alliance are personal growth strategies, life decision-making strategies, conflict resolution strategies, developmental adjustment strategies, prevention strategies, and spiritual growth strategies.

Client characteristics may also affect the outcome of a strategy, and thus affect the identified counseling goals. The choice of therapeutic strategies that meet client expectations and preferences has been found to influence positive therapy outcomes (Devine & Fernald, 1973). One reason for this success is probably that clients identify with strategies that are congruent with their deeply held values and beliefs. When counselors propose an action plan that is too much at variance with the client's beliefs and values, clients are likely to resist the plan outright or to work with it superficially but not really invest themselves in the process.

In the last decade there has been an important change in the client's role and status in counseling. The client has become an active consumer, not just a passive recipient of services. As a result, counselors need to ensure that client rights are made explicit and that clients are informed about and consent to the use of various intervention approaches. Accordingly, counselors need to provide clients with accurate information about all available intervention strategies, including:

1. A description of all relevant and potentially useful treatment approaches for this particular client with this particular problem
2. A rationale for each procedure that will be used
3. A description of the counselor's role in each intervention
4. A description of the client's role in each intervention
5. Possible discomforts or risks that may occur as a result of the intervention
6. Expected benefits that will occur as a result of the intervention
7. The estimated time and cost of each intervention

(Cormier & Cormier, 1991)

## Strategy Selection

In addition to choosing strategies that reflect client expectations and preferences, counselors also must consider available client resources and characteristics. For example, does the client have sufficient internal ego strength or self-discipline to carry out a particular intervention? Does the client live and work in a context in which support from others is fully given or withheld? Is the client likely to apply a particular procedure outside the counseling session? Does an intervention require the client to do something (such as engage in imagination), and is the client capable of doing this? Are certain types of interventions outside the clients' experience or *worldview*?

Proposed strategies also need to take into account previous client attempts to solve their problems. Often in dealing with problems, clients arrive at solutions that are both inadequate and irrelevant. When this happens, an all-too-common situation arises: *The solution becomes the problem*. This can be illustrated by the person whose world contains so many pressures that relaxation is very difficult. Seeing the need to escape from the pressures and routines, the client embarks on a course of action that includes hobbies, travel, and reading. Soon the client realizes that these diversions have taken on the same character as the original problem. Hobbies have become compulsive activities, travel necessitates extraordinary planning, and reading has become a quest to absorb more books than last month's record. In other words, the solutions only added more pressure; consequently, the problem is exacerbated by the solutions.

It is important for the counselor to understand, as well as possible, the client's world. It is also important to understand the frustrated needs the client is experiencing in that world. Finally, it is vitally important to understand what the client has been doing or thinking as part of the solution. We often find that clients have a very limited repertoire of "solutions," and they apply these limited solutions indiscriminately. The result is a more complicated, less successful world than even before the "solution" was applied.

## *Categories of Counseling Interventions*

Counseling interventions may be described within the major categories through which problems are enacted: affectively experienced problems; cognitively experienced problems; behaviorally experienced problems; and problems that are interactional/systemic in nature.

*Affective interventions* (see Chapter 7) elicit and respond primarily to feelings and emotions. They may also involve body awareness activities that focus on somatic components of a problem, as emotional states often involve the musculature and the expenditure of physical energy (Zajonc, 1980).

*Cognitive interventions* (see Chapter 8) deal with thoughts, beliefs, and attitudes one has toward self and others. Such interventions are intended to help the client *think differently* about a situation, person, fear, enemy, boss, spouse, etc.

*Behavioral interventions* (see Chapter 9) are used to help the client develop new behaviors or skills and/or control or eliminate existing behaviors that are counter-productive. They may be used to modify habits, routines, or interaction patterns with others.

*Interactional (systemic) interventions* (see Chapter 10) address relationship patterns with other persons, tasks, or situations. The source may be one's family, work setting, neighborhood, church community, or any social setting in which interactional patterns have been established.

*Table 6-1* describes therapeutic interventions used by counselors to accomplish these tasks. They are classified under the four categories

**TABLE 6–1  Counseling Strategies and Corresponding Manifestations of Client Problems.**

| Affective | Cognitive | Behavioral | Systemic |
|---|---|---|---|
| **Person-centered therapy; Gestalt therapy; body awareness therapies; psychodynamic therapies; experiential therapies:** Active listening; empathy; positive regard; genuineness; awareness techniques; empty chair; fantasy; dreamwork; bioenergetics; core energetics; radix therapy; free association; transference analysis; dream analysis; focusing techniques. | **Rational-emotive therapy; Beck's cognitive therapy; transactional analysis; reality therapy:** A-B-C-D-E analysis; homework assignments; counter–conditioning; bibliotherapy; media-tapes; brainstorming; identifying alternatives; reframing; egograms; script analysis; problem definition; clarifying interactional sequences; coaching; defining boundaries; shifting triangulation patterns; prescribing the problem (paradox). | **Skinner's operant conditioning; Wolpe's counter-conditioning; Bandura's social learning; Lazarus' multimodal therapy:** Guided imagery; role-playing; self-monitoring; physiological recording; behavioral contracting; assertiveness training; social skills training; systematic desensitization; contingency contracting; action planning; counter-conditioning. | **Structural therapy; strategic family therapy; intergenerational systems:** Instructing about subsystems; enmeshment and differentiation; addressing triangulation, alliances and coalitions; role restructuring; clarifying interactional systems; reframing; prescribing the problem (paradox); altering interactional sequences; genogram analysis; coaching; defining boundaries; shifting triangulation patterns. |
| *Manifestations* Emotional expressiveness and impulsivity; instability of emotions; use of emotions in problem-solving and decision-making; sensitivity to self and others; receptive to feelings of others. | *Manifestations* Intellectualizing; logical rational, systematic behavior; reasoned; computer-like approach to problem-solving and decision-making; receptive to logic, ideas, theories, concepts, analysis, and synthesis. | *Manifestations* Involvement in activities; strong goal orientation; need to be constantly doing something; receptive to activity, action, getting something done; perhaps at expense of others. | *Manifestations* Enmeshed or disengaged relationships; rigid relationship boundaries and rules; dysfunctional interaction patterns. |

mentioned above and include typical client presentations which might call for their use. This categorization system is based on previous classification systems, particularly Hutchin's (1979; 1982; 1984) T-F-A (thought-feeling-action) model, and L'Abate's (1981) E-R-A (emotionality, rationality, activity) model.

As you will recall from Chapter 4, client problems typically are multidimensional (include any combination of feeling, thinking, behaving, and interacting with others). In categorizing counseling interventions along these dimensions, the intent is to illustrate how selected interventions may be suitable for specific expressions of client problems. The intent is not to oversimplify the therapeutic process but rather, to lay out the range of options that counselors have when working with specific client problems. And, of course, affective interventions may be effective with more than affectively expressed problems, and so too with the other three categories. In fact, if one views human beings as total persons rather than parts to be added together, then interventions into any of these four dimensions will produce effects in all of the other dimensions of the problem. Let us revisit Angela, our fictional client from Chapter 4, to illustrate how the working alliance and intervention selection might be implemented.

## *Case Illustration of Strategy and Interventions Selection*

Based on information derived from an intake interview with Angela, the counselor summarized Angela's complaints, using the four-dimensional analysis (see *Figure 6-2*).

Next, the counselor examined the six factors for establishing a counseling strategy for this case. These include the following:

**1.** *The counselor's theory:* The counselor prefers an affective approach, with elements of person-centered theory and existentialism. The counselor also subscribes to systemic explanations of human problems.

**2.** *Counseling experience:* The counselor has practiced for about four years and has taken several training workshops since completing her formal counselor preparation program. She has worked with several depressed clients.

**3.** *Character of the problem:* Angela's problem may have a medical dimension in addition to an affective, cognitive, behavioral, and systemic dimension. Her presenting concern is how to have better control over her moods.

**4.** *Typical responses to her problem:* Based on her training and experience, the counselor knows that clients who feel inadequate will need to examine their support system, identify what ends their moods may be serving, and develop alternative and more facilitative behavior patterns.

**5.** *Character of the goal:* Angela identified three main goals (see Chapter 5) that she would like to achieve in counseling: (a) to become significantly more positive about herself over the next three months; (b) to control any negative effect the PMS may be contributing to her

---

**AFFECTIVE**

Angela often feels irritable, upset, or depressed; feels sorry for herself when things go wrong; feels inadequate; feels abandoned by her ex-husband.

**BEHAVIORAL**

Angela retreats into her room when she feels blue; takes out her feelings on her children and students; occasional sleep problems; avoids social contact; has no regular recreational activities.

**ANGELA'S PRESENTING PROBLEMS**

Angela (see Chapter 4) is seeking counseling to learn how to have better control over her moods. She indicates that she often "flies off the handle" for no reason with her children or with her students in the classroom. She suffers from PMS and occasional difficulties sleeping. She feels like a failure as a wife and mother, primarily because of her divorce and her mood swings. Her self-description is primarily negative.

**COGNITIVE**

Angela has a lot of negative self-talk. She thinks her divorce was primarily her fault. She blames herself for her inability to control her moods. She thinks she is not giving her children the atmosphere they need.

**SYSTEMIC**

Angela doesn't date; she seems to have no support network; has little contact with her family of origin; "uses" her children to avoid others; ex-husband takes children when she is overwhelmed.

**FIGURE 6-2   Four-Dimensional Analysis of the Case of Angela**

moods; and (c) to become more aware of the meaningfulness of her daily activities and relationships.

**6.** *Client's characteristics:* Angela appears to be functioning at a minimal level, personally and socially. She was raised in a family in which she was not expected to be responsible for attending to her needs, she does not seem to be able to create social support, and she quickly feels overwhelmed when life's demands begin to accumulate. In her former marriage, her husband took responsibility for "cheering her up."

## Defining a Counseling Strategy

The first step in developing a counseling strategy is to synthesize what is known about the case and define a plan of action that is consistent with those factors. This synthesis would take into account both the four-dimensional analysis and six factors for establishing a counseling strategy. We note that: (a) Angela presented her problem *as affective* (mood swings, feels inadequate) and the counselor is predisposed toward an *affective approach*; (b) the presence of a possible *medical concern* should be addressed by a physician; (c) Angela set as a goal *to become more positive about herself,* which corresponds to her cognitive negativity; (d) Angela tends to *retreat from others* (behavioral and systemic) as well as from her problem (cognitive) and hides in her *affective self* when stress builds up; and (e) Angela's problem has spilled over to *interpersonal relationships* (children, students, social life) which relates to the counselor's *systemic interests*. In addition, she continues to lean on her ex-husband for help when she is in emotional distress and this tends to undermine her self-confidence even more.

### Applicable Strategies

The counselor has several viable choices of direction to take. She might choose to work from an affective context because she suspects that Angela is carrying several unresolved issues from her former marriage (failure feelings) and her mood swings, the effect of which produce increased stress, interpersonal issues, and possible exacerbation of her PMS difficulties. This would seem to be a promising approach, particularly since the counselor does have an affective predisposition and Angela's initial complaints were affective in nature.

Angela's problem could support a different strategy. Rather than address her emotional baggage from her former marriage, the counselor might choose to examine how Angela presently places herself into situations that remind her of her former marriage. In other words, she might address the cognitive links that connect Angela's present to her past and in so doing, seek to establish more facilitative cognitive responses. In addition, with the counselor's aid, Angela might challenge her self-defeating thinking about her past, her potential, and her interpersonal relationships. This approach might allow Angela to reassess her priorities, view her unchangeable life factors in a more positive light, and identify new goals and activities that would support a more desirable lifestyle. Since the counselor has not shown a strong inclination toward cognitive counseling approaches, this strategy could be more difficult to implement.

Yet a third way that the counselor could conceptualize the case is to focus on Angela's behavior patterns, both in terms of how she responds to herself and to her children, students, and adults. The fact that Angela withdraws when she feels depressed probably exacerbates her affective response and becomes self-defeating. It was noted that Angela appears to be functioning at a low level, personally and socially. It may be appropriate to help Angela identify and strengthen certain behavior patterns that she could turn to when she begins to feel overwhelmed, depressed, or self-negative. The rationale would be that if she could intervene in this downward spiraling pattern, then she would be spared the undesirable consequences.

Finally, there seem to be clear links between Angela's present functioning and her role in her family-of-origin and her relationship with her ex-husband. The counselor may wish to explore this linkage with Angela, by seeking to clarify how her interaction patterns reflect her family's views of interdependency and family unity, how she manifests these patterns with her children and her students, and how her social linkage with her family is similar to her social linkage to other adults. She might encourage Angela to examine how this pattern has repeated itself with her reliance on her ex-husband, and help Angela address issues of differentiation vs. unity. In other words, is Angela in conflict with her ethnic (family) values? The counselor may wish to include the children in the counseling process as a means of revealing patterns of interaction, assumptions, family rules, roles, and structure. This might logically lead to a cognitive reassessment of Angela's approach to family and social groups, using a strategic family therapy approach. Because the counselor does subscribe to systemic explanations, this is an attractive approach, except that the counselor does not feel adequately prepared to conduct this type of counseling.

## Selecting Interventions

Each of these four strategies embraces a repertoire of counseling interventions which are theoretically consistent with the assumptions of each strategy. For example, the affective approach emphasizes exploration of feelings in a safe and understanding environment, the development of insight into one's feelings, and ultimately, the acceptance of oneself. Such counselor activities as empathic understanding of the client's situation, active listening, and acceptance are endemic to this strategy. Similarly, the cognitive, behavioral, and systemic approaches also identify counselor interventions that support the objectives of these respective strategies. Chapters 7 through 10 examine these interventions and illustrate how they complement the strategy in question.

### Choosing the Right Strategy

The character of the problem may be addressed through any one of a variety of counseling strategies, including: behavioral; cognitive; affective; systemic; or any combination of these, (e.g., cognitive-behavioral, cognitive-systemic). Your choice of strategy probably will reflect your personal explanation of human problems and how they can best be resolved (your personal theory). On the other hand, multiple or sequential strategies may be needed to work with the entire character of the defined client problem. For example, anxiety may be experienced somatically (behaviorally), cognitively (anticipatory), affectively (depression), and systemically (emotional distancing from others). When more than one component is involved, usually more than one intervention is also necessary. You may still approach the case from your preferred vantage point for conceptualization, but you may find that your interventions should address all aspects of the problem.

### Strategies for Working with Children

Children pose special issues in the counseling relationship, since they have little power or control over their environment. How a child views herself or himself (self-esteem) is bound to have environmental linkages. Similarly, how a child behaves is interconnected to the behaviors of others in the world. The child's potential to change that environment, be it the home, the neighborhood, or the school, is highly problematic without the involvement of significant others. Consequently, any effort to intervene in a child's problems will necessarily involve relationships with siblings, parents, friends, teachers, and other adults. For this reason, a systemic view of the problem, if not a systemic strategy, will prove appropriate. The systemic view involves relationship patterns, and their concomitant behavioral and cognitive components. The counselor can work with the child on an individual basis and seek to produce systemic change *through* the child, or the counselor can involve other participants in the child's system and seek to invoke direct change in the interactional patterns of the system.

The school counselor may include in this systemic counseling process other children, the teacher and the child, or the parents, teacher(s), and child. If the problem, and thus the goal, is primarily learning-related, then the process may be contained totally within the school setting. But if the problem is familial, then the counselor's goal may be to generate parental awareness and responsibility for the problem, at which time a referral to a family counselor would be appropriate. Counselors working with children in community settings probably will seek to include the family in the counseling process. Given the more diffuse nature of community counseling clientele, child problems that come to the counselor probably require family participation if successful resolution of the presenting problem is to be achieved.

## Adapting Strategies to Multicultural Issues

In all client cases, the strategy that is developed should reflect the assessment that had previously occurred. In multicultural client populations, the assessment will often identify the problem as residing partly in the environment. When people experience prejudice, or when stereotyping, devaluing, or insensitivity and ignorance affect persons of color, women, the physically disabled or gays and lesbians, the problem is both what society imposes on the individual and how the individual reacts to that imposition. Increasingly, the counseling profession is recognizing that strategic planning may involve interventions that are directed to the environment rather than the client. Sue and Sue (1990) address this point, saying that:

> *Mental health professionals have a personal and professional responsibility to . . . develop appropriate help-giving practices, intervention strategies, and structures that take into account the historical, cultural, and environmental experiences/influences of the culturally different client.* (p. 6)

Some counselors may find this activist role to be uncomfortable but culturally different clients may have right, as well as reason, to expect it as a part of counseling.

## Summary

Counseling strategies constitute the plan within which most therapeutic work and change take place. The strategic plan of action must reflect a number of divergent factors, including those related to the counselor's theory, experience, and expertise, as well as the client's presenting problem, goals, and environmental contingencies. In the case of children, the other significant players in the child's world assume a particularly significant role. Culturally different clients also reflect needs that are both personal and environmental. Counselors must work with clients to identify interventions that will address both the character of the problem and the goals that have been identified. Client expectations, preferences, capabilities, and resources are other important criteria to consider in choosing workable strategies. In the following four chapters, we shall examine different counseling interventions, how they are implemented, what they are intended to achieve, and how clients typically react to their introduction in the counseling process.

## *Exercises*

**I.** *Choice or Change Issues and Related Counseling Strategies*

**A.** By yourself, or with a partner, list four to six issues or problems you are currently experiencing in your own life. Identify whether each is a *choice* issue or a *change* issue. Remember, choice issues are ones in which you have the skills and opportunities to follow a course of action but feel conflicted about which direction to follow. Change issues are ones in which you need to develop new options and behaviors or modify existing ones. Finally, note whether the choice or change for each issue is under your control and can be initiated by you. If not, identify the other people in your life who are also a part of this choice or change.

**B.** With a partner, or in a small group, brainstorm possible strategies that might be suitable interventions for one of the issues or problems from your list in Part A. Next, evaluate the probable usefulness of each strategy. In your evaluation, consider the six guidelines for selection of counseling strategies described in this chapter.

**1.** Is the strategy consistent with your theoretical orientation?

**2.** Do you have any expertise and experience in working with this strategy?

**3.** Are you knowledgeable about typical responses to and effects of this strategy?

**4.** Does the strategy fit the character or nature of the problem?

**5.** Does the strategy fit the character or nature of your desired goal?

**6.** Does the strategy meet your expectations and preferences and does it avoid repeating or building on prior unsuccessful solutions?

*Note: You do not have to select complex or sophisticated counseling strategies. If you have not yet been exposed to counseling theories and techniques, rely on common-sense approaches and interventions, since the emphasis in this activity is on the process of strategy selection rather than on the actual strategies you select.*

**C.** Continue this activity with your partner or group. For the strategy your group selected in Part B as the best or most effective one, generate the following information about the strategy:

1. A rationale—how it seems to work.
2. A description of the counselor's role in the strategy.
3. A description of the client's role in the strategy.
4. Possible discomfort, negative effects, or "spin-offs" from the strategy.
5. Expected benefits of the strategy.
6. Estimated time involved in using this strategy.

**D.** Role-play the strategy information in Part C. One person will assume the client's role and present the issue. The other person will assume the counselor's role and suggest the recommended strategy and provide the client with enough information about the strategy to help the client make an informed choice about accepting or rejecting the suggestion. Additional members of the group will function as observers and will take notes and provide feedback to the counselor after the role-play. Follow up with a group discussion of the exercise.

***II.*** *Relationship of Problem Components to Strategy Selection*

In this exercise, we present three client cases. For each case, determine the primary component(s) of the problem that would need to be addressed during the intervention strategy phase of counseling. There may be more than one significant component. (Feedback for the exercise can be found in the next section.)

1. Mario is a sixteen-year-old sophomore in high school who wants to lose forty pounds. He states that he has been overweight most of his life and has never really attempted to lose weight before. He says that he eats just about "whatever he wants, when he wants." He indicates that he has no real knowledge of diets, calories, or behavior modification techniques for weight loss. Additionally, he asserts that it is hard to refuse food in his family. His parents are slightly overweight, and he has two teenage brothers who are not overweight but who need to eat a lot to keep up their energy. Pasta and homebaked bread are a part of every meal except breakfast. Mealtime is important in Mario's family and plentiful around the house.

   **Primary components:**
   Affective: _____
   Cognitive: _____
   Behavioral: _____

Systemic: _____
Cultural: _____
**Preferred strategy:** _____

**2.** Rodolfo is an older (sixty-six-year-old) man who reports vague but distressing feelings of nervousness and anxiety. Apparently, these feelings were precipitated by the death of his wife two years ago and his recent retirement. He states that he is most aware of these feelings at night when he is alone in the house with nothing to do and no one around to talk to. Rodolfo lives in a Hispanic neighborhood, attends the local Catholic church daily, and uses the public library extensively. He knows most of the people in his neighborhood but doesn't socialize. He also reports some somatic symptoms—waking up several times each night, loss of appetite, and some stomach distress.

**Primary components:**
Affective: _____
Cognitive: _____
Behavioral: _____
Systemic: _____
Cultural: _____
**Preferred strategy:** _____

**3.** Vanessa is a twenty-two-year-old who is currently working as a fashion model. She lives with her parents and her younger sister. After much discussion, she reveals her primary reason for seeking help—binge eating. She states that what started out as a rather routine way to keep her weight under control in order to model has turned into a pattern she feels little or no control to change. She describes herself as generally unattractive despite her job as a model. She feels that her parents have constantly compared her to her younger sister and she has always come out "on the short end." However, she also says that her father is harder on her sister than on her. She has difficulty describing anything positive about herself. She also indicates that she feels increasingly resentful of the control and strict standards imposed on her by her parents, even though she is no longer a minor.

**Primary components:**
Affective: _____
Cognitive: _____
Behavioral: _____
Systemic: _____
Cultural: _____
**Preferred strategy:** _____

## Feedback for Exercises

**II.** *Problem Components and Strategy Selection*

**1.** There are three components to this problem that would need to be addressed by counseling interventions:
*Behavioral*—excess weight

*Systemic*—role of his family in contributing to and maintaining his weight problem

*Cultural*—What is Mario's family's cultural background? Does eating play a role in family relationships? How important is this to Mario? Others?

**2.** The major component of this problem is the *affective* one. Rodolfo presents feelings of distress and anxiety, accompanied by somatic manifestations such as sleep disturbance, appetite loss, and stomach distress. There is a possible systemic component in terms of Rodolfo's support network, friends, church. Finally, is he Hispanic? If so, what role do his cultural values play in both maintaining his problem and in solving his problem? Is the fact that he is male part of the problem?

**3.** There are three major components to Vanessa's problem that can be identified with the information at hand: an *affective* one—negative feelings about herself; a *behavioral* component—binge eating; and a *systemic* issue—the role her parents play both in her relationship to them, to her sister, and to her self-perceptions. There is also a *cultural* issue— young, female, ambitious. Do these qualities have anything to do with Vanessa's problems?

## Discussion Questions

**1.** Identify and discuss the attributes of a good counseling strategy. Of a poor counseling strategy. From your perspective, what factors make a strategy good or effective?

**2.** How much influence do you believe a person's cultural values have? How aware do you think people are of their cultural values?

**3.** What has been your exposure to people of different cultures? What knowledge have you gained from this? What cultural knowledge deficits do you possess? How will that affect your counseling?

**4.** Identify a problem situation that you have experienced (or have observed in a close relationship) in which the attempted solution became the new problem or made the existing problem worse. To what extent was the person in question aware of this complication? How was the problem finally resolved?

## Recommended Readings

Arredondo, P. (1991). Counseling Latinas. In C.C. Lee and B.L. Richardson, Eds., *Multicultural Issues in Counseling: New Approaches to Diversity*, Alexandria, VA: ACA Press.

Axelson, J.A. (1993). *Counseling and Development in a Multicultural Society*, Pacific Grove, CA: Brooks/Cole. Chapter 3: Profiles of the

American people: Native Americans, Anglo-Saxon Americans, with ethnic Americans. Chapter 4: Profiles of the American people: Black Americans, Hispanic Americans, Asian Americans.

Cook, E.P., Ed., (1993). *Women, Relationships, and Power: Implications for Counseling*, Alexandria, VA: ACA Press.

Fassinger, R.E. (1991). The hidden minority: Issues and challenges in working with lesbian women and gay men, *The Counseling Psychologist, 19*, 157–176.

Ivey, A.E., Ivey, M.B., and Simek-Morgan, L. (1993). *Counseling and Psychotherapy: A Multicultural Perspective*, Pacific Grove, CA: Brooks/Cole. Chapter 4: Decisional counseling: The basis of all counseling and therapy.

Sue, D. and Sue, D.S. (1991). Counseling strategies for Chinese Americans. In C.C. Lee and B.L. Richardson, Eds., *Multicultural Issues in Counseling: New Approaches to Diversity*, Alexandria, VA: ACA Press.

Vásquez, J.M. (1991). Puerto Ricans in the counseling process: The dynamics of ethnicity and its societal context. In C.C. Lee and B.L. Richardson, Eds., *Multicultural Issues in Counseling: New Approaches to Diversity*, Alexandria, VA: ACA Press.

$$C \quad h \quad a \quad p \quad t \quad e \quad r \quad 7$$

# Affective Interventions

### *Purpose of This Chapter—*

Feelings are often thought to be the reason why people seek counseling. While this is not the case with many counseling problems, it is nevertheless true that many people seek counseling for help with overwhelming emotions. This chapter discusses the role feelings play in the process of counseling and describes counseling interventions that are used to help clients identify emotions, modify troublesome feelings, and, when appropriate, to accept feelings that are present.

### *Considerations as You Read This Chapter—*

- Feelings have been described as basic to all human experience. And yet, many people do not seem to understand their feelings. Some will disavow having certain feelings. Others will treat their feelings as embarrassments or signs of weakness. Some cultures treat feelings as private events.

- What are your views? Would you be described as "wearing your feelings on your coat sleeves?" Or would you be the stoic type?

- What role does emotion play in our problems? Is it the source? The result?

- How do people change the way they feel about something? If a feeling changes, for example, from indifference to liking, will that be reflected in the person's perceptions of his or her world?

"Therapy is not simply an intellectual exercise in which clients talk about and analyze their problems; they also *feel* them" (Kleinke, 1994, p. 20). We feel happy when things are going well, sad when we experience loss, angry or frustrated when our desires are thwarted, and lonely when we are deprived of contact with others. Many times, feelings can be accessed only indirectly through the client's verbal expression or behavior. The client may "feel" depressed but only through verbal and nonverbal communication, physical cues, or acting out can the counselor make contact with that feeling state. The impact of this fact is that " . . . we cannot manipulate emotions in the sense that we can manipulate thinking or behaving" (Corsini & Wedding, 1989, p. 7). Consequently, the counselor works with client feelings by generating client awareness and subsequent client valuing and integration of those feelings.

The role that feelings play in counseling and psychotherapy is an unsettled issue. Corsini and Wedding (1989) observe that

> *Some people see emotions as epiphenomena accompanying but not affecting therapeutic change, while others see emotions as a powerful agent leading to change and still others see emotions as evidence of change.* (p. 7)

Whichever the case may be, most, if not all, of our thoughts and behaviors have a feeling dimension. Perhaps, because this is so, feelings can be the source, or a significant part of the problems we experience. We noted above how the counselor accesses the client's affective state, but the client may also lack access to feelings. This bottling up of feelings may be due to one's early training or to the intensity of the emotion which threatens and overpowers the person. We know that boys are often taught to deny those feelings that are associated with weakness, failure, or powerlessness. Similarly, girls are often taught to deny feelings associated with such characteristics as dominance, control, power, or even intellect. Or, consider the child who is raised in a perfectionist environment. If that child internalizes the environmental demands, then the need to be perfect without the skills to do so will lead to excessive threat and emotional difficulties throughout childhood and into adulthood. The result is that when these unacknowledged or even undetected feelings begin to build up, some people are ill-equipped to find release, and counseling or psychotherapy becomes an appropriate recourse.

Helping the individual to develop the capacity to find release of emotional difficulties and to cope better with life demands is a central goal of many therapeutic approaches. The affect-oriented theories have made major contributions to the counselor's repertoire of affect interventions. Generally speaking, those theories with an affective orientation rely heavily upon the development of affect awareness, exploration, and integration of feelings. They do not discount thought processes or behavior patterns. Rather, they emphasize the emotional context in which thought patterns, beliefs, and behaviors occur.

## Theories That Stress the Importance of Feelings

Most affective or emotion interventions derive from the *phenomeno-logical* therapies. Phenomenologists make a distinction between what is (reality) and our *perceptions* of what is. This inner world of our perceptions becomes *our* reality. By far the most dominant of these therapies is Carl Rogers' person-centered therapy. Probably next in its impact would be the contributions of Gestalt therapy, followed by the existential approaches (Binswanger, Boss, Viktor Frankl, and Rollo May). Other therapeutic approaches that are sometimes identified as affective therapies include Kelly's psychology of personal constructs (Rychlak, 1973; Hansen, Rossberg, & Cramer, 1994); Gendlin's experiential counseling ((Hansen, Rossberg, & Cramer, 1994); psychoanalytic therapy (Frey, 1972; Shertzer & Stone 1980); and the body work therapies, such as bioenergetics (Lowen, 1974) and core energetics (Pierrakos, 1990).

All of these approaches place the individual in a context of self-struggle. The internal issues which are experienced may relate to self-identity, self-worth, self-responsibility, or self-actualization. Whatever the issue or the goal, the process involves exploration of feelings, anxieties, defenses, values, perceptions, and the meaning of life. It is within this phenomenological context that the affective therapies attempt to define the human condition.

## Affective Interventions

In one respect, referring to affective interventions is a philosophical contradiction. The affect-focused counselor is more likely to emphasize the personhood of the client and the interpersonal relationship between counselor and client, rather than the techniques that would be used. Nevertheless, the affective counselor is doing something in this process, and it is these behaviors that are the focus of this chapter. As we explore these interventions, the reader should keep in mind that the interventions become gimmicky and ineffective if the therapeutic relationship between counselor and client has been given a lesser priority.

### The Goals of Affective Interventions

The primary goals of affective interventions are: (a) to help the client express feelings or feeling states; (b) to identify or discriminate between feelings or feeling states; (c) to alter or accept feelings or feeling states; or (d) in some cases, to contain feelings or feeling states.

Some clients come to counseling with an awareness that something is wrong in their lives but are unable to articulate or discuss that condition. Talking about problems or feelings may be a new experience for them. This is often the case for the person who grew up in a family or culture where problems were never discussed openly, or the expression of feelings was discouraged or forbidden through injunctions such as "Don't be angry," "Don't cry," "Don't feel." Child clients may not have reached the developmental stage where skills and affect sensitivity are acquired; consequently, they may lack both the skills of expression and the awareness that expression of feelings can be helpful.

At a somewhat more complicated level, the client may come to counseling flooded with emotional reactions. When this happens it is experienced as an emotional overload, and the protective response often is to tune out the emotions, to become emotionless. Or the response may be confusion or disorientation. When this happens the client must be helped to recognize and sort out or to contain the variety of affect responses that are being experienced. This condition is frequently found when a person has experienced a long period of emotional turmoil, such as occurs in a divorce, death of a family member, poor physical health, or other life tragedy; or it may be a more serious psychopathologic blocking of affect.

At the most complex level of affect intervention, the counselor and client are involved in the integration of or alteration of feeling states. This may include value clarification, acceptance of hitherto unacceptable feelings, reconsideration of old feelings, or even redefinition of self-perceptions. This process is common when the client is beginning to differentiate self from family, self from spouse and children, self from job or career, self from culture, or is otherwise laboring with the question "Who am I?"

In this chapter we describe and illustrate the more common affective interventions that facilitate the expression and examination of feelings. These interventions include feeling inventories, counselor *modeling*, scripting and role rehearsal, dialoguing and alter-ego exercises, identifying affect *blocks*, differentiation between competing feelings, role reversal, the *empty chair*, affect focusing, and dreamwork.

## Helping Clients Express Affect

Experiencing a feeling, even knowing that somehow feelings are related to one's problems, does not lead naturally to the expression and examination of the feeling. A part of the counselor's role is to help clients find ways to express feelings, both in ways that capture the meaning of the feeling and convey that meaning to others. The counselor's task may be a matter of setting the stage, creating the proper conditions for a reticent client to open up.

Many authors have described the conditions that are necessary for such an involvement (Sexton & Whiston, 1994). These conditions—an accurate understanding of the client's situation and an unconditional valuing of the client—were discussed in Chapter 3. Beyond the conditions that create the atmosphere of helping, the counselor becomes involved in the client's process of emotional exploration through selective attention and reflective listening, also described in Chapter 3.

The exploration of emotions is a *process* more than a set of verbal responses, involving the counselor's conceptualization of what the client is trying to understand and the acknowledgment of that effort. Sometimes the process also serves to focus the client's awareness on what he or she *seems to be saying*. And usually, the process involves sharing the satisfaction of having accomplished the task. Given that it is a process rather than a series of behavioral events, the counselor must rely, nonetheless, on verbal interaction with the client and close observation of nonverbal communication. This metacommunication interaction incorporates many stylistic responses of counselor and counseling.

### Cultural Variables and Affect Expression

The expression of affect runs counter to the values of some cultures. Argyle et al. (1986) report from their research that the English and Italians endorse the display of distress and anger across relationships more than do the Japanese. This is also born out in research by Noesjirwan (1978) who "found that Indonesians agreed with the rule of keeping quiet and hiding feelings when one is angry at one's boss, while Australians endorsed expressing anger in the same situation" (Gudykunst & Ting-Toomey, 1988 p. 181). Sue and Sue (1990) observe that Asian Americans value the restraint of strong feelings and that self-disclosure is particularly difficult for Black clients working with White counselors. Similarly, the expression of inner thoughts and feelings by Native Americans cannot be expected to occur until trust is well established. It is not that affect is less accessible in some cultures than others but rather, that, in collectivistic cultures (as opposed to individualistic cultures) affect expression is more likely to be withheld (Gudykunst & Ting-Toomey, 1988, p. 179).

### Nonverbal Affect Cues

A major way in which clients show feelings is through nonverbal cues or body language. Nonverbal information can be inferred from such elements of the client's communication as head and facial movement, position of body, movements and gestures, and voice qualities. Although no single nonverbal cue can be interpreted accurately in isolation, each does have meaning as part of a larger pattern or gestalt. Thus, there are relationships between nonverbal and verbal characteristics of client messages. In addition to these relationships, nonverbal cues may also communicate specific information about the relationship between individuals involved in the communicative process, in this case the counselor and client. Some nonverbal cues convey information about the nature and intensity of emotions more accurately than verbal cues. The nature of the emotion is communicated nonverbally primarily by head cues; for example, setting of the jaw, facial grimaces, narrowing of the eyes. The intensity of an emotion is communicated both by head cues and body cues such as muscular rigidity (Ekman & Friesen, 1967).

The counselor may or may not choose to acknowledge these nonverbal cues. In some cases, acknowledging them ("You've been looking very tight since you started talking about this matter") can invite the client to share the intensity of the emotion. At other times, the counselor's observation may be rejected outright or may bring out a defensive response. Thus, timing as well as accuracy of perception is a factor in what the counselor chooses to say.

### *Nonverbal Cues and Cultural Differences*

Ekman (1993) reports finding high agreement of persons of "diverse Western and Eastern literate cultures" in the emotional identification of facial expressions in experiments where subjects were shown pictures of faces in various emotional expressions. This would suggest that different cultures infer the same meanings for different nonverbal facial gestures and therefore those meanings are not culture-specific. On the other hand, Sue and Sue (1990) point out Edward T. Hall's research that differentiates between high context cultures and low-context cultures. High-context cultures are those in which communication relies heavily on nonverbals while low-context cultures rely much less on nonverbals for communication purposes. They point out that U.S. culture (presumably the majority White culture) is a low-context culture, though not as low as Germany, Switzerland, or Scandinavia. On the other hand, Asian Americans, Blacks, Hispanics, Native Americans, and other minority groups in the United States emphasize high-context cues (p. 58). This would suggest that certain ethnic groups in the United States are much more attuned to and adept at reading nonverbal messages. However, Ekman (1993, p. 384) emphasizes that "no one to date has obtained strong evidence of cross-cultural disagreement about the interpretation of fear, anger, disgust, sadness, or enjoyment expressions."

## Verbal Affect Cues

Although there are many different kinds of feelings, most feelings that we identify by words fit into one of four classifications: affection, anger, fear, or emotional pain. Many of these feelings can be identified by certain affect word usage. In addition, there are subcategories of affect words for each of the major affect categories. In using words to identify affect, it is important to remember that these words may occasionally mask more intense feelings or even different feelings. As Ivey (1994) notes, "a common mistake is to assume that these words represent the root feelings. Most often, they cover deeper feelings" (p. 132). Ekman (1993) adds that if the language of a culture does not have a word for a specific emotion, it does not mean that the emotion is not present in that culture but simply connotes the lack of specific terms to represent certain feelings.

### Verbal Cues for Positive Affect

Feelings of affection reflect good or accepting feelings about oneself and others and indicate positive aspects of interpersonal relationships. Verbal cues in a client's communication are revealed by the presence of words that connote certain feelings. For example, if a client uses the word *wonderful* in describing an event, a location, or a person, that descriptor suggests an accepting, preferred or desirable mental set toward the referent. This is a positive affect response. Some examples of word cues that connote this positive affect are shown in *Table 7-1*.

Often nonverbal cues occur simultaneously with these positive affect cues. The most frequent nonverbal cue correlates are facial ones. The corners of the mouth may turn up to produce the hint of a smile;

**TABLE 7-1  Positive Word Cues**

| Enjoyment | Competence | Love | Happiness | Hope |
|-----------|------------|------|-----------|------|
| beautiful | able | close | cheerful | luck |
| enjoy | can | friendly | content | optimism |
| good | fulfill | love | delighted | try |
| nice | great | like | excited | guess |
| pretty | wonderful | need | happy | wish |
| satisfy | smart | care | laugh(ed) | want |
| terrific | respect | want | thrill | |
| tremendous | worth | choose | dig | |

SOURCE: T.J. Crowley. "The Conditionability of Positive and Negative Self-reference Emotional Affect Statements in a Counseling-like Interview." Doctoral dissertation, The University of Massachusetts, 1970. Reprinted by permission.

the eyes may widen slightly; worry wrinkles may disappear. There may be a noticeable absence of body tension. The arms and hands may move in an open-palm gesture of acceptance, or the communicator may reach out as though to touch the object of the affect message lightly. When clients are describing feelings about an object or event, there may be increased animation of the face and hands.

### Verbal Cues of Anger

Feelings serve functions. While anger may sometimes represent an obstruction to be removed, anger can also be a signal to protect one-self or to fight for one's rights. Anger feelings are not pleasant to ex-perience and many clients seek counseling with the idea of having this feeling relieved or eliminated. Making the feelings go away with-out looking to see what function they may serve might not be in the client's best interest, therapeutically. Sometimes, clients need help in learning how to understand the origins of their anger responses. Or, they may need to learn how to express their feelings in an assertive way rather than an aggressive way. Oftentimes, anger masks a more vulnerable reaction like hurt, shame, or inadequacy. Most people are well acquainted with the words that represent anger (see *Table 7-2*). These verbal cues can be classified into four general categories, to which you may want to add other words.

There are certain vocal qualities also associated with anger. Many times the voice will become louder, deeper, or more controlled. The pacing of the communication may become more rapid or more de-liberate. What is important is that communicators make distinct de-partures from their normal communication pattern when anger is ex-pressed.

It is not often that one experiences anger without being aware of it. But it can happen that a person carries old anger all of the time and releases the anger at inappropriate times. It is also possible that some angry people do not realize that their anger is perceived by oth-

**TABLE 7-2   Word Cues of Anger**

| Attack | Grimness | Defensiveness | Quarrelsome |
|--------|----------|---------------|-------------|
| argue | dislike | against | angry |
| attack | hate | protect | fight |
| compete | nasty | resent | quarrel |
| criticize | disgust | guard | argue |
| fight | surly | prepared | take issue |
| hit | serious | | reject |
| hurt | | | (don't) agree |
| offend | | | |

**TABLE 7-3　Word Cues of Fear**

| Fear | Doubt | Pain | Avoidance | Mistrust |
|------|-------|------|-----------|----------|
| anxious | failure | awful | flee | doubt |
| bothers | flunk | hurt | cop out | sneak |
| concerns | confused | dismay | escape | dislike |
| nervous | unsure | aches | cut out | suspect |
| scare | stupid | fester | run from | lie |
| freak out | stuck | suffer | neglect | |
| recoil | insecure | torn between struggle | | |

ers. Thus, the counselor may acknowledge a client's apparent anger either to invite exploration of its source or to provide confirmation that the client is being heard. This can be accomplished by a simple, tentative observation, "You sound as though you might be angry." Or the counselor might focus on the affect cues with a statement like "You have referred to him as disgusting several times now. Could you talk about how he is disgusting?"

## *Verbal Cues of Fear*

Fear is a reaction to some kind of danger to be avoided. It may signal a need to withdraw from a painful or stressful situation, from one's self, or from other people and relationships. The person experiencing fear may also feel isolated. The implicit presence of danger that is signaled by the fear response is the likely focal point for counseling. Cultural characteristics will certainly be linked to the expression of fear. Generally speaking, males have been schooled not to show fear even when they feel it. Verbal cues that suggest fear in a client's communication may be classified into five categories (see *Table 7-3*).

　　As was the case with the anger response, there are some physical cues associated with fear. The face may express surprise or suspicion, the body may recoil or appear ready to spring into action. The breathing rate may become more rapid and shallow. Or as anxiety and tension increase, the number of speech disturbances, such as errors, repetitions, stuttering, and omissions, may increase. The person may speak at a faster than normal rate, or the voice may take on a more guarded quality.

　　When the client appears fearful, the counselor may wish to explore the ramifications of that fear. How realistic is the fear? How physically threatening is the feared situation? Is the situation more threatening to one's identity or spiritual self than to one's physical self? How accurate are the client's perceptions of the feared situation?

Often the most appropriate intervention is to encourage the client to discuss the fear. But if the fear is inordinately strong, the client may be inclined to avoid any discussion. Consequently, the counselor may wish to move gently and supportively, but at the same time persistently. One way of doing this is through the use of self-disclosure. An anecdote from the counselor's own experience in which fear was felt, confronted, and ultimately overcome can communicate that fear is a normal feeling and that it can be faced down. The effect of a brief self-disclosure is like an invitation for the client to approach his or her fear, to talk about it, and to normalize it. Ultimately the acceptance and expression of a fear can also increase the feeling of trust (Kelley, 1979).

### Verbal Cues of Emotional Pain

Sadness, loneliness, or depression are fairly common emotional conditions presented by clients. Such conditions can be a response to relationships, environmental conditions, physiological imbalances, or even diet. *Table 7-4* lists verbal cues that indicate that the client may be experiencing emotional pain. Sadness, often associated with loss, is one of the milder forms of this emotional state. It may be accompanied by a tendency to withdraw from social contact in some clients or a dependency reaction in others. Only the most preoccupied counselor would fail to notice some of the behavioral correlates of sadness. Looking *down in the mouth*, whipped, or about to cry are common characteristics of sadness. The real issue, perhaps, relates to how sad the client is. In other words, is the client approaching clinical depression, thus necessitating a different form of treatment.

Physical cues that accompany these emotions can be misleading. They may include poor posture or slouching in the chair, eyes averted downward and little eye contact with the counselor, talking in a monotone, staring into space, or a general lack of awareness or attention to personal qualities or to self-care. However, some cultural groups,

**TABLE 7-4  Word Cues of Emotional Pain**

| Sadness | Loneliness | Depression |
|---------|------------|------------|
| unhappy | alone | depressing |
| adrift | abandoned | depressed |
| sorrowful | isolated | disillusioned |
| distressed | missing | weary |
| grieving | missed | listless |
| mourning | empty | discouraged |
| heartsick | | despondent |
| | | gloomy |

notably Native Americans and Asian Americans, may avert eyes downward and avoid eye contact as a sign of respect for the counselor.

When you become aware that your client is experiencing feelings associated with sadness, loss, or depression, it is appropriate to ask some questions that would reveal the extent of the mood in order to identify any self-destructive inclinations and to determine whether your client needs medical attention for mood control. The following are some questions that would help determine the extent and nature of your client's emotional pain.

---

*Exploring Dimensions of Depression*

How well do you sleep at night?
　Do you have difficulty going to sleep?
　Do you wake up in the middle of the night and find it difficult to go back to sleep?
　Are you sleeping less (more) than is your typical pattern?
What are your eating patterns?
　Are you disinterested in eating?
　Are you eating obsessively?
　Do you feel guilty about your eating?
What is the state of your physical well-being?
　Do you feel normal?
　If not, what seems unusual about your physical well-being?
　Is this a recent change?
　Do you experience lengthy bouts with fatigue?
　Do you have a high, medium or low energy level?
　Do you consider your sexual feelings to be normal?
What kinds of social contact do you have?

Has your social pattern changed recently?
　Do you prefer to be alone or with people?
　Do you have friends or relatives that you are comfortable calling at inconvenient times?
What are your self-views like?
　What do you think about yourself?
　When do you tend to think about yourself?
　How much time do you spend thinking about yourself?
　What kinds of things distract you from thinking about yourself?
Do you ever think about suicide?
　If so, have you thought about how you might commit suicide?
　Do you have a current suicide plan?
　Have you ever attempted suicide? When?
　Has any member of your immediate family ever attempted or committed suicide?

---

Questions such as these provide cumulative information about the client's inner well-being. If the client appears to be withdrawing from social contact, sleeping poorly, eating poorly or erratically, and focusing extensively on self, then the counselor should seek consultation or refer the client to a physician or psychologist. If the client is contemplating suicide or has attempted suicide before, referral may be made to a physician, or psychiatrist since medication may be a necessary part of treatment.

## Helping Clients Sort Out Feelings

Some clients enter counseling aware of their emotions but overwhelmed by either the complexity or quantity of their unresolved feelings. Such a condition is often triggered by a traumatic life event, such as the death of a parent, spouse, or child; a divorce; or the loss of a career. These traumatic events stimulate feelings associated with the event, and perhaps more significantly, feelings associated with the person's self-worth. Typically, the person is attempting to resolve unanswerable questions such as: "Why did it happen?" "Why did it have to happen to me?" "Could I have prevented it from happening?"

The counselor's role in this situation is that of facilitator, guide, and supporter. Counseling interventions include being a sounding board as the client attempts to unfold a complex series of feelings, helping the client recognize the source of various emotional reactions, and helping the client develop a sense of emotional control. Sometimes the counselor will begin this process with a simple paper-and-pencil exercise if the client is unable to address feelings. At other times, the counseling scene takes on the qualities of a play rehearsal. Often the scene is one of intensely experienced emotions, tears, fears, relived hurts, and anger. Ultimately, it leads to hope, clearer understandings, and new decisions.

A second condition can occur in which the client enters counseling with an overload of emotions. When this happens, a common survival mechanism is to deny or screen out the intensity of the emotion while still acknowledging the emotion.

Whether the crux of the client's problem is the quantity or complexity of emotional experience, the process is to help clients develop some structure or system for managing those feelings. This process is not so simple as it might sound. The tendency, particularly for the inexperienced counselor, is to offer a structure, a way of viewing the client's concerns. External structures may make cognitive sense, but they usually miss the point. The point is, of course, that most emotional overloads are illogically structured by clients. Therefore, when the counselor provides a logical structure, it does not speak to the client's illogic. Instead, the counselor must encourage the client to reprocess situations, personal explanations, and conclusions in such a way that an alternative, and more logical structure may emerge. This process allows clients to conceptualize their life situation in new ways that are personally meaningful.

There are a number of interventions, exercises, and discussions that help clients sort out feelings. No one intervention is effective with all clients. Thus, you must explore and experiment with each new client to find those activities that are acceptable and meaningful for that client. The interventions range from very simple paper-and-pencil exercises to rather complicated and dramatic reenactments of emotional experiences.

Early in counseling, the most appropriate strategy is to use activities that generate expression and classification of feelings. These would include counselor recognition and reflection of client's expression of feelings, verbal statements, and counselor empathy for the client's emotional description. Chapter 3 contains a full discussion of empathy, affective reflections, and restatements. Other activities include the emotional percentages chart and emotions checklist (which is very effective for the client who says, "I can't describe my feelings"), and the emotions balloons chart (which is a helpful aid for young children).

Finally, it may be surprising to learn that not all counselors are comfortable with their own feelings or the feelings of their clients. Teyber (1992) describes counselor avoidance of client feelings as *blocking* and lists a number of ways in which counselors may avoid dealing with client affect appropriately:

Changing the topic
Emotionally withdrawing from the discussion
Becoming very directive
Interpreting the meaning of the client's feelings
Self-disclosing own feelings
Rescuing the client from conflict
Trying to solve the client's problem

(Teyber, 1992, p. 106)

### Emotions Checklist

The emotions checklist is a good exercise to use prior to beginning or during the first counseling session (see *Figure 7-1*). It allows the client to identify the various feelings that contributed to seeking help

| | | |
|---|---|---|
| _____ discouraged | _____ confused | _____ afraid |
| _____ optimistic | _____ uneasy | _____ mad |
| _____ lonely | _____ relaxed | _____ insecure |
| _____ angry | _____ doubtful | _____ uptight |
| _____ hurt | _____ unsure | _____ furious |
| _____ pessimistic | _____ content | _____ satisfied |
| _____ defensive | _____ bewildered | _____ hassled |
| _____ skeptical | _____ outraged | _____ panicked |
| _____ depressed | _____ hopeless | _____ cheerful |
| _____ unhappy | _____ disoriented | _____ irritated |
| _____ resentful | _____ frustrated | _____ scared |
| _____ worried | _____ excited | _____ tense |
| _____ disillusioned | _____ annoyed | _____ offended |

**FIGURE 7-1  Emotions Checklist**

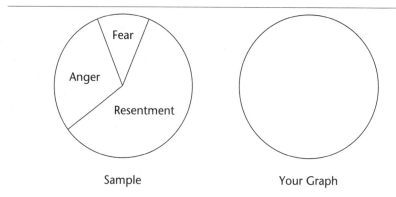

Sample                    Your Graph

**FIGURE 7-2  Emotional Percentages Chart**

and provides a basis for early discussion and exploration of the client's concerns. The client is instructed to indicate in the checklist those feelings that describe his or her life experience in the past three months, underlining those feelings that are of the greatest concern.

### Emotional Percentages Chart

The emotional percentages chart is an example of an exercise that can be quite effective early in counseling (see *Figure 7-2*). On a sheet of paper, two circles are shown. One is drawn as a pie graph and illustrates a number of different feeling states and how much of the total "pie" each emotion occupies. You may want to refer your clients to the emotions checklist if they are having difficulty labeling personal emotions to use in the chart. The emotional percentages chart allows the client to identify the intensity or preoccupation with a particular set of emotions. It also allows the counselor to invite the client to discuss the interrelationships of those identified emotions in the chart.

### Emotions Balloons Chart

Young children pose a special problem for the counselor. Emotional awareness is a process that develops as the child develops. Very young children may only know happy, sad, mad, and bad. As children grow and as their vocabularies increase, they are able to recognize the subtleties that exist within these emotions. Even so, the counselor must relate to the child at the child's level of experience. In part this means that you will use the toys and tools of the child's world to relate to the child's emotions. One example of this is the emotional balloons chart (see *Figure 7-3*).

The child is given the following instructions about this activity:

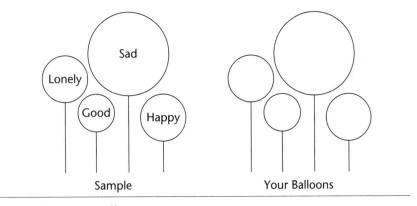

**FIGURE 7-3   Balloons**

*Sometimes people have several different feelings at the same time. Some of those feelings are strong and are very hard to forget, while others are important but are sometimes forgotten. Using the chart I am going to give you, write into the large balloons which of your feelings are biggest and hardest to forget. Then write into the small balloons the feelings you do sometimes forget. You can use feelings like* mad, happy, lonely, scared, upset, proud, *or* excited *to label your balloons.*

## *Focusing Techniques*

Focusing techniques are used to encourage and facilitate introspection in such a way that problems can be clarified and conceptualized by the client. Focusing emphasizes present feelings toward either present or past circumstances. Iberg (1981) described this process as

> *. . . holding one's attention quietly at a very low level of abstraction, to the felt sense. Felt sense is the bodily sense of the whole problem. In focusing, one doesn't think about the problem or analyze it, but one senses it immediately. One senses all of it, in all its complexity, as the whole thing hits one bodily.* (p. 344)

After suggesting that the client find a comfortable sitting position, the counselor invites the client to become quiet and to allow feelings to enter into consciousness. The client is then asked to associate words with this undifferentiated mass of feelings and to allow awareness to generate naturally. The instructions for using this intervention that follow have been adapted from Gendlin (1969, p. 506).

*Affect Focusing Instructions*

*I am going to explain how you can focus on a general or overall feeling you have about some concern or problem. Be silent for a moment and relax . . .* [Pause: Have the client close his or her eyes and relax] . . . *Now let the tension drain from your body . . .* [Longer pause] . . . *See what comes to you when you ask yourself, "How am I now?" "How do I feel?" Let any thoughts emerge. Try not to screen your response . . .* [Longer pause] . . . *Think about what is a major problem or concern for you. Choose whatever seems most meaningful to you . . .* [Shorter pause] . . .

*Focusing Process*

*Try to pay attention [focus] to what all of the problem [concern] feels like. Allow [let] yourself to feel the entire mass of the feeling . . .* [Longer pause] . . . *As you pay attention to [or receive] the entire feeling of your problem, you may find that one spe-cial concern comes up. Let yourself pay attention to that one aspect or feeling. Don't explain it or talk to yourself about it. Just feel it . . .* [Extended pause] . . . *Keep following one feeling. Don't let it be just words or pictures. Wait and let words or pictures emerge from the feelings . . .* [Extended pause] . . . *If this one feeling changes, or moves, let it do so. Whatever it does, follow the feeling and pay attention to it. Feel it all. Don't decide what is important about it. Just experience it . . .* [Extended pause] . . . *Now take your fresh and new feeling about your problem and give it space. Try to find some new words or images or pictures that capture what this feeling tries to say. Find words or images to say what you are feeling now . . .* [Extended pause]

Following the focusing instructions, the counselor should ask the client to describe the words or pictures that entered awareness during the exercise. This description can be continued for the remainder of the session.

## Case Illustration of Focusing

*The Case of Constance*

Constance is a twenty-six-year-old divorced woman who requested counseling to help her deal with her divorce. In the first session, she reported feeling overwhelmed by emotions and the demands of her two-year-old daughter. She vacillated between anger, resentment, guilt, and back to anger (usually directed at her ex-spouse). When this circular process really gained control of her, she would begin to feel stuck, caught, or lost (her words). She showed strong evidence of being rational, realistic, and in control, except for these emotional bouts. There was no past history of depression or life-threatening acts by either herself or any other family member. She did have her good days as well as her bad days and could say that she believed this terrible time would pass eventually.

Based on this information, the counselor decided that she did not show suicidal tendencies, but did ask her to make an appointment with her family physician for a complete physical examination. The counselor also decided that paper-and-pencil exercises were

*Continued*

not needed, since the client seemed quite able to verbalize her feelings and did not seem confused or unable to differentiate between anger and guilt. On the other hand, it did seem desirable to help Constance examine these various feelings and to find the meaning or relevance of the pattern in which they seemed to occur (anger . . . resentment . . . guilt . . . anger . . . ).

By providing facilitative conditions (understanding, accurate empathy, respect) the counselor gradually produced an atmosphere in which Constance began to relax and do some self-confrontation. She was able to talk about her misgivings regarding the causes of the divorce. She began to talk about the heavy burden of single parenthood. Invariably, however, she would reach a dead end (which she referred to as an insurmountable wall) in talking about these feelings.

After three such sessions, Constance began to feel frustrated and the counselor suggested that they try a focusing exercise. Following an explanation of the process and its purpose, they decided together to use the next session as a focusing experiment. Constance arrived at the next session showing some nervousness, but this soon dissipated. The counselor began the focusing exercise and Constance quickly became a cooperative participant. At its completion, Constance reported that when she tried to let the anger, resentment, and guilt merge into one larger feeling, the word *responsibility* kept entering her awareness. The counselor wisely suggested that they repeat the exercise, but that Constance should focus on the *responsible* response this time. At the end of the second round, Constance talked with a sense of discovery about the experience.

"I think I have been running away from my responsibilities, my responsibility for the end of the marriage, my responsibility for my daughter, and most of all, my responsibility for myself. In the exercise I reached the point of 'giving these responsibilities away,' but there is no one I would want to give them to. They are too valuable to give away."

"What do you mean, they are too valuable?" the counselor asked.

"If I give them away, I must also give away my independence, my freedom to be who I am. And that is very valuable to me. I must learn to accept some of these fears about causing the divorce or not liking some parts of being a mother if I'm going to be independent. Otherwise, I'd be right back in the same place I was as a child."

## Helping Clients Integrate or Change Feeling States

It was noted in the preceding section that clients sometimes cope with emotions by creating a psychological distance from their feelings. This can happen when the person is bombarded by multiple affect reactions stemming from traumatic life situations. It can also happen when a person is confronted by a strong but unacceptable emotional situation. The result of this affect distancing is to postpone the immediate demand to respond to the affect. A normal example of this condition is the grieving process. But to postpone an adaptive demand is not a long-term solution. Thus, even the grieving individual must ultimately come to grips with the loss and alter perceptions in whatever way the loss demands.

The process of integrating feeling states, or when appropriate, changing feeling states, can require professional assistance, particularly when the client is insensitive to or unskilled in affective matters. Thus, the process of sorting out and identifying feelings that was discussed in the previous section may lead to a need to integrate those newly felt feelings. A case in point might illustrate this.

---

*The Case of Paulo*

Paulo was married soon after graduating from college. Within two years, he and his wife had a child. As a result, he decided to give up his graduate studies in business and take a job as a department store assistant manager. This decision fit his personal value of providing for his family. After about six months, Paulo began to feel restless and showed irritability at work and at home. When these feelings occurred, he would chastise himself and remind himself that the job had been a choice based on his need to be a good family provider. Still, the feelings persisted.

Paulo decided to seek counseling through the company's EAP program. Counseling helped him become became aware that his restlessness was related to some unmet personal needs for achievement and recognition, putting those values in conflict with his need to be a good provider. The issue for Paulo was twofold: Should he allow these recurring feelings to be admitted into his perceptions of self and family? And if he did acknowledge these feelings, what would be the implications for the family and for his value system?

---

Paulo's situation illustrates how emotional undercurrents can intrude into a person's consciousness and disrupt emotional commitments and daily routines. It also illustrates the interrelatedness of feeling, thought, and behavior, as well as the need to come to some resolution of value conflict and incompatible emotional states.

A number of counseling interventions are derived from person-centered, Gestalt, and existential counseling to aid the client with such problems. In this section we shall examine *role reversal, alter ego,* the *empty chair* (or two-chair) *exercise,* and *dreamwork,* all of which may be used with Paulo's problem.

## Role Reversal

The *role reversal* is a useful exercise when a client is experiencing a conflict of values or feelings or a conflict with his/her self-image but is unable to isolate and understand the nature of the conflict. The purpose of role reversal is to project the client into a paradoxical examination of views, attitudes, or beliefs. This exercise may meet initial resistance, since it asks the client to challenge safe (albeit dysfunctional) roles or attitudes. However, if the client is encouraged to try playing the devil's advocate, to demonstrate that he or she is, in fact, able to discuss both sides of an issue, the exercise can be quite effective.

The counselor becomes an active participant in the role reversal enactment. He or she must be able to identify the splits or different roles that the client is experiencing. In the following case, Vincent has approached counseling because of a problem he is having at work. The counselor soon realized that the conflict was between Vincent and his boss and decided to set up a role reversal to help Vincent explore all aspects of his conflict. The counselor reversed Vincent's role by having him enact an encounter *as his boss*. The counselor also participated in the enactment in the role of *Vincent*. Thus, Vincent's role was reversed.

### Case Illustration of Role Reversal

*The Case of Vincent*

Vincent entered counseling for the purpose of solving "career problems." As counseling progressed, the problem became more clearly defined as an interpersonal conflict between Vincent and his boss. Vincent found it very easy to explore his feelings toward his boss, even though he liked his job. However, these explorations always seemed to lead up blind alleys if the counselor raised the question of solutions. Vincent would become flustered and would jump to the conclusion that the only solution was to change jobs. After this pattern repeated itself for four sessions, the counselor suggested that they try the role reversal exercise. Vincent responded somewhat suspiciously, but after some discussion of what the exercise involved, he agreed to participate. The next session began as follows:

*Vincent:* I don't know what this exercise is going to prove. Every time we discuss my problem, I end up at the same place. My boss is insensitive and completely unconcerned about my situation. He'll never change, and I'm not going to change, so the only solution is for me to look for another job.

*Counselor:* Before we reach that conclusion, let's try the role reversal exercise we discussed last week. It may not change anything, but at least we can say we looked at the problem every way we could imagine. Are you still game?

*Vincent:* Well, I can't imagine what you have in mind, but I'll go along with whatever it is.

*Counselor:* Good. I'd like you to play devil's advocate with your problem for a few minutes. I'd like you to imagine that you are your boss, and I'll be you, and we'll talk about the problem. Try to be as accurate as possible in your boss role. That way, I'll have a much better idea what your boss is like. And I will try to be as accurate as possible in my role as you. If I tend to respond inaccurately, stop the exercise and give me coaching on how I should respond. Are you ready?

*Continued*

*Vincent:* I suppose so. I know I can imitate him. I know him like the back of my hand. But I don't see how it can do any good.

*Counselor:* Maybe you're right. Let's give it a try and see what you think. You begin as your boss.

*Vincent:* Vincent, I see you have missed another deadline for *(as boss)* the production report. What the hell's going on?

*Counselor:* I couldn't get the information I needed, and I didn't *(as Vincent)* want to bother you because you were busy yesterday.

*Vincent:* What the hell do you mean, "You didn't want to bother me?" If you have to bother me to get the report done, then bother me. But don't miss another deadline. Do you understand?

*Counselor:* O.K., O.K. I hear you. But I knew you would have lost it if I interrupted you yesterday too.

*Vincent:* Look Vincent, you can't have it both ways. If you don't ask for help when you need it and that leads to missing deadlines, then you have to expect some consequence. And if anger is the consequence, then you had better understand that it is due to your avoiding me. You've got to stop avoiding me.

*(End of role reversal)*

*Counselor:* Well, Vincent, what do you think of that scene?

*Vincent:* I guess it took an unexpected turn. His anger does upset me, but I haven't been thinking about bringing it on myself.

*Counselor:* Do you think it might help to work on how you react to his anger?

As can be seen in this illustration, Vincent acknowledges his avoidance in a safe confrontation with his boss. This acknowledgment does not mean that Vincent will return to his job with new methods for coping. It may be that counseling will move on to an exploration of how Vincent can develop new approaches to working with his boss. Or it may be that he will end up changing jobs. For the moment, however, Vincent has broken through a resistance that would otherwise block the resolution of his job difficulties.

### Alter Ego

The *alter ego* exercise is similar to role reversal, but with a novel twist. Webster's dictionary defines *alter ego* as "another side of oneself, another self." The notion is that each of us has another dimension of our personality that is more aware, more honest, more perceptive of personal motives, values, and hidden agendas. It is our alter ego that nags us when we neglect our duties or avoid our responsibilities. Thus, the alter ego knows and is a more honest report of our inner motivations.

In this exercise, the client is asked to become his or her alter ego, and the counselor assumes the client's public self. Because the counselor must produce an accurate portrayal of the client's public self, and because the client must feel safe enough with the counselor to allow the alter ego to emerge, this exercise should not be used early in the counseling relationship. When the alter ego exercise is effective, it allows clients to confront themselves more honestly. This kind of self-confrontation can be far more effective than confrontations provided by the counselor. The result is that the client can introduce issues, refute self-rationalizations, or question self-motives in a therapeutic encounter with the self. The following illustrates the use of the alter ego exercise in a counseling setting.

### *Case Illustration of the Alter Ego*

*The Case of Wanda*

Wanda was a thirty-five-year-old homemaker. She was married to a fifty-year-old auto mechanic. She had an eleven-year-old son, Tim, by a previous marriage. Wanda entered counseling because she was concerned about Tim's emotional and academic development. Tim had been identified as a gifted child by the school he attended. However, his grades had deteriorated in the past six months and this had become a source of family concern. As Wanda discussed her concerns for Tim, she would shift from her personal issues to how she felt her husband did not recognize Tim's needs. When this occurred, she would become angry toward her spouse, and then Tim's issues would become lost.

The counselor had asked Wanda to involve the stepfather and Tim in counseling, but Wanda said her spouse refused and that Tim's school schedule would not permit his participation. While the counselor wondered about these explanations, she accepted Wanda's judgment. Because Wanda was a bright and introspective client, the counselor decided that she was a good candidate for the alter ego exercise which, she believed, would help Wanda better understand her own emotional reactions. Wanda, who liked counseling, readily agreed to the counselor's suggestion.

*Counselor:* In this exercise, I am going to be you, as I have come to know you. I'll try to represent you honestly and accurately. I want you to be the private Wanda, the person I don't really know yet. In this exercise we are going to talk to each other, the public you (my role) and the private you (your role). We might even have an argument, but that's okay. Do you understand?

*Wanda:* I think so. I'll try.

*Counselor:* Good, I'll go first.

*(as Wanda)* I just don't know what to do with Tim. He is so bright, but he is wasting his ability.

*Wanda:* You always think you ought to know what to do, *(alter ego)* and you don't.

*Counselor:* Yeah, and that's why I think Bob (husband) ought to be helping. He disappears when I need him most.

*Wanda:* You think Bob knows more about Tim than you do? You just don't want to be responsible for Tim.

*Counselor:* It's not that I don't want to do it alone. I don't think I can do it alone. And besides, I want Bob and Tim to have a parent-child relationship, and that isn't happening.

*Continued*

*Wanda:* It's not happening because you won't let Bob do the important parenting jobs, like discipline.

*Counselor:* What do you mean "I won't let Bob be a parent?"

*Wanda:* I think you're afraid to let Bob be a real parent because Tim might decide he likes Bob better than he likes you. So you keep Bob away.

*Counselor:* That's not true. Bob really doesn't love Tim enough to worry about him.

*Wanda:* That's not true, Wanda, and you know it. Bob loves Tim a lot. He worries about Tim. But he worries more about you and your relationship to Tim, and that's why he doesn't get involved.

*Counselor:* I hate it when you say these things.

*Wanda:* I know it hurts, but you better wake up, Wanda, or you're going to lose both of them someday.

The counselor and Wanda ended the exercise at this point. Wanda had said some very self-revealing things and was beginning to show some discomfort with her revelations. Sensing that Wanda was beginning to reach a saturation level, the counselor decided to allow her some time to integrate the ideas and feelings that had been aroused. After stopping the exercise, they took time to discuss the confrontation. During this discussion, Wanda began to relax and look more comfortable with herself. It was a very significant session and proved to be a turning point in Wanda's counseling, when she acknowledged to herself for the first time that her husband was conflicted between his love for Tim and his concern for her relationship with Tim.

### The Empty Chair

The *empty chair* is a dialoguing exercise made popular by Gestalt therapists but used increasingly by counselors from a wide range of orientations. It is used to help clients explore and develop awareness of subtle feelings that are not surfacing but are affecting client functioning. The exercise may be used with *interpersonal* issues (in which case, the enactment will be between the client and the other relevant person) or with *intrapersonal* issues (in which case, the enactment will be between the client and the client's *other self*).

The counselor begins by explaining that this is a dialogue or imaginary conversation either with oneself or with a specific person who is also involved in the client's problem. The counselor explains that his or her role will be to observe, choreograph the conversation, and at times interrupt to ask questions or share observations. If the client agrees, the next step is to define who the two principals in the conversation will be; that is, who the client will converse with. This might be the *embarrassed self* or the *intimidated self,* or it might be the client's parent, spouse, or significant other.

The counselor must be able to recognize the splits in awareness or the potential conflicts in order to define the elements of the dialogue. The next step is to explain to the client how the process works.

> *In this exercise you will be both the "caring you" and the "angry you." And the two "yous" will talk it over and explore both points of view, both sides. Let's start by having the caring you explain why you don't want to talk to your parents about their decision. Then I'd like the angry you to react to the caring you. Is it clear what you will do? Remember, I'll be right here, coaching when you need help.*

Greenberg (1979) refers to this arrangement as the *experiencing chair* and the *other chair.* The experiencing chair is similar to what happens in most therapeutic settings. The other chair represents the internal objects—opposing will, conflicting values, or motivations—of which the client is possibly unaware but which have a significant effect on the client's emotions, actions, and choices. The case of Paula illustrates how the counselor helps the client begin this exercise.

### Case Illustration of the Empty Chair

*Paula and the Empty Chair*

Paula is a young woman in her mid-twenties who has just landed the job of her life. In addition to this, she is currently involved in a most fulfilling intimate relationship with another woman, Sue, who is in medical school and will be starting her residency next year. Sue has an opportunity to stay at the local hospital but she also is exploring several opportunities to do specified residencies in other states. Paula has very mixed feelings about this. On the one hand, being in love with Sue, she wants what is best for her even if that means Sue has to leave town to get the best training. On the other hand, Paula has her own interests to look out for and she doesn't want Sue to leave because the relationship is so good.

Paula wanted to explore these conflicting feelings and the counselor suggested the empty chair intervention as a way to do this. When Paula agreed, the counselor described the exercise and then asked Paula which of her conflicted feelings seemed the strongest. She identified the feelings associated with Sue's leaving. Then the counselor asked Paula to begin in one chair by explaining to the empty chair across from her those feelings associated with Sue's possible departure.

*Paula #1 (who wants Sue to stay to Paula #2):*

I just don't want her to go. We have such a good thing going. I don't understand why she has to leave when she could do her residency here.

*Continued*

[Counselor directs Paula to move to the other chair and be the other Paula]

*Paula #2 (part who wants Sue to do what is best for Sue):*
Well, you know the answer to that. Staying here probably isn't the best thing for her—she'll get better training somewhere else. She's so talented she needs to get the best training she can.
[Counselor moves Paula back to Chair #1]

*Paula #1:*
But if she really loved me, she'd stay . . .
[Moving to Chair #2]

*Paula #2:*
And if you really loved her, you'd feel freer to let her go . . .
*(starts to cry)*

*Counselor:* Let's stop a minute. What are you aware of right now Paula?

*Paula:* I feel sad, really sad.

*Counselor:* Okay, stay with that feeling and see where it takes you.

*Paula:* You mean from this chair?

*Counselor:* Yes.

*Paula #2 (still weeping):*
The sadness feels deep. It feels like I really do want to let her go—I wouldn't want her to stay just because of me—but letting go is hard for me and I do feel sad (weeps now more easily).

*Counselor:* Try to accept how you are feeling and allow it to exist for a little while. (silence)

After a few minutes, Paula began to talk again. While she didn't feel wonderful, she felt much clearer about her feelings and her position on this issue.

Note that the counselor directed Paula's awareness to her feelings and then encouraged her to be accepting of those feelings that were aroused.

There are two distinct advantages to be derived from this technique: (a) the client's defenses that characterize the conflicting elements tend to diminish as she enacts the dialogue, thus permitting her to see elements of the relationship that she could not easily let herself see; and (b) Paula is able to accept two seemingly incompatible feelings and say to herself, both of these feelings are me.

### Dreamwork

A number of counseling approaches, including psychoanalysis, Gestalt therapy, individual (Adlerian) therapy, and analytical (Jungian) therapy, make use of dreams in the therapeutic process. In some cases, the dream content is taken as relevant insight into the client's psyche. In other cases, the dream is a metaphor to be used in the session to explore alternative realities. This can be illustrated through the Gestalt treatment of dreams in which the client is asked to explore the different elements of the dream to search for or allow awareness to emerge. The meaning of the various elements of the dream is always provided by the client. The following is an example of this type of dream treatment (Dye & Hackney, 1975).

### Case Illustration of Dreamwork

*Linda and Her Dream*

A college student (we shall call her Linda) reported that she had had the following dream:

*I was picked up by this very expensive limousine. When I got in, I was struck by the plushness of the seats, the fine woodwork on the dashboard, the extreme comfort. It was like all my needs were being taken care of. As we were driving, I turned and noticed the driver for the first time. He was an Oriental and was dressed in this chauffeur's uniform. He was unusually concerned for my welfare and my needs. I really felt taken care of by him too. We drove to this large, impressive house. It sat on a knoll and it had huge pillars in front, like a Southern mansion. We got out of the car and went into the mansion, which turned out to be a restaurant. I was relieved to discover this. Discovering it was a restaurant eased my concerns because I knew how to behave in a restaurant. After we were seated (the chauffeur and me), the waiter came and offered us menus to study. It was then I re-* *alized I was very hungry. We waited and waited for the waiter to return and take our orders, but no one came. As I started to look around for our waiter, I noticed that all the other customers in the restaurant were Orientals, and this surprised me. Finally I spotted our waiter, and I got up from the table and went to him and asked him to come take our order. He said he would be there momentarily. Again we waited for what seemed like a long time. Finally, I got up again and went to the waiter and asked him to please serve us. He apologized for the delay and asked us to move to another table where we would be served immediately. We were led out of the main dining room into another empty room that was all white and had one wall of glass windows. I sat down and then realized that there was only one chair at the table. I looked up to see the waiter and my chauffeur both smiling at me. Then I looked and saw for the first time that the windows had bars on them. I was trapped. For the first time, I realized that I was in a mental institution and I was the patient.*

This dream reflects several significant people, objects, and events that the client can be asked to role-play. She could be asked to be the limousine, the chauffeur, the large mansion, the restaurant, the waiter, the Oriental clientele, the white secondary dining room, the table with only one chair, the windowed wall, the bars on the windows, and the smiling waiter and chauffeur—a rich dream indeed. To try to role-play all of these options would require quite a bit of time. So the counselor might select from this list a smaller number of enactments. In that case, it is best to enact each role-play in the sequence in which it occurred in the dream.

The role-play is a dialogue that the client carries on with herself. As a result, it demands that the client use her imagination, often supplying information or details that were not in the original dream. This may be difficult for some clients to do, and it may be necessary to illustrate what you would have the client do in order that she understand. For example, Linda was first asked *to be the limousine.*

*Linda:* What do you mean?

*Counselor:* Be the limousine. If you were the limousine and could talk, what would you be saying to Linda.

*Linda:* I still don't think I understand.

*Counselor:* All right, I'll give you some help. Let's pretend that I am the limousine, and this is what I might be saying: "Hi, little one. Get in and let me show you how good I am."

*Linda:* Okay, I think I know what you mean.

*Counselor:* Good, now, you be the limousine. What would you be saying to Linda?

*Linda:* Hello, Linda. Get in and let me show you how good I can be for you. I want to wrap you in comfort and make you feel really good.

*Linda:* Thank you, I would like you to do those things to me. I want to feel safe, secure, and comfortable.

This first segment may be abbreviated (as it was with Linda). Getting into the spirit of the exercise takes time, and the counselor should not push the client to identify any potential relevance of the enactment to her life. For example:

*Counselor:* Linda, is there any significance in the dialogue between you and the limousine?

*Linda:* No, except that I like to be taken care of, and I think a lot of people would like to have that. That doesn't seem too unusual.

*Counselor:* Okay, let's go on to the next part of the dream, the driver that you suddenly notice. Can you describe the driver again?

*Linda:* Yes. He is a large, kindly looking man. He is Oriental. He doesn't smile or anything. But I can tell that he doesn't mean me any harm.

*Counselor:* Will you be the chauffeur now, talking to Linda?

*Linda:* Yes. Hello, Linda. I am glad you joined me. I have been worried about you. I want to help you decide where to go so you will make the right decision. I want to make these decisions for you because you can't make them for yourself.

*Counselor:* Now be Linda and respond to the chauffeur.

*Linda:* All right. I will do what you say. I know you can make better decisions than I can. I will do what you think is best.

*Counselor:* Linda, does the chauffeur remind you of anyone you know?

*Linda:* Yes, my father.

*Counselor:* Is he your father?

*Linda:* Yes, he is.

*Counselor:* You said he was Oriental.

*Linda:* Well, I had an Oriental friend who always masked his feelings, and that is the way it was with Dad. He *never* let me know where he was or what he was feeling.

Linda began to find meaning as she progressed through other elements of the dream with increasing investment. She was asked to be the large mansion talking to Linda, and the dialogue led her to identify the mansion as the imposing social system that she had been taught to respect and obey. Linda talked about her mixed emotions regarding the social system. She could feel lost in it, and that brought on anger and resentment that was bigger than she was.

Her discovery that the mansion was really a restaurant after she had entered it was also relevant to her. She compared the relief that she had experienced on discovering the restaurant to the relief she also felt when she realized that the social system was something she was very familiar with and knew how to play. The waiter who appeared so solicitous yet did not serve her was a further extension of her frustration at being unimportant within the system.

As Linda took on the role of the other customers in the restaurant, it became apparent to her that they were society sitting in judgment of her. She identified this through the cue that they were all faceless; thus she could not read their emotions. She drew the conclusion that they must be reacting to her, and the hiding of their emotions had to mean that judgment was harsh.

It was when Linda began to enact and interpret the final portions of her dream that the gestalt began to emerge. Finding herself alone in the second dining room—the total whiteness (the absence of stimuli), the discovery of the windowed wall that was covered with bars—led her to an intense emotional experience. She cried softly. The counselor asked her to talk about her tears. Where were they coming from? Who was she crying for?

Linda saw the final portions of the dream tying into an old fear. She confided that since she had been in high school, she had feared that she would go crazy someday and have to be committed to a mental institution. She said that while she was in high school, her father had had a nervous breakdown and had been in a mental hospital for several months. The mother had kept the details from the children, and they had had to create the details in their imaginations. Linda said she related strongly to her father and feared the same would happen to her. Feeling her weakness and vulnerability, identifying the chauffeur as her father, who wanted to take care of her but on his own terms, feeling the pressure of society, all of this Linda identified as the constant underlying heaviness that she carried around. She could also see that there were moments of strength, points at which she could exercise control. This came through her sense of the roles of society that she understood, and it was apparent to her in her ability to deal with the reluctant waiter.*

The use of dreamwork is limited, whether it be used as a Gestalt therapy intervention, a transactional analysis intervention, a Jungian intervention, or a psychoanalytic intervention. It does not always give the client instant insight. Nor it is predictably useful with culturally different clients where the content of dreams may have different cultural meanings. But it can offer material that the client can work with and thus generate awareness of underlying tensions. It allows the client to focus.

There are several guidelines to follow while working with dreams:

1. As a first step, have the client describe the dream from beginning to end without interruption.
2. Describe the procedure for role-playing the dream (dialoguing).
3. If the client appears uncertain about the process, give an example.
4. Be the *director* of the role-play. Ask the client to be each of the several parts of the dream.
5. Proceed with different parts of the dream in the order of their occurrence in the dream.
6. Do not allow yourself to make interpretations of the elements of the dream. Only the client can do that. Ask the client if he or she can find any relationships. If not, proceed to the next part of the dream.

*From H.A. Dye & H. Hackney, *Gestalt Approaches to Counseling*, Boston: Houghton Mifflin, 1975, pp. 62–67. Reprinted by permission.

## *Body Work Therapy*

An increasing number of affective interventions are derived from body work therapy known as bioenergetics (Lowen, 1974), core energetics (Pierrakos, 1990), and Radix (neo-Reichian) therapy (Kelley, 1979). The end goals of body work therapies are to help clients to express feelings when appropriate, and contain feelings when appropriate. Although each method varies in format, body work therapy generally works with muscular armor and breathing patterns to aid clients in reaching these two goals. Practitioners who use body work methods must have specialized training beyond a degree in counseling or its equivalent.

## *Client Reactions to Affective Interventions*

The point was made at the beginning of this chapter that many clients lack the introspective and interpersonal skills to express their feelings accurately and adequately. This does not mean that they do not experience feelings, nor does it mean that they do not need to express their feelings. The inability to express what one is feeling is often experienced as a pressure-cooker effect in which the bottled-up emotions accumulate and add to the person's tensions and anxiety. Eventually, the emotions find an outlet, either through psychosomatic illness, substance abuse, physical violence, temper tantrums, or some other socially destructive expression.

Given this kind of condition and its very limited alternatives, most clients experience relief at the expression of feeling states. Some also feel a kind of embarrassment, as though they had broken some unwritten rule about their behavior. The counselor can facilitate this effect by normalizing the feeling. To *normalize* is to point out that this reaction is a normal reaction and will pass in a matter of time. Occasionally, a client will continue, almost without limits, to talk about current or old feelings. It is as though an emotional dam has finally been broken. With White middle-class clients, the most common client response is a sense of relief, catharsis, and renewal that can lead to further change. Clients of some minority cultures in which the expression of feelings is not part of the culture's values, will not find a sense of relief and may, in fact, experience intense personal embarrassment.

## *Summary*

In this chapter we have examined the very complex subject of human emotions and their expression. You may think of affective interventions as efforts to aid clients in the expression of their innermost fears, hopes, hurts, resentments, and frustrations. Such expression often involves teaching clients how to express their feelings, and helping them to give themselves permission to express emotions. At another level, you may work with clients who are able to express emotions, but who are unable to sort out or conceptualize what they feel. Finally, at the most complex level, you may become involved in helping clients either to accept or integrate affect states, or to change affect states.

Whatever your involvement might be, it is vitally important to recognize that human emotions are central to human functioning. Consequently, when we work with emotions, we are working near the core of most human beings' reality. Thus, we are creating and walking through what amounts to a highly vulnerable passage for clients. Respect for this condition, and appreciation that clients invite us into their inner world, is both appropriate and essential.

## *Exercises*

1. Choose a partner. One of you will be the speaker; the other will be the listener. The speaker should select one of the four emotions identified (positive affect, anger, fear, and emotional pain) and communicate that feeling state to the other person. The listener should record on paper all verbal and nonverbal cues observed, but should not respond to the speaker. After three to five minutes, the exercise should be concluded, and the listener should identify the speaker's feeling state and the cues that support that choice. Check with the speaker to verify your choice.

2. The following is an exercise in verbal affect identification. Identify the feeling state(s) in each of the four client communications, which have been taken from actual counseling interviews. If more than one feeling state is present in the client response, place an asterisk (*) next to the one that you believe has the greatest bearing on the client's concern. After identifying the feeling states, discuss your choices with other class members.

   A. "Well, uh, I'm happy just being in with people and having them know me."
   B. "And, and, uh, you know, they always say that, you know, some people don't like to be called by a number; well, I don't either."
   C. "In speech, I'm, uh, well, in speech I'm not doing good because I'm afraid to talk in front of a bunch of people . . . "
   D. "It seems to me like working in that lab is really harmful; I mean, I enjoy my work, and the people, but that lab, that worries me."

3. This exercise is to be done in triads. One of you is to be identified as the first respondent; the other one listener; the third is the observer/recorder. Rotate all roles twice so each person is in each of the three roles.

    Listed below are some incomplete sentences. The observer's role is to feed each sentence to the respondent and to record the respondent's response. The respondent's task is to respond as quickly as possible *without thinking*. If as the respondent, you can't come up with a response, just go "blah, blah, blah." The listener's job is simply to face the respondent directly—watch, listen, and receive. After you have completed each round, give the respondent time to observe and process his/her affective states.

    Incomplete Sentences:
    1. Something I want you to know about me is . . . .
    2. Something I don't want you to know about me is . . . .
    3. Being angry for me is . . . .
    4. When I'm angry, I just want to . . . .
    5. Being sad for me is . . . .
    6. When I'm sad, I just want to . . . .
    7. Right now I'm feeling . . . .

## Discussion Questions

1. Does any part of working with client affective states worry you? How?

2. Two goals of affective interventions are: (1) to help the client express feeling states; and (2) to help the client identify and discriminate between feeling states. This implies that clients may be able to express feelings but still not be able to identify or sort out those feelings. Do you think this is possible? Isn't it likely that the expression of a feeling carries with it the awareness of what it is? Discuss this with other classmates or colleagues.

3. Which nonverbal cues communicate anger? Do these same cues communicate some other emotion? If yes, what emotion? How would you know which emotion is being communicated?

4. What are the potential therapeutic gains when using role reversal with a client? What kinds of clients might not be able to participate effectively in a role reversal exercise?

5. Referring back to the dreamwork example in this chapter, what was the counselor's role? What was the counselor's most chal-

lenging moment during the exercise? What was the client's most challenging moment?

## Recommended Readings

Cashdan, S. (1988). *Object Relations Therapy*, New York: W.W. Norton.

Gladding, S.T. (1988). *Counseling: A Comprehensive Profession*, Columbus, OH: Merrill. Chapter 4: The theory and practice of individual counseling: Affective approaches.

Hardy, R. (1991). *Gestalt Psychotherapy*, Springfield, IL: Charles C. Thomas.

Jacobs, E. (1992). *Creative Counseling Techniques*, Odessa, FL: Psychological Assessment Resources.

Kepner, J. (1993). *Body Process: Working with the Body in Psychotherapy*, San Francisco: Jossey-Bass.

Wegscheider-Cruse, S., Cruse, J., and Bougher, G. (1990). *Experiential Therapy for Co-dependency*, Palo Alto, CA: Science & Behavior Books.

Weiss, L. (1986). *Dream Analysis in Psychotherapy*, New York: Pergamon.

$$C \quad h \quad a \quad p \quad t \quad e \quad r \quad 8$$

# Cognitive Interventions

### Purpose of This Chapter—

How many times have you gotten yourself in trouble by thinking too much? Or by talking to yourself? Or because you had a bad attitude? This chapter examines the ways clients think themselves into problems, and describes interventions that the counselor can use to reverse this situation. These interventions operate on mistaken beliefs, attitudes or patterns of thinking and give the client the tools to change to more productive and accurate thoughts. Some cognitive interventions are quite simple. Others (e.g., the paradox) can be quite sophisticated. In this chapter we describe a variety of interventions and the manner in which they are applied in counseling.

### Considerations as You Read This Chapter—

- Many people apparently find it difficult to differentiate between their thoughts and their feelings. It is fairly common to hear a person say "I feel like you're right," when the more accurate statement is "I *think* you are right." A lot of thinking people have mislabeled their thoughts as feelings. Is this also the case with you?

- Thinking is a very special quality that human beings possess. But it also can be misused. When this happens, people can become depressed, physically ill, even suicidal. How does one get out of such difficulties? How does one get into these difficulties in the first place?

- What skills does a skilled helper need in order to be able to help people who have thought themselves into trouble?

Cognitions include our thoughts, beliefs, attitudes toward ourselves and others, and our perceptions of the world around us. Many people would say that they determine who we are, what we do, and how we feel. This view holds that *errors* in thinking, sometimes called faulty thinking, are especially likely to produce distressing emotions and/or problematic behavior. For example, the person who expects to fail, thinks that she is going to fail, and the result is that she approaches life events from a *failure* orientation. With this much going against her, the probability is great that she will fail. She could be described as having low self-esteem or lack of confidence, but in fact, she is approaching life with a self-defeating mentality, an "I don't think I can do it" life view. This type of person may benefit from strategies that focus primarily on changing beliefs, attitudes, and perceptions about self and others (Beck, 1976; Lazarus, 1981).

The application of cognitive therapeutic interventions is extensive. They have been applied as the primary intervention for such problems as anxiety reduction, stress management, anger control, habit control, obesity, depression, phobic disorders, and sexual dysfunction. Characteristics of clients who seem to have most success with cognitive interventions include:

Persons of average to above-average intelligence

Persons with moderate to high levels of functional distress

Persons with the ability to identify feelings and thoughts

Persons not in a state of crisis, psychotic, or severely debilitated by the problem

Persons possessing an adequate repertoire of skills or behavioral responses

Persons able to process information visually or auditorily

Persons whose cultural orientation is toward analytical activity

## Goals of Cognitive Intervention

The overall aim of any cognitive intervention is to reduce emotional distress and corresponding maladaptive behavior patterns by altering or correcting errors in thought, perceptions, and beliefs. Changes in behavior or feelings occur once the client's distorted thinking begins to change and is replaced by alternative, more realistic ways of thinking about self, other persons, or life experiences (Beck, 1976). Thus, a cognitive intervention is intended to alter a client's manner of thinking about a particular event, person, self, or in the larger context, life. Clients are viewed as direct agents of their own changes, rather than as helpless victims of external events and forces over which they have little control; although, there are some cognitive interventions that help clients by nudging them out of habitualized ways of thinking. Isn't this a little bit like mind control or brainwashing? No. With cognitive interventions, the issue of responsibility always remains with the client. That can only happen when the client *chooses* to think a particular way, or *chooses* to change the way he or she is thinking about something. This even includes choosing to participate in a cognitive intervention as part of the counseling strategy.

## Culture and Cognitive Processes

Culture embraces how we think about ourselves and how we view (think about) the world. Culture and cognition are very closely related. Our thought processes, especially when considered within a cultural context, are powerful and pervasive. They affect how we *feel* about ourselves, our *behavior*, and our *relationships with others*. Cognitive processes reflect one's cultural determinants more than feelings, behavior, or even interaction with other persons. The differentiations that must be made, when a counselor works with clients of differing cultures, is understanding the difference between those cognitions that are culturally determined (thus shared by others in that culture) and the cognitions that are individually unique to a specific client. In addition, the counselor must strive to understand how the client's cultural cognitions affect his or her feelings, behavior, and interactions with others. Cognitive patterns can change, but when they are as fundamental as one's cultural values and beliefs, they are more resistant to change. Indeed, it is ethically questionable whether the counselor should embark on such change.

## Analysis of Cognitive Problems

Cognitive strategies are heavily reliant on a particular manner of problem assessment. We begin with the assumption that people construct their reality according to their beliefs and attitudes. Some of that *construction* is distorted if our perceptions of self or others is distorted. Why would anyone distort perceptions? We learn these distortions from our parents, our peer groups, our teachers, our cultural group. Then we apply these distortions, along with our more accurate perceptions, to our construction of *our* reality. Problem assessment requires that the counselor and client, together, analyze these perceptions, looking for the flaws, errors, or inaccuracies that underlie one's conclusions. Only at that point can cognitive interventions be applied to change errors in thinking, repair cognitive flaws, or correct the inaccuracies.

## A-B-C-D Analysis

The A-B-C-D analysis is a cognitive strategy associated with rational-emotive therapy (Ellis, 1989). This approach was created in the 1950s by Albert Ellis who developed a *formula* for counselors to follow as they analyzed the client's patterns of thought. A represents the *activating event* which begins the faulty thinking pattern; B is the client's *belief system*, through which all life experiences are filtered; C represents the *consequence*, emotional or cognitive, that is produced by the interaction of A and B. These three steps represent the analysis portion of the formula. Once the cognitive errors have been detected, the counselor moves on to the therapeutic intervention, which involves disputation (D) of the irrational beliefs or thought patterns.

Differentiating between *rational* and *irrational beliefs* is the responsibility of the counselor. Rational beliefs are those that are truly consistent with reality—in the sense that they can be supported with data, facts, or evidence and would be substantiated by a group of objective observers. Rational beliefs may result in moderate levels of consequence (Cs), or emotional consequences, and are useful in helping people attain their goals. Irrational beliefs, on the other hand, are those that are not supported by reality through data, facts, or evidence and *would not* be substantiated by a group of objective observers.

Most irrational beliefs are reflected in one or more of Ellis's eleven irrational beliefs (see *Table 8-1*). According to Ellis (1989), people both create and maintain unnecessary emotional distress by continually reindoctrinating themselves with their irrational beliefs. Self-

**TABLE 8-1  Eleven Irrational Beliefs About Life**

1. I believe I must be loved or approved of by virtually everyone with whom I come in contact.
2. I believe I should be perfectly competent, adequate, and achieving to be considered worthwhile.
3. Some people are bad, wicked, or villainous, and therefore should be blamed and punished.
4. It is a terrible catastrophe when things are not as I would want them to be.
5. Unhappiness is caused by circumstances that are out of my control.
6. Dangerous or fearsome things are sources of great concern and their possibility for harm should be a constant concern for me.
7. It is easier to avoid certain difficulties and responsibilities than it is to face them.
8. I should be dependent to some extent on other persons and should have some person on whom I can rely to take care of me.
9. Past experiences and events are what determine my present behavior; the influence of the past cannot ever be erased.
10. I should be quite upset over other peoples' problems and disturbances.
11. There is always a right or perfect solution to every problem, and it must be found or the results will be catastrophic.

indoctrination is analogous to playing an audio tape in one's head over and over again until the tape's contents are the only reality the person knows. In the A-B-C analysis, the client learns to recognize activating events (A), corresponding *beliefs* about the event (B) that are in one's head, and the emotional-behavioral consequences (C) of interpreting the activating event by using the irrational belief(s). The counselor then teaches the client a variety of ways to *dispute* (D) the emotional beliefs that are leading to the consequence, and to replace these irrational beliefs with more accurate and rational beliefs. An example of the irrational thinking is illustrated in the following description of the case of Marguerite.

---

*The Case of Marguerite*

Marguerite entered counseling with the complaint that she was unable to establish and maintain long-term relationships with people. Her self-description was that of a lonely person, caring for others but not receiving the same caring in return from others. She also described herself as shy, sensitive, reserved, and socially inept. As counseling proceeded, Marguerite explained that her real problems were with men. She believed men were untrustworthy, self-serving, and insensitive to themselves and others. Asked how she had come to such conclusions, Marguerite explained that she and her mother had shared these "feelings" for years, probably resulting from the time her father abandoned the family. She illustrated this by describing a recent relationship with a male acquaintance, who at first, seemed to be pleasantly different from her experiences. After two or three weeks of casual conversations, however, he told her that he had taken a new job in another city and would be leaving in a few days. Marguerite took this announcement (A), screened it through her long-established views of men (B), and concluded that he had been dishonest with her from the beginning, withholding information about his new job, and thus, like all other men, could not be trusted by her (C).

---

## Getting to the A, or Activating Event

The *activating event* is usually some obnoxious or unfortunate situation or person in the client's life, and often the presence of this situation or person is part of what prompts the client to come for counseling. A client may say "I can't stand my husband. He's a slob," or "My marriage is a real disappointment to me." In helping clients identify the A, it is important for clients to understand that this external situation or event does not *cause* their feelings (which are their reactions to *a husband who is a slob*, or the reaction to *a disappointing marriage*).

It is also important to discriminate between activating events that can be changed and those that cannot. For those that can be changed, clients can use good problem-solving skills to bring about change. For those situations that are outside the client's control, it is important to focus on *reactions to the event* rather than the event itself.

### Getting at the C

C represents the emotional *consequences* of the activating event and often is what propels the client into counseling. People cannot tolerate bad or uncomfortable feelings too long, and if such feelings persist, they may be motivated to seek outside assistance. Examples of emotional consequences that lead clients into counseling include guilt, long-term anger, depression, and anxiety.

In order to identify the C accurately, the counselor must be alert to the presence of affect words the client uses and supporting body language or nonverbal cues indicative of emotion. The counselor then proceeds to ask the client what he (or she) is saying to himself about the activating event. Often this question must be asked several times before the client begins to realize what the message is. In particular, clients often fail to realize the self-evaluative component of the message (i.e., "My marriage is a disappointment to me, *and therefore I will be unhappy as long as I am married to this person"*).

### Getting at the Bs

Identifying the Bs, or the client's *belief system*, is a major focus of this particular therapeutic intervention. The client's beliefs about a specific activating event may be exhibited in one of two forms—rational beliefs (RBs) or irrational beliefs (IBs). Both RBs and IBs represent a client's evaluations of reality and self.

Rational beliefs are truly consistent with a person's reality—in the sense that they can be supported with data, facts, or other evidence and would be substantiated by a group of objective observers. RBs result in *moderate* levels of Cs, and tend not to be destructive. It is the IBs that cause people problems. And as a person accumulates more IBs, that person becomes more troubled, not realizing that it is his or her belief system that is the source of the problem.

### Disputing (D) the IBs

Generally clients have to be convinced that their belief systems are at the root of their problems. This is done by questioning and challenging the conclusions they have drawn regarding a particular event. Even when challenged, deeply committed irrational thinking must be addressed again and again until it transforms from *"I feel hurt by my marriage"* to *"I choose to feel hurt by my marriage."* At the point of recognizing *choice*, the client gains control of the situation and is free to choose a different reaction. The goal of disputation is twofold:

1. To eliminate the IBs
2. To acquire and internalize a new, more rational belief system

In order to achieve this twofold goal, disputation occurs in two stages: first, a sentence-by-sentence examination and challenge of any IBs must take place; and second, the irrational belief system must be replaced by a more rational and self-constructive belief system. Disputation can take any of three forms. It can be *cognitive*, or based on one's thoughts. It can be *imaginal*, drawing on one's fantasies of how life is. Or it can be *behavioral*, based on things that happen to the client.

## Case Illustration of A-B-C-D Analysis

The case of Yvonne illustrates how A-B-C-D analysis can be used with a case that extends over a period of time. The client was seen weekly for approximately twenty sessions.

---

*The Case of Yvonne*

Yvonne is a thirty-year-old who enters counseling because of "mood swings" and "depression." Assessment reveals that Yvonne's depression began about three years ago, following her divorce. During the last three years, Yvonne reports periodic bouts of depression that seem to stem largely from thoughts of failure and guilt. Specifically, Yvonne blames herself and feels like a failure because of the divorce. She states that she cannot get rid of thoughts that she is a failure and that she is to blame for the breakup of the marriage.

History and intake reveal Yvonne is of above-average intelligence and possesses a master's degree in business administration. She is currently employed as a marketing analyst for a large chain of fast-food restaurants. She dates some men from time to time but has not been involved in a serious or steady relationship since her divorce. She apparently is in excellent health.

After the intake and assessment sessions, the counselor proposed the use of the A-B-C-D analysis to Yvonne, explaining that perhaps Yvonne's problems were intensified by how she thought them through. This was acceptable to Yvonne.

First, the counselor asked Yvonne to identify any situations which she believed might be contributing to her

*Continued*

emotional distress. She stated, "If I were still happily married, I wouldn't feel this way." At this point, the counselor helped Yvonne to explore that statement and determine whether she had the power to change or not. When Yvonne indicated she did not, the counselor pointed out that her thoughts and feelings about the situation might change, even though the marriage was ended. Yvonne could not seem to separate these two ideas from one another, the divorce and the feelings of failure. The counselor tried again. If the two thoughts were *really* connected, then it would be true that if Yvonne were *still* married, she would be guaranteed happiness. Yvonne thought this could be true but didn't have to be true. The coun-

selor took this opening to point out that the opposite also didn't have to be true—that is, that because Yvonne was divorced, she didn't have to be unhappy.

This theme was to repeat itself over the next several sessions. With each repetition, Yvonne was more accepting of the possibility that marriage did not necessarily lead to happiness and that divorce did not necessarily lead to unhappiness. During this process, Yvonne was also starting to change her self-perception from that of a person who was vulnerable to life's misfortunes to that of a person who could weather life's misfortunes without having to be unhappy, defeated, or worthless.

At this point, the counselor and Yvonne are ready to spend some time working with the Bs—her beliefs, thoughts, or internal "self-talk." The counselor reiterates that some beliefs can cause unnecessary levels of emotional distress, particularly those that are self-defeating or cannot be supported by external evidence. The counselor gives some examples of Yvonne's irrational beliefs, and then contrasts them to more rational or self-enhancing beliefs. Thoughts such as "I'm a failure," "It's my fault the marriage didn't work," are presented to Yvonne as self-defeating and inaccurate. Thoughts such as "The marriage failed—but that doesn't mean the future has failed," and "The marriage fell apart but I am still intact," are more consistent with external evidence and thus more rational (and coincidentally, more self-enhancing). The counselor also has Yvonne practice saying to herself, "Just because my marriage ended does not mean *I have to* feel terribly upset and depressed."

As Yvonne grew increasingly able to dispute her IBs without the counselor's interventions, and to make a shift to different feelings and responses in her imagination, the counselor introduced systematic homework assignments designed to help Yvonne think and behave in new ways in her real-life environment. Through these homework assignments and her continued discussions with the counselor, Yvonne became increasingly skilled at recognizing her vulnerable trouble spots in her belief system and was able to replace them with more rational self-statements. As this process unfolded, she also realized that she was more comfortable and in greater self-control when she was in her cognitive context as opposed to her affective context. Counseling was terminated when Yvonne decided she was able to advance her progress on her own.

## *Cognitive Disputation*

*Cognitive disputation* makes use of persuasion, direct questions, and logical reasoning to help clients dispute their IBs. This is one of the few times in counseling where "why" questions are useful. Some examples of questions suggested for cognitive disputation by Walen, DiGuiseppe, and Dryden (1992, p. 159–162) include:

Is that good logic?

Is that true? Why not?

Can you prove it?

Why is that so?

Could you be overgeneralizing?

What do you mean by that term?

If a friend held that (self-downing) idea, would you accept it? In what way?

Is that very good proof?

Explain to me why (e.g., . . . you're so stupid you don't belong in college.)

What behaviors can you marshall as proof?

Why does it have to be so?

Where is that written?

Can you see the inconsistency in your beliefs?

What *would* that mean about you as a person?

Does that logically follow?

What's wrong with the notion that you're "special"?

How would you be destroyed if you don't . . . ?

Why must you?

Lets assume the worst. You're doing very bad things. Now why must you not do them?

Where's the evidence?

What would happen if . . . ?

Can you stand it?

As long as you believe that, how will you feel?

Lets' be scientists. What do the data show?

Counselors who use cognitive disputation need to recognize that this method can lead to client defensiveness. Counselors who rely on this disputation method need to be sensitive to resulting client responses, particularly to their nonverbal cues. It is important to realize that clients may have difficulty with the disputation process because they are unable to discriminate between IBs and RBs. When this occurs, persistence is called for, often supplemented by counselor modeling of the difference between an IB and RB.

*Imaginal disputation* relies on client imagery, and particularly on a technique known as *rational-emotive imagery*, or REI. This intervention is based on the assumption that the emotional consequences of imagery stimuli are similar to those produced by real stimuli. There are two ways this intervention can be applied. First, clients imagine themselves in the problem situation (the A) and then try to experience their usual emotional turmoil (C). Clients are instructed to signal to the counselor (usually with a raised index finger) when this occurs. As soon as they signal, the counselor asks them to focus on the internal sentences they are saying to themselves (usually IBs). Next, the counselor instructs them to change their feelings from extreme to moderate. The counselor points out that in doing this they are making the cognitive shift they need to make in real life.

In the second application of rational-emotive imagery, clients are asked to imagine themselves in the problematic situation, and then to imagine themselves feeling or behaving differently in this situation. As soon as they get an image of different feelings and behavior, they are instructed to signal to the counselor. The counselor then asks them to notice what they were saying or thinking to themselves in order to produce different feelings and responses. The counselor points out that these are the kinds of sentences or beliefs they need to use in real-life situations to produce different effects.

According to Maultsby (1984), rational-emotive imagery is an excellent therapeutic technique for taking rational ideas and mental pictures that initially 'feel wrong' and make them quickly start feeling right. He recommends that for maximum results, clients use REI several times daily for at least a week or two.

Counselors who use REI may do well to forewarn clients not to expect instant success and to remember to be patient with themselves, even to the point of expecting the new feelings and responses generated during the imagery to feel a little strange at first. Some clients may report that distracting thoughts intrude during REI. In these instances, it is usually helpful to encourage clients to let these thoughts pass and ignore them, but not force the distracting thoughts out of their awareness. Other clients may report difficulty in doing REI work because they cannot generate clear and vivid images during the imagery process. Maultsby (1984) indicates that the production of strong images is not crucial to the success of the technique, as long as clients continue to focus on rational self-talk and on expected new feelings and behaviors as intensely as possible during their daily practice sessions. Also, clients who cannot *picture* rational self-talk and new feelings and behaviors can be instructed to *think about* these aspects of the process instead (McMullin & Giles, 1981).

## *Behavioral Disputation*

In *behavioral disputation*, the client issues a challenge to the IBs by behaving in different ways, often in the opposite manner from previous ways of responding. Ultimately, behavioral disputation is almost crucial if the client's adoption of a more rational philosophy is to result in behavior change. Behavioral disputation usually takes the form of bibliotherapy (reading books and self-help manuals) and systematic homework assignments that involve both written and in vivo practice. Two specific disputation interventions are *desibels* (Ellis, 1971) and *countering* (McMullin & Giles, 1981).

---

*Desibels Intervention*

The *desibels intervention* (which stands for DESensitizing Irrational BELiefs) is used to help clients become aware of disturbances in thinking which simultaneously eliminate consequent distressing feelings. The intervention is usually introduced during the counseling session and then assigned as daily homework. Clients are asked to spend ten minutes each day asking themselves the following five questions and either writing responses on paper or recording their answers on a tape recorder:

1. What irrational belief do I want to desensitize and reduce?
2. What evidence exists for the falseness of this belief?
3. What evidence exists for the truth of this belief?
4. What are the worst things that could actually happen to me if I don't get what I think I must (or if I do get what I think I must not)?
5. What good things could I make happen if I don't get what I think I must (or if I get what I think I must not)?

---

The desibels intervention may be more effective if daily compliance with it is followed by some form of client self-reinforcement, such as engaging in an enjoyable activity.

*Countering* involves the selection and application of thoughts that argue against other thoughts. It consists of such activities as "thinking or behaving in an opposite direction, arguing in a very assertive fashion, and convincing oneself of the falsity of a belief" (McMullin & Giles, 1981, p. 6).

*Countering Intervention*

The *countering intervention* involves a process similar to desibels. Clients are asked to identify, both orally and in writing, counter arguments for each of their significant irrational or problematic beliefs, using the following six "rules" (from McMullin & Giles, 1981, pp. 67–68).

**1.** Counters must directly *contradict* the false belief. For example, if the irrational belief is "I'm a failure if my wife leaves me," a contradicting counter would be, "My wife's behavior is independent of my own success and accomplishments."

**2.** Counters are *believable* statements of reality. For example, a reasonable or believable statement of reality is, "I don't have to get straight *A*s in high school in order to get a reasonably good job," while "I don't have to go to high school to get a reasonably good job" is not.

**3.** Develop *as many* counters as possible in order to counteract the effects that the irrational beliefs have produced over time.

**4.** Counters are created and owned by the client. The counselor's role in developing counters is limited to coaching. This rule is important because clients are likely to be more invested in counters that they themselves generate. Also, effective counters are often highly idiosyncratic to specific clients.

**5.** Counters must be *concise.* Lengthy, long-winded counters are easily forgotten. The most effective counters are ones you can summarize in a few words.

**6.** Counters must be stated with *assertive and emotional intensity.* McMullin and Giles (1981, p. 68) explain the reason for this: "many clients begin countering in an automatic, mechanical and unconvincing way. [Instead], we have them repeat a counter nasally, then mechanically (i.e., without feelings), and then with vigor, filling their lungs with air and vehemently stating the new belief [similar to the popular TV advertisement, "I'm not going to pay a lot for this muffler!"]. This latter style of countering is what we are trying to produce.

After counters are developed, clients practice them in counseling and at home until *they convince themselves* of the wisdom of the counter. When this has occurred, their thinking pattern has changed from an irrational and dysfunctional thought to a rational and highly functional thought.

## *Injunctions and Redecision Work*

Transactional analysis (TA) offers us another type of cognitive intervention called the *injunction.* An injunction is defined as a parental-like message (verbal and/or behavioral) that tells children what they have to do and be in order to survive and to get recognition and approval. According to TA, children make early decisions based on the kinds of injunctions they have been taught about life. Although many of these early learnings have been appropriate for the situations in which they were taught, they are often inappropriate when carried into adulthood and applied to dissimilar situations. This cognitive TA intervention is meant to help clients become aware of the specific injunctions they accepted as children, to reexamine the effect of the intervention(s) for an adult, and then *to decide* whether they want to continue living according to the injunction(s) or to make a new decision. In the application of this technique, specific attention is given to thoughts or beliefs that accompany the long-ago learned injunction that may no longer be true or valid. These are then replaced (with the client's help) by new or different beliefs and thoughts that are needed to support a new decision.

---

*Transactional Analysis Injunction*

The *injunction intervention* uses the following counselor monologue with clients:

**1.** When you were growing up—say between the ages of four and eight—what things did Mom say to you that sounded negative or bad to do?

**2.** Now recall anything that Dad said to you that sounded negative or bad to do.

**3.** From the following list of injunctions, recall two or three that were used most frequently in your home when you were growing up:

Don't
Don't be
Don't be close
Don't be important
Don't be a child
Don't grow
Don't succeed
Don't be you
Don't be sane
Don't be well

Don't belong
Don't feel

**4.** Select one of these injunctions. Write or talk about the decision you made about yourself or your life based on that injunction.

**5.** What thoughts occur to you about this decision? Are they true? Should they affect how you feel and behave?

**6.** Determine whether this decision is appropriate for you now. If not, rewrite the decision in a way that makes it appropriate for the present. In your new decision, specify what you can realistically do to change your behavior. How will this new decision make you feel?

**7.** Develop a plan to put the new decision into effect. What could interfere with this? What thoughts could undermine this? What thoughts do you need to support your plan?

Redecision work may be particularly useful with clients whose current behavior is inappropriate in many situations and appears to be based on one or two parental-type messages they still hear or "play" as tapes in their heads.

## Case Illustration of Injunctions and Redecision Work

### The Case of Marie

Marie is a forty-year-old woman who is married, has two teen-aged children, works outside the home as an attorney, and cannot understand why she is so fatigued, overworked, and generally burned out. Moreover, in the past year, she has developed chronic tension headaches and a stomach ulcer. Marie discloses that she has attempted "to do it all and do it all perfectly" and has never really considered asking for help from family or friends; nor has she expressed her growing irritation and resentment over their lack of help and support.

In the second session, the counselor asked Marie to close her eyes and recall what it was like as a child growing up in her house. Next, the counselor asked Marie to recall anything she remembered Mom telling or showing her not to do when Marie was a child, or anything Mom said that sounded negative. Marie revealed that her mother always told her to do things as well as possible, preferably without any help. Marie recalled that her mother was a perfectionistic, an independent woman who never seemed to have any needs of her own and was always doing things for others.

When the counselor asked Marie to recall what she remembered Dad saying or doing, she stated that Dad always said, "Hold your tongue. Don't get upset or angry with other people, even if they really make you mad." Marie described her father as a very calm person outwardly, who never showed much feeling. He died of heart disease at the age of fifty.

The counselor helped Marie identify the typical injunctions she heard as a child that she still hears or follows in her present life. Marie identified three:

Don's ask for help or show needs or weaknesses.

Do everything as perfectly as possible.

Don't get angry.

She also revealed that she had decided to "work as hard and as independently as possible," and "keep all negative feelings to myself."

The counselor helped Marie explore how these decisions may have been useful as a child. For example, Marie learned to please her Mom and get strokes from her by doing things without error and by not "bugging" her for help. Similarly, she learned to please Dad and obtain recognition from him by being "just like Dad—a chip off the old block—able to handle anything without getting upset." [From a feminist perspective, the counselor has a responsibility to help Marie develop awareness of how growing up in a patriarchal culture produces and reinforces these sorts of injunctions, especially for women. So part of Marie's redecision work would be to develop consciousness about ideas she learned from her family and culture as a way to "keep her in her place" or to be a "nice girl." Part of becoming a woman is reevaluating those societal injunctions that prevent Marie from reaching her full potential as a person.] The counselor and Marie considered whether these two decisions were useful or were interfering in her present life. Marie concluded that her decisions to work independently and contain her feelings had resulted not only in severe stress for her, but also had kept her family and friends at a distance. When she expressed a desire to change these decisions, the counselor helped her to identify what new decisions would be helpful and realistic.

Over the next few sessions, Marie decided she would like to continue to be a hard worker but to ask for help and to express negative feelings whenever her stress approached a certain level. The counselor helped her develop a plan to supplement the new decisions with specific attention to the thoughts or cognitions that could impede or support the plan. Marie identified the following thoughts that could interfere with the plan:

I don't have the right to ask for help.
I should be able to do it all by myself.
I shouldn't burden anyone else with my feelings or needs.

Together, Marie and the counselor developed some alternative thoughts to support the plan:

I am a person who is worthy of asking for and getting help from others.
It is unrealistic for me to do everything alone.
I want my family and friends to be more involved in my life.

During the remaining sessions, the counselor continued to encourage Marie while she tried to implement her plan based on the new decisions she had made for herself. Gradually, she realized that she, rather than other people, presented the main obstacles to making the plan a success. She continued to work on ways in which she would support and carry out her new decisions.

## Cognitive Restructuring

*Cognitive restructuring* (Meichenbaum, 1972, 1991), also called *rational restructuring* (Goldfried, DeCenteceo, & Weinberg, 1974), involves identifying and altering irrational or negative self-statements of clients. It has been used to help athletes modify high performance anxiety (Hamilton & Fremouw, 1985), to change unrealistic expectations of couples in marital therapy (Baucom & Lester, 1986), and to alter cognitions around food for bulimic clients (Wilson, Rossiter, Kleifield, & Lindholm, 1986). This strategy also has been used successfully in treating depression in children, adolescents, and older adults (Matson, 1989; Yost, Beutler, Corbishley, & Allender, 1986), influencing career indecision (Mitchell & Krumboltz, 1987), treating phobias and panic disorders (Mattick & Peters, 1988; Clark & Salkovskis, 1989), and enhancing self-esteem (Pope, McHale, & Craighead, 1988; Warren, McLellarn, & Ponzoha, 1988).

Cognitive restructuring (CR) begins with an exploration of the client's typical thoughts when in a troublesome situation. These thoughts may include both self-enhancing (rational) thoughts as well as self-defeating (irrational) thoughts. The counselor queries the client regarding specific thoughts that occur *before, during*, and *after* the problematic situation (Fremouw, 1977). If the client has trouble recalling specific thoughts, the counselor may want to ask the client to maintain a record of self-statements during future problematic situations, using a daily log sheet (see *Figure 8-1*). Although this inquiry process is similar to RET, it is more specific in that thoughts are linked to situations, and the antecedents and consequences of these situations.

Another way to help clients identify their thoughts in problem-

---

Name: _____

Date: _____

Week: _____

| Negative Self-Statements: | | Situations: |
|---|---|---|
| 1. | 1. | |
| 2. | 2. | |
| 3. | 3. | |
| 4. | 4. | |
| 5. | 5. | |
| 6. | 6. | |
| 7. | 7. | |

SOURCE: M. Fremouw, *A Client Manual for Integrated Behavior Treatment of Speech Anxiety* (JSAS Catalogue of Selected Documents in Psychology, 1977). Reprinted by permission of author.

**FIGURE 8-1  Example of Daily Log**

related situations is to describe situations and ask them to attend to their inner dialogue. For example, "Imagine yourself boarding a commercial airplane. Listen to your internal dialogue as you sit down and strap yourself into the seat. Look out of the window at the plane wing. What are you looking for? What are you saying to yourself?"

Transactional analysis counselors will use a situation such as the above to help clients become more aware of *who* is talking in the dialogue. For example, is it a critical or nurturing parent, a reasonable, logical adult, an impulsive or spontaneous child, or a feeling child? (These are referred to in TA as *ego states*.)

## *Introduction and Use of Coping Thoughts*

After the client has identified typical negative self-statements or thoughts surrounding problem situations, the learning process begins for substituting a variety of coping self-statements or thoughts. These are similar in both content and function to the assertive thoughts used in the thought-stopping procedure. The use of coping thoughts is crucial to the overall success of the CR intervention. Awareness of negative or irrational self-statements is necessary but not usually sufficient to result in enduring change unless the client learns to produce incompatible self-instructions and behaviors as well (Meichenbaum, 1977).

When introducing coping thoughts, the counselor emphasizes their importance and their role in affecting the client's resulting feelings and behaviors. To help the client understand the difference between coping and noncoping thoughts, the counselor may give examples of each. Often it is helpful to teach clients a variety of coping thoughts when the need to cope or intensity of a feeling may vary with the situation. For example, the client may find it helpful to use particular coping *before* a problematic situation occurs. Or *during* the situation, the client may need to utilize coping thoughts that help to confront a challenge or to cope with a difficult moment. *After* the situation, clients can learn coping thoughts to encourage themselves or to reflect on what they learned before, during, and after the problem situation occurrence. A list of potentially useful coping statements for before, during, and after problem situations appears in *Table 8-2*. It is not helpful, however, to give a list of coping statements to clients.

---

*Example of a coping thought:*

Self-defeating statement: *I am afraid of this airplane.*

Coping statement: *This airplane has just been inspected by a specialist in aviation safety.*

**TABLE 8-2  Examples of Coping Thoughts Used in Cognitive Restructuring**

| | | | |
|---|---|---|---|
| **Before Situation** | *Preparing for a stressor* (Meichenbaum & Cameron, 1973a)<br><br>What is it you have to do?<br>You can develop a plan to deal with it.<br>Just think about what you can do about it. That's better than getting anxious.<br>No negative self-statements; just think rationally.<br>Don't worry; worry won't help anything.<br>Maybe what you think is anxiety is eagerness to confront it. | *Preparing for a provocation* (Novaco, 1975)<br><br>What is it that you have to do?<br>You can work out a plan to handle it.<br>You can manage this situation.<br>You know how to regulate your anger.<br>If you find yourself getting upset, you'll know what to do.<br>There won't be any need for an argument.<br>Time for a few deep breaths of relaxation. Feel comfortable, relaxed, and at ease.<br>This could be a testy situation, but you believe in yourself. | *Preparing for a painful stressor* (Turk, 1975)<br><br>What is it you have to do?<br>You can develop a plan to deal with it.<br>Just think about what you have to do.<br>Just think about what you can do about it.<br>Don't worry; worrying won't help anything.<br>You have lots of different strategies you can call upon. |
| **During Situation** | *Confronting and handling a stressor* (Meichenbaum & Cameron, 1973a)<br><br>Just "psych" yourself up; you can meet this challenge.<br>One step at a time; you can handle the situation.<br>Don't think about fear; just think about what you have to do.<br>Stay relevant.<br>This anxiety is what the counselor said you would feel. It's a reminder to use your coping exercises.<br>This tenseness can be an ally, a cue to cope.<br>Relax; you're in control. Take a slow deep breath. Ah, good. | *Confronting a provocation* (Novaco, 1975)<br><br>Stay calm. Just continue to relax.<br>As long as you keep your cool, you're in control here.<br>Don't take it personally.<br>Don't get all bent out of shape; just think of what to do here.<br>You don't need to prove yourself.<br>There is no point in getting mad.<br>You're not going to let him get to you.<br>Don't assume the worst or jump to conclusions. Look for the positives.<br>It's really a shame that this person is acting the way she is.<br>For a person to be that irritable, he must be awfully unhappy.<br>If you start to get mad, you'll just be banging your head against the wall. So you might as well relax.<br>There's no need to doubt yourself. What he says doesn't matter. | *Confronting and handling the pain* (Turk, 1975)<br><br>You can meet this challenge.<br>One step at a time; you can handle the situation.<br>Just relax, breathe deeply and use one of the strategies.<br>Don't think about the pain, just what you have to do.<br>This tenseness can be an ally, a cue to cope.<br>Relax. You're in control; take a slow deep breath. Ah, good.<br>This anxiety is what the trainer said you might feel. That's right! it's the reminder to use your coping skills. |

196

| | Coping with the feeling of being overwhelmed (Meichenbaum & Cameron, 1973a) | Coping with arousal and agitation (Novaco, 1975) | Coping with feelings at critical moments (Turk, 1975) |
|---|---|---|---|
| During Situation | When fear comes, just pause. Keep the focus on the present; what is it you have to do? Label your fear from 0 to 10 and watch it change. You should expect your fear to rise. Don't try to eliminate fear totally; just keep it manageable. You can convince yourself to do it. You can reason your fear away. It will be over shortly. It's not the worst thing that can happen. Just think about something else. Do something that will prevent you from thinking about fear. Describe what is around you. That way you won't think about worrying. | You're muscles are starting to feel tight. Time to relax and slow things down. Getting upset won't help. It's just not worth it to get so angry. You'll let him make a fool out of himself. It's reasonable to get annoyed, but let's keep the lid on. Time to take a deep breath. Your anger is a signal of what you need to do. Time to talk to yourself. You're not going to get pushed around, but you're not going haywire, either. Try a cooperative approach. Maybe you are both right. He'd probably like you to get really angry. Well, you're going to disappoint him. You can't expect people to act the way you want them to. | When pain comes just pause; keep focusing on what you have to do. What is it you have to do? Don't try to eliminate the pain totally; just keep it manageable. You were supposed to expect the pain to rise; just keep it under control. Just remember, there are different strategies; they'll help you stay in control. When the pain mounts you can switch to a different strategy; you're in control. |

| | Reinforcing self-statements (Meichenbaum & Cameron, 1973a) | Self-reward (Novaco, 1975) | Reinforcing self-statements (Turk, 1975) |
|---|---|---|---|
| After Situation | It worked; you did it. Wait until you tell your therapist about this. It wasn't as bad as you expected. You made more out of the fear than it was worth. Your damn ideas—that's your problem. When you control them, you control your fear. It's getting better each time you use the procedures. You can be pleased with the progress you're making. You did it! | It worked! That wasn't as hard as you thought. You could have gotten more upset than it was worth. Your ego can sure get you in trouble, but when you watch that ego stuff you're better off. You're doing better at this all the time. You actually got through that without getting angry. Guess you've been getting upset for too long when it wasn't even necessary. | Good, you did it. You handled it pretty well. You knew you could do it! Wait until you tell the trainer about which procedures worked best. |

SOURCE: D. Meichenbaum and D. Turk, "The Cognitive-Behavioral Management of Anxiety, Anger, and Pain," in P.O. Davidson (Ed.), *The Behavioral Management of Anxiety, Depression and Pain.* Copyright 1976 by Brunner/Mazel, Inc. Reprinted by permission.

They appear to benefit far more when they individualize their own coping statements and choose ones that reflect both their preferences and realistic alternatives (Chaves & Barber, 1974).

### *Shifting from Self-Defeating to Coping Thoughts*

After identifying coping thoughts, the client must still learn how to shift from well-practiced self-defeating thoughts to the new coping thoughts. This is not an easy or natural process. It must be practiced, once the client has learned to recognize the intrusion of the self-defeating thought. Sometimes it helps for the counselor to model this process for the client first. For example, a counselor could model the shift for a client who is waiting for an important job interview:

> *Okay, I'm sitting here waiting for them to call my name for this interview. Wish I didn't have to wait so darn long. I'm getting really nervous. What if I blow it (self-defeating thought)? Now, wait a minute. That doesn't help (cue to cope). It will probably be only a short wait. Besides, it gives me a chance to sit down, relax, pull myself together, take some deep breaths, and review not only what I want to emphasize, but also what I want to find out about this employer. I'm going to be sizing up this person, too. It's not a one-way street (coping thought established before the situation in the form of planning).*
>
> *Okay, now they're calling my name. I guess it's really my turn now. Wow, my knees are really shaking. What if I don't make a good impression (self-defeating thought and cue to cope)? Hey, I'm just going to do my best and see what I can learn from this, too (coping thought).*

### *Differences Between RET and Cognitive Restructuring*

It is important to note that Meichenbaum's cognitive restructuring procedure differs from Ellis's RET approach in several ways. First, Meichenbaum (1991) believes that the "C" or consequence in Ellis's A-B-C-D model is not just the result of beliefs, but also feelings, physiological processes, and environment. Second, he holds that emotional consequences play a large role in the development and resolution of the client's issues. Finally, Meichenbaum believes that the "Bs" or beliefs in Ellis's A-B-C-D model are not the sole cause of problematic emotional consequences. Instead, specific beliefs are parts of larger cognitive organizing patterns which Meichenbaum calls *personal schemas*. His research has revealed that primary cognitive

schemas associated with *anxiety* are loss of control and well-being; cognitive schemas associated with *depression* are loss and rejection; and primary schemas associated with *anger* are equity and fairness.

## *Paradoxical Interventions*

Another form of cognitive restructuring is often referred to as paradoxical thinking. The paradox often is just the opposite of what would seem rational to the client, although it may be rational from a different perspective. It perhaps comes as no surprise that not everything that you or I think is rational. But, unless questioned or challenged, I choose to think of my cognitive processes as rational. The meanings that I attach to objects, persons, or situations may not all pass the test of rationality. Many may not. How does one challenge a client's irrationality? The most commonly used paradoxical interventions include *reframing, symptom* or *problem prescription, restraining*, and *positioning* (Dowd & Milne, 1986).

## *Reframing*

*Reframing* is the gentle art of viewing or thinking about a situation differently. Within a counseling context, it is much more than a Pollyanna view of life. In fact, reframing (also called reformulation) is the counselor's attempt to take the definition of the problem and redefine it in such a way as to open the door to viable solutions. It has been favored by an interesting variety of theories, ranging from existentialists to strategic family therapists. Sometimes reframing amounts to redefining an unsolvable problem as solvable or viewing the problem as not a problem at all. Other times, the reframe cuts through unfounded assumptions about either the person or the problem and provides a fresh and uncomplicated approach to the issue at hand. Madanes (1981) even included bizarre behavior as reframable, suggesting that it be relabeled "as discourteous communication, in that others cannot understand it or in that it upsets others" (p. 130). In its simplest form, reframing takes a relatively simple thought or opinion that is subject to interpretation, and offers a differing interpretation to that which is held.

Therapeutic reframing is most effective when it redefines an offensive motive or behavior as inept but well intended, thus making the behavior more personally or socially acceptable. It may be used equally well with the individual client who is dealing with intrapersonal issues or with the person who is reacting to interpersonal issues. The critical test for an effective reframe is that the alternative meaning is totally credible and believable. Thus, the mother's over-bearing behavior may also be viewed as her inability to communicate her love, or the student's compulsive behavior may be viewed as her attempt to lighten her mother's parenting responsibilities. Only when this credibility criterion has been met is the client likely to accept the new meaning and discard the dysfunctional older meaning.

### Symptom Prescription

Symptom (or problem) prescription involves instructing the client:

> to perform the problem behavior deliberately or even to exaggerate it; for example, an anxious individual is told to deliberately become as anxious as possible in problem situations. (Dowd & Milne, 1986, p. 263)

When a paradoxical intervention is given, it produces a therapeutic double bind. If the client follows the instruction, and deliberately becomes more anxious, that compliance with the instruction actually brings the anxiety under the control of the client. Discovering that the anxiety is controllable is a first and necessary step toward symptom control.

Types of problems that lend themselves to *symptom prescription* are those in which the client feels no sense of control, such as compulsive worrying. The earlier example of thought stopping included the assignment that the client should set aside five minutes of each hour to worry. This part of the assignment was an example of prescribing the problem. Another example would involve the client who suffers from insomnia and reports a long list of solutions that have been tried but found lacking. Insomnia tends to be accompanied by excessive or even compulsive rumination. The typical complaint is that "I just can't seem to turn my mind off when I go to bed."

Given this complaint, the counselor may wish to prescribe the symptom, which would be for the client not to try to go to sleep, even if it requires doing some other task. The point of this intervention is that we can be trapped into fighting ourselves when we try to control a spontaneous process (falling asleep). Trying to control its opposite (staying awake) somehow manipulates our internal processes such that we can then let go. Yet another example, one that is used frequently and with considerable success, is to warn the client not to expect to get over a crisis too quickly. By prescribing the symptom, in this case, the client's fear that the crisis will not recede, the counselor may actually help the client recover more quickly. Such is the paradoxical nature of the psyche.

### *Resisting Therapeutic Change*

A final paradoxical intervention comes in the form of cautioning clients against change or warning them that they are improving too quickly. When used in this manner, the paradox is called *restraining*. It offers a preventive prescription to client resistance to change. Fisch, Weakland, and Segal (1982) described this intervention with a variety of presenting problems. It can be used alone or as part of a more complex intervention. There are many cases in which the counselor can outline what needs to be done to improve a situation but can then add a caution to the considered change. Clients can be warned that they are improving too rapidly and should slow down the process of change. For example a client in divorce counseling might be cautioned if he or she is feeling "single" too soon (sooner than the statistics indicate is normal). If the person suffers a relapse, the counselor has buffered the setback by saying it is normal; if the person continues to change in a therapeutic direction, then the implication is that the client is making a better than normal recovery.

---

*The Case of Sue*

Sue is a twenty-nine-year-old divorcee of three months. She has made a dramatic adjustment to the divorce, a fact she attributes to her long and emotionally draining pre-divorce separation. Nevertheless, she sometimes wonders if she is moving too quickly.

The counselor picked up on this concern and decided to introduce a paradoxical restrain. Suggesting that she might be deceived by the rapid progress she had made, the counselor cautioned that Sue might encounter a temporary relapse during the course of her adjustment. She accepted this caution and thanked the counselor for the warning. The caution achieved two important results: (1) it was indeed possible that she would have a temporary relapse and should it happen, Sue would be less likely to fear that all her gains were imagined; and (2) the notion that she remained somewhat vulnerable led her to exercise some caution as she made new growth decisions. As a postscript, the relapse never happened.

---

### *Positioning*

We have all encountered persons who seemed to elicit positive statements from others by being overly negative about themselves. Examples include the office worker who volunteers that she is poorly organized to draw praise from others regarding her good organization, or the student who complains about not understanding, when clearly the student is in full command of the subject. When this occurs in the counseling session, if the counselor agrees with a client's negative self-assessment, it sabotages the client's power game that is implicit in such communication patterns. In fact, "the counselor can enhance the power of the strategy by exaggerating the negative statement, often eliciting a response such as 'I'm not *that* bad!' from the client" (Dowd & Milne, 1986). The *positioning* response can be effective with clients who use negative self-assessments as a manipulative tool. It should not be used with clients who have *truly negative self-images*, however, because it could exacerbate their problem.

### A Final Point

Paradox is both subtle and sophisticated as an intervention, and it takes a good amount of practice to master. On the other hand, you may find yourself saying, "The paradox could be true. Maybe the symptom *is* hiding another problem, or perhaps the person *is* afraid to change." If you had either of these reactions, you are experiencing an important aspect of the therapeutic paradox. A good paradox contains a deeper truth. This is precisely why the intervention is so powerful. Some proponents suggest that you not use paradox unless you firmly believe you are addressing the truth . . . a truth the client cannot yet acknowledge, except in symbolic form.

## Client Reactions to Cognitive Strategies

Clients are likely either to respond beautifully to cognitive interventions or find them totally meaningless. When clients respond positively to these approaches, they are likely to be people who are intelligent, witty, present neurotic symptoms, generate pictures or internal dialogue easily, and value the art of logical thinking. Clients who are turned off to cognitive approaches may be in crisis or have more severe problems, want or need a great deal of emotional support and warmth from the counseling relationship, process information kinesthetically, and react to issues and make decisions emotionally. It is difficult to use cognitive strategies successfully with clients who are resistant to them. Other types of interventions may be more useful with these clients.

In addition to the above reactions, there are other typical reactions which are likely to occur initially after introducing cognitive interventions. By anticipating these reactions, you will be better able to handle them when and if they occur.

One reaction has to do with the language or labels used by some counselors when using cognitive interventions. When the counselor describes the client's thoughts or beliefs as *irrational, mistaken,* or *il-*

*logical*, clients sometimes perceive that they themselves, as well as their ideas, are being attacked. This may be especially true for some types of clients (rebellious teenagers or rigid adults, for example). Clients are also likely to have negative reactions if the counselor's labels are given in the context of highly directive, active, and confrontational therapeutic style, particularly if the counselor has not established a strong rapport with the client at the outset.

There are several possible ways you can circumvent this reaction from clients. One is to avoid the use of emotionally charged terms. One study (Baker, Thomas & Munson, 1983) found that teenagers, for example, were much more amenable to a cognitive approach when the term "clean up your thinking" was used in place of "irrational thoughts." Another way to avoid this potential pitfall is for you to remove yourself from the position of determining which of the client's beliefs are rational or irrational. Instead, this procedure can be performed by the *client (if he/she is capable)*, thus eliminating the possibility of a power struggle or misunderstandings between you and the client.

A second fairly typical client reaction is initial disbelief at the counselor's proclamation that their thoughts, rather than external events or other persons, cause distressing feelings. A client may say, "I told you I wouldn't feel this way if it weren't *for her*," or "*for it*" (it meaning an outside event). In fact, in initial interviews with clients, many of them believe that everything *except their thinking* is causing the problem. In their eyes, the problem is a parent, or a spouse, their family-of-origin, how they were raised as children, unconscious material, and so on.

How can a counselor deal with a client's disbelief in a sensitive and yet informative manner? One way is to spend an adequate amount of time describing the rationale on which cognitive interventions are based, thus providing an adequate conceptualization of these strategies to the client. Often this may mean that the counselor devotes at least one session to instructional purposes regarding the nature of human problems, and possible corresponding treatment approaches. It is important for counselors to do this with clinical sensitivity in a way that avoids blaming or repudiating the client's ideas. As Meichenbaum (1977) has observed:

> [t]he purpose of providing a framework is not to convince the client—perhaps against his will—that any particular explanation of his problem is valid but rather to encourage him to view his problem from a particular perspective and thus accept and collaborate in the therapy that will follow. (pp. 150–151)

For cognitive interventions to work, it is important in your rationale to refute the "situation/people cause problems/feelings" theory and to subsequently explain how thoughts create undesired feelings and behaviors. This explanation usually is more helpful if realistic examples and analogies are used. For example, McMullin and Giles (1981) use the following sorts of examples with clients:

> *When my daughter was three, she used to watch monster shows on TV and get scared. When she was five, she watched the same shows and laughed like crazy. The situations were the same, but the consequences were different. Why do you think this was so?*
>
> *A New Yorker went to Texas to visit his friend. As they were driving in the desert, the New Yorker spotted what he thought was a boulder in the road, and frantically tried to grab the wheel. The Texan, however, said, "Relax. It's just a mesquite bush." Do you see how it was what the New Yorker thought about the bush that caused his panic? (Snygg & Combs, 1949).*
>
> *Two men over-ate one night and woke up the next morning feeling sick. One went to the doctor in a panic, and the other simply took it easy until he felt better. The first man was saying something pretty scary to himself. What do you think that might have been?* (p. 34)

Clients can also be asked to describe examples from their life in which beliefs affect feelings or to provide examples of how a belief affects the behavior or feeling of a friend or relative. Another technique involves asking clients to describe a myth, fairy tale, or superstition they believed as a young child but no longer believe as an older child, teenager, or adult (McMullin & Giles, 1981).

Clients can be helped to realize that their thoughts can affect feelings and behaviors by using the *distancing* technique (Beck, 1976; McMullin & Giles, 1981). The client is given a list of either irrational beliefs or beliefs that often contribute to emotional distress and asked to pick one belief from each list (for example, "Other people should do what I want them to do.") and to imagine that this belief is *injected* into the head of a passer-by. The client is then asked to state how this person's behavior and feelings would be affected by having this new belief in his head.

Finally, there is always the possibility that cognitive interventions do not produce desired changes in particular clients' feelings and behaviors. If after repeated use of a cognitive procedure the client's level of distress does not diminish, the counselor's original assessment of the client's problem may have to be reexamined.

## Summary

In this chapter, we discussed a variety of interventions that deal primarily with influencing changes in clients' cognitions, beliefs, and "self-talk." Cognitive interventions may be used to reduce emotional distress and modify inappropriate behavioral patterns by correcting errors in client's thoughts and beliefs.

A core cognitive intervention we described is the A-B-C-D analysis. This intervention is used to teach clients to recognize that beliefs, not external events, cause distressing emotional and behavioral consequences. Accepting this notion carries with it accepting responsibility for one's feelings and behaviors as well. Clients then are taught a variety of ways to dispute irrational beliefs.

A cognitive intervention associated with transactional analysis is redecision work. This involves helping clients identify injunctions *(don'ts)* they learned at an early age and any decisions they made based on such injunctions. Clients then learn to evaluate the appropriateness of early decisions for their present life and, if necessary, to revise the decision. Particular attention is paid to the thoughts and beliefs that support or underlie old and new decisions.

Finally, we examined cognitive restructuring, which includes identification and alteration of negative or self-defeating thought patterns and the more subtle paradox interventions, including reframing, symptom prescription, restraining, and positioning. All of these interventions have the same ultimate objective, to identify and modify those thought patterns that lead to self-defeating behaviors or thinking.

## *Exercises*

**I.** *Conduct an A-B-C-D analysis for a problem you experience personally.*

1. Identify an external event (person or problem situation) that consistently evokes strong and unpleasant feelings for you. Identify and list in writing typical thoughts you have about this situation. Examine them. Do your usual thoughts indicate that you believe this situation is what causes your distressed feelings? If so, try to write examples of different or new thoughts about the situation in which you take responsibility for your feelings. For example, you might try using an "I" message: "I feel _____ ," rather than "This situation or person makes me feel _____ ."

2. Identify the specific emotions or feelings that are distressing or uncomfortable. List them. Next, rate the usual intensity of such feelings on a scale of 1 to 10 (1 = not intense; 10 = very intense).

3. For each emotion or feeling you listed in Step 2 above, identify any thoughts or self-talk that goes on before and during the occurrence of these feelings. If this is difficult for you, ask yourself questions such as: What goes through my mind when I feel this way? What am I thinking about before and during these feelings?

List these thoughts in writing for each emotion. Examine your list and categorize your thoughts as either rational, true beliefs, or irrational, false beliefs. Remember that if the belief can be supported by data, facts, or evidence and can be substantiated by an objective observer, it is an RB. If it cannot be supported, it is an IB.

You may need to continue Step 3 during actual situations. As these distressing feelings actually present themselves, become aware of your thoughts surrounding these feelings.

**4.** Examine and challenge each IB you listed in Step 3 above on a sentence-by-sentence basis. Use questions such as the following to challenge each of these beliefs:

What makes it so?

Where is the proof?

Let's be scientists—find the supporting data. Where is the evidence for that? Next, for each IB on your list, develop at least two "counters" for that belief. Recall that a counter is a statement that is directly opposite to the false belief, yet is a believable statement of reality. Make each counter as concise as possible. After developing these counters, repeat them aloud—first, mechanically, next with as much vigor and emotional intensity as possible. Finally, practice countering your IBs by whispering or thinking the counter to yourself. During the next two weeks, use the counters with actual situations. Each time you become aware that you are starting to think an IB, whisper or think to yourself the counters you have developed to challenge that IB.

**5.** Become aware of any new effects of using this process over the next few weeks. Identify and list any *behavioral effects*—new or altered responses—as well as any *emotional effects*—new or altered feelings. Discover what has happened to the frequency and intensity of the feelings you listed earlier in Step 2.

**II.** *TA Redecision Work*

Use the list of injunctions and the outline of the process of redecision work described on pages 190–192 to identify any injunctions you used as the basis of an early decision. Determine whether this decision is still appropriate for you. If not, rewrite the decision in a way that makes it appropriate for the present. Develop a plan to put the new decision into effect, with particular consideration to any thoughts and beliefs that could undermine your plan and any thoughts and beliefs necessary to support your plan. Although you can complete this activity on your own, it might help to stimulate your thinking by sharing this process in a group setting.

**III.** *Cognitive Restructuring*

This activity can be done either for yourself or for another person.

**1.** Identify a situation in which your performance or behavior is altered or inhibited because of unproductive thought patterns. It may be something such as making a presentation in front of a group, a job interview, encountering a difficult person, taking a test, and so on.

2. During the next two weeks, keep a log of the kinds of thoughts that occur before, during, and after this situation, whenever the situation (or thoughts and anticipation of it) occurs. Identify which of these thoughts are negative or self-defeating.

3. For each negative or self-defeating thought from you list in Step 2, develop an incompatible thought or a coping thought. Try to develop coping thoughts that will help you before, during, and after the problematic situation. You may find it helpful to refer to *Table 8-2* but make sure the coping thoughts are suitable for you. Try them out and see how they sound. Practice saying them aloud, in the sequence in which you would actually use them. Use an appropriate level of emotion and intensity as you engage in such practice.

4. Practice making a deliberate shift from the negative or self-defeating thoughts to the coping thoughts. Learn to recognize and utilize the self-defeating thoughts as a signal to use the coping thoughts. First, talk yourself through the situation. Later, practice making this shift subvocally. Use role-play, if necessary, to help you accomplish this. Gradually, start to engage in this process whenever the trouble situation occurs in vivo.

**IV.** *Application of Cognitive Intervention Strategies*

In this exercise, you are given six client descriptions. Based on the information we give you, decide whether cognitive strategies would be appropriate or inappropriate treatments for each client. Explain your decision. An example is given (feedback follows the exercise).

***Example:*** The client is a young boy who is acting out in school (third grade) and, because of limited ability, is having difficulty working up to grade level. Cognitive interventions are not suitable for this client. Because of his developmental age and possible ability limitation, it would be too difficult for him to systematically apply logical reasoning to faulty thinking.

1. The client is a young Asian American male adult who is a college senior. He feels depressed over the recent deterioration of his grades and its effect on his graduate school plans for next year.

2. The client is a six-year-old boy who is an only child. According to his teachers, he is having trouble interacting with the other children in his class and spends much of the time alone. His parents confirm that previous opportunities for interactions with other children have been very limited and have occurred on a sporadic basis.

3. The client is a middle-aged man who is referred to you by his family. From talking with him, you observe flat affect coupled with "loose" or incoherent talk. Occasionally, the client refers to acting on instructions he has been given by a saint.

4. The client is a middle-aged woman who is employed as an elementary school teacher. She was recently elected to a national office and reports feeling terrified by the prospect of having to get up and speak in front of a very large audience. She explains that she is constantly worried about making a mistake, forgetting her speech, or in some way embarrassing herself.

5. The client is a twelve-year-old seventh grader who comes in to talk to the school counselor because she doesn't think she's as pretty or as smart as the other girls in her class and as a result, feels sad.

6. The client is a seventy-two-year-old retired woman who complains abut her retired husband's chronic dependency on her. According to the client, her husband seems unable to get tasks accomplished without her help. The client is well-defended, seems unable to identify any feelings she is having about this issue in her life, and appears to have strongly held beliefs, which are expressed in a rather dogmatic and rigid fashion.

## Feedback for Exercises

### IV. *Application of Cognitive Intervention Strategies*

1. This client is possibly suitable for cognitive approaches and strategies. He is likely to be sufficiently intelligent to apply logical reasoning and to understand the concepts of cognitive interventions. Additionally, it is probable that his distress over the recent grades is maintained by self-defeating thoughts or self-talk. However, another significant factor in this case is that the counselor needs to recognize and respect that his cultural background might also suggest that he experiences a sense of shame over his recent performance.

2. This client is not likely to benefit from cognitive approaches and strategies. First, he is probably too young to have mastered the kind of cognitive developmental tasks necessary in order to use a cognitive intervention effectively. Second, it appears that his presenting problem is more related to skill deficits and lack of opportunities to develop social skills than to inappropriate cognitions or beliefs.

3. Cognitive strategies are inappropriate for this client because of his flat affect, loose associations or stream of thinking, and the presence of auditory hallucinations, all of which suggest severe pathology.

4. Cognitive interventions are likely to be quite helpful for this client. Her stress and anxiety appear to be directly related to troublesome cognitions ("If I should fail, it will be awful"). Additionally, she is likely to have the intellectual capacity to understand the principles and rationale of cognitive strategies.

5. Cognitive strategies will probably be helpful to this client. She is just about at the age where she has probably mastered enough cognitive developmental tasks to understand the concepts of these strategies and to apply logical reasoning to problem situations. Ad-

ditionally, her sad feelings seem to be directly related to errors in thinking.

6. Cognitive strategies are probably not going to be too helpful for this client. Although she can probably understand the principles of these strategies, her strong defenses, lack of self-awareness, dogmatism, and need to disavow responsibility for any part of the relationship problem do not make her a very suitable candidate for cognitive strategies.

## *Discussion Questions*

1. A basic assumption of any cognitive intervention is that thoughts cause feelings. What is your reaction to this assumption? What effect might your reaction have on your application of cognitive interventions with clients?

2. Discuss the characteristics of people you think would be very suitable for cognitive strategies. For what kinds of clients or problems might cognitive interventions not be appropriate?

3. In what ways might some clients resist working with a cognitive strategy? What might this resistant behavior mean? How could you handle it?

## *Recommended Readings*

Ascher, L.M., Ed. (1989). *Therapeutic Paradox*, New York: Guilford.

Beck, A.T. and Weishaar, M.E. (1989). Cognitive therapy, Chapter 8 in Raymond J. Corsini and Danny Wedding, Eds., *Current Psychotherapies,* 4th Ed., Itasca, IL: F.E. Peacock.

Bennett, D. (1976). *TA and the Manager*, New York: AMACOM

Berne, E. (1964). *Games People Play*, New York: Grove Press.

Dowd, E.T. and Milne, C.R. (1986). Paradoxical interventions in counseling psychology, *The Counseling Psychologist, 14*, 237–282.

Ellis, A. (1989). Rational emotive therapy, Chapter 6 in Raymond J. Corsini and Danny Wedding, Eds., *Current Psychotherapies,* 4th Ed., Itasca, IL: F.E. Peacock.

Kantowitz, R. and Ballou, M. (1992). A feminist critique of cognitive-behavioral therapy. In L. Brown and M. Ballou, Eds., *Theories of Personality and Psychotherapy*, New York: Guilford.

# Chapter 9

# Behavioral Interventions

## *Purpose of This Chapter—*

In this chapter we examine how persons change patterns of behavior that may have been in place so long that they are not aware of when or how the pattern begins. Some of these patterns relate to behaviors that interfere with the client's goals, hopes, or needs. Others are behaviors that are missing from the client's patterns of interaction, leading to a failure to achieve desired goals, hopes, or needs. Perhaps the most important aspect of this chapter is the emphasis on the client's responsibility in this process of change, and how the client and counselor work together to accomplish the client's objectives. A variety of symptoms can be treated using the behavioral interventions described herein, including affective symptoms such as phobic responses, cognitive symptoms such as compulsive thought patterns, and behavioral/systemic patterns.

## *Considerations as You Read This Chapter—*

- Behavior is that part of human existence that communicates to others how we feel, what we think, and who we are. Because it is available to others through their observations of us, behavior becomes the communication channel that connects us to other people.
- Behavior is also the tool or means by which we accomplish, perform, or in other ways achieve that which we set as our goals.
- Behavior is very important to us. But it can also be the cause of our failures, or of our mistakes or disappointments.
- Because behavior is the outward manifestation of our inner selves, it may sometimes seem to be unconnected to us.

> Whatever, the case, many client problems involve some manifestation of behavior. And oftentimes, the best approach to working with client problems is by addressing behavioral changes.

Thus far, we have examined how feelings and thinking can lead to human problems, and how affective and cognitive interventions can alleviate those same problems. In this chapter, we address problems that are established in behavior patterns, the things people do, or fail to do. Behavioral interventions are intended to help clients change their behavior when that behavior interferes with achievement of their goals, ambitions, or values, or when it contributes to negative outcomes. Behavioral strategies on which specific interventions are based utilize theories and processes of learning. Although a large number of strategies can be classified as behavioral in nature and focus, perhaps the most common ones derive from social modeling approaches, skills training, operant conditioning and contracting, relaxation training, systematic desensitization, covert conditioning, and self-management exercises (Cormier & Cormier, 1991; Wolpe, 1990). Behavioral interventions were first introduced in 1954 by Skinner and Lindsley and in 1960 by Eysenck. During the 1960s, social modeling became an increasingly popular therapeutic approach. Contemporary behavioral counseling practice has grown increasingly closer to cognitive therapy and has spawned a new identity known as "cognitive behavioral therapy."

Behavioral approaches also share much in common with other action-oriented approaches to helping, particularly William Glasser's (1965; 1985) *reality therapy*. As Glasser and Zunin (1979) note, changes in behavior that occur from reality therapy strategies also involve learning. They observe that "[W]e are what we do, and to a great extent, we are what we learn to do, and our identity becomes the integration of all learned and unlearned behavior" (p. 316). The reader will note that this sounds very much like the cognitive theorist's observation that "we are what we think."

Behavioral interventions share certain common elements:

1. Maladaptive behavior (that which produces undesirable personal or social consequences) is the result of learning, not illness, disease, or intrapsychic conflict.
2. Maladaptive behavior can be weakened or eliminated, and adaptive behavior can be strengthened or increased through the use of psychological principles, especially principles of learning that enjoy some degree of empirical support.
3. Behavior (adaptive or maladaptive) occurs in specific situations and is functionally related to specific events that both precede

and follow these situations. For example, a client may be aggressive in some situations without being aggressive in most situations. Thus, behavioral practitioners attempt to avoid labeling clients using such arbitrary descriptors as "aggressive." Instead, emphasis is placed on what a client *does or does not do* that is "aggressive" and what situational events cue or precipitate the aggressive response, as well as events that strengthen or weaken the aggressive response. A thorough assessment phase (or behavior analysis) similar to the process we described in Chapter 5 is the basis for choosing behavioral interventions.

4. Clearly defined outline or treatment goals are important for the overall efficiency of these interventions and are defined individually for each client. Thus, counselors attempt to avoid projecting their desires for change onto clients. Instead, they help clients specify precise outcomes they want to make as a result of counseling.

5. Helping interventions focus on the present rather than the past or future and are selected and tailored to each client's set of problems and concerns. Behavioral approaches reject the "all-purpose counseling" notion that assumes that one method or approach is generally appropriate for most clients.

Characteristics of clients who seem to have the most success with behavioral interventions include:

- People with a strong goal orientation—motivated by achieving goals or getting results.
- People who are action-oriented—need to be active, goal-focused, participating in the helping process (this includes several cultural groups, including Asians and African Americans).
- People who are interested in changing a discrete and limited (two to three) number of behaviors.

Behavioral interventions have also been used extensively and found to be very suitable in schools, agencies, or situations with time-limited counseling.

## *Goals of Behavioral Interventions*

The overall goal of behavioral interventions is to help clients develop adaptive and supportive behaviors to multifaceted situations. The term *behavior* has grown in recent years to include covert or private events such as thoughts, beliefs, and feelings (when they can be clearly specified), as well as overt events or behaviors that are observable by others. Developing adaptive behavior often involves weakening or eliminating behaviors that work against the desired outcome (i.e., eating snacks when you wish to lose weight), acquiring or strengthening desirable behaviors, (i.e., asking for things that you want or need), or both. Unadaptive or maladaptive behaviors can be harmful to a person's health, lifestyle, or welfare. Adaptive behaviors help a person meet biological and social needs and avoid pain and discomfort (Wolpe, 1990).

Behavioral interventions have been used in many different settings (such as schools, business and industry, and correctional institutions), with a great variety of human problems (including learning and academic problems, motivational and performance problems, marital and sexual dysfunction, skills deficits, and anxiety), and with maladaptive habits (such as overeating, smoking, procrastination, and so on). In this chapter, we focus primarily on the behavioral interventions that seem to be most useful for working with people in the general population (as opposed to those in institutional settings). These include social modeling, behavioral rehearsal and skills-training approaches, relaxation training, systematic desensitization, and self-management interventions. Cognitive-behavioral strategies are not discussed because of their inclusion in the previous chapter.

## *Social Modeling*

Social modeling, also called observational learning or vicarious learning (learning by observing others learn), refers to a process "in which individuals learn by the examples of others" (Rosenthal & Steffek, 1991). Much of the work associated with social modeling has been initiated or stimulated by Bandura (1977).

As adults, much that we learn occurs by watching others. It is a safe way to learn because we don't have to take the risk of failure. It is informative because we can observe both the behavior and the payoff or consequence of that behavior. Often it is entertaining. This observing quality is characteristic of all human beings. It can also be used to help people change, in which case it is called modeling. As a counseling strategy, modeling is used to help a client conceptualize and acquire desired responses as far ranging as how to cash a check, buy a car, rent a video, or address the Queen of England. As a process, it is only limited by the observational powers of the person who would be the learner (see *Table 9-1*). As a result, casual observational learning can also produce inaccurate learning when the observer reads more or less into the process than was actually there. Undoubtedly, some adult learning is inaccurate learning for this reason, if no other. This is a particular concern for immigrants who are new to American culture.

## TABLE 9-1  Three Social Modeling Approaches

A. *Overt* model(s). One or more persons (or trained animals) illustrate the behavior to be learned or refined. The overt model may be a live tutor, recorded on film or videotape (or, mainly for aural responses on audiotape).

B. *Symbolic* model(s). Animated cartoon or fantasy characters, schematics, narratives or slides replace the overt tutor. For example, to teach student auto mechanics how to assemble and troubleshoot the drive-train, the parts can be shown moving into or out of their proper arrangement. The steps needed to illustrate repairs can be repeated a number of times, either as a fixed program or a program that lets the learner control the amount of repetition.

A limiting case is a *target* model. Here, the desired product or work sample is arranged to help learners infer how to create similar correct responses from studying the sample. Examples include charts, diagrams, and such epitomes as correct place-settings, tactful letters, and completed jigsaw or crossword puzzles. Also among target models are illustrations that satisfy some governing rule—such as forceful phrasing to teach assertiveness, the winning move in a chess or a bridge game, or a list of antonyms and synonyms—even though the learner does not witness the actions or the reasoning that brought the target into being.

C. *Covert* model(s). The tutor—whether a person, beast, cartoon character, or schematic diagram—is *imagined* rather than shown. Covert models may be oneself (called self-modeling) or others performing some behavior with increasing deftness. Various cues (e.g., specifying sensory images or inner reactions) can be supplied to support the scenario imagined. To remove fears, covert modeling by self blends into systematic desensitization in clinical structure and format. Depending on observer characteristics, some covert models will surpass others. For instance, to reduce fear in devout clients, visualizing Jesus or Mohammed as a helper will excel over secular tutors.

SOURCE: Rosenthal, T. and Steffek, B. (1991). Modeling methods. In F.H. Kanfer and A.P. Goldstein, Eds., *Helping People Change,* 4th ed., New York: Pergamon, p.76.

### *Live* (in vivo) *Modeling*

With live modeling, the desired behavioral response is performed in the presence of the client. Live models can include the counselor, the teacher in a developmental guidance class, or the client's peers. Usually the counselor will provide a modeled demonstration via a role-play activity, in which he/she takes the part of the client and demonstrates a different way that the client might respond or behave.

Live modeling can be a most versatile tool for the school counselor, the correctional counselor, or the family counselor, to name only a few. Scenarios can vary from (a) helping seventh graders understand how to begin thinking about careers (by observing a video tape of other seventh graders talking about career study); (b) helping high school students deal with peer pressures (through group counseling in which students talk about their successes in resisting pressures), to helping family members see a new way to communicate. The counselor's role can vary from being an actor in the scenario to being the choreographer or being the narrator of the scenario. The following is a modeling session in which the counselor served as narrator. The scene is a group guidance session involving twelve seventh graders. The counselor has been working with six of the students on a project, "Using the Library to Learn About Careers." The second six students are new to the group and are just beginning the project.

---

*Using Live Modeling with Middle School Students*

*Counselor:* Today, we have some new faces in our group. I think all of you already know each other. For convenience, I'm going to call you the "old timers" and the "new bunch." (*Talking to the new bunch*) The old timers have have been working on a project to learn about jobs. I'm going to ask them to demonstrate some of the things they have been doing. We will use something called a "fishbowl." What that means is that the old timers will sit in a small circle. The rest of us will sit outside the circle and observe the old timers as they talk about their project. We will do this for about fifteen minutes and then we will trade places. The "new bunch" will come into the inner circle and the old timers will sit around the outside. Any questions? (*Nervous noises, chairs moving, people getting settled. The old timers are familiar with this exercise. They were introduced to it when they were in the role of the new bunch a few weeks earlier.*) Now, if everyone is ready, old timers, I would like for you to talk to each other about the topic: "Fifty ways to choose a career—all in the library."

*Old timers:* A discussion begins, slowly at first, about how to use the library to find out about careers. Different members of the group talk about how they got started, who in the library helped them find the right books, which books were most helpful, how they preferred the computer career software for some of the research, funny things they discovered about some careers, and so on. There is a lot of joking. It doesn't look like a great learning experience, but the point is made that learning about jobs can be fun and that the library is a neat place to get career information. They also learned the process of approaching the right librarian and knowing what to ask for. (*After about fifteen minutes, the counselor interrupts, summarizes what was said, and asks the two groups to trade places. Many groans, teasing, playful putdowns follow as students change seats.*)

*Counselor:* Now, new bunch, it's your turn. I'd like for you to show the old timers what you can do. This time the topic will be "Things I am going to do in the library to learn about jobs."

*New bunch:* (*More groans, jokes, moving of chairs.*) Talk begins slowly. Someone makes a joke. All laugh. Finally, someone gets into the spirit and says she would like to find out about becoming an astronaut. Everyone laughs. (*Counselor intervenes, commends student for her question, challenges group to come up with a plan for using the library to help her find out about becoming an astronaut.*) The group begins, more or less in earnest, and the information that characterized the first group's discussion comes out again, this time focusing on the topic of finding out about becoming an astronaut.

Live modeling is particularly useful in instances in which the client does not have appropriate response alternatives available. The modeled demonstration provides cues that the client can use to acquire those new responses. For example, a client who wishes to be more assertive may benefit from seeing the counselor or a peer demonstrate such behaviors in role-played situations. The following exchange between the counselor (model) and client (wishing to be more assertive) illustrates how such a session might go:

---

*Modeling Assertive Responses*

*Counselor:* Today, Nancy, I thought we might do a role-play, that's where you and I enact someone other than ourselves, and our "play" will be a scenario in which you are returning some unusable merchandise to a local store.

*Nancy:* That sounds awful. I don't like to have to return things to the store.

*Counselor:* I know. But you said you wished you could do that sort of thing without getting so upset. Don't worry. I'm going to play you and you are going to play the part of the store employee. O.K.?

*Nancy: (smiling)* Well, that's a little better. O.K.

*Counselor:* You will begin first, by asking me if I need some help.

*Nancy (as employee):* Hello, can I help you?

*Counselor (as Nancy):* Yes. I purchased this baptismal gown for my daughter's baby but after the baby was born, she realized it was too small. I'd like to exchange it if I may.

*Nancy (as employee):* How long ago did you purchase it?

*Counselor (as Nancy):* Two months ago, I'm afraid. I know your return policy is 30 days but I hope you will accept it in exchange.

*Nancy (as employee):* Well, since you only want to exchange it, I think we can do that.

---

Following the role-play, the counselor and Nancy discussed the interaction and then they conducted a second role-play, this time with Nancy as herself and the counselor as the store employee. Then they evaluated Nancy's performance and identified some ways she could improve. This was followed by a third role-play in which Nancy again was herself. Her performance in the third role-play was much improved and she felt successful. Live modeling in which the client is a participant is limited by the client's willingness to participate in an imagined situation as an actor, unless the two can take an impending real situation that they can rehearse. If your client is particularly withdrawn, you may wish to use other persons as the modeling participants.

### Symbolic Modeling

Although live models have much impact on the client, they are some-times difficult to use because the counselor cannot control the accu-racy of the demonstration of the behavior being modeled. To correct for this, many counselors make use of symbolic models through video-tapes, audiotapes, or films in which a desired behavior is introduced and presented. For example, symbolic models could be used with clients who want to improve their study habits. Reading about effec-tive study habits of successful people and their scholastic efforts is a first step to help clients identify desired behaviors. Next, clients can listen to an audiotape or watch a videotape illustrating persons who are studying appropriately (such a tape can be produced by the coun-selor with the help of the school librarian). Once effective symbolic models are developed, they can be stored easily and retrieved for fu-ture use by the same or different clients.

### Covert Modeling

*Covert modeling*, also called *imaging*, is a process in which the client imagines a scene in which the desired behavior is displayed (Cautela, 1976; Cautela & Kearney, 1993). The imagined model can be either the client or someone else. This approach is used frequently and with much success by professional and amateur athletes. The first step is to work out a script that depicts the situation(s) and desired responses. For example, if an avoidant client desires to learn to com-municate more successfully with a partner, scenes would be devel-oped in which the client is having a successful discussion. One scene might be:

> *It is Friday night. You would like to go to a movie but your part-ner is very tired. You acknowledge your partner's tiredness but sug-gest that a movie might prove relaxing as well as entertaining. Your partner thinks about it for a moment and then agrees.*

Imaging serves two purposes. It brings the appropriate behaviors into focus. It also serves to construct a success image into the person's self-concept. Both are desired outcomes. Perhaps the best example of this is the Olympic diver who, while standing on the high platform, imag-ines herself balancing, then springing, then turning, and finally en-tering the water, all perfectly. The behavior then follows the pattern established by the image. This procedure is also referred to as *covert self-modeling*, and has the potential for augmenting the client's per-sonal involvement in the process and subsequently effecting greater facilitation of desired behavior (Rimm & Masters, 1979, p. 130).

### *Characteristics of the Modeled Presentation*

The modeled presentation can affect the client's ability to attend to and remember the modeled demonstration. As Rosenthal and Steffak (1991) have noted, the counselor must present the model in such a way that it captures the client's attention (p. 105). The first part of the modeled presentation should include instructions and cues about the features of the modeled behavior of activity. Prior instructions can minimize competition for the client's attention. A rationale for the use of modeling should also be given to the client prior to the modeled display.

Scenerios or responses to be modeled should minimize the amount of stress that the client might experience in the presentation. Distressing and anxiety-provoking modeled stimuli may interfere with the client's observation powers, processing, or remembering.

Complex patterns of behavior should be broken down and presented in smaller, more easily understood sequences. If too may behaviors or an overly complex model is presented to the client at one time, the likelihood of learning is greatly diminished. You can seek the client's input about the presentation of modeled responses to ensure that the ingredients and pace of the modeled demonstration are presented in a facilitative manner.

Perry and Furukawa (1980, p. 139) advise the counselor to "have either the model or a narrator comment on the important features of the modeled behavior as well as on the general principle or rule which governs the model's performance" when a modeling scenerio is particularly complicated. They provide an example of how this might be done:

> *Suppose a model were demonstrating assertive behavior to a withdrawn, socially inept observer. The scene involves ordering dinner in a restaurant and discovering that the steak is too tough to eat. The model exhibits an assertive response in this situation by requesting the waitress to bring him another steak. The model can comment at this point: "That was an example of an assertive response. I was entitled to a good steak and was willing to pay for it. I explained the difficulty in an open and friendly manner to the waitress and asked her to bring me another steak. Afterwards, I felt good about myself and enjoyed my meal." By listening to the model highlight the essential characteristics of an assertive response, the observer is more likely to remember the behavior and is in a better position to apply this form of response in a variety of different situations. As an additional aid to retention, the observer can be asked by the therapist to summarize the main features and general rules associated with the model's behavior. Several studies (for*

*example, Bandura, Grusec, and Menlove, 1966) have found that observers who actively summarize the model's behavior are better able to learn and retain this information.* (Perry and Furukawa, 1980, p. 139)

Practicing the goal behavior or activity also increases the effectiveness of the modeling procedure. In addition to practice in the counseling session, the counselor might assign homework to the client for practice outside the session. Self-directed practice can enhance the generalization of the modeling treatment from within the session to real-life situations. If a client experiences difficulty in performing a particular activity or behavior, instructional aids, props, or counselor-coaching can facilitate successful performance.

## *Modeling and Self-Efficacy*

Self-efficacy refers to the perception a client has about the ability and confidence to handle a situation or to engage in a task successfully. It has been found to be a major variable that affects the usefulness of modeling interventions (Bandura, 1988). As Rosenthal and Steffek (1991) point out, it is not sufficient to assume that clients will simply observe a model—either live, symbolic, or covert—and acquire the skills to achieve desirable results. Clients "must also gain enough self-efficacy (confidence) that they can perform the needed acts despite stress, changes, moments of doubt, and can persevere in the face of setbacks" (p. 75). Thus, modeling interventions must be designed that emphasize not only outcomes but also attitudes and beliefs about oneself. As an example, Ozer and Bandura (1990) developed a modeling program to teach women self-defense skills. The modeling program not only included modeling various self-defense skills but also modeled ways in which the women could acquire trust in their self-defense skills, particularly in the face of adverse situations. Rosenthal and Steffek (1991) conclude that self-efficacy is not a global concept—that is, it does not reflect self-confidence in general—but rather the confidence in oneself to deal with "specific aims" (p. 78). Modeling interventions will be more successful when they also teach clients how to develop confidence for the tasks being modeled.

## *Desirable Characteristics of Models*

Clients are more likely to learn from someone whom they perceive as similar to themselves. Such characteristics as age, gender, prestige, ethnic background, and attitudes should be considered when selecting potential models. However, in the case of cross-cultural counseling, cultural sensitivity may be sufficient to account for perceived competence and modeling effectiveness. Atkinson, Casas, and Abreu (1992) studied the differential effects of cultural similarity and cultural sensitivity and found that "counselors who acknowledge the importance of culture in client problems are perceived as more culturally competent by ethnic minorities than are counselors who ignore cultural variables" (p. 518). On the other hand, gender sensitivity may not be sufficient to enhance modeling effects. Citing Carli (1989), Nelson (1993, p. 203) has suggested that gender plays a significant role in the social influence (modeling) process, in that same sex dyads tend to reflect different patterns of interaction than do different sex dyads.

Similarity between model and client assures clients that the behaviors shown "are both appropriate and attainable" (Perry & Furukawa, 1980, 136). With some clients there is no better model than the client. Hosford and deVisser (1974) found that arranging conditions so clients see themselves performing the desired response can be a very powerful learning tool. In their procedure, called *self-as-model*, the client is captured on video or audiotape actually performing the desired response. For example, a client who wishes to stop stuttering listens to and practices with a tape in which all stuttering has been edited out. Hosford, Moss, and Morrell (1976) found that having a client observe both inappropriate and appropriate behaviors may actually weaken acquisition of the desired responses and promote the undesired behavior. Presumably this is explained by the erosive effect on the client's confidence when hearing the problem behavior.

Meichenbaum (1971) has suggested that a coping model might be more helpful to clients than a mastery model. A client may be able to identify more strongly with a model who shows some fear or some struggle in performing than the model who comes across perfectly. Clients can also learn more from modeling when exposed to more than one model. Multiple models may have more impact on a client, because the client can draw on the strengths and styles of several different persons (Kaxdin, 1973). Warmth and nurturance by the model also facilitates modeling effects.

When modeling fails to contribute to desired client changes, reassess the characteristics of the selected model(s) and the mode and format of the modeled presentation. In many cases, modeling can provide sufficient cues for the client to learn new responses or to extinguish fears. In other instances, modeling may have more effect when accompanied by practice of the target response. This practice can occur through role-play and rehearsal in the counseling session, or as assigned homework.

## *Role-Play and Behavior Rehearsal*

*Role-play* and *behavior rehearsal* interventions promote behavior change through simulated or in vivo enactment of desired responses. Role-play and behavior rehearsal originated from Salter's conditioned reflex therapy (1949), Moreno's psychodrama technique (1946), and Kelly's fixed-role therapy (1955). Common elements in the application of role-play and rehearsal interventions include:

1. A reenactment of oneself, another person, an event, or a set of responses by the client
2. The use of the present, or the "here-and-now," to carry out the reenactment
3. A gradual shaping process in which less difficult scenes are enacted first, and more difficult scenes are reserved for later
4. Feedback to the client by the counselor and/or other adjunct persons

Depending on the therapeutic goal, role-playing procedures are often used by dynamic therapies as a method to achieve catharsis; by insight therapies as a means to bring about attitudinal changes; by Gestalt therapy as a tool to promote conflict resolution and increased self-awareness; and by behavior therapy as a way to facilitate behavior changes. In this chapter, we discuss role-play as a way to achieve the latter objective. Gestalt dialogue work and role-playing to promote attitudinal change were discussed in Chapter 7.

## *Role-Play as a Method of Behavior Change*

*Behavior rehearsal* uses role-play and practice attempts to help people acquire new skills and to help them perform more effectively under threatening or anxiety-producing circumstances. Behavior rehearsal is used primarily in three situations:

1. The client does not have but needs to learn the necessary skills to handle a situation (*response acquisition*).
2. The client needs to learn to discriminate between inappropriate and appropriate times and places to use the skills (*response facilitation*).
3. The client's anxiety about the situation needs to be sufficiently reduced to allow the client to use skills already learned, even though they are currently inhibited by anxiety (*response disinhibition*).

Let us say that you have a client who wants to be able to be more self-disclosing with others but doesn't know where to start learning how. In this case, the client *might have* a deficit repertoire (lack of skills and knowledge) in self-disclosure and needs to learn some new communication skills. Or, the client may have the necessary communication skills but needs clarification or discrimination training to learn *when and how* to use those skills to self-disclose. We have all known persons who have the skills but use them inappropriately. A person may self-disclose too much to disinterested persons and then withhold with persons who are interested in them. In another case, the client's anxiety can inhibit the use of these skills. Role-play and behavior rehearsal can then be used to help the client gain control over the anxiety reaction.

In addition to the practice effects gained from behavior rehearsal, the intervention can often provide important clues as to how the client actually behaves in real-life situations. This is particularly helpful in instances where the client's self-reported descriptions of a behavior are at odds with the client's portrayed behavior under simulated conditions. In this context, Rimm and Masters (1979) have noted that, "[c]ontradictions of this nature are not at all uncommon, and when they occur, it is likely that the role-played behavior is far more accurate than the client's verbal characterization of how he typically handles such a situation . . ." In this respect, behavior rehearsal "is an invaluable diagnostic technique [as well] . . ." (p. 68).

The nuts and bolts of behavior rehearsal consists of a series of graduated practice attempts in which the client rehearses the desired behaviors, starting with a situation that is manageable and is not likely to backfire. Psychologists call this process *successive approximation*. The rehearsal attempts may be arranged in a hierarchy according to level of difficulty or gradiations of stress. Adequate practice of one situation is required before moving on to a scene with more advanced skills. The practice of each scene should be very similar to the situations that occur in the client's environment. To simulate these situations realistically, you may wish to use props and portray the other person involved with the client as accurately as possible. This portrayal should include acting out the probable response of this person to the client's new or different behavior.

Behavior rehearsal can be either overt or covert (*imaged*). Both seem to be quite effective (McFall & Twentyman, 1973). Probably a client could benefit from engaging in both of these approaches. Initially, the client might practice by imaging and then move on to acting out the scenerio with the counselor. Covert rehearsal can also be assigned as a homework intervention. Lazarus (1966) has provided guidelines for knowing when to move from one scenerio to the next level:

1. The client is able to enact the scene without feeling anxious.
2. The client's general demeanor supports the client's words.
3. The client's words and actions would seem fair and reasonable to an objective onlooker.

Feedback is an important part of role-play and behavioral rehearsal interventions. Feedback is a way for the client to recognize both the problems and successes encountered in the practice attempts. To be effective, evaluative feedback should be measured by the client's willingness to change and by the potential for helping clients identify other effective alternatives (McKeachie, 1976). Feedback also should be nonpunitive, constructive, and directed toward behaviors the client can potentially change. Feedback may be supplied by videotaped and audiotaped playbacks of the client's practices. These taped playbacks are often more useful objective assessments of the client's behavior than verbal descriptions alone. You may find that your evaluations are more important early in the feedback process, but eventually, it is desirable for the client to begin using accurate self-assessments in the feedback process.

## *Modeling, Rehearsal, and Feedback: Components of Skill Training*

*Skill training* is an intervention that is composed of several other interventions we have already discussed: successive approximation, modeling, behavioral rehearsal, and feedback. Skill training may take a variety of forms, including problem-solving skills, decision-making skills, communication skills, social skills, and assertion skills. To develop a skill training program, first you must identify the components of the skill to be learned. Then those components are arranged in a learning sequence that reflects a less difficult to more difficult continuum. Training then proceeds by modeling each skill component, having the client imitate the modeled behaviors, provide evaluative feedback and repeat the sequence if appropriate. Skill training protocols exist for most skills that might be taught in the counseling setting and may be found in the professional counseling literature. To illustrate how a training package might be developed, we will describe an *assertion training* protocol.

Assertion training is a means of overcoming social anxiety that inhibits a person's interactions with others (Wolpe, 1990). Typical assertion skills involve the ability to make requests, to refuse requests, to express opinions, to express positive and negative feelings, and to initiate, continue, and terminate social conversations. In assertion training, you begin by having the client identify one situation in which he or she wants to be more assertive. Then identify what assertive behaviors are involved and what the client would like to say or do. The situation is modeled and role-played consistently in the interview until the client can be assertive without experiencing any anxiety. Then the learned skill is transferred to situations outside the counseling setting through homework assignments. Once the client is able to exhibit the desired skills independently of counseling, the process is deemed successful. Successes at assertiveness will generalize to other situations as well; that is, it will be increasingly easier for clients to be assertive on their own without assistance and feedback.

As an illustration, suppose you are working with a student who reports a lack of assertive classroom behaviors. You and your client would first specify the desired classroom skills. You may need to observe the student in the classroom setting to identify these target behaviors. In counting the number of times the student engages in assertive classroom behavior (asking questions, voicing opinions, engaging in group discussion, giving reports, volunteering for chalkboard work, initiating conversations with the teacher, etc.), you can obtain a fairly accurate idea of the kind of assertive behaviors that are most prevalent in the client's repertiore and the ones the client needs most to strengthen. After identifying the desired behaviors to strengthen, you must choose the type of modeling to use to teach the target behaviors: live, symbolic, or covert modeling, or some combination of these. After the client has seen, listened to, read about, or imagined these modeled behaviors, he/she can demonstrate and practice brief senerios in which they are demonstrated. Following practice and successful demonstration, in which the client is becoming comfortable with the new behaviors, the client is asked to begin to transfer the skill to classroom settings.

Wolpe (1990) observes that many persons who need assertiveness training present an early history in which they have been taught that the rights of others supercede their own rights (p. 136). This is not to imply that in assertion training one learns to be aggressive, but rather to treat oneself and others with a reasonable amount of respect. In some cases assertion training involves helping clients learn the legitimate expression of anger so that their rights are not consistently violated. Laidlaw, Malmo, and associates (1990) observe that the expression of anger and consequent inhibited assertive expression are often particularly hard for some female clients who have been socialized to "put others first and yourself last." Assertion training may be useful for women as long as it simply doesn't encourage women to develop skills just to meet the prevailing patriarchal social standards (Kantrowitz & Ballou, 1992, p. 70). Assertion training also may be useful to assist gay, lesbian, and bisexual clients who are in the coming out process, that is the process of asserting their identity to friends, family, co-workers and so on. However, it must also be recognized that the meaning of assertiveness varies among culturally diverse groups. As Ivey, Ivey, and Simek-Morgan (1993) observe, "what is assertive for European-American cultures may be considered intrusive and aggressive by those from other cultural groups" (p. 245). Cheek (1976) has illustrated some of the problems of meaning in assertion training with African American clients:

> *You see the authors on assertiveness have not sufficiently considered the social conditions in which Blacks live—and have lived. That blind spot in many ways alters or changes the manner that assertiveness is applied . . . Current assertive authors have a great approach—it's an approach which can really aid Black folks, in fact they need it—but at the time these authors are unable to translate assertiveness training into the examples, language and caution that fit the realities of a Black lifestyle.* (pp. 10–11)

## *Case Illustration of Skill Training*

### *The Case of Jack*

Jack is a twenty-seven-year-old caucausian male who initially sought counseling because he wanted to improve his social relationships. Assessment revealed that Jack has had a series of interpersonal encounters in which the relationship ended when Jack began to feel dominated by the woman involved. As this pattern repeated itself, Jack reported that his confidence sagged to new depths and lately he has avoided social relationships as a result. He describes himself as weak and powerless in relationships. At this point, the counselor determined that Jack might need some skill training related to interpersonal skills in addition to the exploration of his feelings and thoughts about himself.

First, the counselor explained the process of assertion training, noting that it involves a good bit of role-playing. The counselor also drew on paper a contin- uum of a possible range of behavior— ranging from passive to assertive to aggressive—to illustrate the differences between being passive, assertive, and aggressive. This distinction is very important, because formerly passive people often attempt to overcompensate initially in their interactions with others by behaving aggressively rather than assertively. In Jack's case, this could have a very negative effect on future relationships.

Then Jack and the counselor discuss Jack's past relationships and identify a series of situations in which Jack has trouble being assertive with women. Most of these center around his social relationships but several also involved his mother. Each social skill was discussed thoroughly so that there was a good idea what actually happened in the social encounters. Then Jack and the counselor arranged the identified skills

*Continued*

in a hierarchy—starting with ones that were the least difficult for Jack and presented the least difficulties when he wished to be assertive. Jack and the counselor identified six situations which Jack wanted to work on:

1. When shopping with a companion, not following her shopping plan only, but also identifying a shopping plan he would like to include
2. Choosing what to wear on a date without asking his companion's opinion first
3. Identifying some places to go to before asking a companion out to dinner
4. Telling his mother he can't come over to see her
5. Telling his mother he can't fix something for her
6. Telling his date that he really doesn't want to see a particular movie

At this point Jack was ready to start working with the first situation on the list. The counselor had him participate in an imaginary shopping trip to the local mall, beginning with the drive to the mall. She took on the role of the companion and described what she wanted to do when they got there. Jack had to describe what he wanted to do. They imagined themselves getting out of the car and walking to the entrance. She said to him, "Do you have something you want to get or do you want to come with me?"

Jack's role was to describe to her what he wanted to do and then to negotiate when and where they would meet. Over the next few counseling sessions, they rehearsed this senerio until Jack was quite comfortable with his role. At that point, the counselor gave Jack a homework assignment to invite a date to go shopping. He announced that he had already done so the past weekend and that the experience had worked out very much to his liking. The remaining items on Jack's list went much faster as he gained self-confidence and skill.

Booraem (1974) has noted that during skill training there is a tendency for counselors to terminate role-playing with too few trials, possibly because the counselor has a higher skill level than the client and becomes bored, or assumes clients are more comfortable with the new skills than they really are. The counselor may also want to discuss how the client can handle unexpected or varied responses from the other party who is involved in the scenerio. For example, in Jack's situation (above) Jack and the counselor discussed ways that he could respond if his date insisted he accompany her into the store she selected.

## Anxiety Reduction Methods

Many clients who seek help do so because of strong negative emotions labeled *fear* or *anxiety*. Lehrer and Woolfolk (1982) define several types of anxiety, including *somatic anxiety*, which may manifest itself in body sensations such as stomach butterflies, sweaty palms, rapid pulse rate; *cognitive anxiety*, which may be apparent in an inability to concentrate or in intrusive, repetitive, panicky, or catastrophic thoughts; and *performance* or *behavioral anxiety*, typically manifested by avoidance of the anxiety-arousing situation.

While some amount of anxiety is believed to be helpful and actually lead to successful performance, when it reaches an intolerable or uncomfortable level, a person should seek help for it. Various strategies are used for anxiety reduction. In this chapter, we describe two of the more common behavioral interventions: relaxation training and systematic desensitization.

## *Relaxation Training*

The most common form of relaxation training used by behavioral counselors is called *progressive relaxation* or *muscle relaxation* (Jacobson, 1939). Muscle relaxation has long been used to treat a wide variety of problems, including generalized anxiety and stress, headaches and psychosomatic pain, insomnia, and chronic illnesses such as hypertension and diabetes. Relaxation training is often used as an adjunct to short-term counseling. Rimm and Masters (1979) have observed that relaxation can be a very effective way of establishing rapport and a sense of trust in the counselor's competence (p. 35). Muscle relaxation is also a major component of systematic desensitization which we discuss in the next section.

The basic premise of using muscle relaxation to treat anxiety is that muscle tension exacerbates or adds to anxiety and stress. At the same time, relaxation and anxiety are not compatible states. Consequently, an individual can experience a reduction in felt anxiety by causing relaxation to occur in muscle groups on cue or self-instructions. The procedure involves training clients to contract and then relax various muscle groups, to recognize differences between sensations of muscle contraction and relaxation, and to induce greater relaxation through the release of muscle tension and suggestion. Suggestion is enhanced by counselor comments throughout the procedure, directing the client's attention to pleasant (relaxed) sensations, heavy or warm sensations, and so on. These suggestions are not unlike hypnotic inductions; however, muscle relaxation is not hypnosis, and some clients may need to know that they are not going to be hypnotized. After going through the procedure several times with the counselor's assistance, clients are encouraged to practice it on their own, daily if possible, and often with the use of audiotape-recorded instructions as a guide. (Commercially prepared relaxation audiotapes are available, or you can record the session in which you are teaching the client how to relax muscle groups and send that tape home with the client to practice.)

Relaxation training should occur in a quiet environment free of distracting light, noise, and interruptions. The client should use a couch, reclining chair, or lie on a pad on the floor. (This latter option is most practical when working with a relaxation training group.) The counselor uses a quiet, modulated tone of voice when delivering the relaxation instructions. Each step in the process (tensing and relaxing a specific muscle) takes about ten to fifteen seconds, with a ten- to fifteen-second pause between each step. The entire procedure takes twenty to thirty minutes. It is very important not to rush through any of the procedure. The process is illustrated in the following instructions:

*Tension Release Through*
*Muscle Relaxation*

*First, let your body relax. Close your eyes and visualize your body letting go. (Pause) Now we are going to the muscles of your face. First, smile as broadly as you can. Tighter. Relax. (Pause) Good. Now again, smile. Smile. (Pause) Relax. Now your eyes and forehead. Scrunch them as tightly as you can. Like a prune. Tighter. (Pause) Relax. Good. Note the difference between the tension and relaxation. Feel the warmth flow into the muscles as you relax. Now, again. Make a prune face. Tighter. (Pause) Relax. Relax.*

*Let all of the muscles in your face relax. Around your eyes, your brow, around your mouth. Feel your face becoming smoother as you let go. (Pause) Feel your face become more and more relaxed.*

*Now, focus on your hands. Clench them into fists and make the fists tight . . . tighter. Study the tension in your hands as you tighten them. (Pause) Now release them. Relax your hands and let them rest. (Pause) Note the difference between the tension and the relaxation. (Pause) Now, tighten your hands into fists again. Tighter . . . tighter. Relax. Let them go. Feel the tension drain out of your hands as they release. (Pause)*

*Now bend both hands back at the wrists so the muscles in your lower arms*
*tighten. Tighter. . . . Relax. Again feel the tension flow out of your arms and hands. As the tension releases, a warmth enters your muscles to replace the tension. Try to recognize the warmth flowing in. (Pause) Bend both hands back and tense your lower arms again. Tighter. Relax. Feel the warmth replacing the tension. Relax further. Deeper. Good.*

*Now we will move to your upper arms. Tighten your byceps by pulling your bended arms to your chest. Tighter. Tighter. (Pause) Relax. Let your arms drop. Let the tension flow out. Let the warmth flow in. Relax. Deeper. Try to reach an even deeper level of relaxation of your arms.*

*And now your shoulders. Shrug your shoulders and try to touch them to your ears. Feel and hold the tension. Tighter. (Pause) Now relax. Relax. Let go. Feel the tension leave. Deeper. Good. Tighten your shoulders again. (Pause) Relax. (Pause) Relax. Feel all of the muscles in your hands, arms, shoulders, face. Feel them letting go. Deeper into relaxation. Deeper.*

*As these muscles relax, direct your attention to your chest muscles. Tense them. Tighter. (Pause) Relax. Again. Pull your chest muscles tighter and tighter. Tighter. (Pause) Relax, relax. (Pause) Now your stomach*

*Continued*

muscles. Tighten your stomach. Harder. Tighter. (Pause) Relax. Feel the tension flow out of those muscles. Feel them grow softer. Relax. Feel the warmth. Relax. (Pause) Now tense the stomach muscles again. Good. Tighter. Relax, relax. Feel the difference. Good.

Focus now on your buttocks. Tense your buttocks by holding them in or contracting them. Feel the tension. Tighter. Relax. (Pause)

Now tighten them again. Tighter. (Pause) Relax. Let you whole body go. Feel the tension flow out of your body. Feel the warmth flow into your body. Feel the warmth pushing the tension out. Let go. Relax. (Pause)

Now locate your legs. Tighten your calf muscles now by pointing your toes toward your head. Tighten them. Relax. Let your feet drop. Feel the muscles letting go. Again now. Tighten your calf muscles. Point your toes toward your head. Tighter. (Pause) Relax. Good. Feel the muscles go soft, smooth, warm.

Stretch both legs out from you. Reach as far as you can with your legs. Extend them. Extend them. (Pause) Relax. Let them drop. Feel the difference in your muscles. Feel the leg muscles relax. Concentrate on the feeling. Now stretch your legs again. Point your toes. Extend; extend. (Pause) Relax. Drop your feet. Relax. Deeper. Feel the warmth rush in. Let the tension go. Let your legs relax even deeper. Let them relax deeper

still. Feel your whole body letting go. Feel it. Remember the feeling. Relax.

Now I am going to go over all of the muscle groups again. As I name each group, try to notice whether there is any tension left in the muscle. If there is, let it go. Let the muscle go completely soft. Think of draining all of the tension out. Focus on your face. Explore your face for tension. If you feel any, drain it out. Let the face soften, become smoothe. Your hands. Let the tension drip from your fingertips. Visualize it dripping out, draining from your hands, your arms. (Pause) Your shoulders. Is there any tightness, tension there? If so, let it loose. Open the gates and let it flow outward, filing the space with warmth. Now your chest. Let your mind explore for any tension. Your stomach. Let the tightness go. Softer. Your buttocks. (Pause) If you find any tension in your buttocks, let it flow out. Down through your legs, your calfs, your feet to your toes. Let all of the tension go. Sit quietly for a moment. Experience the relaxation, the tension is gone. Your body feels heavy, soft, relaxed. (Pause) With your eyes still closed, record this memory in your mind. What it feels like to be so relaxed. (Pause)

Now, before you open your eyes, think about how relaxed you are. Think of a scale from 0 to 5 where 0 is complete relaxation, no tension. A 5 is extreme tension, no relaxation. Tell me where you place yourself on that scale right now.

## Systematic Desensitization

*Systematic desensitization* is an anxiety-reduction intervention developed by Wolpe (1958; 1990) and based on the learning principles of classical conditioning. This type of learning involves the pairing (occurring close together) of a neutral event or stimulus with a stimulus that already elicits or causes a reflexive response such as fear. Desensitization employs *counterconditioning*—the use of learning to substitute one type of response for another—to desensitize clients to higher

levels of fear or anxiety. In desensitization, a counteracting stimulus such as relaxation is used to replace anxiety on a step-by-step basis. Wolpe (1982) explains this process:

> *After a physiological state inhibiting anxiety has been induced in the [client] by means of muscle relaxation, [the client] is exposed to a weak anxiety-arousing stimulus for a few seconds. If the exposure is repeated, the stimulus progressively loses its ability to evoke anxiety. Successively stronger stimuli are then similarly treated.* (p. 150)

Desensitization is often the first treatment of choice for *phobias* (experienced fear in a situation in which there is no obvious external danger) or any other disorders arising from specific external events (Rimm & Masters, 1979; Morris, 1980). It is particularly useful in instances where the client has sufficient skills to cope with the situation or perform a desired response but avoids doing so or performs below par because of interfering anxiety and accompanying arousal.

On the other hand, desensitization is inappropriate when the target situation is inherently dangerous (such as sky diving) or when the person lacks appropriate skills to handle the target situation. In the latter case, modeling, rehearsal, and skills-training approaches are more desirable. Counselors can determine whether a particular client's anxiety is irrational or is the result of a truly dangerous situation or a skills deficit by engaging in a careful assessment of the presenting problem. Effective desensitization usually also requires that a client be able to relax and to engage in imagery, although occasionally responses other than relaxation or imagery are used in the intervention.

The intervention involves three basic steps and, on average, takes about ten to thirty sessions to complete, depending on the client, the problem, and the intensity of the anxiety. Those steps are:

1. Training in deep muscle relaxation
2. Construction of a hierarchy representing emotion-provoking situations
3. Graduated pairing through imagery of the items on the hierarchy with the relaxed state of the client

Training in deep muscle relaxation follows the procedure we discussed earlier. If the client is unable to engage in muscle relaxation, some other form of relaxation training, such as that associated with yoga or meditation may be used.

### *Hierarchy Construction*

Hierarchy construction involves identification of various situations that evoke the conditioned emotion to be desensitized, such as anxiety. It may involve either situations the client has already experienced or anticipates in the future. It may also involve something extrinsic to the client, such as snakes or airplanes, as well as something intrinsic, such as feelings of "going nuts." (Wolpe, 1990) The counselor and client can discuss these situations in the counseling sessions, and the client can also keep track of them as they occur in the in vivo setting using notes. As each situation is identified, it is listed separately on a small index card.

There are three possible types of hierarchies one can use in desensitization, depending on the parameters and nature of the client's problem. The three are: *spatio-temporal, thematic,* or *personal.* The *spatio-temporal hierarchy* consists of items that relate to physical or spatial dimensions, such as distance from a feared object, or time dimensions, such as time remaining before a feared or avoided situation such as taking a test. Spatio-temporal hierarchies are particularly useful in reducing client anxiety about a particular stimulus object, event, or person.

*Thematic hierarchies* consist of items representing different parameters surrounding the emotion-provoking situation. For example, a client's fear of heights may be greater or less depending on the contextual cues surrounding the height situation and not just one distance from the ground. Or a client's social anxiety may vary with the type and nature of various interpersonal situations.

*Personal hierarchies* consist of items representing memories or uncomfortable ruminations about a specific person. Dengrove (1966) suggested that personal hierarchies are very useful in desensitizing a client to conditioned emotions produced either by a loss-related situation such as loss of one's job or dissolution of a relationship through death, divorce, separation, and so on. Personal hierarchies can also be used to countercondition a client's avoidance behavior to a particular person who, perhaps because of negative interactions, has become aversive to the client. *Table 9-2* provides an illustration of these three different types of hierarchies.

Regardless of which type of hierarchy is used, each usually consists of ten to twenty different items. After each item is listed on a separate index card, they are arranged by the client in a graduated order from the lowest or least anxiety-provoking to the highest or most anxiety-provoking. The ordering process is also facilitated by a particular scaling and spacing method. Although there are several possible, the most commonly used scaling method is referred to as SUDS or *Subjective Units of Disturbance* (Wolpe & Lazarus, 1966). The SUD

## TABLE 9-2   Three Different Hierarchies Used in Systematic Desensitization

| Spatial-Temporal (Test-Anxiety) | Thematic (Sensitivity to Criticism) |
|---|---|
| 1. It is two weeks before an examination.<br>2. A week before an examination.<br>3. Four days before an examination.<br>4. Three days before an examination.<br>5. Two days before an examination.<br>6. One day before an examination.<br>7. The night before an examination.<br>8. The examination paper lies face down before her.<br>9. Awaiting the distribution of examination papers.<br>10. Standing before the unopened doors of the examination room.<br>11. In the process of answering an examination paper.<br>12. On the way to the university on the day of the examination. | 1. Friend on the street: "Hi! How are you?"<br>2. Friend on the street: "How are you feeling these days?"<br>3. Sister: "You've got to be more careful so they don't put you in a hospital."<br>4. Wife: "You shouldn't drink beer while you are taking medication."<br>5. Mother: "What's the matter? Don't you feel good?"<br>6. Wife: "It's just you yourself. It's all in your head."<br>7. Service station attendant: "What are you shaking for?"<br>8. Neighbor borrowing rake: "Is there something wrong with your leg? Your knees are shaking."<br>9. Friend on the job: "Is your blood pressure okay?"<br>10. Service station attendant: "You are pretty shaky; are you crazy or something?" |

### Personal (Termination of Intimate Relationship)

| | |
|---|---|
| 1. You have been with Susie every day for the last month. You're sitting holding her in your arms and feeling like she's the only woman you'll ever love like this.<br>2. You and Susie are sitting on the floor in your apartment, drinking wine and listening to your records.<br>3. You've just returned from taking Susie to her first race. She's ecstatic about the experience.<br>4. You and Susie are studying together in the library.<br>5. You and Susie are drinking beer at the local pub.<br>6. You and Susie aren't spending every day together. Sometimes she wants to study alone now. You're in the library by yourself studying. | 7. You call Susie up late at night. The phone rings constantly without any answer. You wonder where she is.<br>8. You call Susie to ask her out for dinner and she turns you down—says she doesn't feel well.<br>9. You're walking down the street by the court. You see Susie playing there with another person. You wonder why she hasn't told you about him.<br>10. You go over to Susie's. She isn't there. You wait until she comes. She sees you, goes back to the car, and drives away.<br>11. You call Susie on the phone. She says she doesn't want to see you any more, that she never really loved you, and hangs up on you. |

SOURCES: J. Wolpe, *The Practice of Behavior Therapy*, 4th Ed. (New York: Pergamon Press, 1990), p. 152; J.N. Marquis and W.G. Morgan, *A Guidebook for Systematic Desensitization* (Palo Alto, CA: Veterans Workshop, Veterans Administration Hospital, 1969), p. 28; W.H. Cormier and L.S. Cormier, *Interviewing Strategies for Helpers: Fundamental Skills and Cognitive-Behavioral Interventions*, 3rd Ed. (Monterey, CA: Brooks/Cole, 1991).

scale ranges from 0 to 100. Zero represents absolute calm or no emotion; 100 represents panic or extreme emotion. The client is asked to specify a number between 0 and 100 that best represents the intensity of his or her reaction for each item. Effective hierarchies usually consist of items at all levels of the SUDS scale. If there are more than ten SUDS between any two items, probably another item should be inserted.

After the hierarchy has been constructed and you have trained the client in muscle relaxation or some variation thereof, you are ready to begin the pairing process. This aspect of systematic desensitization can be summarized in the following steps adapted from Wolpe (1990):

**1.** You and your client discuss and agree on a signaling process which the client can use to let you know if and when anxiety begins to be felt. A common signaling system is to have the client raise an index finger if any anxiety (or other conditioned emotion) is experienced.

**2.** You then use the exercise to induce a state of relaxation for the client.

**3.** When your client is deeply relaxed (this will be apparent to you by such things as deeper and slower breathing, changes in body posture, and so on), you describe the first (least emotion-provoking) item on the hierarchy to the client and ask him/her to imagine that item. The first time, you present the item only briefly, for about ten seconds, provided the client does not signal anxiety first. If the client remains relaxed, you instruct him/her to stop visualizing the scene and either to relax or to imagine a pleasant (or comforting) scene (e.g., a sandy beach in summer). Stay with this scene for about thirty seconds.

**4.** Return to the first anxiety hierarchy item, describe it again, and remain with it for about thirty seconds. This second presentation should include as much detailed description as you gave the first time.

**5.** If the client again indicates no anxiety, you have the option of repeating Steps 3 and 4, or moving to the second item in the hierarchy. Typically, an item may require from three to ten repetitions before achieving a SUDS of zero. Scenes that have been desensitized in a prior session may need to be presented again in a subsequent session.

**6.** When your client signals anxiety present (by lifting an index finger), you immediately return to the relaxation process (Step 2), until the client is fully relaxed again. Then you return to the anxiety hierarchy at a lower level (one where the client experienced no anxiety) and begin the process again. Gradually you work back to the hierarchy level where anxiety was experienced. If anxiety is experienced again, repeat this process. Usually within two to three repetitions, the client is able to move through this level of the hierarchy without experiencing anxiety. If a client continues to experience anxiety in a given item, Cormier and Cormier (1991) note there are at least three

things a counselor can do to eliminate continued anxiety resulting from presentation of the same item: add a new, less anxiety-
provoking item to the hierarchy; present the same or the previous
item to the client again for a shorter time period; or assess if the client
is revising or drifting from the scene during the imagery process.

There is one note of caution regarding the manner in which the
counselor responds to a client who is indicating *no* anxiety. The tendency is to respond to the client's relaxed state by saying "good," or
some similar remark. The counselor's intent is to communicate to the
client that "you are doing just what you should be doing." However,
Rimm and Masters (1979) have noted that this could have just the
opposite effect, reinforcing the client's *not signaling* anxiety, and thus
disrupting the process. For this reason, it is better if the counselor
gives no response as long as the client is not indicating the presence
of anxiety.

Each new desensitization session begins with the last item successfully completed during the previous session and ends with a no-
anxiety item. The pairing process is usually terminated in each session
after successful completion of three to five hierarchy items, or after a
duration of twenty to thirty minutes (ten to fifteen minutes for children), although occasionally a client may be able to concentrate for a
longer period and complete more than five items successfully.

Because systematic desensitization may continue over several
weeks, it is important that you keep accurate written notations about
what you did and your client's success each session. Using a note card,
write the date of the session, ending item number, brief description
of the item, and indicate the duration of the last two presentations
of the item (i.e., 30 seconds; 40 seconds). The counselor writes the
scene, followed by how many presentations of the scene were given
as well as the SUDS scores for each presentation. As items are successfully completed without anxiety within the counseling session,
you may assume that your client will be able to confront them in real
life settings also without experiencing undue anxiety or discomfort.
However, you should caution your client not to attempt to encounter
the hierarchy situations in vivo until 75 to 80 percent of the hierarchy desensitization process has been successfully completed.

### *Eye Movement Desensitization*

A promising new variation of desensitization has been developed by
Shapiro (1989) that involves the use of eye movements. This method
of desensitization was developed originally for a condition described
in the *DSM*-IV as post-traumatic stress disorder or PTSD. The procedure has been used more frequently in recent years to inhibit and de-

condition persistent anxiety (Wolpe, 1990) as well as desensitization of traumatic memories. It begins with the elicitation of rhythmic eye movements from clients while they simultaneously hold in imagination the most important feature of a traumatic scene. The apparent advantage of this intervention is that relief is induced without clients having to discuss the trauma in specific ways. Clients treated with this method continued to show freedom from anxiety of traumatic memories up to twelve months following treatment. The mechanism that is activated by the procedure is not clear; Wolpe (1990) cites Jacobson's (1939) observation that relaxation of the extrinsic eye muscles has great potency for emotional relief. For specific instructions in the use of this intervention, counselors should attend a training workshop offered by Shapiro or others skilled in the intervention.

## Case Illustration of Anxiety Reduction

### The Case of Pam

Pam is a ten-year-old fourth grader who has recently refused to go to school. According to her parents, about one month earlier, she got very upset at school and begged her teacher to send her home; her teacher referred her to the school nurse who did so. In the last two weeks, Pam has become physically ill on school mornings and protests strongly when her parents insist that it is time to leave. Her teacher reports that she continues to have periods of being upset and of crying at school. Pam's mother took her to the family doctor who could find no physical cause for her complaints. The parents are perplexed, since Pam has always enjoyed school and seems relatively well adjusted in other areas of her life.

Pam was referred to the school counselor whose assessment revealed that probably Pam became upset initially when a classmate teased her about the fact that she walks with a slight limp. Unfortunately, her feelings of anxiety and stress were terminated by being sent home, rather than being encouraged to stay at school and to deal with the upsetting situation. Pam's reaction to the upsetting experience has remained in her awareness, and she has learned that by staying at home, she can avoid a repetition of the experience. The counselor explained to the parents how this may have occurred and suggests systematic desensitization as a successful treatment method, after determining that Pam's ability to engage in imagery would support this approach. With the parents' signed approval, she began working with Pam, first discussing the procedure thoroughly, explaining that it is an imagination game that will help with fears, and they began to identify the things Pam fears most at school. Together they developed an anxiety hierarchy. Pam indicated that she became most upset as the time for school approaches, so a *spatiotemporal hierarchy* was constructed with time as the significant dimension. At this point, the counselor taught Pam

*Continued*

how to relax, using the relaxation method described earlier. The hierarchy consisted of:

1. It's Friday night. School's over for a whole weekend, and you are thinking about the fun things you will do.
2. It's Saturday. You play most of the day but in the evening, you remember some homework your teacher gave you. It is a game that you think will be fun to do.
3. It's Sunday night. You are tired but had a lot of fun this weekend. It is time to get your books, pencils, and notebook together for school tomorrow morning.
4. It's Monday morning. You wake up feeling funny in your stomach.
5. Mom calls you for breakfast. You are thinking about school and remember the homework you did.
6. You eat cereal and a piece of toast. Mom checks you to see if you look okay. You do. It's almost time for the bus.
7. You stand at the front door. The bus turns the corner and you go down to the curb to be picked up.
8. The bus stops, you get on. Your best friend waves you to the seat she has saved for you.
9. The bus arrives at school. You see your teacher standing on the sidewalk waiting for you. She gives you a big smile.
10. You walk with your teacher to your classroom as she tells you about the exciting project she has for you to do today.

The counselor led Pam through relaxation training and they began the desensitization process. During the first session, she explained the signaling system and then spent about fifteen minutes helping Pam become relaxed. Then she presented the first hierarchy item, "It's Friday night. School's over for a whole weekend . . ." reminding Pam to raise her index finger if or when she felt any discomfort, nervousness, etc. Pam got through the first item with no problem. After two more repetitions to familiarize Pam with the process and increase her relaxed state, the counselor moved to the second item, "It's Saturday. You play most of the day but in the evening, you remember some homework your teacher gave you." Pam raised her index finger. The counselor immediately stopped the item and returned to the relaxation exercise, suggesting to Pam that she think about her cat, Toby. Pam relaxed quickly and the counselor returned to the first item, "It's Friday night. School's over for a whole weekend . . ." This pattern continued until Pam could focus on the Saturday night homework item for 40 seconds without feeling any anxiety. The counselor terminated the counseling session at this point.

In the next counseling session, after making Pam feel comfortable and after talking about what she was doing, the counselor began the desensitization process with the second item, "It's Saturday . . . " Pam experienced no anxiety. The process continued as before, returning to relaxation exercises and thinking about her cat whenever she experienced tension, nervousness, or anxiety.

After nine sessions, Pam was able to go through the entire hierarchy without any anxiety, she no longer had any physical reactions to going to school in the morning, and her confidence was back. The counselor and teacher met twice to discuss how Pam's progress could be supported in the classroom. Pam felt she had successfully beaten her problem, and the case was concluded.

## Self-Management

Many people are legitimately concerned about the long-term effects of counseling. In an effort to promote enduring client changes, counselors have become more concerned with client self-directed change. This interest has led many counseling researchers and practitioners to explore the use of a variety of strategies called *self-control, self-regulation,* or *self-management* (Kanfer & Gaelick-Buys, 1991).

The primary characteristic of a self-management strategy is that the client administers the strategy and directs the change efforts with minimal assistance from the counselor. Kanfer and Gaelick-Buys (1991) note that these strategies are based on a participant model of therapy which emphasizes the client's responsiblity (p. 305). Self-management strategies are among the best strategies designed to strengthen client investment in the helping process. Self-management may eliminate the counselor as a middle person and ensure greater chances of client success because of the investment made by the client in the strategies for change.

### Using Self-Management Interventions

According to Kanfer and Gaelick-Buys (1991), self-management interventions are most easily applied:

> *(1) To help the client acquire more effective interpersonal, cognitive, and emotional behavior*
> *(2) To alter the client's perceptions and evaluative attitudes of problematic situations*
> *(3) To change either a stress-inducing or hostile environment or learn to cope with it by accepting that it is inevitable.* (p. 307)

Self-monitoring, self-reward, and self-contracting are among the more frequently used interventions.

#### Self-Monitoring

*Self-monitoring* involves two processes: self-observation and recording. In *self-observation,* the client notices or discriminates aspects of his/her behavior. *Self-recording* involves using very specific procedures to keep a record of what the client is doing. Taken together, self-monitoring involves having your client count and/or regulate a target behavior, for example, an undesirable habit, or a self-defeating thought or feeling. The process of self-monitoring seems to interfere with the target by breaking the stimulus-response association and drawing the behavior into consciousness or awareness where a choice or decision to enact the behavior can occur. Kanfer (1980) has observed that "[a] person who is asked to observe and record his own behavior is helped immediately to become more aware of its occurrence" (p. 354). Such awareness helps clients to obtain more concrete information about their problem and to collect evidence of changes in the behavior pattern over time.

The initial step in setting up a self-monitoring intervention with a client is selection of the behavior to be monitored or changed. Usually clients will achieve better results if they start by counting only one behavior. The type of behavior can also affect the degree and direction of change that occurs as a result of monitoring. Self-monitoring seems to increase the frequency of postive or desirable behaviors and to decrease the frequency of negative or undesirable behaviors. This effect is called *reactivity*. Self-monitoring of neutral (neither positive nor negative) behaviors results in inconsistent behavior change. For this reason, it is important to have clients monitor behaviors they value or care most about changing.

Deciding how to monitor the behavior is dependent on the circumstances of the client's environmental context and the nature of the behavior to be monitored. Generally, clients are asked to count either how often a behavior occurs or how long a particular condition lasts. If we are interested in focusing on *how often* a behavior occurs, frequency counts are obviously appropriate. But if we simply want to reduce the amount of time dedicated to a particular behavior pattern, then recording the length of time spent talking on the telephone, studying, or playing a computer game is appropriate. Occasionally, clients may wish to record both time and frequency of a behavior.

In some cases where the target behavior occurs very often or continuously, or when the onset and termination of the behavior is difficult to establish, the client might use an *interval method* of recording, which involves dividing the day into half-hour time intervals and then noting whether or not the behavior occurred in each time interval with a yes or no. Mahoney and Thoresen (1974) refer to this as the "all-or-nothing" recording method. Where the observed behavior is qualitative—i.e., better or worse, warmer or colder, happier or sadder—a response scale may be used in which 0 represents one extreme, 7 represents the other extreme, and the client is asked to rate the quality of his/her behavior somewhere between 0 and 7 at each interval. For example, on a scale of 0 to 7, rate how confident you are feeling right now.

According to Watson and Tharp (1993), "[r]ating scales are useful in recording emotions and feelings because intensity is the crucial issue" (p. 79). In the example described above, the monitoring gives the client information about when she felt calm and when she felt anxious. Clients are helped to see that they are not anxious *all of the time*, and that often their anxiety may not be as intense as they imagined it was.

Clients will need to record with the assistance of some "device" for recording. These can range from simple note cards, log sheets, and diaries for written recording, to more mechanical devices such as golf score counters worn on the wrist, kitchen timer, or tape recorder. The device should be simple to use, convenient, portable, and economical.

The timing of self-monitoring can influence any change that is produced by this intervention. If the client wishes to *decrease* the frequency or duration of a monitored behavior (e.g., reduce the number of cigarettes smoked), it is more effective to record the event *prior to* lighting the cigarette. If the objective is to *increase* the frequency or duration of a monitored behavior (e.g., a positive self-statement), then the intervention is more effective if the client records the event *after* its occurrence.

Counting behaviors is the initial step in self-monitoring. The second, and equally important, step is charting or plotting the behavior counts over a period of time. This permits your client to see progress that might not otherwise be apparent. It also permits your client to set daily goals that are more attainable than the overall goal (successive approximation). Clients can take weekly cumulative counts of self-monitored behaviors and chart them on a simple line graph. After initial recording efforts are successful in initiating change, it is useful for clients to continue recording in order to maintain change. Often clients' motivation to continue self-monitoring is enhanced if they reward their efforts for self-monitoring.

### Self-Reward

Self-reward involves intentionally giving oneself a reward following the occurrence of a desired response or behavior. Self-rewards seem to function in the same way as rewards that are external reinforcements. Watson and Tharp (1993, p. 221) draw on work by Nelson, Hays, Sprong, Jarrett, and McKnight (1983) and Catania (1975) to explain this as: "You are teaching yourself to discriminate between correct and incorrect performances. You are reminding yourself of your long-term goals and of your rules for getting there. You are learning self-awareness."

There are three major factors to consider in teaching clients how to use the self-reward intervention: choosing the *right* reward, knowing *how* to give the reward, and knowing *when* to give the reward. Rewards can be objects, contact with other persons, activities, images and ideas and positive self-talk. Watson and Tharp (1993) observe that "[t]he most important reinforcers are those that will eventually maintain [a] new behavior, once it is solidly in place" (p. 212).

Self-reward is a very common practice by people. You go shopping and see a new pair of exercise shoes and say to yourself, "I'm going to buy those and start exercising." The only problem is that the self-reward was not predetermined and it was given *before* the desired behavior. We have already noted that if you wish to *increase* a particular behavior, you should reward yourself *after* the behavior occurs. Thus, self-reward must be a *planned strategy, systematically applied*, and *consistently practiced*. That is unlikely to happen unless you have developed a plan for the self-reward intervention.

Specific types of self-rewards include *verbal-symbolic* (self-praise, such as thinking to yourself, "I really did that well"), *imaginal* (visualizing pleasant scenes—e.g., a new dress or a new suit you plan to buy), or *material* (tangible events or objects that you give yourself at the time of reinforcement).

The most effective self-rewards are perhaps similar to what Glasser and proponents of reality therapy term *positive addictions*—different from conventional addictions in that they bring both short- and long-term benefits, not just immediate gratification and delayed pain. According to Glasser (1985), a positive addiction is anything you do regularly that is also noncompetitive, easy to do, beneficial to you, and results in both self-improvement and self-acceptance.

Clients can be asked to create a "reward menu," which would vary from small to quite large rewards and which they would value and like to receive. These can be further defined as *current reinforcers* (something enjoyable that occurs on a daily basis, such as eating, reading, etc.) and *potential reinforcers* (something that could occur in the future that would be satisfying and enjoyable—e.g., going out to dinner with friends, taking a trip, etc.). Watson and Tharp (1993, pp. 213–214) have developed a reinforcement survey that can be used to help clients identify the things in their world that they find rewarding (see *Table 9-3*).

The rewards clients select should be potent but not so valuable that they would not give them up in the event the target behavior was not achieved. In other words, the reinforcer should be strong enough to make working for it worthwhile and, at the same time, not so indispensable that the client refuses to make it something that must be earned.

After identifying what the reward(s) will be, clients must be instructed on what must be done in order to give themselves a reward. The plan should be defined before starting the self-reward intervention rather than during the intervention. Clients should know, and it helps if it is written out, just what the desirable outcome will be for achieving a particular sub-goal. This plan can be defined with the client's assistance. It is also important that clients know when they should administer a self-reward. It is perhaps more effective to en-

**TABLE 9-3   Example of Reinforcement Survey**

1. What will be the *rewards* of achieving your goal?
2. What kind of praise do you like to receive, from yourself or from others?
3. What kinds of things do you like to have?
4. What are your major interests?
5. What are your hobbies?
6. What people do you like to be with?
7. What do you like to do with those people?
8. What do you do for fun?
9. What do you do to relax?
10. What do you do to get away from it all?
11. What makes you feel good?
12. What would be a nice present to receive?
13. What kinds of things are important to you?
14. What would you buy if you had an extra $20? $50? $100?
15. On what do you spend your money each week?
16. What behaviors do you perform every day? (Don't overlook the obvious or the commonplace.)
17. Are there any behaviors that you usually perform instead of the target behavior?
18. What would you hate to be?
19. Of the things you do every day, which would you hate to give up?
20. What are your favorite daydreams and fantasies?
21. What are the most relaxing scenes you can imagine?

SOURCE: D.C. Watson and R.J. Tharp, *Self-Directed Behavior: Self-Modification for Personal Adjustment,* 6th Ed. (Monterey, CA: Brooks/Cole. 1993), pp. 213–214.

courage them to reward themselves for *gradual* progress toward the desired goal. Daily rewards for small steps are more effective, by and large, than one big reward that is given only when major progress is made. Watson and Tharp (1993, p. 222) illustrate how this what/when schedule can be defined:

> *If the dieter arranges the reinforcement of, say, watching an enjoyable TV program immediately after (or even during) self-restraint, dieting is more likely to be observed than if he or she depends entirely on the long-range rewards of being slim someday. In other words, it is the TV program that right now competes with an extra bowl of spaghetti, not the dim dream of slimness in what, at the moment, may appear as a faraway future.*

Immediate reinforcement is especially critical in cases where the undesired behavior consists of consummatory or fear responses (Watson & Tharp, 1993). The ice cream cone or piece of candy you eat right now is more reinforcing than the change in the scale next week or the drop in your clothing size next month. If clients select material rewards that aren't portable enough to be carried around for immediate reinforcement, they might consider the following intermediate options as immediate rewards:

**1.** Tell a significant other about their behavior to elicit their encouragement. Social reinforcement can be very powerful in helping clients to find extra opportunities to be reinforced and also to ward off urges and temptations.
**2.** Assign points to each occurrence of the desired behavior; after accumulating a specified number of points, trade it in for a larger reinforcer. Points (sometimes called tokens) are useful because they make it possible to employ a variety of reinforcers and also make it easy to increase a behavior gradually (Watson & Tharp, 1993, pp. 224–227).
**3.** Engage in imagined or verbal-symbolic rewards; see, hear, and feel what it is like to be ten pounds slimmer, or praise yourself covertly for refusing that second helping (granted, this doesn't work for everyone).

### *Self-Contracting*

Clients who are able to identify and be responsible for their behaviors often acknowledge that their current actions are resulting in some undesirable consequences. They can see how they would like the consequences to be different. They may or may not realize that in order to change those consequences, they must first modify the behaviors producing them. Behavior change of any kind can be slow. Therefore, getting clients to make behavior changes is not easy. You must first obtain the client's *commitment* to change.

The behavioral contract is a useful intervention for gaining the client's cooperation and commitment. Behavioral contracting is used by a growing number of theoretical approaches but has been popularized by behavioral and reality therapists. The contract specifies what actions the client agrees to take in order to reach the desired goal. Kanfer and Gaelick (1991, p. 303) observe that "contracts can reduce clients' fears that they will never overcome their problems by requiring only small behavior changes at first." The contract contains a description of the conditions surrounding the action steps: *where* the client will undertake such actions; *how* (in what manner) the client will carry out the actions; and *when* (by what time) the tasks will be completed. Because these contract terms are specified in writing and signed by the client, we refer to this intervention as *self-contracting*. The most effective contracts have terms that are completely acceptable to the client, are very specific, and reflect short-range goals that are feasible (Kanfer & Gaelick, 1991). Self-contracts often are more successful when they are paired with self-reward.

In some cases a self-contract may also include sanctions that the client administers for failure to meet the contract terms. However, the rewards and sanctions should be balanced, and a self-contract that emphasizes positive terms is probably more effective. When clients do not fulfill terms of their self-contract, some theoretical orientations—i.e., Glasser's reality therapy—believe it is important for the counselor not to accept excuses, but at the same time, not be critical or punative.

Self-contracts are very useful in working with children and adolescents because the conditions are so concrete. When contracts are used with children, several additional guidelines are applicable (Homme, Csanyi, Gonzales, & Rechs, 1969; Kanfer, 1980):

**1.** The required behavior should be easy for the child to identify.

**2.** The total task should be divided into subtasks, and initial contracts should reward completion of each component or subtask. Other steps can be added later, after each successive target behavior is well established.

**3.** Smaller, more frequent rewards are more effective in maintaining the child or adolescent's interest in working for change than larger, less frequently administered rewards.

**4.** In the case of a self-contract, rewards controlled by the child or teenager are generally more effective than those dispensed by adults. For example, a child who completes his workbook pages at school by lunchtime may dispense a variety of accessible rewards to and for himself, such as free time, visiting the library, drawing, and so on. This helps the child to view the reward "as recognition of accomplishments and not as payment for obedience" (Kanfer, 1980, p. 351).

**5.** Rewards follow rather than precede performance of the target behavior to be increased. The client must agree to complete the specified activity first before engaging in any part of the reward.

**6.** The client must view the contract as a fair one which, in an equitable way, balances the degree of work and energy expended and the resulting payoffs or consequences.

**7.** The most effective self-contracts for children and adolescents facilitate their overall growth and development and are used daily. "[T]he very essence of the effectiveness of the contract procedure, as of many other self-management techniques, lies in the fact that it becomes a rule for everyday conduct. Neither contract management nor other methods can be reserved for use only as special occasions, on weekends, or in difficult situations" (Kanfer, 1980, p. 352).

### Client Commitment to Self-Management

A critical problem in the effective use of any self-management intervention is having the client use the intervention regularly and consistently. Clients will be more likely to carry out self-management programs if certain conditions exist, including the following:

**1.** The use of the self-management program will provide enough advantages or positive consequences to be worth the cost to the client in terms of time and effort.

**2.** Clients believe in their capacity to change. Since beliefs create one's reality, the belief that change is possible helps clients try harder when they get stuck or are faced with an unforeseen difficulty in their change plans (Watson & Tharp, 1993, p. 43).

**3.** Clients' utilization of self-management processes reflects their own standards of performance, not the standards of the counselor or of significant others. Karoly (1982, p. 22) addresses this problem of borrowed goals: "[S]elf-mananagement efforts are unlikely to be maintained if clients are merely learning how to behave in accordance with standards that are foreign to them." He recommends that an important ingredient of any self-management program, particularly for clients who are ambivalent about their choices, is *values clarification*.

**4.** Clients use personal reminders about their goals when tempted to stray from the intervention plan. A written list of self-reminders that clients can carry at all times may prove helpful in this respect.

**5.** If the client se..etly harbors an escape plan ("I'll study every day except when my friend drops over" or "I'll diet except on Sundays") this should be made explicit. Concealed escape plans are likely to wreak havoc onto the best-conceived self-management programs. Watson and Tharp (1993) note that some escape clauses may be particularly detrimental to change, particularly those that reactivate an irresistible craving. However, they recommend that any plan "should clearly state all intended escapes, whether or not they are wise" (p. 55).

**6.** The self-management program is directed toward maintenance as well as initial acquisition of target behaviors. For this to occur, you must take into account the client's lifestyle.

> *Self-management requires more than a temporary change in setting conditions or the acquisition of specific strategies. For therapeutic change to be maintained, the individual must be prepared, by virtue of his or her mode of information processing, the adequacy of active coping skills, and by dint of having selected a supportive social setting (friends, co-workers, spouse, etc.) to deal with unforeseen challenges, conflicts, periods of depression, and/or the periodic malfunctioning of "best laid plans."* (Karoly, 1982, p. 22)

**7.** The client's use of the program may be strengthened by enlisting the support and assistance of other persons—as long as their roles are positive, not punishing. Former clients, peers, or friends can aid the client in achieving goals through reinforcement of the client's regular use of the self-management strategies and reminders to resist temptations.

**8.** The counselor maintains some minimal contact with the client during the time the self-management program is being implemented. Counselor reinforcement is quite important in successful implementation of self-management efforts.

You can provide reinforcement easily through oral approval or by acknowledging progress. Have the client drop in or telephone regularly during the course of the self-management program. This enables you to provide immediate encouragement and, if necessary, to modify the program if it is flawed.

## *Case Illustration of Self-Management*

*The Case of Kareem*

Kareem is a fourteen-year-old boy who has scored very high on ability tests but has performed consistently below his ability level in school. He admits that his poor grades are due, for the most part, to what he calls "not really trying." When asked by the counselor to define and give examples of this, Kareem noted that he rarely took homework home, or if he did, he didn't complete it. He also said that he rarely opened a book and often had not studied for tests. As a direct result of a series of events that occurred in his neighborhood, Kareem sought out the counselor for help in changing his ways. He has decided that he wants to go to college and was starting to realize that his bad grades would adversely affect this possibility unless he pulled them up. He was concerned because he did not know how to change what he referred to as bad study habits.

The counselor supported his newly found goals and explained some of the rationale and process of a strategy called self-management. She pointed out that Kareem, rather than herself, would be in charge of setting specific goals for his performance and monitoring his progress. She assured him that she would be there to help him start the process and to assist whenever he needed help. This appealed to Kareem, who stated that he is tired of having so many other people on his back about doing better in school.

Because Kareem's present base rate for studying was almost zero, the counselor initially discussed some realistic goals that he might want to set for himself as part of a self-contract. She helped him build in a self-monitoring system and a self-reward process. Kareem decided to set the following goals and action steps for his contract:

*Goal:* To improve my rate of homework assignment completion during the next nine-week grading period from zero to 85 percent.

*Action Steps:* To keep a daily record of assigned homework and to establish a time and place at home where he

*Continued*

would work on homework *every day*. On Fridays, he would do Monday's homework. On Saturdays he would be free from school work but on Sundays, he would review his assignments and organize his books for the next school day.

In addition, he completed a reinforcement survey like the one in *Table 9-3* and selected eight potential rewards that he could use to reinforce his action steps. Kareem included a *bonus clause* in his self-contract which specified an additional reward any week he exceeded the 85 percent level of homework completion. His self-contract is illustrated in *Figure 9-1*.

The counselor explained a self-monitoring system which Kareem could use to track his progress. She suggested that he use a daily log to record completion of each homework assignment (a large poster board with each school day of the month and a thermometer-like graph to show the percentage of his homework that he completed). She also asked Kareem if he wanted to use any outside source to verify completion of assignments but he indicated that he didn't need that. Finally, she and Kareem agreed to meet each Monday morning and he was to show her his monitoring chart (which he could roll up and store in his locker easily). Kareem's log for the first week is shown in *Figure 9-2*.

Kareem found the self-management strategy to work. Several conditions contributed to this outcome: he was highly motivated; he did not want others to be monitoring him; he chose a reasonable goal and action steps; he liked the counselor; the counselor liked him and was clearly supportive of his goal, his motivation, and his plan; and the counselor followed up religiously on the Monday morning commitments.

## Client Reactions to Behavioral Interventions

Behavioral interventions are often very appealing to clients, particularly in the initial stages of counseling when clients are highly motivated and want something to be done about their situations. The specificity, concreteness, and emphasis on action that these interventions offer, help clients to feel as if something important is being done on their behalf. Even nonbehavioral counselors sometimes use a behavioral intervention such as relaxation to capitalize on this phenomenon, which can increase the counselor's credibility with the client and the client's sense of trust that counseling can and will make a difference.

As the helping process continues, some of the clients' initial enchantment with the procedures may wear thin as they discover the

Name of Contractor: _____

Date of Contract: _____

### *This I Will Do:*

*Goals of Contract:* To improve my grades by improving my homework assignment completions from zero percent to 85 percent.

*Action Steps:*  1 a.  I will keep a homework assignment book and will write down each homework assignment before leaving my desk after each class period.

  1 b.  I will transfer my homework assignments from my book to my record poster before I become involved in any other activity at home.

  2 a.  I will clear space in my room and move the old desk from the basement into the room as a working place.

  2 b.  I will start my homework assignment no later than 4:00 P.M. each day and will not stop until it is completed (unless dinner interrupts my plans, in which case I will return to homework until it is finished).

  3 a.  I will indicate on my record poster which assignments I completed and I will record the percentage at the end of the week.

  3 b.  I will bring my record poster to Miss Bancroft on Mondays at 7:45 A.M. and will review my progress before classes begin.

*Rewards:*  1. Watch the sports channel news at 11:00 P.M.
  2. Listen to my music between the end of school and 4:00 P.M.
  3. Play pool with the guys on Friday night.
  4. Go to the mall and take in a movie on Saturday night.
  5. Hang out.
  6. Buy a new CD.
  7. Talk to girls on the phone.
  8. Get a pizza.

Date contract will be reviewed: _____

Signatures: _____ Kareem L. (client) _____

_____ Miss Bancroft (counselor) _____

**FIGURE 9-1  Behavioral Self-Contract**

different and often painful work of changing fixed and established behavior patterns. Successful use of behavioral interventions requires a significant investment of time, energy, and persistence from clients—daily practice, homework assignments, accurate recordkeeping, and so on.

To counteract any potential pitfalls or letdowns, counselors who rely heavily on behavioral interventions during the helping process must also generate involvement with the client through a positive re-

*Scoreboard*

Name: _____ Kareem L. _____

Behavior Record: 1. _____ Management of homework assignments _____

2. _____ Completion of homework assignments _____

Week of: February 5

| Day | Assignments | Done | Reward |
|-----|-------------|------|--------|
| Monday | English (read) | | |
| | Math (problems) | X | |
| | Biology (lab report) | X | Listen to music |
| | History (read) | | |
| Tuesday | English (nothing-read Monday's) | X | |
| | Math (problems) | | |
| | Biology (read) | X | Listen to music |
| | History (questions) | X | Watch sports news |
| Wednesday | English (read) | X | Listen to music |
| | Math (nothing) | | |
| | Biology (questions) | X | Watch sports news |
| | History (read) | X | Call Clarice - talk |
| Thursday | English (study for quiz) | X | |
| | Math (problems) | X | Listen to music |
| | Biology (read) | X | Watch sports channel |
| | History (questions) | X | Call Felicia |
| Friday | English (theme) | | |
| | Math (study for test) | X | Listen to music |
| | Biology (read) | X | Watch sports news |
| | History (study for quiz) | X | |

Amount completed: 15 out of 19 assignments.

//////////////////////////////////////////////////////////////////////

**FIGURE 9-2 Assignment Record**

lationship and commitment to action. When counselors use behavioral approaches, they must find ways to strengthen the client's compliance with the demands of the intervention. Compliance can be enhanced in a number of ways. Additional techniques for fostering compliance include creating a positive expectancy set, providing detailed instructions about the use and benefits of an intervention, having the client rehearse the intervention, and having the client visualize and explore beneficial aspects of change.

## Summary

In this chapter, we have explored a variety of counseling interventions based on action-oriented helping approaches. These approaches focus on direct modification of a client's behavior and rely heavily on principles of learning to facilitate behavior change.

The modeling and rehearsal interventions we described are major components of skill training programs such as assertion training, job interview skills training, and social skills training. These interventions are most useful when clients have skill deficits or lack effective skills for selected situations.

Anxiety reduction strategies such as muscle relaxation, sensory relaxation, and systematic desensitization are useful for dealing with the behavioral excess of fear, worry, and anxiety. Muscle relaxation is used as either a single strategy or as part of systematic desensitization.

Self-management intervention programs are growing in their usage and success. Clients are put in charge of their change program; the counselor acts as a facilitator of that process. Common components of a self-management program include self-monitoring, self-reward, and self-contracting.

Behavioral interventions are very appealing to many clients because they offer specificity, concreteness, and something that can be done by the client. A major problem with continued use is management of the appropriate level of client commitment to ensure success.

## Exercises

*I. Modeling*

Listed below are four hypothetical clients who might derive benefit from a modeling intervention. Based on the description given about each client, select the model that might be most effective for the client.

**1.** The client is an African American male in a graduate program who is avoiding a required statistics course because of his fear of math.
   **a.** An older African American male who has already succeeded in statistics.
   **b.** A white male who has overcome his fear of statistics.
   **c.** An African American male of similar age who is also enrolled in a graduate program that requires statistics.

**2.** The client is a young, White, male who lost a leg in a car accident and is trying to learn to get around in a wheelchair without soliciting assistance from other people.
   **a.** A female who has been in a wheelchair since birth.
   **b.** A White male who survived a motorcycle crash.
   **c.** An older white male who is successfully employed.

**3.** The client is a middle-aged woman who is enrolled in a special treatment program for alcoholics.

**a.** Another middle-aged woman who has successfully overcome alcoholism through a similar program.

**b.** Another woman who is an active alcoholic.

**c.** The woman's husband or a close relative.

**4.** The client is a young woman who is institutionalized in a state hospital because she has refused to go out of her house for two years, believing that people were after her.

**a.** Another institutionalized patient who is in the prerelease program.

**b.** A staff psychiatrist.

**c.** A female staff aide.

## II. *Behavior Rehearsal*

With a partner, try out the process of behavior rehearsal. One of you should take the client's role, and the other can assume the role of helper. Have the client present a problem in which the desired behavior change is to acquire a skill or to extinguish a fear. The counselor should try out the behavior rehearsal intervention to help the client meet this goal. Here are the things to remember to do:

**1.** Specify the target behavior(s).

**2.** Determine the situations in which the skills need to be used or the fear needs to be reduced.

**3.** Arrange these situations on a hierarchy, starting with the least difficult or least anxiety-producing situations and gradually moving up to situations of greater difficulty, complexity, or threat.

**4.** Beginning with the first situation on the hierarchy, have the client engage in covert rehearsal of the target response(s). Following this practice attempt, ask the client to analyze it.

**5.** Using the same situation, have the client engage in a role-play (overt) rehearsal. Give the client feedback about the strengths and limitations of this practice. Supplement your feedback with an audiotape or videotape analysis, as feasible.

**6.** Determine when the client has satisfactorily demonstrated the target skills or reduced anxiety within the interview rehearsals. Assign homework consisting of in vivo rehearsal of this one situation.

**7.** Repeat Steps 4 through 6 for the other situations on the hierarchy.

## III. *Relaxation*

Using triads or small groups, practice providing muscle relaxation training for someone in the group. You can utilize the instructions found on pages 229–230. After the procedure, obtain feedback both from your role-play "client" and from observers. Some of the items you may wish to solicit feedback about are:

**a.** Your voice—pitch, tempo, volume

**b.** The pacing or speed with which you took the person through the procedure

**c.** The clarity of your instructions

After you have practiced with this intervention and received feedback from another person, you may want to put the instructions on an audiotape and critique it yourself.

**IV.** *Systematic Desensitization*

Instructions:

**1.** Match each of the client descriptions listed below with the type of hierarchy that would be most appropriate to use with that particular client. Explain your choice. Be sure to give a rationale for your choice.

**2.** Pick one of the client descriptions from this list and develop a corresponding hypothetical hierarchy for the client. Consult with a colleague or instructor after your hierarchy is completed.

*Type of Hierarchy*
   **a.** Spatio-temporal
   **b.** Thematic
   **c.** Personal

*Client Descriptions*

**1.** The client is very stressed after the recent dissolution of a five-year relationship.

**2.** The client becomes increasingly anxious about a speech as the time of the speech draws near.

**3.** The client becomes anxious in situations that involve other people.

**4.** The client becomes more anxious as she gets farther away from her house.

**5.** The client is very upset after the death of her spouse two years ago.

**V.** *Self-Management*

This exercise is designed to help you modify some aspect of your helping behavior with the use of a self-management program.

**1.** Select and define a behavior you wish to increase or decrease that, when changed, will make you a better helper. The behavior may be an overt one, such as asking open questions instead of closed questions. Or the behavior may be covert, such as reducing the number of apprehensive thoughts about seeing clients or increasing some self-enhancing thoughts about your helping potential.

**2.** Record the occurrence of the behavior for a week or two to obtain a baseline measure; the baseline gives you the present level of the behavior before applying any self-management interventions.

**3.** After obtaining some baseline data, deliberately try to increase or decrease the behavior (depending on your goal) using self-monitoring. Remember, prebehavior monitoring to decrease a response and postbehavior monitoring to increase a response. Do this for about two weeks. Does the behavior change over time in the desired direction? If so, you may want to continue with self-monitoring for a few more weeks. Charting and posting the data will help you see visible progress.

**4.** Work out a self-reward plan or write out a self-contract related to the behavior change you are seeking.

**5.** Continue to self-record the occurrence of the behavior during Step 4; then compare these data with the data you gathered during baseline (Step 2). What change occurs?

## Discussion Questions

**1.** Behavioral approaches assume that much maladaptive behavior is acquired through learning. What is your reaction to this assumption?

**2.** In what ways does learning occur through counseling?

**3.** In using behavioral approaches with clients, to what extent do you think that you are treating real problems or merely symptoms?

**4.** In what counseling settings do you think behavioral interventions would be most useful?

## Recommended Readings

Cautela, J.R. and Kearney, A.J. (1993). *Covert Conditioning Casebook*, Pacific Grove, CA: Brooks/Cole.

Cormier, W.H. and Cormier, L.S. (1991). *Interviewing Strategies for Helpers: Fundamental Skills and Cognitive-Behavioral Interventions*, 3d ed. Pacific Grove, CA: Brooks/Cole.

Deffenbacker, J., Thwaites, G., Wallace, T., and Oetting, E. (1994). Social skills and cognitive-relaxation approaches to general anger reduction, *Journal of Counseling Psychology, 41,* 386–396.

Glasser, W. (1985). *Positive Addiction*, New York: Harper & Row.

Kanfer, F.H. and Goldstein, A.P., Eds. (1991). *Helping People Change*, 4th ed. New York, Pergamon.

Karoly, P. and Kanfer, F.A., Eds. (1982). *Self-Management and Behavior Change*, New York: Pergamon Press.

Lazarus, A.A. (1989). *The Practice of Multimodal Therapy*, Baltimore: Johns Hopkins University Press.

Öst, L.G., Westling, B.E., and Hellström, I. (1993). Applied relaxation, exposure *in vivo* and cognitive methods in the treatment of panic disorder with agraphobia, *Behaviour Research and Therapy, 31,* 383–394.

Watson, D.L. and Tharp, R.G. (1993). *Self-Directed Behavior: Self-Modification for Personal Adjustment*, 6th ed. Pacific Grove, CA: Brooks/Cole.

Wilson, G.T. and Agras, W.S. (1992). The future of behavior therapy, *Psychotherapy, 29,* 39–43.

Wolpe, J. (1990). *The Practice of Behavior Therapy*, 4th ed. New York: Pergamon Press.

# Chapter 10

# Systemic Interventions

***Purpose of This Chapter—***

Much that we have studied considers the individual client separate from his or her social environment. But of course, that is not how humans function. In this chapter we shall consider a theoretical alternative to those psychologically based interventions that have been discussed in preceding chapters. We shall examine a variety of counseling interventions that assume (a) human problems are not based in the individual but rather, in the system in which the individual functions; (b) change in any part of the system affects all parts of the system, and thus, the individual who is experiencing the problem; and (c) systemic change must reflect not only the immediate social system in which it occurs but also other systems—for example, gender, culture, race—as they contribute to the system's characteristics and values.

***Considerations as You Read This Chapter—***

• Central to systemic thinking is the notion that problems are rooted in systems. One criticism of this is that it removes from the individual any responsibility for that person's problems. Do you agree? How might this impact the individual's participation in counseling?

• You will also note that the systemic counselor seems to be quite active and emphasizing change rather than insight. What advantages could you predict from this approach. What problems could you foresee?

• Finally, to what problems in social units other than the family might these interventions be applied? How do you think the process would be different than that in which the family is the focus?

Systemic interventions are drawn from a variety of approaches that view the individual as part of a larger social context. Seen this way, the individual constantly interacts with that larger context, contributing and responding in ways that can best be understood by understanding the social context. Thus, the system's role becomes more meaningful and impactful and the individual's role is diminished, when compared to most psychological views of human behavior. This way of viewing human functioning can be likened to ecological systems in which all elements are interrelated, and in which change at any level of those interrelated parts will lead to alteration of the whole system. One of the better ways of illustrating this is through the functioning of the family unit.

Recent years have witnessed a maturing of the systemic therapy movement. Its roots date to the 1950s, when Gregory Bateson was first studying the relationship between schizophrenia and interpersonal functioning within the family. Stimulated by Bateson's early thinking, the next twenty years witnessed an explosion of new concepts on the functioning of family systems. These concepts have begun to crystallize into four recognizable schools of family therapy: the *object relations* school which includes writers such as Framo (1982) and Zuk (1975); the *family systems* school, represented by Bowen (1978); the *structural family therapy* school, identified in the writings of Minuchin and Fishman (1981); and the *strategic intervention* school which embraces a ranging group of theorists and therapists. Strategic intervention became recognized as a result of the work and writings of therapists associated with the Mental Research Institute of Palo Alto (MRI). These included Jackson (1961), Jay Haley (1963, 1973, 1976, 1980), and Weakland, Fisch, Watzlawick, and Bodin (1974). Haley later established his own Family Therapy Institute in Washington, DC, where he and Cloe Medanes continue to develop their particular variations of systemic thinking. The strategic intervention approach is also represented in other cultures, particularly in the work of the Milan *systemic therapy* school (Palazzoli, Cecchin, Prata, & Boscolo, 1978), which is also reflected in the work of the *Ackerman Institute* group of New York City (Hoffman, 1981). These groups reflect a theoretical continuum that extends from a highly psychoanalytic orientation (object relations) to an ecological basis (Foley, 1989).

The different schools all occupy prominent positions in the practice of marriage and family therapy in the United States and have a growing list of practitioners and advocates in Great Britain, Israel, Germany, and Finland. One might ask why the systemic approach has been particularly successful in moving into other cultures. One answer undoubtedly is that the philosophical underpinnings of this approach lend themselves to different cultural perspectives. Even in cultures as individualistic as the British or Finnish, an ecological perspective of human interaction seems to be more facilitative than some of the more individualistic approaches.

As with the interventions we discussed in earlier chapters, the interventions associated with the systemic model have received criticism by feminist therapists who believe that so many of the family therapy models were developed without attention to the female experience, and, as a result, contain covert gender bias (Goodrich, Rampage, Ellman, & Halstead, 1988; McGoldrick, Anderson, & Walsh, 1989). Enns (1993), one of the more recent critics observes that:

> *The notion that all persons within a system contribute equally to problems ignores the reality of power differentials within the family and results in the minimalization or trivialization of acts of violence associated with battering, incest, and child abuse. By removing individual responsibility for behavior, these "neutral" systems also contribute to mother blaming. Family therapies have also contributed to the idealization of White, middle class family structures and may subtly reinforce stereotyped gender roles. Finally, terms such as enmeshment, fusion, and symbiosis are sometimes used to pathologize women's relational qualities and concepts such as complementarity and hierarchy encourage role differentiation along traditional lines.* (p. 31)

Similarly, family therapy models that embrace systemic thinking have been criticized with respect to their lack of attention to the ethnicity of the [American] family in treatment. Rigazio-DiGillio (1993) observes that "ethnicity is a filter through which families and individuals understand and interpret their symptoms, their attitude toward helpers, and their preferred treatment methods" (p. 338).

These criticisms may be more directed at what has been written about family therapy in the professional journals than by what is practiced in family therapy. Even if this is the case, it is important to recognize that the structure and social organization of families are strongly influenced by cultural and ethnic factors, thus producing wide-ranging variations among families in what is typically thought of as a "melting pot" American culture. In many respects the White middle-class American family has come to represent a standard against which all other families are measured. However, what the White middle-class American family finds acceptable as therapeutic interventions may alienate or completely miss the mark with many American families. For example, Berg and Jaya (1993, p. 32) note that American children [presumably that middle-class White standard] seem to fight their way out of the family in order to emancipate or individuate themselves. By contrast, Asian families view being excluded from the family as the worst possible punishment one can endure. Emancipation and individuation are alien concepts.

Hierarchy within the therapy relationship and the family system, however, takes on a different meaning for African American families, who confront racism and oppression on a daily basis, again making their experience different from majority culture clients (Stevenson & Renard, 1993; Cheatham & Stewart, 1990). As these authors note, an awareness and acknowledgement of the role and presence of racism and oppression is very important in working with African American families because it is a part of their system. Otherwise the counselor may become an agent for illegitimate and abusive power in the hierarchy of the relationship and also may stimulate too many feelings of mistrust (Stevenson & Renard, 1993).

## Interpersonal Systems Thinking

In systemic thinking, families and other social systems have inherent structure, dictated by rules, roles, boundaries, and patterns of behaving. These structural qualities are explained through principles of interpersonal functioning of family members.

*Cohesive interpersonal systems develop a self-sustaining quality.* The integral parts (members) of the system collectively seek to maintain the system, even when the system may be failing to meet the needs of an individual member. Thus the system's preservation becomes the dominant motive for functioning. This can be illustrated by the many ways families adapt to children's growing up and becoming adults.

*The internal organization of the cohesive system is defined by systemic "rules."* Systemic rules are a euphemism for interactions between individual members that are so predictable that one might think a rule exists to govern the behavior. An example might be the manner in which the father reenters the family system each evening (no one is to disturb him until he has had time to read his paper or drink a beer) or the manner in which a particular child is disciplined (only the mother may discipline Billy). Such rules contribute to the family's drive to sustain the system. When rules are broken, the violator may be dealt with by the entire system or by a designated enforcer. For example, if the father is an incorrigible grouch, family rules will evolve that attempt to control those stimuli that will put him in a bad mood. Strong pressure will be exerted on maverick family members to keep them from breaking the rules that might lead to father's bad temper.

*Most individuals function within a network of systems embedded within systems.* As we begin to conceptualize how and, perhaps, why the individual functions as he or she does, we must realize that more is involved than just the sociological family unit. Clearly, families also function within other systems. One of those systems is the family's cultural heritage, whether it be visibly obvious or only apparent through the family's ceremonial patterns (Preli & Bernard, 1993). Szapocznik and Kurtines (1993) point out that this is particularly observable with the family that has a distinct cultural heritage, such as Hispanic or African American. Culture is not the only system in which families function. Socioeconomic status also contributes to functioning systems (e.g., families below the poverty level or those families that are in the "upper-middle class" and identify with labels such as "yuppies", "beamers", etc.).

These examples suggest that the family functions as an integral system imbedded within other systems. When counseling is sought, the counselor must make the decision either to treat family members individually, or to view the family system as the client. When treating the system, the counselor's conceptual approach must reflect an awareness of governing rules, structure, systems within systems, and other ecological factors. For this reason, systemic therapy has evolved by using traditional interventions in new ways or by developing new kinds of interventions that are more effective with system change.

The major portion of this book has addressed counseling interventions in an individual context. By increasing the number of individuals involved in any intervention, interpersonal dynamics (current or historical) become a a significant dimension of the therapy process. This fact has led to the emergence of communications approaches.

*Dysfunctional systems tend to develop rigid boundaries.* The psychological boundaries that define the family (separate the family from other social units such as neighbors) identify and sustain the family unit. Because dysfunctional families experience greater vulnerability, the systemic tendency is to become more rigid and resistant to change. Thus, the dysfunctional family finds change to be more difficult to accomplish than the family with more flexible boundaries. This can be particularly problematic when the dysfunctional family is of a cultural background in which family identity and solidarity are emphasized (e.g., the Italian American family), thus possibly magnifying the intensity of the problem.

The fact that family system rigidity is related to the group's level of dysfunction has caused theorists to search for more effective interventions. Thus, the structural and strategic approaches have emerged. The first of these, *structural therapy*, has focused on redefining the system by altering interpersonal rules and boundaries in a behavioral manner. The second, *strategic therapy*, has developed cognitive interventions as a means of entering and altering family members' conceptualizations of the system and how it should function.

In this chapter, we shall examine how many individual interventions are also adaptable and effective in achieving better communication, structural change, and strategic change. In addition, attention will be directed to systemic interventions that are associated with the newer family approaches.

## Altering Communication Patterns

Family or group dysfunctions may be approached from a variety of directions. Sometimes the underlying issue appears to be a fundamental misunderstanding among family members. This misunderstanding may relate to members' expectations, roles in the family organization, or responsibilities. When communication appears either to have broken down or fails due to lack of communication skills, the counselor may use a variety of interventions to teach or develop insight and skills for family or group members to use. Nichols and Schwartz (1994) observe that most of the techniques used by communications family therapy consist of teaching rules of clear communication, analyzing and interpreting communication patterns, and manipulating interactions through a variety of strategic maneuvers.

## Communication Skill-Building

Often communication skill-building begins with an introduction to basic rules of communication. These "rules" are really guidelines to sending and receiving clear and concise messages. Gestalt therapy, reality therapy, transactional analysis, and rational emotive therapy all emphasize these rules. In addition, the work of Jackson and Weakland (1961) and programs such as the Minnesota Couples Communication Program have contributed to communication rules training. Effective communications rules are fairly simple. They include: (a) speaking in the first person singular; (b) speaking for self; and (c) speaking directly to the person for whom the communication is intended.

These simple rules often prove to be rather difficult to master, particularly when they run counter to the individual's habitual or cultural patterns of communication. Consequently, the acquisition of a new pattern may require instruction, rehearsal, evaluation, and continued practice. (These elements of skill training are discussed in Chapter 9.) For example, some people develop a communication style in which the personal pronoun "I" is almost never used. In its place, the impersonal second person (you) or the collective (we or people) is used. This is illustrated by a brief dialogue between Bob and his wife, Janet.

*Janet:* Bob, are you going to cut the grass tomorrow?

*Bob:* You know people don't cut the grass on Sunday.

*Janet:* Well, I just thought it would be good to cut it before Monday.

*Bob:* Well, that's just not what one does on a Sunday.

The counselor might point out to Bob that when he uses such referents as "people" and "one," he is speaking in terms that Miller, Wackman, Nunnally, and Miller (1989) refer to as *underresponsible.* This notion of responsible communication is the same as the Gestaltist notion of *claiming ownership.* In other words, if Bob were to say, "You know I don't cut the grass on Sunday," he would be taking responsibility for the claim rather than attributing it to unknown "people."

Underresponsible communication is a style. It does not necessarily reflect an intention to avoid responsibility, although it can. The counselor might work with Bob and Janet to increase Bob's awareness both of his style and the consequences of his style.

---

*Counselor:* Bob, when you say, "People don't cut the grass on Sunday," aren't you also saying "I don't cut the grass on Sunday?"

*Bob:* Right

*Counselor:* What would happen if you just said, "I don't want to cut the grass on Sunday"?

*Bob:* Nothing, I guess. Maybe Janet wouldn't understand why.

*Counselor:* Could you tell her why if she didn't understand?

*Bob:* Yeah, I guess so.

*Counselor:* Why don't you tell Janet why you don't want to cut the grass?

*Bob:* O.K. I don't want to cut the grass on Sunday because I don't think it looks good to the neighbors.

*Counselor:* Janet, is it different when Bob says it that way?

*Janet:* Yes, I like it better when Bob tells me what he is thinking but I think it is silly to feel that way.

---

The other type of communication style is the *indirect message.* Janet answered the counselor's question and then added her opinion of Bob's view by saying, "I think it is silly to feel that way." By tacking this opinion onto her answer, she is actually communicating to Bob *through the counselor.* Speaking directly to the person for whom the communication is intended is responsible communication. When the message is made through another person (children, friends, neighbors), the communicator is, once again, using an underresponsible style. In this case, the counselor might turn to Janet and say:

---

*Counselor:* Janet, you answered my question, and then you said something to me that Bob needed to hear.

*Janet:* What do you mean?

*Counselor:* You told me your opinion of Bob's reason for not cutting the grass on Sunday. I think you really wanted Bob to hear your opinion. Is that right?

*Janet:* Well, yes, I guess so.

*Counselor:* Then turn to Bob and tell him.

*Janet:* He already knows now. *(Janet resists being responsible.)*

*Counselor:* I know, but this is just for practice.

*Janet:* I don't think you need to worry about what the neighbors think. They all work on Sunday.

---

At this point, the counselor interrupts the dialogue to review what was happening in the two communication styles and how underresponsible styles lead to ambiguity, confusion, and frustration. This is the teaching time and is as important as the rehearsal. During this time, the counselor can appraise each person's style, the consequences of that style, and its apparent effect on the other person. Sometimes the lesson is enhanced by asking the participants to exaggerate their underresponsible style (be even more underresponsible).

It should be noted here that these rules may not be as transferrable across cultures as we once thought. For example, the Native American culture views the person as part of a larger ecosystemic context and thus may not place the emphasis on individuals as these "rules" seem to imply. Other cultures also deemphasize individuality while raising the importance of the family, community, or society.

Finally, one particularly common communication problem that becomes evident in counseling is what Fogarty (1986) has labeled the "distancer/pursuer" system. This dynamic emerges over time when one partner pursues and the other distances or avoids communicating. Such communication styles are really personality characteristics of the players, one having learned (perhaps from his/her parent) that it is easier to hide or avoid than it is to confront, while the other has learned that it is more effective to approach or confront than to avoid. This systemic issue is illustrated in a case described by Bernard and Hackney (1983).

## Case Illustration of Distancer/Pursuer:

*The Case of Sheila and Eric*

Eric was attracted to Sheila because she was outgoing and fun. Since he was somewhat shy, he admired this friendly quality in her. Sheila found Eric attractive because he was "the strong, silent type." She also liked his gentleness, which made him different from many of the men she had dated. After a year of dating, they were married. They both felt they had found a mate who would complement them, someone who would bring out new things in themselves.

After a year, Sheila found herself edgy with Eric when they went to social gatherings. Although he wished to be friendly, he still acted aloof and distant. At home they also seemed to have "stuck" at an intermediate level of closeness. Eric didn't offer all of the infor-

mation Sheila wanted. He didn't think to tell her about little details at work, funny things that happened. In an attempt to open him up, she would ask questions and more questions. Eric was not comfortable with what felt like an intrusion on his privacy. He wished Sheila were more like him. He was also beginning to feel that Sheila thought he was inadequate.

Ten years later, the scene looks quite different. Sheila is belligerent about her husband's quietness. "You never tell me anything. You don't want me in your world. What do you think it is like to live with a stranger?" Eric has become totally withdrawn. Sheila's role is to nag. Eric's role is to hide. (Bernard & Hackney, 1983, pp. 52–53)

Eric and Sheila's communication difficulties are a product of personal qualities each brought into the marriage. They are complicated and intensified by the couple's lack of awareness of the systemic and personal issues that are involved. Sensitizing Eric and Sheila to the systemic issues will address part of the problem. This may be accomplished by pointing out the pattern and helping them see that it is not Eric's withdrawal or Sheila's demands but the interaction of their unique characteristics.

Awareness should also be focused on interpersonal qualities, since partial awareness of one's needs, motives, or intentions is a frequent source of miscommunication. Miller, Wackman, Nunnally, and Miller (1989, pp. 49–50) use an exercise they call the Awareness Wheel to help couples become aware of these interpersonal patterns. Each communicated message has five stages of development. The first stage is *sensing*, or receiving data into awareness (for example, awareness of discomfort). Stage two is *thinking* about that data (Why am I uncomfortable? What is the source?). The third stage, *feeling*, involves affective processing of the cognitive processes of stage two (How do I feel about being made uncomfortable by that?). In the fourth stage, *intentions*, the individual determines what should be done to respond to the thought and feeling stages (What do I want to change? How should things be?). In the final stage, the individual reaches the level of *action* (What am I going to do?). This is a circular sequence, with the action stage leading back into the sensing stage and beginning the process all over again. (It might help you to draw these stages out in a circular pattern with arrows pointing from each stage to the next.)

This procedure can be used with couples as a means for analyzing each person's communication pattern. Typically, one or more stages is either weak or missing entirely from the process. The counselor can ask partners to select a topic and use the five stages to organize their messages. For example:

> *Sensing:* I sense (observe) that you are irritated.
>
> *Thinking:* This makes me wonder if I did something to make you mad.
>
> *Feeling:* I'm nervous and uncomfortable with that thought.
>
> *Intending:* I would like for you to be friendly and warm toward me.
>
> *Acting:* I will ask you if I did something to upset you. If I did, I will apologize. If I didn't, I will ask what I could do to make your day more pleasant.

An insecure person might be highly sensitive (stage one) and unaware of the thinking or feeling stages. On the other hand, the spouse might be action-oriented (stage five) but relatively unaware of stages one and three. In such an example neither partner could communicate effectively until they were able to identify internal dimensions of their messages. First, one must know the message, and then it can be communicated.

Accurate and responsible communication is only half the goal of good communication patterns. If a message is clearly and responsibly sent, but the receiver does not comprehend, then communication has failed. This may happen if the message is too threatening or if the receiver is preoccupied or otherwise blocked from perceiving the intent of the message. The person trying to communicate the message cannot know this without some feedback from the receiver. In other words the communicator must know if the receiver (a) hears, and (b) hears accurately, what is being said. Miller, Wackman, Nunnally, and Miller (1989) refer to this as a "shared meaning," and they have developed a communication exercise for partners to use whenever they believe miscommunication is occurring. The shared-meaning exercise is a conversation in slow motion. The communicator is asked to phrase a communication (restricting it to not more than two or three parts). After stating the message, the communicator asks, "What did you hear me saying?" The receiver tries to repeat the elements of the communication and ask, "Is that what you meant to say?" If the message was perceived accurately, the communicator adds whatever is required to complete the message. If the message was perceived inaccurately, then the communicator corrects the misperception and proceeds.

Not all communication problems are caused by underresponsible patterns, of course. Very often, the problem has an interpersonal dimension which has developed over time. As a result of her past frustrations, a woman may have come to the conclusion that her partner does not care to communicate. This may cause her to assume a defensive stance when she needs to communicate. Whether or not her perception is accurate, by communicating defensively, she elicits a certain kind of response from her partner. This response, which is in part due to her approach, may give her further reason to think she is right. Such a sequence of events is obviously systemic. The counselor must recognize when poor communication is a systemic problem and develop an intervention that addresses the systemic issue rather than the communication issue. This can be done by observing how the couple interacts in the session, identifying patterns, and intervening in the pattern development. But if the problem is unique to the home environment, the best means for observation is to ask the couple to enact a typical encounter by role-playing.

### Role-Playing

Role-play or role-enactment has already been discussed in Chapter 7 as a useful intervention in individual counseling. It is also used in working with families or peer groups when a particular event or experience must be relived in order to be more real. Thus, the counselor may decide to ask a family member to enact a problematic encounter or to enact the role of another family member. This provides an immediate stimulus to which family members can react. It gives the counselor an opportunity to observe sequences and can lead to discussion of individual perceptions of the family system, individual differences, or conflicting loyalties.

Family members may be surprised by the content that is provoked in role-plays. Often they are able to see the other person's point of view more easily through an enactment than by having the person discuss viewpoints. Role-play also allows the counselor to intervene, ask why the scene develops as it does, and offer alternative patterns the couple might try when they become locked into a sequence of events.

### Negotiation and Conflict Management

Many families find negotiation and decision making to be a time when communication is most likely to break down. In family counseling, negotiation is an ongoing process that involves both process issues and family issues. Consequently, the counseling setting provides an ideal opportunity for the counselor to observe family negotiation skills and to provide strategies the family can use to improve communication and negotiation. This approach also lends itself to situations in which culture is a contributing factor. Berg and Jaya (1993) note that there is a long Asian ritual that focuses on solving problems through negotiation rather than confrontation.

Notarius and Markman (1993) have developed a conflict management skills-training program for couples called PREP (Prevention and Relationship Enhancement Program). This program was based on extensive longitudinal research of distressed couples over time. The authors note that the goal of PREP is not so much to enhance current relationship functioning but to prevent future distress. They have found that a couple's distress is greatly affected by adverse ways of handling conflict. Among the guidelines in PREP for negotiating and handling conflict effectively are the following:

1. Difficult issues must be controlled.
2. Partners may call mutual time-outs as needed.
3. Conflicts that escalate need to be slowed down.
4. Conflicts need to be constructive.
5. Withdrawal of contact should be avoided and involvement maintained.

Marital conflict has also been shown to correlate with poorer physical health (Gottman, 1993). Gottman (1991) has also conducted a series of studies (with Levenson) that examine the specific role of marital conflict in predicting marital dissatisfaction, separation, and divorce. His findings suggest that there are a series of events based around conflict that unfold in predictable ways. For example, conflict begins and the husband becomes highly aroused and stonewalls with his wife by withdrawing as a listener and subsequently by withdrawing emotionally. The husband's stonewalling is very aversive to the wife; she becomes aroused but responds by trying to reengage the husband. Failing to do so, she becomes critical and contemptuous and also withdraws, increasing her husband's fear. Gottman (1991) notes that:

> *The husband's withdrawal from tense marital interaction is an early precursor of the wife's complementary withdrawal. When both withdraw and are defensive, the marriage is on its way toward separation and divorce.* (p. 5)

Gottman has found, however, that if tense marital conflict is offset by positive expressions of communication such as "affection, humor, positive problem-solving, agreement, assent, empathy, and active non-defensive listening" arousal is reduced and the conflict is handled with better contact rather than withdrawal (1991, p. 5). Clearly couples need substantial help in learning effective negotiation and conflict management skills. However, there remains a need for a third party (the counselor) who acts as a mediator. Berg and Jaya (1993) point out that family therapists are in an ideal position with Asian families to assume this role "because of their position of authority and their knowledge of family relationships and therapies that enhance 'face saving' " (p. 32). In addition, some family therapists have developed exercises to use with families for handling of conflictual issues.

Gottman, Notarius, Gonso, and Markman (1976, pp. 62–63) have also developed an exercise that will help build negotiation skills. This activity can be used with a variety of systems or groups in addition to families. Called the Family Meeting, the exercise is divided into three parts: (a) gripe time; (b) agenda building; and (c) problem solving. The counselor should preface the exercise by explaining that all family members can have gripes and resentments and that these gripes are viewpoints rather than truths. They are the way the individual views the moment, the situation, or the relationship. They can change, and if ignored, they can get worse. It is important that each person's viewpoint be respected and aired. The counselor can help ensure each person's cooperation by introducing rules for griping (see *Table 10-1*).

After all family members have been allowed time to express their gripes (and this may require some encouragement from the counselor), the family moves into the second stage, agenda building. The purpose of agenda building is to evaluate the relative importance of gripes that have been expressed and select one or more that family members believe should be remedied. The counselor is an active arbitrator during this process, helping family members define specific dimensions of a particular gripe.

Having identified and defined a particular gripe, the family moves

**TABLE 10-1  Do's and Don'ts**

| | |
|---|---|
| Do state clearly and specifically the gripes you have about other family members. | Don't try to define yourself by showing that the other person is wrong. |
| Do be honest and constructive when you gripe. | Don't sulk and withdraw. |
| Do listen and accept gripes as legitimate feelings. | Don't respond to gripes with a gripe of your own. Don't assume you know what the other person means; make sure you know. |

into the problem-solving stage. This is characterized by identification of positive behaviors that will address the complaint(s) and the writing of a contract that (1) specifies behaviors each family member will change; and (2) specifies incentives designed to increase the frequency of desired behaviors.

Kottler (1994) has written a useful book for couples who are experiencing conflict. As he points out, conflict is not only unavoidable, but without it, relationships would stagnate and not have the opportunity for growth. However, he also notes that it is family conflicts that are most likely to get out of control. He observes that the key to conflict resolution without blame is to avoid holding the other person responsible for your own pain and suffering.

## Altering Family Structure

Family structure refers to the patterns of interaction, the rules and roles that emerge to support these patterns, and the alliances that result from these rules and roles. All structure begins with family transactions which, when repeated, become patterns of behavior. As interaction patterns become well established, they begin to dictate how, when, and with whom family members will interact. For example, a young child falls, skins his knee, and runs to mother for comfort. As this scene repeats itself over and over again, a nurturing alliance forms between mother and child. Thus, mother assumes a nurturant (role) posture and the child learns to seek mother when hurt (rule). The alliance between mother and child defines a subsystem within the family.

All families have subsystems which are determined by interaction patterns, rules, roles, and alliances. The spousal subsystem is the obvious beginning point. When the first child is born, two things happen. The spousal subsystem accommodates a new parental subsystem, and mother-child and father-child subsystems emerge. Subsystems become differentiated from one another by boundaries. Additional children, grandparents, and other family relatives develop alliances within the larger family structure to the point that many subsystems emerge, with individuals occupying significant roles within more than one subsystem. There is a random as well as systematic dimension to the development of family structure. Consequently, families are often at a loss to explain how certain rules or subsystems become so powerful or how they could be changed.

Recognizing the powerful impact structure has on family functioning, a group of family therapists began working with family structures. Significant among these therapists were Salvador Minuchin, Braulio Montalvo, and Jay Haley. They developed a scenario for working with the family based on five basic goals for the counseling process:

1. Joining (establishing rapport) with the family
2. Generating and observing the interaction
3. Diagnosing the family structure
4. Identifying and modifying interactions
5. Reconstructing boundaries

These goals are accomplished through a variety of techniques and interventions, some of which require family cooperation and others of which are therapist manipulations.

## Joining with the Family

The first of these objectives, *joining*, refers to social identification with each family member. This is accomplished in a number of small but meaningful ways: addressing each member by name; shaking hands with each member (including even the smallest); touching the baby; and so forth. This individual and personal contact is seen as quite important to the later process of therapy, since each family member has been given a personal acknowledgement by the therapist. Nichols and Schwartz (1994) note that:

> *It is particularly important to join powerful family members as well as angry ones. Special pains must be taken to accept the point of view of the father who thinks therapy is hooey, or of the angry teenager who feels likes a hunted criminal. It's also important to reconnect with such people at frequent intervals, particularly as things begin to heat up.* (p. 229)

Joining does not mean that the counselor is catering to powerful family members. Rather, it means that the counselor is acknowledging all family members, all of the time, even when a particular member's effect may be negative or overpowering.

## Generating and Observing Interactions

After the family has been joined (in the first session and in subsequent sessions), the counselor turns to the task of setting up and observing family interactions. One of the real benefits of working with family units is that they allow the therapist the opportunity to observe them in realistic interactions (as opposed to the individual client who must *report* interactions). Some interactions are totally spontaneous sequences that emerge when the family is dealing with a current issue. Since spontaneous interactions may not develop, the counselor must help the family become involved in interactions that are representative. One of the first of these is the physical alignment the family displays at the beginning of each session.

### Recognizing Physical Alignments

Prior to each session, the counselor arranges a sufficient number of chairs in a circle. As family members enter the room, they are encouraged to sit wherever they wish. The counselor observes closely who chooses to sit by whom, what kind of negotiation occurs when two members want the same chair, or who moves chairs (increasing or decreasing distance). This early expression of family dynamics is seen as a metaphor for the family's dysfunctioning system.

As the session progresses and subsystems become more apparent through interactions, the counselor may ask specific family members to exchange chairs, thus physically altering a boundary separating subsystems. Or if the counselor senses that the family has excluded a member, he or she may physically move to sit beside that excluded member, again realigning the dynamics of the counseling scene. As counseling progresses in later sessions, family members become aware of this realignment activity and begin to realize that such alterations do change the dynamics of the family interaction.

### Using the Family Genogram

One of the better ways of helping the family recognize its intergenerational structure is the genogram, a type of diagram. The exercise uses symbols to represent family members, typically over three generations (see *Figure 10-1*). This intervention begins by explaining to family members how the genogram is drawn. Then the counselor begins to solicit information about various family members, beginning with the immediate family—e.g., father and mother, each child, including those who might have died or were stillborn, and dates of birth of each. Children of the immediate family constitute the *third (present) generation* while parents (mother and father) constitute the *second generation*. Added to this are the maternal and paternal grandparents (*first generation*) and any other family members who play active roles in the family's functioning.

Once the genogram has been drawn, it may be used to examine the other pertinent facts about the interrelationship of family members, including "physical location of family members, frequency and type of contact, emotional cutoffs of certain family members, issues that create conflict or anxiety, nodal events, and degree of openness or closedness" among family members (Sherman & Fredman, 1986,

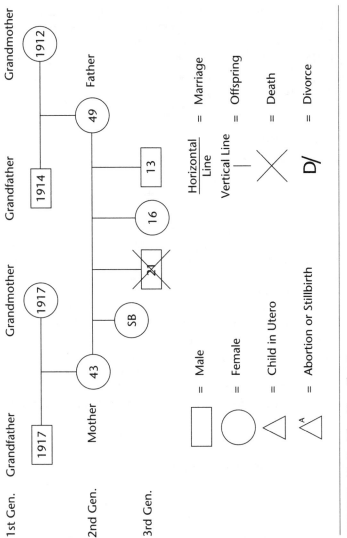

**FIGURE 10-1  The Family Genogram**

p. 83). This discussion yields a *family history* as well as a pictorial format. Both may be used to help family members gain insight into the family's functioning, to repair cutoffs, and to make adjustments in organizational patterns. The genogram is probably most used by counselors of a Bowenian orientation, but is a useful intervention for all schools of family therapy.

### Family Sculpture

Family sculpture (Duhl, Kantor, & Duhl, 1973) also provides diagnostic insights and generates family awareness of perceptions, structure, and sequences. Perhaps a better label would be family choreography (Papp, 1976) because the exercise calls for one family member to choreograph family members' involvement with one another in a typical scenario. It can be used to enact current family sequences or to reenact scenes from the past. Through family sculpture or choreography, family members are placed both in activities and spatial relationship to one another. As the director (the family member who is choreographing the scene) assigns, moves, or directs interactions, all family members respond both to the direction and to the director's perceptions of their interactive relationships.

In the family therapy case of Bob and Jeannette, the therapist used family sculpting as a means to generate awareness of each spouse's perceptions of their problem. The situation that was selected for enactment was the end-of-day scene in which father and mother each arrived home from work.

## Case Illustration of Family Sculpture

*The Case of Bob and Jeannette*

*Counselor:* Bob, I'd like you to produce the scene at home when you and Jeannette arrive from work. We'll assume the kids are also home. Place each person in whatever is the typical activity they would be doing. Do this without discussion. Merely place them in a particular space, and tell them what they should be doing. Do you understand what I want you to do?

*Bob:* I'm not sure. Do I just say, "Jeannette, you yell at the kids or something like that"?

*Counselor:* If that is what Jeannette typically does, yes. And then go on to tell the kids what they should be doing.

*Bob:* O.K. Jeannette, you are sitting in the living room with a martini. Tommy (seven years old), you are downstairs watching cartoons with Karen (nine years old). Then Tommy, you and Karen
*Continued*

come to the living room when I arrive home. [Bob acts as though he is coming in the front door of their house; both children rush up.] Now, I sit down with Mommy, and you start talking and demanding attention. Mommy and I will be trying to talk to each other while you try to talk to both of us. [Both children somewhat sheepishly begin talking about something.] Bob and Jeannette try to begin a conversation but children won't let them complete the conversation.

*Counselor:* O.K. Now, what happens?

*Bob:* Well, if Jeannette and I try to ignore the kids, they end up in a fight. If we stop trying to talk to each other, I end up mad.

*Counselor:* O.K. everyone. Act out that scene that Bob just described.

---

The family members begin to act out their parts. Just as Bob sits down and begins to talk to Jeannette, Tommy comes in to ask Mommy a question. Bob waits until Jeannette answers, at which time Tommy asks another question. Enter Karen, who proceeds to tell Mommy that Tommy ate all the potato chips. Jeannette responds, and it becomes obvious that Jeannette and the children are the focal unit. Bob, trying to look patient, asks the children to return to their activities so he and Mommy can talk. The children leave and Jeannette turns to Bob and tells him that the children need some parent time also after being away from them all day. Bob responds impatiently that he needs some spouse time and accuses her of not noticing that.

### Diagnosing the Family Structure

In the discussion that followed this scene, Jeannette and Bob discussed their reactions. Jeannette was somewhat surprised that Bob was wanting relationship time with her but was unable to have it because the kids were interrupting. She indicated that such interruptions didn't bother her as much as they apparently bothered Bob. Instead, she had been presuming that his reactions to her (this scene was a common one in their home) were merely reflecting a bad day at work. Bob, on the other hand, thought Jeannette understood his relationship needs but was opting to take care of the children. He assumed that her choice was in reaction to feeling guilty that she had been away from the kids all day. As they discussed their individual perceptions, each became aware of the other's needs, motivations, and misperceptions. Throughout this type of interaction, the counselor also observes and looks for ways the couples might sabotage their negotiations.

This process involves the recognition of dysfunctional sequences and the behaviors that maintain the sequences. It also includes recognition of boundaries and how they are creating or sustaining problematic behavior sequences. Diagnosing family interactions does not involve specific therapeutic interventions. However, Minuchin has developed a *family blueprint* which allows the counselor to diagram family boundaries. This tool is discussed at length in *Families and Family Therapy* (Minuchin, 1974). The reader who wishes to develop family diagnostic skills would want to include Minuchin's work.

### Identifying and Modifying Interactions

Having determined what sequences appear to be maintaining the dysfunctional interactions, the structural family counselor proceeds to bring the family's attention to the sequence. This calls for *intensifying* the interaction so family members cannot ignore or avoid the issue.

#### Intensification

Intensification is a communication process through which the counselor draws the client's attention to a particular interaction, behavior, or event in such a way that client awareness is the inevitable outcome. Minuchin (1974, p. 310) provides an example of intensification while working with the family of an anorexic girl. In the dialogue, the daughter (Loretta) has accused her mother of being too money conscious, and the mother responds:

---

*Mother:* Sophia tells me, "Don't do these things. You're killing yourself." Now you, Loretta, you tell me this, see? How many aspirin? I'll get them for you, because when you get nervous, you stop eating. Right away, no food. Not get up from the bed. You don't want to see nobody. You don't want to talk to nobody. And Mama cries.
*(Therapist insists on conflict)*

*Minuchin:* Is your mother saying that you are blackmailing them?

*Loretta:* That's not— . . .

*(Therapist increases stress between mother and daughter)*
*Minuchin:* That's what she's saying. She's saying that you are controlling her by having temper tantrums and not eating.

---

This style of intensifying conflict keeps family members to the task of resolving old issues rather than their typical style of brushing up against the issue and then retreating from it.

#### Confrontation

Another way in which the counselor modifies interaction sequences is through confrontation and direction. In the following example, the parents are attempting to deal with a three-year-old child who is throwing a temper tantrum. The counselor is observing and eventually intervening.

*Mother:* Janice, please settle down or we are going to have to spank you. *(Janice wails louder.)*

*Father:* Janice, you heard what your mother said. (Mother places Janice on her lap and begins to soothe her. Janice continues to wail and resist. Father turns to the counselor and shrugs.)

*Counselor:* Aren't you going to do anything? Are you just going to let her continue to disrupt us?

*Counselor:* Well, do something.

*Father:* (to mother) Let me have her. (Mother hands Janice over to father.)

*Father:* Janice, stop now or you will have to go to the other room. (Janice doesn't stop.)

*Counselor:* (to mother) Does he really mean that he will send her away until she stops?

*Mother:* I don't know.
*(Father carries Janice to waiting room and returns. Janice wails for five minutes.)*

*Mother:* Don't you think we should go check on her?

*Father:* I don't know.

*Counselor:* She can't hurt herself out there.

*Father:* Right. She's just mad.

In this interaction, the counselor is forcing the parents to confront the issue. Mother attempts to intervene, and father withdraws. The counselor turns to father and challenges him to stay involved. Father becomes involved by threatening the child with removal, but they do not follow through. At that point, the counselor increases the tension by asking mother if father intends to do what he threatened. This confronts father, and he follows through. The parents then begin to waiver as daughter turns up the intensity from the other room. The counselor assures them that the daughter is really all right, and they regain their resolve to win this battle of wills.

The process of identifying and modifying interactions is one way in which the counselor is attempting to alter the family structure by altering sequences of behavior. A second approach involves the manipulation of subsystem boundaries.

### Reconstructing Boundaries

As the counselor works with families (or other systems), the concept of *family identity* becomes increasingly apparent. Families develop qualities that define their internal structure and interdependent characteristics. One family may be so cohesive that individual identities are relegated to a low priority, while the total family unit is elevated to the highest priority. In such a family, often referred to as *enmeshed*, group activities are emphasized over individual activities, the welfare of the family unit is emphasized over the individual, the group *will* is more important. (Minuchin illustrated this by squeezing the teenage daughter's wrist and asking how many family members felt the pain. All but one raised their hands, and that person was apologetic for not feeling the pain.)

Family enmeshment is one end of a family organization continuum. The other end of the continuum is represented by the *disengaged* family. In disengagement, family members have little or no connection to one another. The family group identity is deemphasized, and individualization is held supreme. In the disengaged family, members' activities are planned without consultation or consideration of other family members. Group activity is rare.

Both enmeshment and disengagement are considered to be problematic in the family therapy literature. However, when cultural factors are taken into account, both arrangements might be considered normative for specific cultural groups. For example in Asian American families, family identity and cohesiveness are highly valued by family members. It is considered both appropriate and healthy to deemphasize individuality and emphasize family agendas (Berg & Jaya, 1993).

Within the family system, boundaries function to differentiate between subsystems. They allow members to function in appropriate roles and to interact with other subsystems. But families can generate many different types of subsystems, and some subsystems exist to maintain a dysfunctional situation. For example, one parent may create an alliance with one or more children that effectively excludes the other parent from decision making or other family functions. In such situations, the counselor may wish to intervene in the system in ways that will reintegrate the excluded parent. This can be done through assignments (as discussed under *Family Sculpture*).

The use of assignments in the counseling setting to manipulate subsystem boundaries can resemble family sculpture in one respect. For example, if the counselor believes parents are failing to respect the sibling subsystem by interfering or invading the system, the counselor might invite the invading parents to join the counselor in an observing, "adult" group because children "think differently these days than in our time and may have solutions the we couldn't even imagine" (Minuchin & Fishman, 1981, p. 149). By creating an "adult observer" group, the counselor has pulled the parents away from the sibling subsystem and assigned them the role of observer. Since one cannot be an effective observer and participant at the same time, the counselor has created a new boundary separating parents from siblings.

The counselor also manipulates the spatial relationships that reflect boundaries between subsystems. It was noted earlier that the counselor may use the seating arrangements in the counseling room as a means of observing how subsystems operate. By moving family members to other chairs, thus altering the spatial arrangements, the counselor also alters the spatial expression of boundaries. Imagine a counseling scene in which the clients are a stepfamily composed of mother, teenage son, and stepfather. The stepfamily has existed for about twelve months. During this time mother has created an obvious boundary between herself and son on the one side, and stepfather on the other. By moving the stepfather's chair in such a way that he now sits beside stepson, the counselor has made a symbolic intervention into the family system. This intervention can be extended by asking the mother to become an observer of stepfather/stepson interactions, thus encouraging the stepfather and stepson interaction to happen, and removing mother from active involvement.

By altering family structure, the objective is to interrupt habitual and dysfunctional sequences and patterns in such a way that the family must create new patterns. With the counselor's help, these new patterns can be more functional and constructive for family relationships and individual needs.

Szapocznik and Kurtines (1993) observe that in structural family work, not only does an individual client need to be understood in the context of one's family, but also that a family needs to be understood in the context of its culture. All three of these contexts overlap as shown in *Figure 10-2.*

In these authors' studies of Hispanic families, they found that understanding of the family dynamics was enhanced when the families were viewed not just from a Hispanic context but from a culturally pluralistic or diverse context (see *Figure 10-3*).

As an example, they found that the conflict in these families resulted often from parents who had strong generational Hispanic cultural alliances while the youth in the families rapidly had become acculturated or Americanized. The elders struggled for greater connectedness; the youth for greater freedom.

Szapocznik and Kurtines (1993) have developed a bicultural ef-

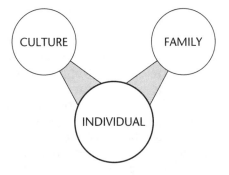

**FIGURE 10-2   The Individual in the Context**

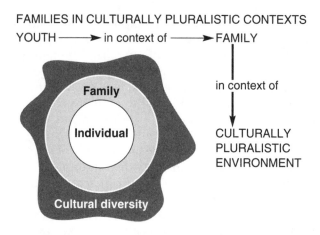

FAMILIES IN CULTURALLY PLURALISTIC CONTEXTS
YOUTH ⟶ in context of ⟶ FAMILY

Family

Individual

in context of

CULTURALLY
PLURALISTIC
ENVIRONMENT

Cultural diversity

**FIGURE 10-3   Model for the Imbeddedness**

fectiveness training model which combines aspects of structural family therapy with a cultural understanding of family conflicts. One of their intervention strategies is to create crossed alliances between elders and youth and between Hispanic and acculturated values as shown in *Figure 10-4.*

## *Working with Families Strategically*

The area of strategic family therapy includes a diversified group of family therapists, among whom are Cloe Madanes, Milton Erickson, Jay Haley, Maria Selvini Palazzoli, Paul Watzlawick, Lynn Hoffman, John Weakland, and Richard Fisch. With this variety of major contributors, one might expect the approach to be diffuse; in fact, strategic therapists have a significant core of agreement in their approaches.

Compared to the structural therapy approach, strategic therapists emphasize problem definition (including how the family perceives itself and its problems); brief or short-term therapy; interventions that focus on redefinition of the problem or perception; and interventions that affect sequences outside the session. It should also be said that strategic therapists often use structural interventions, just as structural therapists use strategic interventions.

The term *strategic therapy* was coined by Jay Haley in describing the work of Milton Erickson. Erickson "assumed that deep down, patients knew what to do; they just didn't have access to that wisdom. One way to get access was to break out of habitual patterns of behavior or thinking, so Erickson developed many ways of getting people to simply do something different in the context of the old behavior, or to do the old behavior in a new context" (Nichols &

Establishing crossed alliances

(a)  Family boundaries are made more permeable at this time to foment crossed alliances and encourage Parent/Acculturated Value and Youth/Hispanic Value relationships. Crossed alliances are expected to further weaken existing generational-cultural alliances.

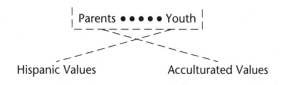

(b)  By viewing culture conflict as a common foe and by weakening existing generational-cultural alliances new crossed alliances are fostered, the overall level of biculturalism in families is enhanced, and parents and youth strengthen their relationship vis a vis cultural alliances.

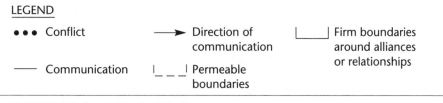

LEGEND

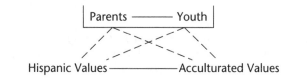

**FIGURE 10-4  A Change Strategy**

Schwartz, 1994, p. 412). Haley was one of the first to bring Erickson's work to the attention of professionals.

Another source of strategic thinking was the Brief Therapy Center, part of the Mental Research Institute of Palo Alto, California. Led by Don Jackson, this group came from a communications orientation to change, and included Richard Fisch, Paul Watzlawick, and John Weakland, among others. They emphasized a close examination of how people tend to generate their problems and how families tend to generate unworkable solutions to those problems; when the solution does not work, the next solution tends to be more of the first solution. You may note that although many of the interventions used in strategic therapy tend to be cognitive in nature, they do not originate in the more traditional individual therapies, nor does the rationale for using them have a parallel in most individual cognitive approaches.

## *Preparing for the Intervention*

Although the ultimate goal of strategic family therapy is to prescribe an intervention that will cause change, the process leading to that objective is critical if strategic therapy is to work. Joining with each family member is very important, just as it is with structural family therapy. Indeed, family interactions in early sessions will be closely scrutinized by the counselor. Typically, once a brief social interaction has been completed between the counselor and each family member, the counselor sets the stage for counseling to occur. This is similar to what a counselor does in individual counseling, and includes alerting the family to observers for taping purposes, receiving demographic data, having clients sign consent forms, etc. An additional condition set on strategic therapy that is often not part of individual counseling is an agreement that counseling will last a certain number of sessions, usually no more than ten. By definition, strategic therapy is brief therapy.

### *Defining the Problem*

Because of the limit put on the number of counseling sessions, it is very important that the problem be well defined. In many ways, strategic family counselors mirror a behavioral approach *in defining* the family's problem. There are four guidelines the counselor would follow in defining the problem:

1. Each family member must contribute to the definition without having to become argumentative or defensive.
2. The problem must be stated in specific behavioral language.
3. If there is more than one problem, the most troublesome must be identified and that made the target of counseling.
4. Unsuccessful attempts to solve the problem are described in detail.

Although each family member will see the problem from his or her own perspective, usually there is some agreement about the behavioral manifestation of the problem. For example, a father might see his teenage son's behavior as disrespectful, while the son experiences his father as overbearing. With the counselor's help, however, they might both be able to agree that they can define the problem as "the number of times they get into explosive arguments." Thus, the problem becomes the frequency of their arguments rather than each person's bad attitude. If the arguments tend to gravitate toward a specific theme, for example, the son getting home too late with the family car, then the problem would be defined as getting home too late. It is important not to rush this phase of counseling and to be willing to negotiate and renegotiate until one problem is identified as the goal of counseling.

Finally, it is imperative that the counselor collect information regarding attempted solutions that have failed. There are several reasons for doing this. First, a great amount can be learned about the family system by hearing them describe their attempts to solve their problems. This information will be essential when attempting to identify an appropriate intervention for the family. Second, this discussion of failed solutions establishes the fact that the family does, indeed, have a problem that it has been unable to solve. Since most families continue to deny their problem even in counseling, this admission is important. Third, the process establishes that the counselor respects the efforts put forth by the family thus far. The counselor is saying, "I know you take your problem seriously and that you have already invested considerable energy in trying to solve it. Furthermore, I won't frustrate you by asking you to do what you have already tried without success." This part of the counseling process also gives the counselor another opportunity to watch the family operate and to determine the distribution of power in the family through such mechanisms as alliances within the family.

### Setting Realistic Goals

It is not enough for the family and counselor to define the problem. The family must also agree on what degree of improvement would be considered a therapeutic success. The description of success must be as concrete and well-defined as the description of the problem. Using our example of father and teenage son, it would not be appropriate to switch from "too many arguments" as the problem to "having a better relationship" as the measure of success (relationship quality not being of the same category as frequency). Rather, the goal might be "going from daily arguments to weekly arguments." Once the arguments were under control, it might be appropriate to work toward positive goals such as "spending more leisure time together." The consequence of reducing the number of arguments added to spending more enjoyable time together might result in having a better relationship, but this cannot be measured and therefore is not considered an appropriate counseling goal.

## Directives for Change

The crux of strategic family therapy is the *therapeutic directive*, or intervention. Most strategic directives are paradoxical in nature; that is, they may seem to defy logic. The rationale behind the paradoxical directive is that most problems are more emotional than logical. Consequently, a solution that follows the typical laws of logic completely misses the point and simply will not work. Watzlawick, Weakland, and Fisch (1974) noted that most attempted solutions in counseling are linear in nature, that is, they describe relationships that lead from a causal event to a responsive event. For example, if a child is punished for the weekend for misbehaving, the problem is presumed to have been addressed by the punishment. But what if the child misbehaves again? The linear solution might be to punish the child similarly for an entire week. In this illustration, can it be said that the punishment had the desired effect? In this example, punishment was intended to produce good behavior in the future, a *linear* solution. These types of solutions are called more-of-the-same solutions, and rarely work as they are intended. Paradoxical interventions attempt to come at the problem from a different perspective.

In Chapter 8 we discussed paradoxical interventions as cognitive interventions. Their effect is to reformat the individual's frame of reference in such a way that misbehavior *appears to the child* to be illogical or inappropriate, rather than something that might lead to punishment. For more information on this topic, you may wish to consult the original sources that are dedicated exclusively to a discussion of the strategic intervention (Haley, 1973; Watzlawick, Weakland, & Fisch, 1974; Madanes, 1981).

## *Summary*

As we have noted, systemic interventions do not originate in the traditional theories of counseling or personality. Instead, they derive from an ecological epistemology that many trained counselors find both unique and effective. The systemic orientation begins with a set of assumptions about human behavior that include: (a) a self-sustaining quality known as *homeostasis*; (b) the tendency of dysfunctional systems to develop rigid boundaries; and (c) an internal system organization that is determined by systemic "rules" as defined by repeated behavioral interaction patterns.

Effective counseling with social systems begins by recognizing these conditions and then developing interventions that address the system character rather than individual psychological characteristics. The dominant approaches are represented by communication-oriented counseling, object relations, structurally oriented counseling, and strategic counseling. In almost all cases, systemic counselors feel free to draw on interventions from all three orientations and from individual therapy models as well.

Systemic counseling fits quite well into the five-stage model for the helping process. Particular emphasis is placed on assessment as well as intervention. A frequent admonition of the systemic counselor is that the problem cannot be treated until it has been accurately identified. Systems thinking has particular relevance in working with couples and families. Indeed, many family interventions make no sense unless you think of the family as an ecosystem that is self-reinforcing and self-sustaining. Therefore, we recommend that you become well informed in family systems approaches if you plan to work with families or use family interventions.

## Exercises

1. Consider your family of origin. On a sheet of paper, write the names of your parents first. Then, as you add the names of siblings, place the names nearest that parent with whom you think there was a primarily identification. Draw lines connecting the subsystems you believe were operating in your family.

2. This is a two-part exercise. With a group of three to four class members, define yourselves as a family. Each person should assume a family member role: father, mother, oldest sibling, and so on. Given this "system," the family should discuss and make plans for a week-long vacation at the beach. After the plan has been finalized, step out of your roles and analyze the process and the system.

   In the second part of the exercise, the family is to repeat the exercise, assuming the same roles. However, one family member in this second exercise is to be a dysfunctional member (exhibiting a marginal level of functioning). Given this condition, repeat the planning of the vacation. Once the plan has been finalized, step out of your roles once again and analyze the process and the system. How did a dysfunctional family member alter the system? How did the individual family member roles accommodate this change?

3. In the case of Eric and Sheila (p. 263) the communication problem was identified as the product of personal qualities each brought into the marriage. Identify two or three individual goals of both Sheila and Eric that would have a positive effect on the communication problem.

## Discussion Questions

1. In a small group of class members, discuss what you think would be the most difficult type of family problem to work with. As you discuss the problem(s), consider whether you would choose to work with individuals or the total family in addressing the problem(s).

**2.** In this chapter we compared the family's system to an ecological system. In what ways are the two similar? How is this illustrated by the "empty nest" syndrome?

**3.** In a group of employees who have worked together in the same office area for ten years, what kinds of systemic rules are likely to be developed? How easy would it be to alter those rules?

**4.** In this chapter, very little attention is given to soliciting input from members of the system regarding goal-setting. Why wouldn't the counselor ask members of the system to help identify counseling goals?

## Recommended Readings

Berg, I. and Jaya, A. (1993). Different and same: Family therapy with Asian American families, *Journal of Marital and Family Therapy, 19,* 31–38.

Cheatham, H. and Steward, J. (1990). *Black Families: Interdisciplinary Perspectives,* New Brunswick, NJ: Transactional Publishers.

Gilbert, R. (1992). *Extraordinary Relationships,* Minneapolis, MN: Chronimed Publishing.

Goodrich, T.J., Ed. (1991). *Women and Power: Perspectives for Family Therapy,* New York: W.W. Norton.

Goodrich, T.J., Rampage, C., Ellman, B., and Halstead, K. (1988). *Feminist Family Therapy,* New York: W.W. Norton.

Gottman J. (1991). Predicting the longitudinal course of marriages, *Journal of Marital and Family Therapy, 17,* 3–7.

McGoldrick, M., Anderson, C., and Walsh, F. (Eds.) *Women in Families: A Framework for Family Therapy,* New York: W.W. Norton.

Visher, E. and Visher, J. (1988). *Old Loyalties, New Ties: Therapeutic Strategies with Stepfamilies,* New York: Brunner/Mazel.

*Chapter* *11*

# Termination and Follow-up

## *Purpose of This Chapter—*

Termination, the fifth and final stage of counseling, is the transition from an assisted functioning to counseling-free functioning by the client. In this chapter we discuss the dynamics that affect this transition, the counselor's role and responsibilities in seeing that this transition occurs, and the occasional necessity to make client referrals to other mental health professionals. It is important to keep in mind through each of the counseling stages that the ultimate goal of any counseling relationship is success and termination. How this is accomplished is the focus of this chapter.

## *Considerations as You Read This Chapter—*

- Beginning and endings often prove problematic to people, particularly to sensitive persons. Being sensitive, one is more aware of the importance of good beginnings. And one is particularly aware of the implications of ending relationships that have been productive, rewarding, and meaningful.
- Where do you fit in this picture? What have the beginnings and endings of relationships been like for you? Has it been your tendency to think of endings as a positive experience?
- Can you, as a counselor, put yourself in the client's world? How might termination be seen?
- What is the most constructive way for a client to view termination? How might you as a counselor enhance the client's ability to see termination in that constructive way?

In Chapter 2 we described termination as one of the five stages of counseling. This suggests that it functions as part of the therapeutic process and is not just a significant moment in the counseling relationship. The dynamics of a termination are some indication of just how important the treatment of this stage can be. It has been described as a "loss experience" (Goodyear, 1981), an "index of success" (Pate, 1982), a "recapitulation of the multiple preceding goodbyes in life" (Hansen, Rossberg, & Cramer, 1994), a mixture of sadness and pleasure (Pietrofesa, Hoffman, Splete, & Pinto, 1984), pride and accomplishment (Pinkerton & Rockwell, 1990), and a "transformative growth experience" (Quintana, 1993). However one wishes to describe termination, the emotional dynamics of letting go, trusting their gains, and facing future potential with only partially tested new skills present clients with multiple reactions.

The counselor also experiences pride and regret when a successful counseling relationship ends (Boyer & Hoffman, 1993). Or if the relationship has been something less than successful, the counselor probably feels unfinished or even unsure of the manner in which the counseling case was conducted. In this chapter, we shall consider termination as a therapeutic stage and shall address such issues as who determines when termination should occur, problems in the termination process, and characteristics of successful termination.

## *The Termination Stage*

Termination is not so much an ending as it is a transition from one set of conditions to another. Pate has caught the spirit of this, saying:

> *When counseling is viewed as a process in which an essentially competent person is helped by another to solve problems of living, solving the problem leads to termination, not as a trauma, but as another step forward in client growth.* (1982, p. 188)

At some level, both the counselor and client know from the beginning of the counseling relationship that it will end eventually. But the knowledge that counseling ultimately will end provides no guidelines for making the decision. This raises the question, "What are the determinants for when counseling should terminate?" The answer to this question is based both on theoretical orientations and counselor/client interactions.

## *Theoretical Determinants of Termination*

The counselor operates out of some theoretical view of what counseling is meant to accomplish and how clients change through counseling. This theoretical viewpoint may be formalized (identified with a recognized counseling theory) or it may be idiosyncratic to the counselor's life view. The person-centered counselor might view termination as a decision to be made by the client. However, Pate observes that this position can be taken to the extreme, noting:

> *One point of view builds on the developmental nature of counseling and the goal of client self-actualization. Such a view might (wrongly) lead to the conclusion that a counseling relationship was always growth producing and thus ideally would continue.* (1982, p. 189)

A somewhat different position is reflected in family therapy practice. Madanes suggests that:

> *After the presenting problems are solved, the therapist must be willing to disengage quickly, with the idea of keeping in touch occasionally with the family and to be available if problems arise.* (1981, p. 121)

Finally, "brief therapy" proponents take the position that counseling should be limited to a specified number of sessions (often ten sessions). In this case the counselor may contract with the client(s) in the initial session to terminate at a specific point in time.

In each of these examples, the question of when termination should occur may be answered by the counselor's theoretical stance. However, it should be noted that many counselors do not feel bound to theoretical directives regarding the termination issue. When theoretical determinants are not used, the counselor tends to rely on intuition or other variables.

## *Pragmatic Determinants of Termination*

In practical terms, counseling ends when either the client, the counselor, or the process indicates that termination is appropriate. Even in psychoanalysis, clients have input into the decisions, as Lorand has observed:

> *Often patients themselves bring up the matter of terminating by asking how much longer they will need to come. Sometimes they are*

*more definite and may state, for instance, that they will not come back in the fall. This gives the analyst an opportunity to discuss a tentative time limit for winding up the analysis.* (1982, p. 225)

But Teyber (1992) offers what is probably the most pragmatic answer as to when counseling should end, saying:

*It is time to end when clients no longer have symptoms, can respond more flexibly and adaptively in current situations that arouse their old generic conflicts, and have begun to take steps toward promising new directions in their lives.* (p. 246)

### When Clients Initiate Termination

Clients may elect to terminate for a number of reasons. They may feel that their goals have been accomplished. They may feel that the relationship (or the counselor) is not being helpful or may even be harmful. They may lack the financial means to continue. Or they may move to a new community or, if they are students, may finish the school year. Whatever the client's reason for terminating, it should be emphasized that the counselor's legal and ethical responsibilities do not end with the client's announcement. Preparation for termination and possible referral are issues that must be addressed. These topics will be discussed in greater detail later in the chapter.

### When the Counselor Terminates

Often the counselor is the first person to introduce the notion that counseling is approaching termination. This decision may be based on the client's progress toward identified counseling goals, or the counselor may determine that his or her expertise does not match the client's needs.

When counseling has been predicated on a behavioral or other form of contract, progress toward the goals or conditions of the contract presents a clear picture of when counseling should end. Although clients may be in the best position to experience counseling-based change, they are not always in the objective position needed to recognize change. Thus, the counselor may need to say to the client, "Do you realize that you have accomplished everything you set out to accomplish?" Ordinarily, the counselor can see this event approaching several sessions earlier. It is appropriate to introduce the notion of termination at that time, thereby allowing the client an opportunity to adjust to the transition. A fairly simple observation, such as, "I think we probably have about three or perhaps four more sessions and we will have finished our work," is enough to say. It provides an early warning, opens the door for discussion of progress and goal assessment, and focuses the client's attention on what life may be like after counseling.

Occasionally, as a case unfolds, the counselor may become aware that the demands of the client's problem call for skills or qualities the counselor does not possess. For example, after a few sessions a client may reveal that she is manifesting symptoms of bulimia. If the counselor is unacquainted with the treatment procedures for such a condition, the client should be referred to a professional who is recognized as competent with this problem. Or the client may present a dilemma that poses value conflicts for the counselor such that the counselor could not meet the client's needs without experiencing personal value conflicts. An example might be when a client discovers she is pregnant and wishes to consider abortion as a solution. If the counselor's values will not allow her or him to include abortion as a personal solution, then the counselor might be unable to support an objective examination of this solution with the client. In such cases, the counselor is ethically bound to refer the client to another professional who is able to do so. Obviously, this involves termination and transition to another counselor.

## Premature Termination

Among the more demoralizing effects for inexperienced and seasoned counselors alike is the fact of premature termination. Very often termination occurs almost before a working alliance can be formed. This can be a function of many different conditions. One important reason is *client readiness*. Smith, Subich, and Kalodner (1995) report that clients who were in a "precontemplation" or low potential for change stage were far more likely to terminate after only one session than those who initiated counseling at a contemplation stage. Other reasons for early or premature termination may be related to matching of gender, ethnic, or cultural factors (Lin, 1994; Kim, Lee, Chu, & Cho, 1989; Tata & Leong, 1994).

Sometimes counselors suggest that counseling terminate before an appropriate point has been reached. Because many clients rely heavily on the counselor to be the best judge of such matters, clients may go along with the counselor's recommendation, and the relationship may end prematurely. It has already been suggested that there are some very legitimate reasons why the counselor may decide to terminate counseling and refer the client to another professional. Aside from these situations, three precipitating conditions can lead the counselor to initiate inappropriate premature termination:

1. The counselor experiences interpersonal discomfort.
2. The counselor fails to recognize and conceptualize the problem.
3. The counselor accurately conceptualizes the problem but becomes overwhelmed by it.

Personal discomfort may result from the counselor's fear of intimacy or inexperience with intense counseling relationships. With good supervisory assistance, this situation will remedy itself through continued counseling exposure and awareness. If the counselor's conceptual skills are weak or if the counselor's approach to all problems is to minimize the situation, then the result may be premature termination because the counselor fails to understand the client. This situation obviously calls for a careful reassessment of the counselor's decision to become a helper and whether additional training and supervision can remedy the situation. The third reason for premature termination is that the counselor accurately conceptualizes the client's problem but becomes overwhelmed by its complexity.

Finally, the special case of the counselor-in-training or the counselor who relocates should be acknowledged. In most cases, counselor trainees provide services in a practicum setting that conforms to university semester or quarter schedules. When counselor trainees know that their practicum will end at a certain date and the client will either be terminated or referred to another counselor, ethical practice dictates that the client be informed in the first session that a terminal date already exists. This allows the client a choice to enter into what might be brief counseling or potential long-term counseling with the condition of referral, or to seek another counselor who does not impose this terminal limitation on the counseling relationship.

## *The Termination Report*

Whether counseling is brief or long term, a summary report of the process is appropriate and desirable for several reasons. Assuming that the client may have future need for counseling, the termination report provides an accurate summation of the client's responsiveness to counseling and to specific types of interventions. Should the client request the counselor to provide information to other professionals (physician, psychiatrist, psychologist) or to the legal system, the report provides a base for the preparation of that information.

The counseling case can usually be summarized in two or three typewritten pages and should include the counselor's name, address, date that counseling began, date that counseling concluded, number of sessions, presenting problem(s), types of counseling interventions used and their effectiveness, client reaction to the counseling relationship over time, client reaction to termination, and the counselor's assessment of client's success with counseling. The termination report is a confidential document and should not be released without the client's written permission.

## Termination as a Process

The termination process involves several steps. The first is a careful assessment by the counselor and client of the progress that has been made and the extent to which goals have been achieved. Depending on the results of this assessment, the counselor will take one of two directions: termination or referral. Assuming termination is the appropriate choice, the counselor and client may proceed to discuss in depth the gains that have been made, and how those gains might be affected by future situations, making plans for follow-up, and finally, saying goodbye (Pate, 1982, p. 188). Typically, the termination process is characterized by cognitive discussions interspersed with acknowledgment of emotional aspects of the relationship. When termination is appropriate, the process has a constructive, positive quality.

### Assessing Progress

Quintana (1993) views the role of assessment during termination as:

> [a] particularly critical opportunity for clients and therapists to update or transform their relationship to incorporate clients' growth. For this transformation to occur, clients need to acknowledge the steps they have taken toward more mature functioning. Perhaps most important to clients is for therapists to acknowledge and validate their sense of accomplishment. (p. 430)

This notion of transformation from the helping relationship to a more autonomous and more normal lifestyle is related to the maintenance after counseling of those therapeutic gains that have been made. If the counseling agreement was based on specific goals identified by the client, or if some form of counseling contract was established early in the process, then the assessment of change may take a rather formal character. Each goal that had been set becomes a topic to discuss, changes related to that goal are identified, perhaps environmental consequences that grow out of those changes are enumerated, and so forth. In this approach, there is a sense of structure as the counselor and client review the outcomes. When counseling has involved couples or families, the assessment becomes even more complex, for each member's change is considered as well as systemic changes in patterns of interaction.

## Summarizing Progress

It may seem redundant to suggest that the assessment of progress should be followed by some sort of summary of that progress by the counselor. The rationale for providing a summary is twofold. First, hearing one's progress from another person or another perspective is quite different from hearing oneself describe progress. Most clients benefit from the counselor's statement, even though it is not new information. As one client described it, "I know I have made some gains, but it sure helps to hear you say it, too." Clients' efforts to internalize the counseling relationship are also enhanced when the counselor validates their accomplishments and encourages them to take credit for all of the steps they have taken toward their goals (Quintana, 1993). The second reason for a summary is that the counselor can inject some cautions if some counseling gains need to be reinforced or monitored by the client. This is related to future client efforts to preserve or generalize the progress that has been achieved.

## Generalizing Change

Having identified the changes that have occurred directly or indirectly through counseling, the counselor and client should turn to how those new behaviors, attitudes, or relationships can be generalized to the client's world. This step in the process calls on the client to extend beyond the immediate gains to potential future gains. The counselor might introduce this with questions such as, "In what other situations could you anticipate using these social skills you have acquired?" or "If your husband should develop some new style of obnoxious behavior next month, how do you think you might handle it?" The basic goal of the implementation step is to test the client's willingness and ability to adapt learned skills or new attitudes to situations other than those that provoked the original problem.

## Planning for Follow-Up

Follow-up in counseling refers to the nature and amount of professional contact that occurs between the counselor and client after termination has occurred. Some counseling approaches place greater emphasis on follow-up than others. For example, some systemic family therapists take the position that a family therapist is like a family physician. Over the years, the family will encounter new crises and problems and will reenter counseling as these situations demand. Thus, counseling is viewed as a service that can extend, intermittently, over a portion of the client's lifetime. Other approaches, most notably those that emphasize self-actualization, view counseling as a developmental experience, the object of which is to facilitate the client's growth and capability of dealing with new problems more effectively. In this context, future returns to counseling are not expected, although they certainly are not discouraged.

There is also an ethical aspect to follow-up. Even when the counselor and client agree that sufficient progress has been made to warrant termination, it is appropriate for the counselor to (a) make his or her future services available; and (b) explain to the client how future contact can be made. In so doing, the counselor has established a link between the client's present state and future needs. This link can also be an effective intervention for those clients who believe termination is appropriate but experience anxiety at the prospect. When this is the case, it may help if the counselor suggests a three-month or six-month "checkup." Depending on the client's response to the suggestion, the counselor can even schedule an appointment or suggest that the client call to make an appointment if needed. This is an effective bridging intervention in that it gives the client a sense of security and relationship continuation, even when counseling has terminated. The counselor might also suggest to the client that should the appointment not seem necessary in three months time, a phone call to cancel the appointment would be appreciated. Our experience has been that clients are responsible about either keeping the appointment or cancelling it. Even when they call to cancel, the telephone contact provides some follow-up information on how the client is coping.

Finally, if counseling outcomes include post-counseling activities that the client has decided to pursue, the counselor might want to follow up on the success of these goals. For example, if a client decides to make a career change that involves future job interviewing, then the counselor might ask the client to keep him or her informed of progress, either through a letter or telephone contact.

## The Referral Process

Client referral is a special form of termination. Shertzer and Stone (1980) define it as "the act of transferring an individual to another person or agency for specialized assistance not available from the original source" (p. 327). To this definition might be added: or when the service provider cannot continue providing counseling either for ethical or personal reasons. The referral involves a number of steps: (1) identifying the need to refer; (2) evaluating potential referral sources; (3) preparing the client for the referral; and (4) coordinating the transfer.

## *The Need to Refer*

The most frequent reason for referral is when the client needs some specialized form of counseling. This does not mean that the client is seriously stressed, although that can be the case for referral. It is more likely that the client needs a specific form of counseling that the counselor does not offer (for example, career counseling or marital counseling). Because clients rarely are informed consumers of the various forms counseling can take, counselors should be keenly attuned to specialized needs and their own ability to provide quality services.

Clients may also need or prefer special conditions for counseling. Those conditions might be gender-, ethnicity-, or culturally related. Even when the counselor recognizes the need, the task remains to help the client come to the same conclusion or referral will not be effective.

Clients may resist the first suggestions that a referral is appropriate. After all, having risked themselves by sharing their concerns or vulnerabilities, they probably would prefer not to have to go through the same process with yet another person. If you provide explanations that are complete and answer the client's questions clearly and thoroughly, and support the client's ambivalence, this resistance will ease.

## *Evaluating Potential Sources*

It is important that counselors be familiar with potential referral sources in the community. Some communities publish a mental health services directory that lists public agencies, services, services provided, fees, and how referral can be accomplished. The *Yellow Pages* of the telephone directory also provide information on both public and private sources under such headings as:

Counselors (Counseling)
Marriage and Family Therapists
Mental Health Counselors
Physicians
Psychologists
Psychotherapy

Such lists or directories provide little more than names and possible affiliations. For example, a listing under Marriage, Family, Child, and Individual counselors might read:

---

Psychotherapy Services
Ralph T. Marcus Ph.D.
Center for Psychotherapy
• Marriage Enrichment
• Divorce Bereavement
• Family Mediation
Conveniently located in the Meridian Center
Call for appointment: 555–5555

---

Just what can be learned from this listing? Dr. Marcus offers psychotherapy for marriages that may require enrichment, surviving divorce, and resolving family conflict issues. What is not known is (a) the kind of training Dr. Marcus received; (b) whether his doctorate was earned in psychology or a related mental health field or whether he is licensed as a psychologist; (c) his therapeutic orientation (individual versus family; theoretical base; etc.); or (d) his skill level or success rate with different types of problems. The best way to know answers to such questions is through exposure to different sources. Lacking that, the counselor might want to call Dr. Marcus and ask him such questions. After obtaining this information, the counselor should ask Dr. Marcus if he is accepting referrals and what procedures he prefers to follow when a case is referred to him. Over time, counselors can build up their own listing of referral sources that is based on direct experience. Such a listing is by far the best resource when the need to refer a client arises.

Finally, there is a legal ramification attached to making referrals. Because one can never know with certainty that a referral to a specific mental health provider will prove to be a positive experience for the client, it is probably best to provide the client with choices of referral sources. In that way, your client has the opportunity to choose a professional whose personal characteristics, values, and professional qualities are closest to the client's perceived needs. If the referring counselor provides only one potential referral professional to the client and that proves to be a problematic experience, the referring counselor may be held liable.

## Coordinating the Transfer

Whenever the counselor is referring a client to another professional, it is hoped that the referral will occur successfully and without undue strain on the client. If the client is highly anxious or if the counselor thinks the client might not accept the referral, special attention should be devoted to the client's concerns. In addition, successful referrals require that the counselor make contact with the receiving professional and provide information that will facilitate the referral process.

### *Preparing the Client*

Preparing the client for referral involves both details of the referral and the client's anxieties about the new relationship. It helps if the counselor has discussed the case with the receiving professional and can assure the client that painful details may not have to be repeated. It also helps if the counselor can tell the client some details about the potential new counselor(s), including personal characteristics, professional competency, and their receptiveness to the referral. Referral details may include helping the client identify what he or she should be looking for in a new counselor.

### *Communication with the Receiving Professional*

Before any referral recommendation is made, you should establish whether or not potential receiving professionals are willing or able to accept the referral. This can be accomplished most effectively through telephone communications. Once the client has identified an acceptable receiving professional, the transfer of information about the case must be addressed. Usually, a receiving counselor will want a written case summary, in addition to the demographic information received by telephone. The termination report described earlier will provide sufficient information to meet this requirement. Before sending any written material, however, you must obtain signed consent from the client to provide this information. Most counseling centers use a standard consent form. Private practitioners should develop a statement form that gives the counselor power to transfer written information with the signed consent of the client to other specified professionals, agencies, or authorities (see *Figure 11-1*).

## *Blocks to Termination*

Counseling can be such an intimate and valued personal experience for both the counselor and client that the thought of ending the relationship is most unattractive. From the counselor's perspective, a client who grows, overcomes obstacles, and accomplishes goals is an immensely rewarding experience. Added to this, counselor/client relationships often assume a personal as well as professional dimension. Counselors begin to like clients and appreciate their humanness and

COUNSELING ASSOCIATES, INC.
Consent For Release of Confidential Information

Date: _____

Client's Name: _____ Date of Birth: _____

Permission is hereby granted to COUNSELING ASSOCIATES, Inc., to release psychological, medical, social, educational, and/or other clinical information regarding the client named above to the following professional mental health provider and/or agency.

Person/Agency to
receive information: _____

Address: _____

City/State/Zip: _____

Signature: _____

Name of signer (please print): _____

Relationship to client
(if client minor): _____

**FIGURE  11-1  Sample Consent Form**

finer qualities. Thus, there can be some personal investment in maintaining the relationship. Clients often experience counselors in ways they wish could have happened in their familial relationships. In this context, termination often means saying goodbye to a very good friend.

On the other hand, Quintana (1993) challenges the termination-as-crisis concept, suggesting that it is lacking in empirical support. He advocates an alternative definition of termination-as-development. This notion views termination as a transformation that encourages growth and development in the client "that is applicable across gender, ethnicity, and race." (p. 429)

### *Client Resistance to Termination*

Much has been written in both the theoretical and experimental literature about the termination experience and its effect on clients. Interestingly, the theoretical notions of its impact appear to be in conflict with the empirical results. For example, according to psychoanalytic thinking:

> *The most desirable state of affairs is for the patient to slowly wean himself away, for him to eventually accept his limitations and be*

*willing to relinquish the desires which cannot be realized.* (Lorand, 1982, p. 225)

In his review of the theoretical views of termination, Quintana (1993, p. 427) describes how

*clients are expected to react to termination with a plethora of neurotic affective, cognitive, interpersonal, and defensive reactions related to grief reactions [and] [c]lients' reactions are . . . intense enough to overwhelm positive gains made earlier in therapy.* (Mann, 1973; Ward, 1984)

On the other hand, Quintana (1993) describes the research on termination's effect on client reactions:

*The frequency and intensity of clients' reactions to termination do not reflect inherent crisis over loss. Results [of research by Marx and Gelso, 1987; Quintana and Holahan, 1992] suggest that only a small minority of clients experience a psychological crisis over the end of therapy, and the crisis seems to focus on the disappointing level of client outcome rather than specifically on loss.* (p. 427)

Whatever may be the more likely reaction, it is appropriate for the counselor to evaluate the client's degree of concern with the prospect of termination and respond therapeutically.

### *Counselor Resistance to Termination*

It may be surprising that counselors often resist terminating with clients, even though the client has reached a logical hiatus in the counseling process. And yet, most counselor resistance is understandable. The counselor forms real human attachments to clients. In fact, it might be argued that counselor investment in the person of the client is a prerequisite to successful counseling. When this is part of the relationship, letting go has an emotional impact. Goodyear (1981) identified eight conditions that can lead to the counselor's experience of loss when termination occurs.

**1.** When termination signals the end of the significant relationship.
**2.** When termination arouses the counselor's anxieties about not having been more effective with the client.
**3.** When termination arouses guilt in the counselor about not having been more effective with the client.
**4.** When the counselor's professional self-concept is threatened by the client who leaves abruptly and angrily.
**5.** When termination signals the end of a learning experience for

the counselor (for example, the counselor may have been relying on the client to learn more about the dynamics of a disorder or about a particular subculture).

**6.** When termination signals the end of a particularly exciting experience of living vicariously through the adventures of the client.

**7.** When termination becomes a symbolic recapitulation of other (especially unresolved) farewells in the counselor's life.

**8.** When termination arouses in the counselor conflicts about his or her own individuation. (p. 348)

While the counselor trainee may have a supervisor who can point to any apparent resistance, what does the professional counselor do? In the first place, most experienced counselors know, at some level of consciousness, when the relationship has grown quite important. This is a cue to the counselor that peer consultation or supervision would be both appropriate and desirable. The more human counselors tend to be, the more susceptible they are to personal intrusions in their professional practice. Having a colleague who can provide a level of objectivity through discussion and taped supervision is a valuable asset.

## Case Illustration of Termination: The Case of Alex

In the following case, Alex is a thirty-four year old stockbroker who has been unemployed for six months as a result of his firm's downsizing. He has tried to see this turn of events as an opportunity to move his career in new directions. However, he has decided to seek counseling at this time for two reasons. Although he has extensive outplacement counseling, he really doesn't know in what direction he would like to go with a new career, and, in fact, has growing uncertainties about his potential. Added to this uncertainty, during the past few months he has grown increasingly bitter about being fired and how the outplacement was handled by his supervisor whom he considered a close friend. The case was seen in a private psychotherapy group practice.

### First Session

The first session began with the counselor orienting Alex to the conditions he could expect, including confidentiality, the necessity for the sessions to be tape-recorded, and the fact that the counselor belonged to a consortium of mental health professionals who met periodically to provide and receive peer supervision. In addition, the counselor indicated that he practiced "short-term" psychotherapy which meant that they would contract for ten sessions. If at the end of that time, the client had any remaining issues, they could contract for an additional brief period of counseling.

---

*Counselor:* Alex, one of the things we will be doing at each session is a review of your progress and how it is reflecting your goals. Since you have already had extensive career assessment, I would like your permission to request those results and they will become part of our weekly focus. So, how would you like to begin this ten-week exploration?

*Alex:* If you don't mind my saying so, I don't see how you can solve all my problems in ten weeks.

*Counselor:* You may be right, but of course, it won't be me doing it. It will be the two of us doing it.

*Alex:* Still, I don't see how it can be done. I've been sweating this out for six months already.

*Counselor:* Yes, and hopefully we can find some new and more efficient ways to look at your issues. But the first thing we need to address is which concern we should consider first, your future or your anger.

*Alex:* Well, its my future that brings me here.

*Counselor:* Yes, but do you think your anger and your loss of confidence are having any effect on your ability to make sound decisions about your future?

---

## Fourth Session

As the fourth session was about to end, the topic of termination was initiated by Alex.

---

*Alex:* This was a really tiring session today.

*Counselor:* Yes, we covered a lot of ground. I do think you are making some good progress.

*Alex:* Yeah, I do feel better about things but that worries me too.

*Counselor:* What is it about a good feeling that makes you worry?

*Alex:* Oh, it's not the good feeling. I'm just aware that things have been moving awfully fast and we only have six more sessions. I'm not sure I trust this idea of only ten sessions and boom, you're fixed.

*Counselor:* I don't think we said "Boom, you're fixed," when we started. And we can renegotiate for a couple more sessions when the time comes. But let's not jump to conclusions too quickly now. Most of the time, when clients are feeling good about their progress for several weeks, the feeling can be trusted. I'm glad you raised the issue because we are almost half-way through our ten-week contract. We don't have to do anything about that except to be aware that we will be terminating one of these days.

The counselor took this opportunity to extend Alex's awareness of the termination process. In effect, this discussion became the starting point for the termination process in this case. The seed of awareness was planted, and the client took that awareness with him at the end of the session. Three sessions later, the awareness had grown and matured.

### Seventh Session

Nearing the end of this session, which had been a difficult but significant session, the counselor introduced the termination topic again to Alex.

---

*Counselor:* Well, you've worked hard today Alex. How are you feeling about your progress?

*Alex:* To tell you the truth, I'm exhausted, Doc. But I feel pretty good about how things are going. I'm glad I have gotten over that anger I was feeling toward George. That was really getting in the way.

*Counselor:* About a month ago, you mentioned that one of your fears was feeling too optimistic about your improvement. Do you still feel that way?

*Alex:* When was that?

*Counselor:* Oh, I was reviewing the tape of our fourth session and heard you say that you didn't trust that you could get your situation under control in only ten sessions.

*Alex:* Well, I still wonder about that. But I do feel like I'm a lot clearer on things now than I was then. I don't feel as shaky.

*Counselor:* What about terminating soon. Do you feel shaky about that?

*Alex:* (Laughing) Well, you still owe me three sessions. I'm not ready to terminate today. But, unless the bottom falls out, I don't think I will need another ten sessions.

*Counselor:* (Chuckling) No, if you had another ten sessions, you'd probably begin to lose the ground you have gained.

*Alex:* What do you mean? Do people lose ground if they stay in counseling too long?

*Counselor:* I think so. There's a time to leave your parents, a time to leave your training, a time to leave a job, and in our case, a time to leave counseling. If we don't make that break when it's time, then you could grow dependent and that would be self-defeating.

---

In this dialogue, the counselor is able to present the therapeutic effects of appropriate termination in such a way that it is seen as a normal, developmental process, like growing up. That does not remove all of the client's fears, but it does place termination in a context that is anything but catastrophic. Quintana (1993) suggests that counselors can greatly facilitate the termination process by distinguishing between *losing* and *outgrowing* a valued relationship. He states:

> *If therapy has been constructive . . . clients are likely to have outgrown much of their need for the formal structure of therapy at this time in their ongoing development . . . [Although] therapists should be careful not to imply that clients have outgrown their needs for therapy definitely . . . [as] future therapy should remain an option for clients as a way to support or catalyze their continued development.* (p. 430)

### Ninth Session

The counselor begins this session by introducing the topic of termination.

---

*Counselor:* Well, Alex, this is our next to last session. How shall we use it?

*Alex:* We could call it a tie and go into extra innings.

*Counselor:* You're right, we could say that your weaknesses are still equal to your strengths.

*Alex:* Well, I don't believe that and you don't either, I don't think.

*Counselor:* No, I don't think that at all. In fact, I think your strengths are real and many of your weaknesses were imagined.

*Alex:* Yeah, I am feeling that. But its good to hear you say it too. Maybe that's how I'd like to spend today.

*Counselor:* What do you mean? Talking about your strengths?

*Alex:* Yeah. I think I know what I want to do with my life. The graduate school idea seems right and I did have an interview at the University this week.

---

The counselor intentionally introduced termination at the beginning of the ninth session to allow Alex time to process his feelings about the imminent ending of the relationship. Alex might have dwelt on the insecurity of ending a meaningful relationship; he could have negotiated an extension at this time, or he could try to cement the gains he has realized through discussion and review. In this case, Alex chose the latter.

### Tenth and Final Session

Alex began this session with the acknowledgment that it was the final session.

*Alex:* Well, this is it.
*Counselor:* What do you mean?

*Alex:* This is the last time I'll be seeing you, I think.

*Counselor:* I think so, too.

*Alex:* It's been good. When we started, I really wasn't so sure this was going to work. But things are starting to pull together. Oh, by the way, George and I went out partying last Friday night. It was good to see him again. And, I am filling out application forms for an M.B.A. program.

*Counselor:* That sounds good. Did George call you or did you call him?

*Alex:* No, I called him. And it's neat. I think he's going to be able to help me with some contacts.
*(Later in the session)*

*Counselor:* Before we finish today, I want you to know that I would like to hear from you in six months or so. Just a note telling me how things have been going would be fine. Would you do that?

*Alex:* Sure. What if I need a booster shot between now and then?

*Counselor:* If that happens, you can call and set up an appointment.

In this final session, the counselor provided a bridge to aid the transition by asking Alex to get back in touch in six months with an informal progress report. This is as much for Alex's benefit as it is for the counselor, for it says, "I'm not just dropping you from my appointment book and my consciousness. You will remain my client in absentia." Second, the counselor has provided a termination structure that allows Alex to make contact for future needs, should they arise. This would seem to be assumed, but clients often do not take this privilege for granted or are reluctant about such a move. In summary, an invitation for clients to return seems to result in greater levels of client satisfaction and lower levels of distress (Quintana & Holahan, 1992).

## Summary

Often, termination is viewed as the moment when counselor and client conclude a successful counseling relationship. We have tried to dispel this notion and replace it with a broader definition of termination as a stage in the counseling process. As a stage, termination can be seen as the time when positive change is solidified and the transition to self-reliance is accomplished (Prochaska et al., 1992). Viewed in this way, termination can be as critical to successful counseling as was the assessment or the intervention stages.

When termination is an imminent possibility, the counselor and client should begin discussing the matter several sessions in advance.

Many desirable consequences accrue from this discussion. The client becomes increasingly aware of new strengths and skills, the counselor is able to reinforce those gains, future demands and expectations can be considered, fears and concerns can be assessed. The process addresses unfinished business and enhances a sense of completion. In all of this, the counselor has responsibility to see that the client's well-being is protected and preserved. When termination occurs through referral, the counselor has primary responsibility to see that the transfer to the receiving professional is handled smoothly and sensitively.

Successful termination must be seen as part of successful treatment. Without it, even the most impressive counseling gains are tempered in the client's perception and future needs may be negatively affected.

## Exercises

1. Class members should divide into groups of three. Each should assume a role: counselor, client, or observer. The observer's responsibility will be to record both the counselor's and client's behaviors during the exercise. Both the counselor and client should select a role from the following lists. Do not reveal your role to the other persons.

    | *Counselor* | *Client* |
    | --- | --- |
    | 1. Resisting termination | 1. Resisting termination |
    | 2. Encouraging termination | 2. Requesting termination |
    | 3. Uncertain about termination | 3. Uncertain about termination |

    Conduct a ten-minute counseling session simulation using the roles you selected. Following the session, discuss your reactions to one another. The person who observed them should provide feedback to each of you regarding the dynamics he or she observed.

2. In the following role-play, one person should be the counselor, the second should be the client, and the third will be an observer/recorder.

    The role-play is a client who is being referred to a psychologist. The reason for the referral is that the counselor has realized that the client's problems are beyond his or her level of training and competence to treat. The client has seen the counselor for two sessions. Allow ten minutes for this role-play.

    Following the role-play, discuss among yourselves the dynamics of the interaction. What did you learn from this experience about its effect on the client? On the counselor? What interpersonal skills were required?

## Discussion Questions

1. What are the pros and cons of early discussion of termination?

2. What types of clients are most in need of gradual introduction to the idea of termination? Why?

3. In the chapter, reference is made to premature termination. What are some of the conditions that might lead to premature termination? Can all be controlled by the counselor?

4. Discuss the idea of counselor resistance to termination. Do you possess any characteristics that might cause you to resist terminating a client?

5. Discuss the ways in which referral is similar to termination. How is referral different from termination, in terms of the counselor's responsibilities? What are the interpersonal dynamics of each?

## Recommended Readings

Boyer, S.P. and Hoffman, M.A. (1993). Counselor affective reactions to termination: Impact of counselor loss history and perceived client sensitivity to loss, *Journal of Counseling Psychology, 40,* 271–277.

Quintana, S.M. (1993). Expanded and updated conceptualization of termination: Implications for short-term individual psychotherapy, *Professional Psychology, 24,* 426–432.

Quintana, S.M. and Holahan, W. (1992). Termination in short-term counseling: Comparison of successful and unsuccessful cases, *Journal of Counseling Psychology, 39,* 299–305.

Smith, K.J., Subich, L.M., and Kalodner, C. (1995). The transtheoretical model's stages and processes of change and their relation to premature termination, *Journal of Counseling Psychology, 42,* 34–39.

*Chapter* *12*

## Applying Counseling Skills to Unique Situations

*Purpose of This Chapter—*

In this chapter, we examine three activities that are commonly found in the counselor's practice. In each, the counseling skills that you have studied in earlier chapters form the basis for the activity. The first section, "Crisis Intervention," provides a description of the process and necessary skills for successful intervention. The second section, "Consultation," describes the nature of consultation, desirable conditions for effective consultation to occur, and skills related to consultation. The final section, "Conflict Management and Resolution," presents the theory and skills behind conflict resolution.

*Considerations as You Read This Chapter—*

- Your experiences outside of counseling may have been the reasons you decided to study counseling. No doubt this was because those experiences were similar in important ways to counseling.

- Similarly, the counseling experience can be related to situations outside the definition of counseling. Three such situations are presented here. Try to identify additional circumstances in which your counseling skills could be adapted and applied as you read this chapter.

The counseling skills and interventions that you have studied in the preceding chapters are applicable to a wide variety of settings. Because counseling addresses and seeks to improve human interactions as well as intrapersonal issues, the settings in which such interactions occur and in which intrapersonal issues are likely to rise lend themselves to human relations approaches. In this chapter we examine three of those areas, when human crises occur, when people require the insights and experience of human relations specialists, and when people find themselves locked into conflict with one another.

## Crisis Intervention

Beginning counselors often anticipate the occurrence of a client crisis as a counseling crisis as well. Without realizing that their basic counseling skills are translatable to crisis situations, they fear that they will be immobilized and unhelpful, perhaps even destructive to the client in crisis. In fact, many of the interventions that have been described in preceding chapters are also employed in crisis counseling. There are differences, of course. Crises have an immediacy, a demand for action, and a need for resolution, that differ from most other developmental human problems. There are also some differences in *how* the counselor views or conceptualizes the presenting problem.

### The Nature of Crisis

Human crises come in many forms. Some are natural disasters that affect large numbers of people simultaneously. The Kobe (Japan) earthquake, Hurricane Hugo, massive floods in the midwest and western United States, tornados that wreak devastation on midwest and southwestern communities each year, all of these disasters disrupt the lives of thousands of people. No less devastating are those crises that are violent in nature, such as the Long Island Railroad massacre, the parent suicide, the carload of high school seniors who crash and die the week before graduation, the physical abuse of a woman by her spouse, or the college basketball star who dies of a drug overdose.

What do these different crises have in common? Roberts (1990) describes five criteria that reflect the conditions of a person in crisis:

1. The person perceives the precipitating event as being meaningful and threatening.
2. The person appears unable to modify or lessen the impact of the event(s) with traditional coping methods.
3. The person experiences increased fear, tension, and/or confusion.
4. The person exhibits a high level of subjective discomfort.
5. The person rapidly moves into a state of psychological disequilibrium. (p. 9)

### Models of Crisis Intervention

Contemporary views of crisis intervention draw on three differing models. The first, which is inherent in Roberts' (1990) listing of crisis characteristics, is the *equilibrium model*. Drawing on the psychoanalytic notion of equilibrium/disequilibrium, this model emphasizes the *internal coping mechanisms* of the person experiencing the crisis, and the degree to which the crisis has pushed the person into a state of disequilibrium. The second is the *cognitive model*, which defines crisis not as the event, but in how the individual *interprets* the event and the effects of the event. From this perspective, crisis intervention would involve cognitive restructuring. The third model is the *psychosocial transition* model. This model integrates hereditary and environmental endowments into the individual's ability to respond to crisis situations and involves the assessment of those various contributions. According to Gilliland and James (1993)

> *The psychosocial model does not perceive crisis as simply an internal state of affairs that resides totally within the individual. It reaches outside the individual and asks what systems need to be changed.* (p. 21)

## Stages of Crisis Intervention

Each of the three crisis models identified above has a conception of the stages through which resolution develops. Further, the stages in two of these models varies to some extent from those five stages of counseling that we described in Chapter 2. There are also significant similarities.

Roberts (1990) describes the disequilibrium model as seven stages: (1) making psychological contact and rapidly establishing a relationship; (2) examining the dimensions of and defining the problem; (3) encouraging exploration of feelings/emotions; (4) assessing coping skills; (5) exploring alternative solutions; (6) implementing an action plan; and (7) follow-up.

Gilliland and James (1993) describe an integrative crisis model that encompasses six stages: (1) defining the problem; (2) ensuring client safety; (3) providing support; (4) examining alternatives; (5) making plans; and (6) obtaining commitment.

Similarities of these models to that described in Chapter 2 are fairly obvious. We have described the counseling process as a five-stage model in which relationship and rapport building is the initial stage. It is also a pervasive stage, in that it encompasses the other four stages and is always a matter of concern. The remaining stages are assessment, goal-setting, intervention, and termination/follow-up.

How does the model that has been the underpinning of this book interface with these crisis intervention models? First, the initial attention to *relationship building*, while important, is played down considerably in crisis intervention. When a person is in crisis, action is the most sought response. Relationship is achieved through a compassionate sensitivity to what the client has experienced that induced the crisis. The next step is *assessment* of the problem. This stage is clearly emphasized in the crisis models. Without an assessment of (a) the client's cognitive interpretations of the impact of the event on him or her; (b) the client's behavioral coping skills; (c) the client's social support system; and (d) the client's will to change or adapt, counseling intervention cannot proceed. The third stage, *goal-setting*, is a lesser player in crisis intervention, requiring much less negotiation between counselor and client. The reason is that the goals of crisis intervention are rather obvious: (1) to reduce the stress and pressures by (2) identifying existing coping skills and skill deficiencies, (3) defining behavioral strategies to alleviate distress, and (4) restructuring cognitive interpretations of the event(s) and effects of the event(s). Because crisis intervention is directed toward immediate response to situational factors and should not be confused with crisis remediation, a fifth, counselor-dictated goal is appropriate, (5) to facilitate successful referral to a longer-term counseling setting if appropriate. The fourth step, *intervention*, is inherent in all of the models. Finally, *termination and follow-up* are equally shared by the crisis models and the model we have presented.

## Skills Associated with Crisis Intervention

Many of the skills that have been introduced in preceding chapters are also applicable to the stages of crisis intervention (see *Table 12-1*). Skills are identified with each of the stages except the termination and follow-up stage. The contents of Chapter 11 is equally relevant to the special nature of crisis counseling, however.

### Individual Differences and Crisis Reactions

Each of these models is modified by characteristics of individual clients. Factors such as age, gender, ethnic, and multicultural characteristics will affect both how the individual reacts to different crises and the types of interventions that would be appropriate to use. For example, in cultures where the family is the focal unit, interventions must include family members in addition to the client. Or in cases where social conditions already produce ongoing crisis-like conditions for a cultural group (e.g., Palestinians living in the Gaza Strip, or Israelis living in the Golan Heights), crisis interventions necessarily incorporate the social system's support network as well as the individual's and family's coping skills.

**TABLE 12-1   Crisis Intervention Skills Applications**

| Skill | Application | Refer to |
| --- | --- | --- |
| Communicating empathy, genuineness, acceptance | Establishing a relationship | Chapter Three |
| Facilitative listening | Establishing relationship, assessing the parameters of the problem | Chapter Three |
| Paraphrasing and reflecting feelings | Establishing relationship, assessing the problem | Chapter Three |
| Intake interview | Assessing impact of crisis, assessing for suicide potential | Chapter Four |
| Open-ended and clarifying questions | Assessing severity of crisis and client's current emotional status; assessing alternatives, coping mechanisms, support systems | Chapter Four |
| Closed questions | Assessing for suicide potential | Chapter Four |
| Eliciting affect | Assessing impact of crisis event | Chapter Six |
| Affect focusing | Assessing impact of crisis event | Chapter Six |
| A-B-C-D analysis | Assessing/altering faulty thinking | Chapter Seven |
| Cognitive disputation | Altering faulty thinking | Chapter Seven |
| Introducing coping thoughts | Altering faulty thinking | Chapter Seven |
| Reframing | Altering faulty thinking | Chapter Seven/Ten |
| Self-monitoring | Establishing coping responses | Chapter Eight |
| Behavioral self-contract | Establishing commitment to change | Chapter Eight |

## Doing Crisis Intervention Counseling

How does one actually conduct a counseling session when the client is in active crisis? Gilliland and James (1993) provide a six-step model which can be used by volunteers and professional counselors alike. The model is action-oriented and situationally based.

### Defining the Problem—Step One

This step really involves a combination of focused information gathering and relationship building. The object of this step is that the counselor accurately perceives the crisis *as the client perceives it*. This includes not just the client's affective reactions but also his or her cognitive perceptions and the client's linking of situational events to the crisis. The counselor should use active listening skills and facilitative conditions as described in Chapter 3 as well as open-ended, clarifying, and closed questions. Depending on the setting and conditions, the counselor may also use an abbreviated form of the client intake interview.

### Ensuring the Client's Safety—Step Two

Because crisis can have a life-threatening quality, it is essential that you establish whether or not such a condition exists. Crisis can have other characteristics that are harmful, if not life threatening. Gilliland and James (1993, p. 28) define client safety as "minimizing the physical and psychological danger to self and others." Ensuring client safety is accomplished first by assuming that such a condition *could* exist, and proceeding to listen for and elicit information that might suggest that the hypothesis of danger is confirmed.

### Providing Support—Step Three

Vulnerability is a dominant characteristic of the client in crisis. The feeling of having conditions be out of control and questioning one's potential for achieving control over those conditions are characteristic of clients in crisis. These conditions can also revive and reinforce old feelings of inadequacy or failure, thus, magnifying the crisis. An essential step in the process of intervention is to provide support to the client so he or she does not feel so alone in the crisis. The larger purpose of this support is to help the client struggle back to a place where hope is possible. The counselor can provide this support by understanding, paired with *gradually increasing* degrees of confidence in the client's potential. Verbal responses such as *enhancing responses* (Chapter 3) and the *ability potential* (Chapter 5), paired with the continued core conditions of helping relationships (empathy, genuineness, immediacy, and positive regard—Chapter 3) form the basis for counselor support.

### Examining Alternatives—Step Four

At this step, it is essential that you have established a relationship of accurate understanding of the client's crisis and of the client's perceived world. Otherwise, your input into helping the client identify alternatives will come across as superficial, unrelated, or inappropriate. But, of course, you have established such a relationship by this point. Gilliland and James (1993) identify three different ways that the crisis counselor can think about alternatives:

> *(1) situational supports, which may represent excellent sources of help, people known to the client in the present or past who might care about what happens to the client;*
> *(2) coping mechanisms, those actions, behaviors, or environmental resources the client might use to help get through the present crisis; and*
> *(3) positive and constructive thinking patterns on the part of the*

*client [which] are ways of thinking that might substantially alter the client's view of the problem and lessen the client's level of stress and anxiety.* (p. 29)

As you and your client begin to discuss what to do, where to go, how to think about this crisis, these factors should guide your discussion. The first two, situational supports and coping mechanisms, may be identified by asking open-ended, clarifying, and closed questions. The third factor, identifying positive and constructive thinking patterns, may call for the use of reframing, paradox, or other cognitive strategies as discussed in Chapter 8.

### Making Plans—Step Five
Once the client has begun to recognize and accept the possibility of alternatives, it is important to move to action plans. Crisis intervention calls for action (crisis resolution may also call for insight but our focus is on intervention at this point). It is time now to identify a plan of action that includes persons other than the client who will be involved, actions the client will take, attitudes toward the crisis that the client will try to maintain, and a focus on systematic problem solving. This plan must be a product of the counselor and client's mutual discussions. Most importantly, it must be a plan that the client can endorse without reservation.

### Obtaining Commitment—Step Six
This step is really the beginning of a preventive process as well as a finalization of the intervention process. It calls for the client to move from planning, evaluating, and rethinking, to *doing*. That can be a long leap for some. But it is essential if the process of intervention is to be manifested. This step is preventive because the commitment to action marks a change in the client's outlook, a constructive change.

How does one obtain commitment from a client? Are words enough? Without meaning to diminish the value of the spoken commitment, it may be appropriate to look for additional, and more concrete forms of commitment. For example, the process of developing a plan of action is best acknowledged when the plan is actually written out and signed by the client (see Chapter 6). For whatever reasons, counselors have long found that the act of writing and signing a contract to action carries a lot of force with clients.

## Summary

The process of crisis intervention has a number of points of similarity to traditional counseling, as well as a few distinct differences. Principal among the differences are the urgency of the problem, the need for a quick move into relationship and beyond that to assessment. Identifying goals that relate specifically to the environmental conditions that precipitated the crisis and the client's interpretation of those events then must be cemented by concrete action steps. Finally, the vulnerability that crisis instills calls for the counselor to present and maintain a supportive role while at the same time helping the client move toward a new level of strength and autonomy. All of this occurs in a relatively short time. The similarities are in the counseling skills that are employed by the crisis counselor. They are many of the same skills that are found in other less-crisis-oriented counseling sessions.

Finally, it is important to distinguish between crisis intervention and crisis resolution. Crisis intervention is an intermediate step intended to reduce the situational stress and help the client return to a problem-solving state. Why the crisis was so powerful, and how future similar situations could be made less crisis-ridden is the domain of crisis resolution and involves longer term counseling along more traditional lines.

## Consultation

The delivery of consultation services has grown proportionately to the growing complexity of society. The realization that none of us can be skilled in all areas of performance as demanded by modern day careers, interpersonal relationships, and even child-raising, has led to the need to ask others for advice, instruction, or guidance in a wide spectrum of human functioning. One effect of this complexity is the practice of consultation.

Consultation occurs in a variety of settings. Organizational consultation typically occurs in corporate environments, although it can also occur in community agencies, schools, and governmental agencies. Its focus tends to be that of helping staff solve problems and improve productivity. On the other hand, mental health consultation can occur in a variety of settings, but focuses on people rather than technology (Hansen, Himes, & Meier, 1990). In this section, we will concentrate our attention on mental health consultation and the transfer of counseling skills.

### Consultation Defined

There is a wide divergence of opinion on what consultation is. However, Dougherty (1995) offers a definition that captures those areas in which there is general agreement:

*Consultation is a process in which a human service professional assists a consultee with a work-related (or caretaking related) prob-*

*lem with a client system, with the goal of helping both the consul-*
*tee and the client system in some specified way.* (p. 9)

Based on this definition, the client becomes the indirect receiver of the consultant's services. The kinds of consultation that counselors provide would include services to other counselors regarding their work with clients or institutions; services to groups regarding achievement of their objectives or analysis of their interactions as they seek their objectives; and services to institutions (such as schools and community agencies) regarding the planning and implementing of their programs.

Kurpius (1978) has described four modes of consultation, each of which may be utilized by the professional counselor. The first is the *provision* mode, in which the consultee contracts with the consultant for assistance on a specific need. The second is the *prescription* mode, similar to the doctor-patient relationship, where the consultant is asked to collect information, make a diagnosis, and give directions for treating or solving the problem. A third mode is *collaboration*. This mode requires that the consultant and consultee work as partners in analyzing problems, developing change processes, and evaluating progress. The final mode is *mediation*, in which the consultant generates information about the problem, the system, or the process and initiates action by drawing attention to those data.

## *Models of Consultation*

A variety of views exist on what are basic consultation models. However, there is general agreement on two models, Caplan's (1970) *mental health consultation* and the *behavioral* model. Other models that have been described in the literature include the education and training model, program-centered administrative consultation, consultee-centered administrative consultation, process consultation, and advocacy consultation (Conoley & Conoley, 1991; Dougherty, 1995; Hansen, Himes, & Meier, 1990). Each of these models has relevance for the counselor, according to the nature of the problem and setting in which it occurs. For our purposes, however, we will consider only mental health consultation, behavioral consultation, process consultation, and advocacy consultation.

### *Mental Health Consultation*

Originally defined by Caplan (1970), this model, when applied to a client, addresses not only the problem at hand, but also the underlying causes of this problem and potential future problems of a similar nature. The mental health consultant offers the consultee (typically the counselor) "diagnosis, clarification, or advice, which the consultee is able to accept or reject or use in any manner chosen"

(Hansen et al., 1990, p. 7). The counselor's supervisor is most likely to be the person providing this type of service, although it could also occur in a collaborative group of counselors who are providing consultation services to one another.

### Behavioral Consultation

Behavioral consultation is oriented toward problem-solving. Bergan (1977) is generally credited for applying principles of behavior change to consultation and establishing this model. According to Hansen et al. (1990), "the model assumes that the problems are the result of situational factors (i.e., classroom environment or teacher technique) which can be identified and brought under the control of the consultee" (p. 12). While behavioral consultation is suited to school settings, it is also viable as a consultation method applied to other settings (e.g., parent/child; supervisor/employees; administrator/managers; warden/incarceration officers). With this model, the consultant works on the identified problem *indirectly* through the consultee (1) to identify and correct problem behaviors of the client, and (2) to initiate and maintain consultee behaviors or situational factors that influence the problem behavior (Hansen et al., 1990). This is accomplished through a teaching process and helping the consultee to understand how changes will be accomplished.

### Process Consultation

The process consultation model differs from those already described in that it focuses attention on the *activities* that occur as a target group is interacting—that is, what group members are doing, saying, and enacting as they try to problem solve, perform certain tasks, or resolve disagreements. This model originates in the work of Schein (1978) who viewed the consultant's roles as either facilitator or catalyst of change. When in the facilitator role, the consultant probably knows what viable solutions to the problem may exist, but chooses to guide the consultee to those solutions rather than telling the consultee what they are. On the other hand, when the consultant is in the catalyst role, he or she may not know what the solution is but leads the consultee to possible solutions by using certain consultation skills. The process consultation model has been used extensively in group settings where the goal is to teach members new ways to work together, problem solve, and identify solutions to problems. Industry has used this model to train assembly-line personnel and managers. Community organizations have used this model to learn how to explore community problems using members from divergent interest groups. Schools have employed the model to help teachers with curriculum building and other collective efforts.

### Advocacy Model

Advocacy consultation is a lesser acknowledged model than those we have already described. In this role, the consultant "attempts to persuade the consultee to do something the consultant deems highly desirable" (Dougherty, 1995, p. 29). Conoley and Conoley (1991) suggest that it may be used to work for change when the client is a minority, physically or mentally challenged, or economically disadvantaged. The advocacy consultant addresses such issues as power and how it can be manipulated, and political influence and how it can be used. Advocacy consultation is obviously used in community settings and in the schools. But it also takes the form of the lobbyist in the legislature or the environmental advocate to the town council.

## Stages of Consultation

Consultation has been described as a four-stage process (Dougherty, 1995; Hansen et al., 1990). The first stage is the *initial contact* or *entry* stage. Stage two is the *assessment* and *diagnosis* stage. The third stage is *intervention* or *implementation*, and the final stage is *termination* or *disengagement*. These stages are very similar to the stages described in Chapter 2. Missing is the goal-setting stage which is subsumed under the assessment and diagnosis of the problem.

## Skills Associated with Consultation

Hansen et al. (1990, p. 47) describe three tasks that the consultant has in the first stage: to assess the consultee's readiness for change; to develop a working relationship with the consultee; and to establish some understanding of the consultee's situation and problem. In this stage, the consultant also must formalize a contract or agreement with the consultee regarding the consultation relationship. Dougherty (1995) also notes that in this stage the consultant *psychologically enters the system*, noting that this step "actually lasts the duration of the consultation process" (p. 43). Skills such as facilitative listening, open-ended questioning, and behavioral contracting are used extensively in this stage.

The assessment/diagnosis stage involves a variety of steps, including definition of the problem, goal-setting, and identification of appropriate interventions to be used by the consultant with the consultee. Skills identified in Chapters 4 and 5 are particularly applicable to this stage. Depending on the diagnosed nature of the problem (whether it is communication-based; behaviorally based, or systemically based) the consultant identifies interventions that relate to the consultee's goals. Having identified the strategies, the intervention stage involves a variety of skills and activities that you have already studied, including role-playing, modeling, successive approximation, and positive reinforcement. Finally, in the termination stage, it is important to evaluate the degree to which the consultee has incorporated the proposed changes and to establish a program that the consultee may use to maintain those changes and continue self-evaluation of their effects. While relationship issues are not at issue in termination of consultation, it is desirable to provide the consultee with options for reestablishing a consultation relationship in the future. This may include scheduled future dates in which the consultant and consultee will make contact. Skills that are part of the termination stage include assessing goal achievement, setting up a self-monitoring program for the consultee, and behavioral self-contracting.

### Cultural Differences in Consultation

Jackson and Hayes (1993) observe that consultation often involves consultees and clients who reflect and embrace ethnic and cultural diversity. Because most consultation models fail to address multicultural issues, they have proposed that diversity models can be superimposed on consultation models, thus enhancing the consultant's delivery of services. Multicultural differences can exist between consultant and consultee, consultee and client(s), or among clients (e.g., ethnic/cultural problems within a school or work or community setting). These differences must be recognized and understood from the context of all who are participants. We return to the need to understand *world views* or *the failure to do so*, which may be at the root of the problem. In addition, Jackson and Hayes point to the need to recognize when the consultee or client(s) reflect either high-context or low-context cultural organization. This characteristic would significantly impact the assessment/diagnosis, and intervention stages of the consulting process in ways similar to those we have discussed regarding individual counseling.

## Summary

Mental health consultation involves stages, processes, and skills that are similar to or the same as those of mental health counseling. Significant differences are also apparent, particularly the relationship of the consultant to the consultee, who then relates the process to the client. The four models of consultation presented in this chapter may be applied to psychotherapy issues, institutional change needs, group process issues, and community issues. Of these models the advocacy model represents the greatest divergence, since the consultant using this model is attempting to institute change directly into the system through the consultee.

## Conflict Management and Resolution

Increasingly, the counselor is asked to participate in the mediation of conflict, whether it be conflict between school children, husbands and wives, parents and children, or rival gangs. The ingredients of conflict include misunderstanding, vested interests, competing values, power and control, hostility and aggression. Too often, those who may have some potential effect on the control of conflict are not involved until conflict has grown into hostility and aggression. When this occurs, then the intervener's role is that of mediator and resolver. At an earlier time in the development of conflict, the intervener may also become involved in a preventive approach to conflict which involves teaching potentially conflicting individuals, partners, or groups how to manage their conflictual feelings, perceptions, and actions.

### Conflict Defined

The term *conflict* derives from the Latin word *conflictus*, which means a "striking together with force" (Forsyth, 1990). In its vernacular usage, conflict also includes physical, mental, or emotional aggression. Boardman and Horowitz (1994) provide a working definition of conflict as:

> *an incompatibility of behaviors, cognitions (including goals), and/or affect among individuals or groups that may or may not lead to an aggressive expression of this social incompatibility. This includes such variables as the type of conflict (whether the conflict is over resources, beliefs, values, or the nature of the relationship), the perceived size or consequences of the conflict, and how rigidly the issues are presented.* (pp. 4–5)

The United States is viewed by other countries as a particularly violent and aggressive society. In their examination of human aggression, Lore and Schultz (1993) suggest that this is the result of Americans' attitude that "aggression either cannot or should not be controlled" (p. 16). In their defense of this position, they note that most Americans assume that virtually any societal attempt to control aggression would of necessity be so stringent and repressive as to produce unpredictable and unfortunate side effects. This view reflects not only the rugged individualism of America's past but also the Freudian theme on the adverse effects of repressing aggressive impulses and avoiding frustration. (Lore & Schultz, 1993, p. 17)

However, this attitude may be breaking down when it comes to the effect of violence in the schools, and to some extent, violence in the home. Increasingly, calls for divorce mediation, spouse abuse intervention, gang violence intervention, and similar aggressive expressions are being heard by counselors. Clearly, we must respond to conflict when it attacks the most vulnerable, whether it be individuals or societal fabric.

## The Nature of Conflict

Many beginning counselors look on conflict with aversive reactions, dreading its expression, and feeling somehow responsible. Some counselors, whose personal history includes debilitating negative effects of conflict in childhood, will view conflict as something to be avoided in the counseling session and in their personal lives. In Deutsch's (1973) opinion, however, conflict also has positive value in society. In an open society, conflict is likely to stabilize by permitting immediate and direct expression of rival claims. He differentiates between destructive and constructive conflict, saying:

> [A] conflict clearly has destructive consequences if its participants are dissatisfied with the outcomes and feel they have lost as a result of the conflict. Similarly, a conflict has productive consequences if the participants all are satisfied with their outcomes and feel that they have gained as a result of the conflict. (Deutsch, 1973, p. 17)

Conflict between groups takes on an added dimension. Sometimes a group manages its internal conflict by transferring it to opponent groups. This is particularly apparent in the case of juvenile gangs, where conflict *within* the gang is transferred to other gangs through territorial disputes, perceived insults, etc.

## Stages of Conflict Resolution

In many respects, conflict resolution is a special form of consultation. Hansen et al. (1990) take this position and describe it as "third party consultation." Fisher (1994) describes a three-stage process for conflict resolution, which includes:

**1.** *Conflict analysis.* This involves sources and types of conflict and events that have escalated the conflict to its present state; identifying needs, values, interest, and positions of the parties involved; perceptions of each party and facilitation of the exchange of perceptions and clarifications by each party; and clear and honest communication.

**2.** *Conflict confrontation.* In this stage, parties must engage in face-to-face interaction under established rules of mutual respect, shared exploration, and commitment to resolution; recognize intergroup diversity and gender equality; be sensitive to cultural differences and power imbalances; persistently seek out mutually acceptable outcomes.

**3.** *Conflict resolution.* At this stage, the mediator encourages collaboration and problem-solving activity by both parties; and addresses human needs and seeks to build on the qualities of sustainable relationships between the parties. The parties involved must freely choose a common solution to their disagreement and conflict. (pp. 50–61)

Hansen et al. (1990) also describe a process of conflict resolution that includes:

**1.** *Presence.* This is the most benign of the stages. It implies that the counselor's presence may be enough in itself to influence openness and discussion of viewpoints.

**2.** *Preliminary interviewing.* This step involves interviews with each party to the conflict, assessing substantive and emotional issues, openness to negotiate, and motivation to change.

**3.** *Structured meeting.* This meeting should occur at a neutral site, diminish power differences between conflicting parties, establish rules of engagement, provide open-ended time for discussion, and enhance communication between conflicting parties.

**4.** *Interventions into discussion.* This may take the form of establishing the agenda, directing discussion to issues and alternatives, summarizing, translating, and providing feedback, and identifying alternatives.

**5.** *Follow-up.* When the conflict requires more than a single session, the counselor plans, schedules, arranges meeting conditions, summarizes previous gains, identifies alternative courses of action, and facilitates decision making by both parties. (pp. 262–263)

### *Conflict Management as Prevention*

Fisher (1994) identifies factors that often precede conflict. Among these are sensitivity to intergroup diversity and gender equality, cultural differences, power imbalances, etc. But in addition, skills associated with conflict management and peacemaking are often missing. Active listening, shared meanings, and focused questioning are necessary to the understandings that allow persons to be more tolerant, and less impetuous in their reactions to others. Where do people learn these skills? Some of us have learned them in our families-of-origin. Others of us learn them in our religious training. Most of us learn them through structured socialization experiences in early school years. However, there are many who do not learn these skills and insights. For this reason, prevention programs have been developed that offer exposure and training in how to confront conflict, defuse its energy, and replace it with understanding and acceptance. Schools have begun to adopt peer mediator programs in which students are taught how to be peer helpers when conflict arises. Some school districts have even developed programs in which trained peer mediators wear distinctive shirts that identify them as resources when disagreements occur during schooltime. Johnson and Johnson (1994) describe the mediation procedure as a four-step process that includes: (1) end hostilities; (2) ensure that the disputants are committed to the mediation process; (3) help the disputants to successfully negotiate with each other; and (4) formalize the agreement. If these initial interventions appear to be ineffective, the peer helper refers the participants to professional counselors in the school.

## Skills Associated with Conflict Resolution

The basic skills of conflict resolution involve negotiation and mediation processes. Deutsch (1994, p. 25) identifies several communication skills as basic to resolution intervention. These include: "active listening, taking the perspective of the other, distinguishing between 'needs' and 'positions', using 'I' rather than 'you' messages, reframing the issues in conflict to find common ground, being alert to the possibility of misunderstandings due to cultural differences, etc." In addition, the mediator must know how to use open-ended and clarifying questions to obtain and use feedback, and finally, when and how to respond to existing cultural factors that influence communication. Because the professional counselor will have these skills, conflict resolution programs often rely on the counselor for implementation. But there is another set of skills that contribute to the mediation process. Those skills relate to the identification of the problem, assessment of individual investments in the problem, identification of alternative investments that the participants could accept, and negotiation of agreements that allow for peaceful settlements of differences. These skills also are found in the professional counselor's repertoire.

### Cultural Differences and Conflict Resolution

When cultural differences are an apparent condition of the persons involved in the dispute, a cultural analysis should be conducted to determine whether or not cultural differences are a component of the misunderstanding or disagreement. According to Avruch and Black (1993), this is the first step in the process toward resolution. They describe culture as a lens through which the world is perceived and observe that persons assume their own normality of perceptions and "tend to assert the abnormality, the strangeness and bizarreness of the other" (p. 133). They quote Raymonde Carroll's (1988, p. 2) description of cultural analysis as "a means of perceiving as 'normal' things which initially seem 'bizarre' or 'strange' among people of a culture different from one's own."

The process of cultural analysis involves (a) being on the lookout for what might be interpreted as bizarre; (b) avoiding interpreting such events with value judgments such as "the English are cold," or "the French are just rude"; having noticed the strange and having avoided moralizing it away, locating it within the cultural context of the person from whom it came (Avruch & Black, 1993, p. 136).

## Summary

As conflict and violence grow in our schools, families, neighborhoods and the workplace, it becomes increasingly clear that we must develop more effective means to counter and prevent their occurrence. The skills inherent in professional counseling are transferable to peer mediation training, conflict intervention, and conflict resolution. As a result, the professional counselor has a role to play in this societal dilemma, both as a third party in intervention efforts and as a trainer in prevention efforts. In addition, the growing cultural complexity of our society adds to the potential for misunderstandings among people whose cultural lens shape their attitudes about what is normal or abnormal, natural or bizarre. Here too, the counselor has much to offer in helping people develop communication processes that broaden their understanding of cultural and personal differences.

## The Counselor and Unique Situations: A Postscript

As counselor educators and practicing counselors, we are continuously reminded of the broad applicability of counseling skills to other social situations. Recently a colleague returned from an intensive experience at an internationally recognized corporate Leadership Training Program. Her comment was that while the experience had been excellent, the skills were the same as those we use and teach our counseling students. It is also the case within the eduation community (teacher/learner), the legal profession (mediation), the medical profession (doctor/patient relationship), and many more. The reality is that those skills you have been studying are *human relationship* skills. As you come to accept this fact, you will also grow in your self-confidence when you approach human problems in other settings.

# Recommended Readings

## Crisis Intervention

Congress, E.P. (1990). Crisis intervention with Hispanic clients in a urban mental health clinic. In Roberts, A.R. (1990). *Crisis Intervention Handbook: Assessment, Treatment, and Research*, Belmont, CA: Wadsworth.

Gilliland, B.E. and James, R.K. (1993). *Crisis Intervention Strategies*, Pacific Grove,CA: Brooks/Cole.

Lewis, R., Walker, B.A., and Mehr, M. (1990). Counseling with adolescent suicidal clients and their families. In Roberts, A.R. (1990). *Crisis Intervention Handbook: Assessment, Treatment, and Research*, Belmont, CA: Wadsworth.

Roberts, A.R. and Roberts, B.S. (1990). A comprehensive model for crisis intervention with battered women and their children. In Roberts, A.R. (1990). *Crisis Intervention Handbook: Assessment, Treatment, and Research*, Belmont, CA: Wadsworth.

Schulman, N.M. (1990). Crisis intervention in a high school: Lessons from the Concord High School experiences. In Roberts, A.R. (1990). *Crisis Intervention Handbook: Assessment, Treatment, and Research*, Belmont, CA: Wadsworth.

## Consultation

Conoley, J.C. and Conoley, C.W. (1991). *Consultation: A Guide to Practice and Training*, 2d ed. New York: Pergamon.

Daugherty, A.M. (1995). *Consultation: Practice and Perspectives in School and Community Settings*, 2d ed. Pacific Grove, CA: Brooks/Cole.

Hansen, J.C., Himes, B.S., and Meier, S. (1990). *Consultation: Concepts and Practices*, Englewood Cliffs, NJ: Prentice-Hall.

Jackson, D.N. and Hayes, D.H. (1993). Multicultural issues in consultation, *Journal of Counseling and Development, 72,* 144–147.

Remley, T.P., Jr. (1993). Consultation contracts, *Journal of Counseling and Development, 72,* 157–158.

West, J.F. and Idol, L. (1993). The counselor as consultant in the collaborative school, *Journal of Counseling and Development, 71,* 678–683.

Westbrook, F.D., Kandell, J.J., Kirkland, S.E., Phillips, P.E., Regan, A.M., Medvene, A., and Oslin, Y.D. (1993). University campus consultation: Opportunities and limitations, *Journal of Counseling and Development, 71,* 684–688.

## Conflict Management and Resolution

Avruch, K. and Black, P.W. (1993). Conflict resolution in intercultural settings. In D.J.D. Sandole and H. van der Merwe, Eds., *Conflict*

*Resolution Theory and Practice: Integration and Application*, Manchester, UK: Manchester University Press.

Boardman, S.K. and Horowitz, S.V. (1994). Constructive conflict management and social problems: An introduction, *Journal of Social Issues, 50*, 1–12.

Carroll, R. (1988). *Cultural Misunderstandings: The French-American Experience*. Chicago: University of Chicago Press.

Deutsch, M. (1973). *The Resolution of Conflict: Constructive and Destructive Processes*. New Haven, CT and London: Yale University Press.

Deutsch, M. (1994). Constructive conflict resolution: Principles, training, and research, *Journal of Social Issues, 50*, 13–32.

Fisher, R.J. (1994). Generic principles for resolving intergroup conflict, *Journal of Social Issues, 50*, 47–66.

Forsyth, D.R. (1990). *Group Dynamics*, 2d ed. Pacific Grove, CA: Brooks/Cole.

Goldstein, A.P. and Huff, C.R. (1993). *The Gang Intervention Handbook*, Champaign, IL: Research Press.

Hansen, J.C., Himes, B.S., and Meier, S. (1990). *Consultation: Concepts and Practices*, Englewood Cliffs, NJ: Prentice-Hall.

Johnson, D.W. and Johnson, R.T. (1994). Constructive conflict in the schools, *Journal of Social Issues, 50*, 117–138.

Lore, R.K. and Schultz, L.A. (1993). Control of human aggression, *American Psychologist, 48*, 16–25.

*A p p e n d i x*  *A*

# Code of Ethics, American Counseling Association*

(Approved by the ACA Governing Council, April, 1995)

## Preamble

The American Counseling Association is an educational, scientific, and professional organization whose members are dedicated to the enhancement of human development throughout the lifespan. Association members recognize diversity in our society and embrace a cross-cultural approach in support of the worth, dignity, potential, and uniqueness of each individual.

The specification of a code of ethics enables the association to clarify to current and future members, and to those served by members, the nature of the ethical responsibilities held in common by its members. As the code of ethics of the association, this document establishes principles that define the ethical behavior of association members. All members of the American Counseling Association are required to adhere to the *Code of Ethics* and the *Standards of Practice*. The Code of Ethics will serve as the basis for processing ethical complaints initiated against members of the association.

*©1995, ACA. Reprinted with permission. No further reproduction authorized without permission of ACA.

327

## Section A: The Counseling Relationship

**A.1.** Client Welfare

a. *Primary Responsibility.* The primary responsibility of counselors is to respect the dignity and to promote the welfare of clients.

b. *Positive Growth and Development.* Counselors encourage client growth and development in ways that foster the clients' interest and welfare; counselors avoid fostering dependent counseling relationships.

c. *Counseling Plans.* Counselors and their clients work jointly in devising integrated, individual counseling plans that offer reasonable promise of success and are consistent with abilities and circumstances of clients. Counselors and clients regularly review counseling plans to ensure their continued viability and effectiveness, respecting clients' freedom of choice. (See A.3.b.)

d. *Family Involvement.* Counselors recognize that families are usually important in clients' lives and strive to enlist family understanding and involvement as a positive resource, when appropriate.

e. *Career and Employment Needs.* Counselors work with their clients in considering employment in jobs and circumstances that are consistent with the client's overall abilities, vocational limitations, physical restrictions, general temperament, interest and aptitude patterns, social skills, education, general qualifications, and other relevant characteristics and needs. Counselors neither place nor participate in placing clients in positions that will result in damaging the interest and the welfare of clients, employers, or the public.

**A.2.** Respecting Diversity

a. *Nondiscrimination.* Counselors do not condone or engage in discrimination based on age, color, culture, disability, ethnic group, gender, race, religion, sexual orientation, marital status, or socioeconomic status. (See C.5.a., C.5.b., and D.1.i.)

b. *Respecting Differences.* Counselors will actively attempt to understand the diverse cultural backgrounds of the clients with whom they work. This includes, but is not limited to, learning how the counselor's own cultural/ethnic/racial identity impacts her/his values and beliefs about the counseling process. (See E.8. and F.2.i.)

**A.3.** Client Rights

a. *Disclosure to Clients.* When counseling is initiated, and throughout the counseling process as necessary, counselors inform clients of the purposes, goals, techniques, procedures, limitations, potential risks and benefits of services to be performed, and other pertinent information. Counselors take steps to ensure that clients understand the implications of diagnosis, the intended use of tests and reports, fees, and billing arrangements. Clients have the right to expect confidentiality and to be provided with an explanation of its limitations, including supervision and/or treatment team professionals; to obtain clear information about their case records; to participate in the ongoing counseling plans; and to refuse any recommended services and be advised of the consequences of such refusal. (See E.5.a. and G.2.)

b. *Freedom of Choice.* Counselors offer clients the freedom to choose whether to enter into a counseling relationship and to determine which professional(s) will provide counseling. Restrictions that limit choices of clients are fully explained. (See A.1.c.)

c. *Inability to Give Consent.* When counseling minors or persons unable to give voluntary informed consent, counselors act in these clients' best interests. (See B.3.)

**A.4.** Clients Served by Others

If a client is receiving services from another mental health professional, counselors, with client consent, inform the professional persons already involved and develop clear agreements to avoid confusion and conflict for the client. (See C.6.c.)

**A.5.** Personal Needs and Values

a. *Personal Needs.* In the counseling relationship, counselors are aware of the intimacy and responsibilities inherent in the counseling relationship, maintain respect for clients, and avoid actions that seek to meet their personal needs at the expense of clients.

b. *Personal Values.* Counselors are aware of their own values, attitudes, beliefs, and behaviors and how these apply in a diverse society, and avoid imposing their values on clients. (See C.5.a.)

**A.6.** Dual Relationships

a. *Avoid When Possible.* Counselors are aware of their influential positions with respect to clients, and they avoid exploiting the trust and dependency of clients. Counselors make every effort to avoid dual relationships with clients that could impair professional judgment or increase the risk of harm to clients. (Examples of such relationships include, but are not limited to, familial, social, financial, business, or close personal relationships with clients.) When a dual relationship cannot be avoided, counselors take appropriate professional precautions such as informed consent, consultation, supervision, and documentation to ensure that judgment is not impaired and no exploitation occurs. (See F.1.b.)

b. *Superior/Subordinate Relationships.* Counselors do not accept as clients superiors or subordinates with whom they have administrative, supervisory, or evaluative relationships.

**A.7.** Sexual Intimacies with Clients

a. *Current Clients.* Counselors do not have any type of sexual intimacies with clients and do not counsel persons with whom they have had a sexual relationship.

b. *Former Clients.* Counselors do not engage in sexual intimacies with former clients within a minimum period of two years after terminating the counseling relationship. Counselors who engage in such relationship after two years following termination have the responsibility to thoroughly examine and document that such relations did not have an exploitative nature, based on factors such as duration of counseling, amount of time since counseling, termination circumstances, client's personal history and mental status, adverse impact on the client, and actions by the counselor suggesting a plan to initiate a sexual relationship with the client after termination.

**A.8.** Multiple Clients

When counselors agree to provide counseling services to two or more persons who have a relationship (such as husband and wife, or parents and children), counselors clarify at the outset which person or persons are clients and the nature of the relationship they will have with each involved person. If it becomes apparent that counselors may be called upon to perform potentially conflicting roles, they clarify, adjust, or withdraw from roles appropriately. (See B.2. and B.4.d.)

**A.9.** Group Work

a. *Screening.* Counselors screen prospective group counseling/therapy participants. To the extent possible, counselors select members whose needs and goals are compatible with goals of the group, who will not impede the group process, and whose well-being will not be jeopardized by the group experience.

b. *Protecting Clients.* In a group setting, counselors take reasonable precautions to protect clients from physical or psychological trauma.

**A.10.** Fees and Bartering (See D.3.a. and D.3.b.)

a. *Advance Understanding.* Counselors clearly explain to clients, prior to entering the counseling relationship, all financial arrangements related to professional services including the use of collection agencies or legal measures for nonpayment. (A.11.c.)

b. *Establishing Fees.* In establishing fees for professional counseling services, counselors consider the financial status of clients and locality. In the event that the established fee structure is inappropriate for a client, assistance is provided in attempting to find comparable services of acceptable cost. (See A.10.d., D.3.a., and D.3.b.)

c. *Bartering Discouraged*. Counselors ordinarily refrain from accepting goods or services from clients in return for counseling services because such arrangements create inherent potential for conflicts, exploitation, and distortion of the professional relationship. Counselors may participate in bartering only if the relationship is not exploitive, if the client requests it, if a clear written contract is established, and if such arrangements are an accepted practice among professionals in the community. (See A.6.a.)

d. *Pro Bono Service*. Counselors contribute to society by devoting a portion of their professional activity to services for which there is little or no financial return (pro bono).

**A.11.** Termination and Referral

a. *Abandonment Prohibited*. Counselors do not abandon or neglect clients in counseling. Counselors assist in making appropriate arrangements for the continuation of treatment, when necessary, during interruptions such as vacations, and following termination.

b. *Inability to Assist Clients*. If counselors determine an inability to be of professional assistance to clients, they avoid entering or immediately terminate a counseling relationship. Counselors are knowledgeable about referral resources and suggest appropriate alternatives. If clients decline the suggested referral, counselors should discontinue the relationship.

c. *Appropriate Termination*. Counselors terminate a counseling relationship, securing client agreement when possible, when it is reasonably clear that the client is no longer benefiting, when services are no longer required, when counselor no longer serves the client's needs or interests, when clients do not pay fees charged, or when agency or institution limits do not allow provision of further counseling services. (See A.10.b. and C.2.g.)

**A.12.** Computer Technology

a. *Use of Computers*. When computer applications are used in counseling services, counselors ensure that: (1) the client is intellectually, emotionally, and physically capable of using the computer application; (2) the computer application is appropriate for the needs of the client; (3) the client understands the purpose and operation of the computer applications; and (4) a follow-up of client use of a computer application is provided to correct possible misconceptions, discover inappropriate use, and assess subsequent needs.

b.   *Explanation of Limitations.* Counselors ensure that clients are provided information as a part of the counseling relationship that adequately explains the limitations of computer technology.
c.   *Access to Computer Applications.* Counselors provide for equal access to computer applications in counseling services. (See A.2.a.)

## Section B: Confidentiality

**B.1.** Right to Privacy

a.   *Respect for Privacy.* Counselors respect their clients' right to privacy and avoid illegal and unwarranted disclosures of confidential information. (See A.3.a. and B.6.a.)
b.   *Client Waiver.* The right to privacy may be waived by the client or their legally recognized representative.
c.   *Exceptions.* The general requirement that counselors keep information confidential does not apply when disclosure is required to prevent clear and imminent danger to the client or others or when legal requirements demand that confidential information be revealed. Counselors consult with other professionals when in doubt as to the validity of an exception.
d.   *Contagious, Fatal Diseases.* A counselor who receives information confirming that a client has a disease commonly known to be both communicable and fatal is justified in disclosing information to an identifiable third party, who by his or her relationship with the client is at a high risk of contracting the disease. Prior to making a disclosure the counselor should ascertain that the client has not already informed the third party about his or her disease and that the client is not intending to inform the third party in the immediate future. (See B.1.c. and B.1.f.)
e.   *Court Ordered Disclosure.* When court ordered to release confidential information without a client's permission, counselors request to the court that the disclosure not be required due to potential harm to the client or counseling relationship. (See B.1.c.)
f.   *Minimal Disclosure.* When circumstances require the disclosure of confidential information, only essential information is revealed. To the extent possible, clients are informed before confidential information is disclosed.
g.   *Explanation of Limitations.* When counseling is initiated and throughout the counseling process as necessary, counselors inform clients of the limitations of confidentiality and identify foreseeable situations in which confidentiality must be breached. (See G.2.a.)
h.   *Subordinates.* Counselors make every effort to ensure that pri-

vacy and confidentiality of clients are maintained by subordinates including employees, supervisees, clerical assistants, and volunteers. (See B.1.a.)

i. *Treatment Teams.* If client treatment will involve a continued review by a treatment team, the client will be informed of the team's existence and composition.

**B.2.** Groups and Families

a. *Group Work.* In group work, counselors define confidentiality and the parameters for the specific group being entered, explain its importance, and discuss the difficulties related to confidentiality involved in group work. The fact that confidentiality cannot be guaranteed is clearly communicated to group members.

b. *Family Counseling.* In family counseling, information about one family member cannot be disclosed to another member without permission. Counselors protect the privacy rights of each family member. (See A.8., B.3., and B.4.d.)

**B.3.** Minor or Incompetent Clients

When counseling clients who are minors or individuals who are unable to give voluntary, informed consent, parents or guardians may be included in the counseling process as appropriate. Counselors act in the best interests of clients and take measures to safeguard confidentiality. (See A.3.c.)

**B.4.** Records

a. *Requirements of Records.* Counselors maintain records necessary for rendering professional services to their clients and as required by laws, regulations, or agency or institution procedures.

b. *Confidentiality of Records.* Counselors are responsible for securing the safety and confidentiality of any counseling records they create, maintain, transfer, or destroy whether the records are written, taped, computerized, or stored in any other medium. (See B.1.a.)

c. *Permission to Record or Observe.* Counselors obtain permission from clients prior to electronically recording or observing sessions. (See A.3.a.)

d. *Client Access.* Counselors recognize that counseling records are kept for the benefit of clients, and therefore provide access to records and copies of records when requested by competent clients, unless the records contain information that may be misleading and detrimental to the client. In situations involving multiple clients, access to records is limited to those parts of records that do not include confidential information related to another client. (See A.8., B.1.a., and B.2.b.)

e. *Disclosure or Transfer.* Counselors obtain written permission from clients to disclose or transfer records to legitimate third parties unless exceptions to confidentiality exist as listed in Section B.1. Steps are taken to ensure that receivers of counseling records are sensitive to their confidential nature.

**B.5.** Research and Training

a. *Data Disguise Required.* Use of data derived from counseling relationships for purposes of training, research, or publication is confined to content that is disguised to ensure the anonymity of the individuals involved. (See B.1.g. and G.3.d.)
b. *Agreement for Identification.* Identification of a client in a presentation or publication is permissible only when the client has reviewed the material and has agreed to its presentation or publication. (See G.3.d.)

**B.6.** Consultation

a. *Respect for Privacy.* Information obtained in a consulting relationship is discussed for professional purposes only with persons clearly concerned with the case. Written and oral reports present data germane to the purposes of the consultation, and every effort is made to protect client identity and avoid undue invasion of privacy.
b. *Cooperating Agencies.* Before sharing information, counselors make efforts to ensure that there are defined policies in other agencies serving the counselor's clients that effectively protect the confidentiality of information.

## Section C: Professional Responsibility

**C.1.** Standards Knowledge

Counselors have a responsibility to read, understand, and follow the *Code of Ethics* and the *Standards of Practice.*

**C.2.** Professional Competence

a. *Boundaries of Competence.* Counselors practice only within the boundaries of their competence, based on their education, training, supervised experience, state and national professional credentials, and appropriate professional experience. Counselors will demonstrate a commitment to gain knowledge, personal awareness, sensitivity, and skills pertinent to working with a diverse client population.

b. *New Specialty Areas of Practice.* Counselors practice in specialty areas new to them only after appropriate education, training, and supervised experience. While developing skills in new specialty areas, counselors take steps to ensure the competence of their work and to protect others from possible harm.

c. *Qualified for Employment.* Counselors accept employment only for positions for which they are qualified by education, training, supervised experience, state and national professional credentials, and appropriate professional experience. Counselors hire for professional counseling positions only individuals who are qualified and competent.

d. *Monitor Effectiveness.* Counselors continually monitor their effectiveness as professionals and take steps to improve when necessary. Counselors in private practice take reasonable steps to seek out peer supervision to evaluate their efficacy as counselors.

e. *Ethical Issues Consultation.* Counselors take reasonable steps to consult with other counselors or related professionals when they have questions regarding their ethical obligations or professional practice. (See H.1.)

f. *Continuing Education.* Counselors recognize the need for continuing education to maintain a reasonable level of awareness of current scientific and professional information in their fields of activity. They take steps to maintain competence in the skills they use, are open to new procedures, and keep current with the diverse and/or special populations with whom they work.

g. *Impairment.* Counselors refrain from offering or accepting professional services when their physical, mental, or emotional problems are likely to harm a client or others. They are alert to the signs of impairment, seek assistance for problems, and, if necessary, limit, suspend, or terminate their professional responsibilities. (See A.11.c.)

**C.3.** Advertising and Soliciting Clients

a. *Accurate Advertising.* There are no restrictions on advertising by counselors except those that can be specifically justified to protect the public from deceptive practices. Counselors advertise or represent their services to the public by identifying their credentials in an accurate manner that is not false, misleading, deceptive, or fraudulent. Counselors may only advertise the highest degree earned which is in counseling or a closely related field from a college or university that was accredited when the degree was awarded by one of the regional accrediting bodies recognized by the Council on Postsecondary Accreditation.

b. *Testimonials.* Counselors who use testimonials do not solicit them from clients or other persons who, because of their particular circumstances, may be vulnerable to undue influence.

c. *Statements by Others.* Counselors make reasonable efforts to ensure that statements made by others about them or the profession of counseling are accurate.

d. *Recruiting Through Employment.* Counselors do not use their places of employment or institutional affiliation to recruit or gain clients, supervisees, or consultees for their private practices. (See C.5.3.)

e. *Products and Training Advertisements.* Counselors who develop products related to their profession or conduct workshops or training events ensure that the advertisements concerning these products or events are accurate and disclose adequate information for consumers to make informed choices.

f. *Promoting to Those Served.* Counselors do not use counseling, teaching, training, or supervisory relationships to promote their products or training events in a manner that is deceptive or would exert undue influence on individuals who may be vulnerable. Counselors may adopt textbooks they have authored for instruction purposes.

g. *Professional Association Involvement.* Counselors actively participate in local, state, and national associations that foster the development and improvement of counseling.

**C.4.** Credentials

a. *Credentials Claimed.* Counselors claim or imply only professional credentials possessed and are responsible for correcting any known misrepresentations of their credentials by others. Professional credentials include graduate degrees in counseling or closely related mental health fields, accreditation of graduate programs, national voluntary certification, government-issued certifications or licenses, ACA professional membership, or any other credential that might indicate to the public specialized knowledge or expertise in counseling.

b. *ACA Professional Membership.* ACA professional members may announce to the public their membership status. Regular members may not announce their ACA membership in a manner that might imply they are credentialed counselors.

c. *Credential Guidelines.* Counselors follow the guidelines for use of credentials that have been established by the entities that issue the credentials.

d. *Misrepresentation of Credentials.* Counselors do not attribute more to their credentials than the credentials represent, and do not imply that other counselors are not qualified because they do not possess certain credentials.

e. *Doctoral Degrees From Other Fields.* Counselors who hold a master's degree in counseling or a closely related mental health field, but hold a doctoral degree from other than counseling or a closely related field do not use the title, "Dr." in their practices and do not announce to the public in relation to their practice or status as a counselor that they hold a doctorate.

**C.5.** Public Responsibility

a. *Nondiscrimination.* Counselors do not discriminate against clients, students, or supervisees in a manner that has a negative impact based on their age, color, culture, disability, ethnic group, gender, race, religion, sexual orientation, or socioeconomic status, or for any other reason. (See A.2.a.)

b. *Sexual Harassment.* Counselors do not engage in sexual harassment. Sexual harassment is defined as sexual solicitation, physical advances, or verbal or nonverbal conduct that is sexual in nature, that occurs in connection with professional activities or roles, and that either: (1) is unwelcome, is offensive, or creates a hostile workplace environment, and counselors know or are told this; or (2) is sufficiently severe or intense to be perceived as harassment to a reasonable person in the context. Sexual harassment can consist of a single intense or severe act or multiple persistent or pervasive acts.

c. *Reports to Third Parties.* Counselors are accurate, honest, and unbiased in reporting their professional activities and judgments to appropriate third parties including courts, health insurance companies, those who are the recipients of evaluation reports, and others. (See B.1.g.)

d. *Unjustified Gains.* Counselors do not use their professional positions to seek or receive unjustified personal gains, sexual favors, unfair advantage, or unearned goods or services. (See C.3.d.)

**C.6.** Responsibility to Other Professionals

a. *Different Approaches.* Counselors are respectful of approaches to professional counseling that differ from their own. Counselors know and take into account the traditions and practices of other professional groups with which they work.

b. *Personal Public Statements.* When making personal statements in a public context, counselors clarify that they are speaking from their personal perspectives and that they are not speaking on behalf of all counselors or the profession. (See C.5.d.)

c. *Clients Served by Others.* When counselors learn that their clients are in a professional relationship with another mental health professional, they request release from clients to inform the other professionals and strive to establish positive and collaborative professional relationships. (See A.4.)

## Section D: Relationships With Other Professionals

**D.1.** Relationships with Employers and Employees

a.  *Role Definition.* Counselors define and describe for their employers and employees the parameters and levels of their professional roles.

b.  *Agreements.* Counselors establish working agreements with supervisors, colleagues, and subordinates regarding counseling or clinical relationships, confidentiality, adherence to professional standards, distinction between public and private material, maintenance and dissemination of recorded information, workload, and accountability. Working agreements in each instance are specified and made known to those concerned.

c.  *Negative Conditions.* Counselors alert their employers to conditions that may be potentially disruptive or damaging to the counselor's professional responsibilities or that may limit their effectiveness.

d.  *Evaluation.* Counselors submit regularly to professional review and evaluation by their supervisor or the appropriate representative of the employer.

e.  *In-Service.* Counselors are responsible for in-service development of self and staff.

f.  *Goals.* Counselors inform their staff of goals and programs.

g.  *Practices.* Counselors provide personnel and agency practices that respect and enhance the rights and welfare of each employee and recipient of agency services. Counselors strive to maintain the highest levels of professional services.

h.  *Personnel Selection and Assignment.* Counselors select competent staff and assign responsibilities compatible with their skills and experiences.

i.  *Discrimination.* Counselors, as either employers or employees, do not engage in or condone practices that are inhumane, illegal, or unjustifiable (such as considerations based on age, color, culture, disability, ethnic group, gender, race, religion, sexual orientation, or socioeconomic status) in hiring, promotion, or training. (See A.2.a. and C.5.b.)

j.  *Professional Conduct.* Counselors have a responsibility both to clients and to the agency or institution within which services are performed to maintain high standards of professional conduct.

k.  *Exploitive Relationships.* Counselors do not engage in exploitive relationships with individuals over whom they have supervisory, evaluative, or instructional control or authority.

1. *Employer Policies.* The acceptance of employment in an agency or institution implies that counselors are in agreement with its general policies and principles. Counselors strive to reach agreement with employers as to acceptable standards of conduct that allow for changes in institutional policy conducive to the growth and development of clients.

**D.2.** Consultation (See B.6.)

a. *Consultation as an Option.* Counselors may choose to consult with any other professionally competent person about their clients. In choosing consultants, counselors avoid placing the consultant in a conflict of interest situation that would preclude the consultant being a proper party to the counselor's efforts to help the client. Should counselors be engaged in a work setting that compromises this consultation standard, they consult with other professionals whenever possible to consider justifiable alternatives.

b. *Consultant Competency.* Counselors are reasonably certain that they have or the organization represented has the necessary competencies and resources for giving the kind of consulting services needed and that appropriate referral resources are available.

c. *Understanding with Clients.* When providing consultation, counselors attempt to develop with their clients a clear understanding of problem definition, goals for change, and predicted consequences of interventions selected.

d. *Consultant Goals.* The consulting relationship is one in which client adaptability and growth toward self-direction are consistently encouraged and cultivated. (See A.1.b.)

**D.3.** Fees for Referral

a. *Accepting Fees from Agency Clients.* Counselors refuse a private fee or other remuneration for rendering services to persons who are entitled to such services through the counselor's employing agency or institution. The policies of a particular agency may make explicit provisions for agency clients to receive counseling services from members of its staff in private practice. In such instances, the clients must be informed of other options open to them should they seek private counseling services. (See A.10.a., A.11.b., and C.3.d.)

b. *Referral Fees.* Counselors do not accept a referral fee from other professionals.

**D.4.** Subcontractor Arrangements

When counselors work as subcontractors for counseling services for a third party, they have a duty to inform clients of the limitations of confidentiality that the organization may place on counseling services to clients. The limits of such confidentiality ordinarily are discussed as part of the intake session. (See B.1.e. and B.1.f.)

## Section E: Evaluation, Assessment, and Interpretation

**E.1.** General

a. *Appraisal Techniques.* The primary purpose of educational and psychological assessment is to provide measures that are objective and interpretable in either comparative or absolute terms. Counselors recognize the need to interpret the statements in this section as applying to the whole range of appraisal techniques, including test and nontest data.

b. *Client Welfare.* Counselors promote the welfare and best interests of the client in the development, publication, and utilization of educational and psychological assessment techniques. They do not misuse assessment results and interpretations and take reasonable steps to prevent others from misusing the information these techniques provide. They respect the client's right to know the results, the interpretations made, and the bases for their conclusions and recommendations.

**E.2.** Competence to Use and Interpret Tests

a. *Limits of Competence.* Counselors recognize the limits of their competence and perform only those testing and assessment services for which they have been trained. They are familiar with reliability, validity, related standardization, error of measurement, and proper application of any technique utilized. Counselors using computer-based test interpretation are trained in the construct being measured and the specific instrument being used prior to using this type of computer application. Counselors take reasonable measures to ensure the proper use of psychological assessment techniques by persons under their supervision.

b. *Appropriate Use.* Counselors are responsible for the appropriate application, scoring, interpretation, and use of assessment instruments, whether they score and interpret such tests themselves or use computerized or other services.

c. *Decisions Based on Results.* Counselors responsible for decisions involving individuals or policies that are based on assessment results have a thorough understanding of educational and psychological measurement, including validation criteria, test research, and guidelines for test development and use.

d. *Accurate Information.* Counselors provide accurate information and avoid false claims or misconceptions when making statements about assessment instruments or techniques. Special efforts are made to avoid unwarranted connotations of such terms as IQ and grade equivalent scores. (See C.5.c.)

**E.3.** Informed Consent

a. *Explanation to Clients.* Prior to assessment, counselors explain the nature and purposes of assessment and the specific use of results in language the client (or other legally authorized person on behalf of the client) can understand, unless an explicit exception to this right has been agreed upon in advance. Regardless of whether scoring and interpretation are completed by counselors, by assistants, or by computer or any other outside services, counselors take reasonable steps to ensure that appropriate explanations are given to the client.
b. *Recipients of Results.* The examinee's welfare, explicit understanding, and prior agreement determine the recipients of test results. Counselors include accurate and appropriate interpretations with any release of individual or group test results. (See B.1.a. and C.5.c.)

**E.4.** Release of Information to Competent Professionals

a. *Misuse of Results.* Counselors do not misuse assessment results, including test results, and interpretations, and take reasonable steps to prevent the misuse of such by others. (See C.5.c.)
b. *Release of Raw Data.* Counselors ordinarily release data (e.g. protocols, counseling or interview notes, or questionnaires) in which the client is identified only with the consent of the client or the client's legal representative. Such data are usually released only to persons recognized by counselors as competent to interpret the data. (See B.1.a.)

**E.5.** Proper Diagnosis of Mental Disorders

a. *Proper Diagnosis.* Counselors take special care to provide proper diagnosis of mental disorders. Assessment techniques (including personal interview) used to determine client care (e.g., locus of treatment, type of treatment, or recommended follow-up) are carefully selected and appropriately used. (See A.3.a. and C.5.c.)
b. *Cultural Sensitivity.* Counselors recognize that culture affects the manner in which clients' problems are defined. Clients' socioeconomic and cultural experience is considered when diagnosing mental disorders.

**E.6.** Test Selection

a. *Appropriateness of Instruments.* Counselors carefully consider the validity, reliability, psychometric limitations, and appropriateness of instruments when selecting tests for use in a given situation or with a particular client.

b.   *Culturally Diverse Populations.* Counselors are cautious when selecting tests for culturally diverse populations to avoid inappropriateness of testing that may be outside of socialized behavioral or cognitive patterns.

**E.7.**  Conditions of Test Administration

a.   *Administration Conditions.* Counselors administer tests under the same conditions that were established in their standardization. When tests are not administered under standard conditions or when unusual behavior or irregularities occur during the testing session, those conditions are noted in interpretation, and the results may be designated as invalid or of questionable validity.

b.   *Computer Administration.* Counselors are responsible for ensuring that administration programs function properly to provide clients with accurate results when a computer or other electronic methods are used for test administration. (See A.12.b.)

c.   *Unsupervised Test-Taking.* Counselors do not permit unsupervised or inadequately supervised use of tests or assessments unless the tests or assessments are designed, intended, and validated for self-administration and/or scoring.

d.   *Disclosure of Favorable Conditions.* Prior to test administration, conditions that produce most favorable test results are made known to the examinee.

**E.8.**  Diversity in Testing

Counselors are cautious in using assessment techniques, making evaluations, and interpreting the performance of populations not represented in the norm group on which an instrument was standardized. They recognize the effects of age, color, culture, disability, ethnic group, gender, race, religion, sexual orientation, and socioeconomic status on test administration and interpretation and place test results in proper perspective with other relevant factors. (See A.2.a.)

**E.9.**  Test Scoring and Interpretation

a.   *Reporting Reservations.* In reporting assessment results, counselors indicate any reservations that exist regarding validity or reliability because of the circumstances of the assessment or the inappropriateness of the norms for the person tested.

b.   *Research Instruments.* Counselors exercise caution when interpreting the results of research instruments possessing insufficient technical data to support respondent results. The specific purposes for the use of such instruments are stated explicitly to the examinee.

c.   *Testing Services*. Counselors who provide test scoring and test interpretation services to support the assessment process confirm the validity of such interpretations. They accurately describe the purpose, norms, validity, reliability, and applications of the procedures and any special qualifications applicable to their use. The public offering of an automated test interpretations service is considered a professional-to-professional consultation. The formal responsibility of the consultant is to the consultee, but the ultimate and overriding responsibility is to the client.

**E.10.** Test Security

Counselors maintain the integrity and security of tests and other assessment techniques consistent with legal and contractual obligations. Counselors do not appropriate, reproduce, or modify published tests or parts thereof without acknowledgment and permission from the publisher.

**E.11.** Obsolete Tests and Outdated Test Results

Counselors do not use data or test results that are obsolete or outdated for the current purpose. Counselors make every effort to prevent the misuse of obsolete measures and test data by others.

**E.12.** Test Construction

Counselors use established scientific procedures, relevant standards, and current professional knowledge for test design in the development, publication, and utilization of educational and psychological assessment techniques.

## *Section F: Teaching, Training, and Supervision*

**F.1.** Counselor Educators and Trainers

a.   *Educators as Teachers and Practitioners*. Counselors who are responsible for developing, implementing, and supervising educational programs are skilled as teachers and practitioners. They are knowledgeable regarding the ethical, legal, and regulatory aspects of the profession, are skilled in applying that knowledge, and make students and supervisees aware of their responsibilities. Counselors conduct counselor education and training programs in an ethical manner and serve as role models for professional behavior. Counselor educators should make an effort to infuse material related to human diversity into all courses and/or workshops that are designed to promote the development of professional counselors.

b.   *Relationship Boundaries with Students and Supervisees.* Counselors clearly define and maintain ethical, professional, and social relationship boundaries with their students and supervisees. They are aware of the differential in power that exists and the student's or supervisee's possible incomprehension of that power differential. Counselors explain to students and supervisees the potential for the relationship to become exploitive.

c.   *Sexual Relationships.* Counselors do not engage in sexual relationships with students or supervisees and do not subject them to sexual harassment. (See A.6. and C.5.b.)

d.   *Contributions to Research.* Counselors give credit to students or supervisees for their contributions to research and scholarly projects. Credit is given through coauthorship, acknowledgment, footnote statement, or other appropriate means, in accordance with such contributions. (See G.4.b. and G.4.c.)

e.   *Close Relatives.* Counselors do not accept close relatives as students or supervisees.

f.   *Supervision Preparation.* Counselors who offer clinical supervision services are adequately prepared in supervision methods and techniques. Counselors who are doctoral students serving as practicum or internship supervisors to master's level students are adequately prepared and supervised by the training program.

g.   *Responsibility for Services to Clients.* Counselors who supervise the counseling services of others take reasonable measures to ensure that counseling services provided to clients are professional.

h.   *Endorsement.* Counselors do not endorse students or supervisees for certification, licensure, employment, or completion of an academic or training program if they believe students or supervisees are not qualified for the endorsement. Counselors take reasonable steps to assist students or supervisees who are not qualified for endorsement to become qualified.

**F.2.** Counselor Education and Training Programs

a.   *Orientation.* Prior to admission, counselors orient prospective students to the counselor education or training program's expectations, including but not limited to the following: (1) the type and level of skill acquisition required for successful completion of the training, (2) subject matter to be covered, (3) basis for evaluation, (4) training components that encourage self-growth or self-disclosure as part of the training process, (5) the type of supervision settings and requirements of the sites for required clinical field experiences, (6) student and supervisee evaluation and dismissal policies and procedures, and (7) up-to-date employment prospects for graduates.

b. *Integration of Study and Practice.* Counselors establish counselor education and training programs that integrate academic study and supervised practice.

c. *Evaluation.* Counselors clearly state to students and supervisees, in advance of training, the levels of competency expected, appraisal methods, and timing of evaluations for both didactic and experiential components. Counselors provide students and supervisees with periodic performance appraisal and evaluation feedback throughout the training program.

d. *Teaching Ethics.* Counselors make students and supervisees aware of the ethical responsibilities and standards of the profession and the students' and supervisees' ethical responsibilities to the profession. (See C.1. and F.3.e.)

e. *Peer Relationships.* When students or supervisees are assigned to lead counseling groups or provide clinical supervision for their peers, counselors take steps to ensure that students and supervisees placed in these roles do not have personal or adverse relationships with peers and that they understand they have the same ethical obligations as counselor educators, trainers, and supervisors. Counselors make every effort to ensure that the rights of peers are not compromised when students or supervisees are assigned to lead counseling groups or provide clinical supervision.

f. *Varied Theoretical Positions.* Counselors present varied theoretical positions so that students and supervisees may make comparisons and have opportunities to develop their own positions. Counselors provide information concerning the scientific bases of professional practice. (See C.6.a.)

g. *Field Placements.* Counselors develop clear policies within their training program regarding field placement and other clinical experiences. Counselors provide clearly stated roles and responsibilities for the student or supervisee, the site supervisor, and the program supervisor. They confirm that site supervisors are qualified to provide supervision and are informed of their professional and ethical responsibilities in this role.

h. *Dual Relationships as Supervisors.* Counselors avoid dual relationships such as performing the role of site supervisor and training program supervisor in the student's or supervisee's training program. Counselors do not accept any form of professional services, fees, commissions, reimbursement, or remuneration from a site for student or supervisee placement.

i. *Diversity in Programs.* Counselors are responsive to their institution's and program's recruitment and retention needs for training program administrators, faculty, and students with diverse backgrounds and special needs. (See A.2.a.)

**F.3.** Students and Supervisees

a.  *Limitations.* Counselors, through ongoing evaluation and appraisal, are aware of the academic and personal limitations of students and supervisees that might impede performance. Counselors assist students and supervisees in securing remedial assistance when needed, and dismiss from the training program supervisees who are unable to provide competent service due to academic or personal limitations. Counselors seek professional consultation and document their decision to dismiss or refer students or supervisees for assistance. Counselors assure that students and supervisees have recourse to address decisions made, to require them to seek assistance, or to dismiss them.

b.  *Self-Growth Experiences.* Counselors use professional judgment when designing training experiences conducted by the counselors themselves that require student and supervisee self-growth or self-disclosure. Safeguards are provided so that students and supervisees are aware of the ramifications their self-disclosure may have, on counselors whose primary role as teacher, trainer, or supervisor requires acting on ethical obligations to the profession. Evaluative components of experiential training experience explicitly delineate predetermined academic standards that are separate and not dependent on the student's level of self-disclosure. (See A.6.)

c.  *Counseling for Students and Supervisees.* If students or supervisees request counseling, supervisors or counselor educators provide them with acceptable referrals. Supervisors or counselor educators do not serve as counselor to students or supervisees over whom they hold administrative, teaching, or evaluative roles unless this is a brief role associated with a training experience. (See A.6.b.)

d.  *Clients of Students and Supervisees.* Counselors make every effort to ensure that the clients at field placements are aware of the services rendered and the qualifications of the students and supervisees rendering those services. Clients receive professional disclosure information and are informed of the limits of confidentiality. Client permission is obtained in order for the students and supervisees to use any information concerning the counseling relationship in the training process. (See B.1.e.)

e.  *Standards for Students and Supervisees.* Students and supervisees preparing to become counselors adhere to the *Code of Ethics* and the *Standards of Practice*. Students and supervisees have the same obligations to clients as those required of counselors. (See H.1.)

## Section G: Research and Publication

**G.1.** Research Responsibilities

a. *Use of Human Subjects.* Counselors plan, design, conduct, and report research in a manner consistent with pertinent ethical principles, federal and state laws, host institutional regulations, and scientific standards governing research with human subjects. Counselors design and conduct research that reflects cultural sensitivity appropriateness.

b. *Deviation from Standard Practices.* Counselors seek consultation and observe stringent safeguards to protect the rights of research participants when a research problem suggests a deviation from standard acceptable practices. (See B.6.)

c. *Precautions to Avoid Injury.* Counselors who conduct research with human subjects are responsible for the subjects' welfare throughout the experiment and take reasonable precautions to avoid causing injurious psychological, physical, or social effects to their subjects.

d. *Principal Research Responsibility.* The ultimate responsibility for ethical research practice lies with the principal researcher. All others involved in the research activities share ethical obligations and full responsibility for their own actions.

e. *Minimal Interference.* Counselors take reasonable precautions to avoid causing disruptions in subjects' lives due to participation in research.

f. *Diversity.* Counselors are sensitive to diversity and research issues with special populations. They seek consultation with appropriate professionals. (See A.2.a. and B.6.)

**G.2.** Informed Consent

a. *Topics Disclosed.* In obtaining informed consent for research, counselors use language that is understandable to research participants and that: (1) accurately explains the purpose and procedures to be followed; (2) identifies any procedures that are experimental or relatively untried; (3) describes the attendant discomforts and risks; (4) describes the benefits or changes in individuals or organizations that might be reasonably expected; (5) discloses appropriate alternative procedures that would be advantageous for subjects; (6) offers to answer any inquiries concerning the procedures; (7) describes any limitations on confidentiality; and (8) instructs that subjects are free to withdraw their consent and to discontinue participation in the project at any time. (See B.1.f.)

b.   *Deception.* Counselors do not conduct research involving deception unless alternative procedures are not feasible and the prospective value of the research justifies the deception. When the methodological requirements of a study necessitate concealment or deception, the investigator is required to explain clearly the reasons for this action as soon as possible.

c.   *Voluntary Participation.* Participation in research is typically voluntary and without any penalty for refusal to participate. Involuntary participation is appropriate only when it can be demonstrated that participation will have no harmful effects on subjects and is essential to the investigation.

d.   *Confidentiality of Information.* Information obtained about research participants during the course of an investigation is confidential. When the possibility exists that others may obtain access to such information, ethical research practice requires that the possibility, together with the plans for protecting confidentiality, be explained to participants as a part of the procedure. (See B.1.e.)

e.   *Persons Incapable of Giving Informed Consent.* When a person is incapable of giving informed consent, counselors provide an appropriate explanation, obtain agreement for participation and obtain appropriate consent from a legally authorized person.

f.   *Commitments to Participate.* Counselors take reasonable measures to honor all commitments to research participants.

g.   *Explanations After Data Collection.* After data are collected, counselors provide participants with full clarification of the nature of the study to remove any misconceptions. Where scientific or human values justify delaying or withholding information, counselors take reasonable measures to avoid causing harm.

h.   *Agreement to Cooperate.* Counselors who agree to cooperate with another individual in research or publication incur an obligation to cooperate as promised in terms of punctuality of performance and with regard to the completeness and accuracy of the information required.

i.   *Informed Consent for Sponsors.* In the pursuit of research, counselors give sponsors, institutions, and publication channels the same respect and opportunity for giving informed consent that they accord to individual research participants. Counselors are aware of their obligation to future research workers and ensure that host institutions are given feedback information and proper acknowledgment.

**G.3.** Reporting Results

a.   *Information Affecting Outcome.* When reporting research results, counselors explicitly mention all variables and conditions known to the investigator that may have affected the outcome of a study or the interpretation of data.

b. *Accurate Results.* Counselors plan, conduct, and report research accurately and in a manner that minimizes the possibility that results will be misleading. They provide thorough discussions of the limitations of their data and alternative hypotheses. Counselors do not engage in fraudulent research, distort data, misrepresent data, or deliberately bias their results.

c. *Obligation to Report Unfavorable Results.* Counselors communicate to other counselors the results of any research judged to be of professional value. Results that reflect unfavorably on institutions, programs, services, prevailing opinions, or vested interests are not withheld.

d. *Identity of Subjects.* Counselors who supply data, aid in the research of another person, report research results, or make original data available take due care to disguise the identity of respective subjects in the absence of specific authorization from the subjects to do otherwise. (See B.1.g. and B.5.a.)

e. *Replication Studies.* Counselors are obligated to make available sufficient original research data to qualified professionals who may wish to replicate the study.

**G.4.** Publication

a. *Recognition of Others.* When conducting and reporting research, counselors are familiar with and give recognition to previous work on the topic, observe copyright laws, and give full credit to those to whom credit is due. (See F.1.d. and G.4.c.)

b. *Contributors.* Counselors give credit through joint authorship, acknowledgment, footnote statements, or other appropriate means to those who have contributed significantly to research or concept development in accordance with such contributions. The principal contributor is listed first and minor technical or professional contributions are acknowledged in notes or introductory statements.

c. *Student Research.* For an article that is substantially based on a student's dissertation or thesis, the student is listed as the principal author. (See F.1.d. and G.4.a.)

d. *Duplicate Submission.* Counselors submit manuscripts for consideration to only one journal at a time. Manuscripts that are published in whole or in substantial part in another journal or published work are not submitted for publication without acknowledgment and permission from the previous publication.

e. *Professional Review.* Counselors who review material submitted for publication, research, or other scholarly purposes respect the confidentiality and proprietary rights of those who submitted it.

## Section H: Resolving Ethical Issues

**H.1.** Knowledge of Standards

Counselors are familiar with the *Code of Ethics* and the *Standards of Practice* and other applicable ethics codes from other professional organizations of which they are members, or from certification and licensure bodies. Lack of knowledge or misunderstanding of an ethical responsibility is not a defense against a charge of unethical conduct. (See F.3.e.)

**H.2.** Suspected Violations

a.   *Ethical Behavior Expected.* Counselors expect professional associates to adhere to Code of Ethics. When counselors possess reasonable cause that raises doubts as to whether a counselor is acting in an ethical manner, they take appropriate action. (See H.2.d. and H.2.e.)

b.   *Organization Conflicts.* If the demands of an organization with which counselors are affiliated pose a conflict with Code of Ethics, counselors specify the nature of such conflicts and express to their supervisors or other responsible officials their commitment to Code of Ethics. When possible, counselors work toward change within the organization to allow full adherence to Code of Ethics.

c.   *Informal Resolution.* When counselors have reasonable cause to believe that another counselor is violating an ethical standard, they attempt to first resolve the issue informally with the other counselor if feasible, providing that such action does not violate confidentiality rights that may be involved.

d.   *Reporting Suspected Violations.* When an informal resolution is not appropriate or feasible, counselors, upon reasonable cause, take action such as reporting the suspected ethical violation to state or national ethics committees, unless this action conflicts with confidentiality rights that cannot be resolved.

e.   *Unwarranted Complaints.* Counselors do not initiate, participate in, or encourage the filing of ethics complaints that are unwarranted or intend to harm a counselor rather than to protect clients or the public.

**H.3.** Cooperation with Ethics Committees

Counselors assist in the process of enforcing Code of Ethics. Counselors cooperate with investigations, proceedings, and requirements of the ACA Ethics Committee or ethics committees of other duly constituted associations or boards having jurisdiction over those charged with a violation. Counselors are familiar with the ACA Policies and Procedures and use it as a reference in assisting the enforcement of the Code of Ethics.

# Integrative Practice Exercises

Learning to counsel is somewhat like learning any other complex task. It involves acquiring a set of skills, mastering a set of subtasks, and eventually putting everything together in some integrated fashion. Perhaps you can recall what the process of learning to drive a car was like for you. At first, the mere thought of being able to drive a car was probably an overwhelming idea. Now you drive and hardly pay any attention to the process because it is so familiar and has become such a part of you. In between the initial overwhelming idea of learning to drive and your current state of driving with relative comfort and ease, you practiced and mastered a variety of skills related to driving. You learned how to steer the car, use the accelerator, use the clutch, brake the car, and while doing all of this, watch out for other drivers. And you learned all of this in a relatively short time period—although certainly not overnight.

Now it is time to try to put some things together for yourself—to take what you have learned in somewhat isolated fashion and integrate it in a meaningful way. The purpose of these exercises is to help you put the parts together in a conceptual framework that allows you to make even greater sense of the helping process for yourself. At the same time, it is important to realize that your ability to synthesize the tools and stages of counseling will necessarily stretch beyond the experience of these exercises, particularly if you are not yet in a field or job experience in which you can apply the tools with actual clients.

While simulation such as role-playing can be an invaluable way to learn under conditions of reduced threat, it is not a substitute for actual encounters and interactions with persons whose lives are distressed, whose emotions are conflicted, and who are sitting in front of you somewhat expectantly, relieved, and scared, all at the same time. As you accumulate actual counseling experience, your understanding and integration of the tools and stages of helping will continue to grow, just as you will also continue to grow and develop personally and professionally.

In this appendix, we present a variety of exercises designed to help you pull together the skills and strategies we have presented in this book into some meaningful whole. Additionally, we believe that completion of these activities will enable you to understand better the counseling process as it unfolds over an extended period of time with a client.

## *Exercise 1*

In this exercise, we present three client cases. After reading each case, respond to the questions following the cases. In your responses, indicate issues that may arise in each of the five stages of the counseling process as well as your ideas for dealing with these issues effectively. You may wish to jot down your ideas in writing or use a partner or small group to help you brainstorm with this material.

> *Case 1.* Sally is a college freshman at a large university; she is overwhelmed by the size of the university, having lived in a small town all her life. She is concerned about her "shyness" and feels it is preventing her from making friends. She reports being uncertain about how to "reach out" to people. She is concerned about her performance on tests; although she believes her study habits are adequate, she reports that she "blows" the tests because she gets so uptight about them.
>
> *Case 2.* Mr. and Mrs. Yule have been married for two years. Both are in their sixties, and this is their second marriage; their previous spouses had died within the last ten years. Mr. and Mrs. Yule are concerned that they "rushed into" this second relationship without adequate thought. They report that they argue constantly about everything. They feel they have forgotten how to talk to each other in a "civil" manner. Mrs. Yule states that she realizes her constant nagging upsets Mr. Yule; Mr. Yule discloses that his spending a lot of time with his male buddies irritates Mrs. Yule.
>
> *Case 3.* Arthur is a third-grader at Malcolm Elementary School. Arthur is constantly "getting into trouble" for a number of things. Arthur admits that he starts a lot of fights with the other boys. He says he doesn't know why or how, but suddenly he is punching them. Only after these fights does he realize his anger got out of hand. Arthur realizes his behavior is causing some of the other kids to avoid him, yet he believes he would like their friendship. He is not sure how to handle his temper so that he doesn't lash out at his peers.

### Rapport Relationship

**1.** List specific issues that may arise with this client in terms of establishing rapport and an effective helping relationship.

**2.** How might this particular client respond initially to the counselor?

**3.** How might this client respond to the counselor after several sessions?

### Assessment of Problems

**4.** List what seem to be the major problem areas for this client. Consider the affective, behavioral, cognitive, and interpersonal dimensions.

**5.** What seem to be the client's main strengths, resources, and coping skills?

**6.** Can you identify any probable payoffs of the client's dysfunctional or problematic behavior?

### Goal-Setting

**7.** What might this client seek or expect from counseling?

**8.** What seem to be the ideal outcomes for this person?

**9.** How different might your choice of outcomes for this client be from the client's choice of outcomes? If the difference is great, what impact might this have on the helping process?

### Intervention Strategies

**10.** Develop a list of possible intervention strategies that might be most useful in working with this particular client. Provide a rationale for your selection.

**11.** What theoretical approach underlies each of the intervention strategies on your list?

**12.** Would you *generally* favor using affective, cognitive, behavioral, or systemic strategies with this person? Why?

### Termination and Follow-Up

**13.** What are some indicators you would look for that suggest this client is ready to terminate counseling?

**14.** How would you help this client plan for transfer of learning from the counseling situation to the person's actual environment? What potential obstacles in his or her environment need to be anticipated?

**15.** How would you follow up on the progress of this client once the helping process is terminated?

## Exercise 2

Select one of the three cases described in Exercise 1 to use for the purpose of conducting an extended series of role-play counseling sessions. Enlist the help of a colleague or classmate who can meet with you regularly over the next five weeks. This person's task is to assume the role of the client from one of these cases and to "become" this client in the sessions with you. Your task is to meet with this person for five scheduled sessions during the next five weeks.

The first session should be directed toward establishing rapport and building an effective therapeutic relationship with this person. The second session should be an assessment interview and should reflect the content presented in Chapter 4. In the third session, try to help the client develop outcome goals, using the process and skills described in Chapter 5. In the fourth session, based on the assessed problem areas and defined goals, select one or two intervention strategies from Chapters 7–10 and implement these strategies with the client. Also in this session, begin to prepare the client for termination. In the fifth and last session, help the client summarize and evaluate the helping process and plan for changes in his or her environment. Terminate the counseling process and develop a follow-up plan.

At a minimum, audiotape each session—videotape if possible. After each interview, assess and rate your behavior using the corresponding part of the Counseling Strategies Checklist that follows. Your instructor or supervisor may also want to assess your performance. Your "client" can also provide you with informative feedback. Use this feedback and your ratings to determine which skills and parts of the helping process you have mastered and which areas need additional improvement and practice.

## The Counseling Strategies Checklist (CSC)

The CSC is divided into six parts: (I) The Process of Relating; (II) Assessment; (III) Goal-Setting; (IV) Intervention Strategies; (V) Termination and Follow-Up; and (VI) Individual Skills Summary. The first five parts correspond to each of the five stages of the counseling process. Each of these parts can be used to observe, evaluate, and rate sessions for each of these stages in the counseling process. For example, Part I, the Process of Relating, is used primarily to assess rapport and relationship-building sessions. Part II, Assessment, is used to evaluate assessment interviews, and so on. Part VI, The Individual Skills Summary, is a compilation of all the individual verbal and nonverbal skills associated with each of these stages of counseling. It can also be used following each corresponding type of session to determine the presence or absence of the skills associated with a particular stage of counseling.

### Using the Counseling Strategies Checklist

Each item in the CSC is scored by circling the most appropriate response, either Yes, No, or N.A. (not applicable). The items are worded such that desirable responses are Yes or N.A. No is an undesirable response.

After you have observed and rated each interview, sit down and review the ratings. Where noticeable deficiencies exist, you should identify a goal or goals that will remedy the problem. Beyond this, you should list two or three Action Steps that permit you to achieve this goal.

## Part I: The Process of Relating

**1.** The counselor maintained eye contact with the client.
Yes    No    N.A.

**2.** The counselor's facial expressions reflected the mood of the client.
Yes    No    N.A.

**3.** The counselor demonstrated some variation in voice pitch when talking.
Yes    No    N.A.

**4.** The counselor used intermittent one-word vocalizations ("mm-hmm") to reinforce the client's demonstration of goal-directed topics or behaviors.
Yes    No    N.A.

**5.** The counselor made verbal comments that pursued the topic introduced by the client.
Yes    No    N.A.

**6.** The subject of the counselor's verbal statements usually referred to the client, either by name or the second-person pronoun, "you."
Yes    No    N.A.

**7.** A clear and sensible progression of topics was evident in the counselor's verbal behavior; the counselor avoided rambling.
Yes    No    N.A.

**8.** The counselor made statements that reflected the client's feelings.
Yes    No    N.A.

**9.** The counselor verbally stated his or her desire and intent to understand.
Yes    No    N.A.

**10.** Several times (at least twice), the counselor shared his or her own feelings with the client.
Yes    No    N.A.

**11.** At least one time during the interview, the counselor provided specific feedback to the client.
Yes    No    N.A.

**12.** The counselor encouraged the client to identify and discuss his or her feelings concerning the counselor and the interview.
Yes         No         N.A.

**13.** The counselor voluntarily shared his or her feelings about the client and the counseling relationship.
Yes         No         N.A.

**14.** The counselor expressed reactions about the client's strengths and/or potential.
Yes         No         N.A.

**15.** The counselor made responses that reflected his or her liking and appreciation of the client.
Yes         No         N.A.

## Part II: Assessment

**1.** The counselor asked the client to provide basic demographic information about himself or herself.
Yes         No         N.A.

**2.** The counselor asked the client to describe his or her current concerns and to provide some background information about the problems.
Yes         No         N.A.

**3.** The counselor asked the client to list and prioritize problems.
Yes         No         N.A.

**4.** For each identified problem, the counselor and client explored the
____ affective dimensions of the problem.
Yes         No         N.A.
____ cognitive dimensions of the problem.
Yes         No         N.A.
____ behavioral dimensions of the problem.
Yes         No         N.A.
____ interpersonal dimensions of the problem.
Yes         No         N.A.
____ intensity of the problem (frequency, duration, or severity).
Yes         No         N.A.
____ antecedents of the problem.
Yes         No         N.A.
____ consequences and payoffs of the problem.
Yes         No         N.A.

**5.** The counselor and client discussed previous solutions the client had tried to resolve the problem.
Yes         No         N.A.

**6.** The counselor asked the client to identify possible strengths, resources, and coping skills the client could use to help resolve the problem.
Yes         No         N.A.

## Part III: Goal-Setting

1. The counselor asked the client to state how he or she would like to change his or her behavior ("How would you like for things to be different?")
   Yes       No       N.A.
2. The counselor and client decided together upon counseling goals.
   Yes       No       N.A.
3. The goals set in the interview were specific and observable.
   Yes       No       N.A.
4. The counselor asked the client to state orally a commitment to work for goal achievement.
   Yes       No       N.A.
5. If the client appeared resistant or unconcerned about achieving change, the counselor discussed this with the client.
   Yes       No       N.A.
6. The counselor asked the client to specify at least one action step he or she might take toward his or her goal.
   Yes       No       N.A.
7. The counselor suggested alternatives available to the client.
   Yes       No       N.A.
8. The counselor helped the client to develop action steps for goal attainment.
   Yes       No       N.A.
9. Action steps designated by counselor and client were specific and realistic in scope.
   Yes       No       N.A.
10. The counselor provided an opportunity within the interview for the client to practice or rehearse the action step.
    Yes       No       N.A.
11. The counselor provided feedback to the client concerning the execution of the action step.
    Yes       No       N.A.
12. The counselor encouraged the client to observe and evaluate the progress and outcomes of action steps taken outside the interview.
    Yes       No       N.A.

## Part IV: Strategy Selection and Implementation

1. The counselor suggested some possible strategies to the client based on the client's stated goals.
   Yes       No       N.A.
2. The counselor provided information about the elements, time, advantages, and disadvantages of each strategy.
   Yes       No       N.A.

3. The counselor involved the client in the choice of strategies to be used.
   Yes         No         N.A.
4. The counselor suggested a possible sequence of strategies to be used when more than one strategy was selected.
   Yes         No         N.A.
5. The counselor provided a rationale about each strategy to the client.
   Yes         No         N.A.
6. The counselor provided detailed instructions about how to use the selected strategy.
   Yes         No         N.A.
7. The counselor verified if the client understood how the selected strategy would be implemented.
   Yes         No         N.A.

### Part V: Termination and Follow-Up

1. The counselor and client engaged in some evaluation or assessment of the client's attainment of the desired goals.
   Yes         No         N.A.
2. The counselor and client summarized the client's progress throughout the helping process.
   Yes         No         N.A.
3. The counselor identified client indicators and behaviors suggesting termination was appropriate.
   Yes         No         N.A.
4. The counselor and client discussed ways for the client to apply or transfer the learnings from the helping interviews to the client's environment.
   Yes         No         N.A.
5. The counselor and client identified possible obstacles or stumbling blocks the client might encounter after termination and discussed possible ways for the client to handle these.
   Yes         No         N.A.
6. The counselor discussed some kind of follow-up plan to the client.
   Yes         No         N.A.

### Part VI: Individual Skill Summary

Instructions: Check (✓) any of the skills that were utilized by the counselor in the observed interview. Use the space under Comments to record your qualitative assessment of the use of this skill. For example, how appropriately and effectively was it used?

| Skills of Counseling | Comments |
|---|---|
| *Rapport Relationship* | |
| Nonverbal attending | |
| Verbal attending | |
| Paraphrase | |
| Reflection | |
| Self-Disclosure | |
| Immediacy | |
| Pacing | |
| *Assessment* | |
| Questions<br>  Open<br>  Closed<br>  Clarifying | |
| *Goal-Setting* | |
| Confrontation | |
| Ability Potential | |
| Instructions | |
| *Strategy Implementation* | |
| Information-Giving | |
| Modeling | |
| Rehearsal/Practice | |
| Feedback | |
| *Termination* | |
| Summarization | |

# References

American Psychiatric Association (1994). *Diagnostic and Statistical Manual of Mental Disorders*, 4th Ed. Washington, DC: Author.

Anderson, C.A., Lepper, M.R., and Ross, L. (1980). Perseverance of social theories. The role of explanation in the persistance of discredited information, *Journal of Personality and Social Psychology*, *39*, 1037–1049.

Argyle, M., Henderson, M., Bond, M., Iizuka, Y., and Contarelo, A. (1986). Cross-cultural variations in relationship rules, *International Journal of Psychology*, *21*, 287–315.

Arredondo, P. (1991). Counseling Latinas. In C.C. Lee and B.L. Richardson, Eds., *Multicultural Issues in Counseling: New Approaches to Diversity*, Alexandria, VA: ACA Press.

Ascher, L.M., Ed. (1989). *Therapeutic Paradox*, New York: Guilford.

Atkinson, D.R., Casas, A., and Abreu, J. (1992). Acculturation, ethnicity, and cultural sensitivity, *Journal of Counseling Psychology*, *39*, 4, 515–520.

Atkinson, D.R., Morten, G., and Sue, D.W. (1989). *Counseling American Minorities: A Cross-cultural Perspective*, 3d Ed., Dubuque, IA: William C. Brown.

Avruch, K. and Black, P.W. (1993). Conflict resolution in intercultural settings. In D.J.D. Sandole and H. van der Merwe, Eds., *Conflict Resolution Theory and Practice: Integration and Application*, Manchester, UK: Manchester University Press.

Axelson, J.A. (1993). *Counseling and Development in a Multicultural Society*, 2nd Ed., Pacific Grove, CA: Brooks/Cole, Chapter 1, Culture and counseling.

Baker, S.B. and Butler, J.N. (1984). Effects of preventative cognitive self-instruction on adolescent attitudes, experiences and state anxiety, *Journal of Primary Prevention*, *5*, 10–14.

Baker, S.B., Thomas, R.N., and Munson, W.W. (1983). Effects of cognitive restructuring and structured group discussion as primary prevention strategies, *School Counselor*, *31*, 26–33.

Bandura, A. (1969). *Principles of Behavior Modification*, Englewood Cliffs, NJ: Prentice-Hall.

Bandura, A. (1977). *Social Learning Theory*, Englewood Cliffs, NJ: Prentice-Hall.

Bandura, A. (1988). Self-efficacy conception of anxiety, *Anxiety Research*, *1*, 77–88.

Bandura, A., Grusec, J.E., and Menlove, F.L. (1966). Observational learning as a function of symbolization and incentive set, *Child Development*, *37*, 499–506.

Barrett–Leonard, G.T. (1981). The empathy cycle: Refinement of a nuclear concept, *Journal of Counseling Psychology*, *28*, 91–100.

Baucom, D.A. and Lester, G.W. (1986). The usefulness of cognitive restructuring as an adjunct to behavioral marital therapy, *Behavior Therapy*, *17*, 385–403.

Beck, A.T. (1976). *Cognitive Therapy and the Emotional Disorders*, New York: International Universities Press.

Beck, A.T. and Weishaar, M.E. (1989). Cognitive therapy. In Raymond J. Corsini and Danny Wedding, Eds., *Current Psychotherapies*, 4th Ed., Itasca, IL: F.E. Peacock, Chapter 8.

Bellack, A. and Hersen, M. (1988). *Behavioral Assessment*, 3d Ed., Elmsford, N.Y.: Pergamon Press.

Bennett, D. (1976). *TA and the Manager*, New York: AMACOM.

Berg, I. and Jaya, A. (1993). Different and same: Family therapy with Asian-American families, *Journal of Marital and Family Therapy*, *19*, 31–38.

Bergan, J.R. (1977). *Behavioral Consultation*, Columbus, OH: Merrill.

Bergin, A.E. and Lambert, M.J. (1978). The evaluation of therapeutic outcomes. In S.L. Garfield and A.E. Bergin, Eds., *Handbook of Psychotherapy and Behavior Change: An Empirical Analysis* (pp. 139–189). New York: John Wiley.

Bernard, J.M. and Goodyear, R.K. (1992). *Fundamentals of Clinical Supervision*, Boston: Allyn and Bacon.

Bernard, J.M. and Hackney, H. (1983). *Untying the Knot: A Guide to Civilized Divorce*, Minneapolis: Winston.

Betancourt, H. and López, S.R. (1993). The study of culture, ethnicity, and race in American psychology, *American Psychologist*, *48*, 629–637.

Biggs, D. and Blocher, D. (1987). *Foundations of Ethical Counseling*, New York: Springer.

Biglan, A. and Campbell, D. (1981). Depression. In J.L. Shelton and R.L. Levy, Eds., *Behavioral Assignments and Treatment Compliance*, Champaign, IL: Research Press, pp. 111–146.

Blocher, D.H. (1966). *Developmental Counseling*, New York: Ronald Press.

Boardman, S.K. and Horowitz, S.V. (1994). Constructive conflictmanagement and social problems: An introduction, *Journal of Social Issues*, *50*, 1–12.

Booraem, C.D. (1974). Differential effectiveness of external versus self reinforcement in the acquisition of assertive responses. Unpublished doctoral dissertation, University of Southern California.

Bowen, M. (1978). *Family Therapy in Clinical Practice*, New York: Jason Aronson.

Boyd-Franklin, N. (1989). *Black Families in Therapy*, New York: Guilford.

Boyer, S.P. and Hoffman, M.A. (1993). Counselor affective reactions to termination: Impact of counselor loss history and perceived client sensitivity to loss, *Journal of Counseling Psychology*, *40*, 271–277.

Bradshow, J. (1990). *Homecoming: Reclaiming and Championing Your Inner Child*, New York: Bantam.

Brooks, D.K. and Gerstein, L.H. (1990). Counselor credentialing and interprofessional collaboration, *Journal of Counseling and Development, 68*, 477–484.

Caplan, G. (1970). *The Theory and Practice of Mental Health Consultation*, New York: Basic Books.

Carkhuff, R.R. and Anthony, W.A. (1979). *The Skills of Helping*, Amherst, MA: Human Resource Development Press.

Carli, L.L. (1989). Gender differences in interaction style and influence, *Journal of Personality and Social Psychology, 56*, 565–576.

Carroll, R. (1988). *Cultural Misunderstandings: The French-American Experience*, Chicago: University of Chicago Press.

Carter, R.T. (1991). Cultural values: A review of empirical research and implications for counseling, *Journal of Counseling and Development, 70*, pp. 164–173.

Cashdan, S. (1988). *Object Relations Therapy*, New York: W.W. Norton.

Castro, L. and Rachlin, H. (1980). Self-reward, self-monitoring, and self-punishment as feedback in weight control, *Behavior Therapy, 11*, 388–448.

Catania, A.C. (1975). The myth of self-reinforcement, *Behaviorism, 3*, 192–199.

Cautela, J.R. (1976). The present status of covert modeling, *Journal of Behavior Therapy and Experimental Psychiatry, 6*, 323–326.

Cautela, J.R. and Kearney, A.J. (1993). *Covert Conditioning Casebook*, Pacific Grove, CA: Brooks/Cole.

Cavanaugh, M.E. (1982). *The Counseling Experience*, Pacific Grove, CA: Brooks/Cole.

Celotta, B. and Telasi-Golubscow, H. (1982). A problem taxonomy for classifying clients' problems, *Personal and Guidance Journal, 61*, 73–76.

Chaves, J. and Barber, T. (1974). Cognitive strategies, experimental modeling, and expectation in the attenuation of pain, *Journal of Abnormal Psychology, 83*, 356–363.

Cheatham, H.E., Ivey, A.E., Ivey, M.B., and Simek-Morgan, Lynn (1993). Multicultural counseling and therapy: Changing the foundations of the field. In A.E. Ivey, M.B. Ivey, and L. Simek-Morgan, *Counseling and Psychotherapy: A Multicultural Perspective*, 3d Ed., Boston, MA: Allyn & Bacon.

Cheatham, H. and Stewart, J. (1990). *Black Families: Interdisciplinary Perspectives*, New Brunswick, NJ: Transactional Publishers.

Cheek, D. (1976). *Assertive Black . . . Puzzled White*, San Luis Obispo, CA: Impact.

Ciminero, A., Nelson, R., and Lipinski, D. (1977). Self-monitoring procedures. In A. Ciminero, K. Calhoun, and H. Adams, Eds.,

*Handbook of Behavior and Assessment*, New York: Wiley, pp. 195–232.

Clark, D.M. and Salkovskis, P.M. (1989). *Cognitive Therapy for Panic and Hypochondriasis*, New York: Pergamon.

Congress, E.P. (1990). Crisis intervention with Hispanic clients in an urban mental health clinic. In Roberts, A.R. (1990), *Crisis Intervention Handbook: Assessment, Treatment, and Research*, Belmont, CA: Wadsworth.

Conoley, J.C. and Conoley, C.W. (1991). *Consultation: A Guide to Practice and Training*, 2d Ed., New York: Pergamon.

Cook, E.P. (1993). *Women, Relationships, and Power: Implications for Counseling*, Alexandria, VA: ACA Press.

Coombs, A.W. and Gonzalez, D.M. (1994). *Helping Relationships: Basic Concepts for the Helping Profession*, 4th Ed., Boston, MA: Allyn & Bacon.

Corey, M.S. and Corey, G. (1993). *Becoming a Helper*, 2d Ed., Pacific Grove, CA: Brooks/Cole.

Corey, G., Corey, M.S., and Callanan, P. (1992). *Issues and Ethics in the Helping Professions*, 4th Ed., Pacific Grove, CA: Brooks/Cole.

Cormier, W.H. and Cormier, L.S. (1991). *Interviewing Strategies for Helpers: Fundamental Skills and Cognitive Behavioral Interventions*, 3d Ed., Pacific Grove, CA: Brooks/Cole.

Cormier, L.S., Cormier, W.H., and Weisser, R.J. (1984). *Interviewing and Helping Skills for Health Professionals*, Monterey, CA: Wadsworth.

Corrigan, J.D., Dell, D.M., Lewis, K.N., and Schmidt, L.D. (1980). Counseling as a social influence process: A review, *Journal of Counseling Psychology*, *27*, 395–441.

Corsini, R.J. and Wedding, D., Eds. (1989). *Current Psychotherapies*, 4th Ed., Itasca, IL: F.E. Peacock.

Cross, W.E., Jr. (1971). The negro-to-black conversion experience: Towards a psychology of Black liberation, *Black World*, *20*, 13–27.

Cummings, A.L. (1989). Relationship of client problem to novice counselor response modes, *Journal of Counseling Psychology*, *36*, 331–335.

Davenport, D.S. and Yurich, J.M. (1991). Multicultural gender issues, *Journal of Counseling and Development*, *70*, 64–71.

Deffenbacher, J.L. (1985). A cognitive-behavioral response and a modest proposal, *Counseling Psychologist*, *13*, 261–269.

Dengrove, E. (1966). Treatment of non-phobic disorders by the behavioral therapies. Paper presented at the Association for Advancement of Behavior Therapy, New York.

Deutsch, M. (1973). *The Resolution of Conflict: Constructive and Destructive Processes*, New Haven, CT and London: Yale University Press.

Deutsch, M. (1994). Constructive conflict resolution: Principles, training, and research, *Journal of Social Issues*, *50*, 13–32.

Devine, D.A. and Fernald, P.S. (1973). Outcome effects of receiving a preferred randomly assigned, or non-preferred therapy, *Journal of Consulting and Clinical Psychology, 41,* 104–107.

Dinkmeyer, D. and Dinkmeyer, D., Jr. (1982). *Developing Understanding of Self and Others,* D-1 and D-2, Rev. Ed., Circle Pines, MN: American Guidance Service.

Dixon, D.N. and Glover, J.A. (1984). *Counseling: A Problem-Solving Approach,* New York: Wiley.

Doherty, P.A. and Cook, E.P. (1993). No woman is an island: Women and relationships. In E.P. Cook, Ed., *Women, Relationships, and Power: Implications for Counseling,* Alexandria, VA: ACA Press.

Donley, R.J., Horan, J.J., and DeShong, R.L. (1990). The effect of several self-disclosure permutations on counseling process and outcome, *Journal of Counseling and Development, 67,* 408–412.

Doster, J.A. and Nesbitt, J.G. (1979). Psychotherapy and self-disclosure. In G.J. Chelune, Ed., *Self-disclosure: Origins, Patterns, and Implications of Openness in Interpersonal Relationships,* San Francisco: Jossey-Bass.

Dougherty, A.M. (1995). *Consultation: Practice and Perspectives in School and Community Settings,* 2d Ed., Pacific Grove, CA: Brooks/Cole.

Dowd, E.T. and Milne, C.R. (1986). Paradoxical intervnentions in counseling psychology, *The Counseling Psychologist, 14,* 237–282.

Duhl, F.J., Kantor, D., and Duhl, B.S. (1973). Learning, space and action in family therapy: A primer of sculpture. In D.A. Bloch, Ed., *Techniques of Family Therapy,* New York: Grune & Stratton.

Dworkin, S.H. and Guiterrez, F.J. (1992). *Counseling Gay Men and Lesbians: Journey to the End of the Rainbow,* Alexandria, VA: American Counseling Association.

Dye, H.A. and Hackney, H. (1975). *Gestalt Approaches to Counseling,* Boston: Houghton Mifflin.

Egan, G. (1994). *The Skilled Helper,* 5th Ed., Pacific Grove, CA: Brooks/Cole.

Ekman, P. (1993) Facial expression and emotion, *American Psychologist, 48,* 384–392.

Ekman, P. and Freisen, W.V. (1967). Head and body cues in the judgment of emotion: A reformulation, *Perceptual and Motor Skills, 24,* 711–724.

Ekman, P. and Freisen, W.V. (1969). Nonverbal leakage and clues to deception, *Psychiatry, 32,* 88–106.

Elder, J.P., Edelstein, B.A., and Fremouw, W.J. (1981). Client by treatment interactions in response acquisition and cognitive restructuring approaches, *Cognitive Therapy and Research, 5,* 203–210.

Ellis, A.E. (1971). *Rational-Emotive Therapy and Its Application to Emotional Education,* New York: Institute for Rational Living.

Ellis, A.E. (1989). Rational emotive therapy. In R. J. Corsini and D.

Wedding, Eds., *Current Psychotherapies*, 4th Ed., Itasca, IL: F.E. Peacock, Chapter 6.

Ellis, A.E. (1991). Using RET effectively: Reflections and interview. In M. Bernard, Ed., *Using Rational-Emotive Therapy Effectively*, New York: Plenum, pp. 1–33.

Enns, C.B. (1993). Twenty years of feminist counseling and therapy: From naming biases to implementing multifaceted practice, *The Counseling Psychologist, 21*, 3–87.

Falco, K.L. (1991). *Psychotherapy with Lesbian Clients: Theory into Practice*, New York: Brunner/Mazel.

Farber, B.A. and Heifetz, L.J. (1982). The process and dimensions of burnout in psychotherapists, *Professional Psychology, 13*, 293–301.

Fassinger, R.E. (1991). The hidden minority: Issues and challenges in working with lesbian women and gay men, *The Counseling Psychologist, 19*, 157–176.

Figley, C.R. and Nelson, T.S. (1990). Basic family therapy skills, II: Structural family therapy, *Journal of Marriage and Family Therapy, 16*, 225–239.

Fisch, R., Weakland, J.H., and Segal, L. (1982). *The Tactics of Change: Doing Therapy Briefly*, San Francisco: Jossey-Bass.

Fisher, R.J. (1994). Generic principles for resolving intergroup conflict, *Journal of Social Issues, 50*, 47–66.

Flowers, J.V. and Booraem, C.D. (1980). Simulation and role-playing methods. In F.A. Kanfer and A.P. Goldstein, Eds., *Helping People Change*, New York: Pergamon, pp. 172–209.

Fogarty, T.F. (1986). Marital crisis. In P.G. Euerin, Ed., *Family Therapy: Theory and Practice*, New York: Gardner Press.

Foley, V.D. (1989). Family therapy. In R.J. Corsini and D. Wedding, Eds., *Current Psychotherapies*, 4th ed., Itasca, IL: F.E. Peacock.

Fong, M.L. and Cox, B.G. (1983). Trust as an underlying dynamic in the counseling process: How clients test trust, *Personnel and Guidance Journal, 62*, 163–166.

Forman, S.G. (1980). A comparison of cognitive training and response cost procedures in modifying aggressive behavior of elementary school children, *Behavior Therapy, 11*, 594–600.

Forsyth, D.R. (1990). *Group Dynamics*, 2d Ed., Pacific Grove, CA: Brooks/Cole.

Fox, R. (1993). *Elements of the Helping Process: A Guide for Clinicians*, Binghamton, NY: Haworth Press.

Framo, J. (1982). *Family Interaction: A Dialogue Between Family Therapists and Family Researchers*, New York: Springer.

Frederick, S.L. (1988). Learning to empathize with resistance, *Journal of Counseling and Development, 67*, 128.

Fremouw, W.J. (1977). A client manual for integrated behavior treatment of speech anxiety, *JSAS Catalogue of Selected Documents in Psychology, 1,* 209–217.

Fremouw, W.J. and Brown, J.P. (1980). The reactivity of addictive behaviors to self-monitoring: A functional analysis, *Addictive Behaviors, 5,* 209–217.

Frey, D.H. (1972). Conceptualizing counseling theories: A content analysis of process and goal statements, *Counselor Education and Supervision, 11,* 243–250.

Gazda, G.M., Asbury, F.S., Balzer, F.J., Childers, W.C., and Walters, R.P. (1984). *Human Relations Development: A Manual for Educators,* 3d Ed., Boston: Allyn & Bacon.

Gendlin, E.T. (1969). Focusing, *Psychotherapy: Theory, Research and Practice, 6,* 14–15.

Gendlin, E.T. (1984). The client's edge: The edge of awareness. In J.M. Shlien and R.F. Levant, Eds., *Client-centered Psychotherapy and the Person-Centered Approach,* New York: Praeger.

George, R. and Christiani, T.S. (1981). *Theory, Methods, and Processes of Counseling and Psychotherapy,* Englewood Cliffs, NJ: Prentice-Hall.

Gilbert, R. (1992). *Extraordinary Relationships,* Minneapolis, MN: Chronimed Publishing.

Gilligan, C. (1982). *In a Different Voice: Psychological Theory and Women's Development,* Cambridge, MA: Harvard University Press.

Gilliland, B.E., James, R., and Bowman, J. (1989). *Theories and Strategies in Counseling and Psychotherapy,* 2d Ed., Englewood Cliffs, NJ: Prentice Hall.

Gilliland, B.E. and James, R.K. (1993). *Crisis Intervention Strategies,* 2d Ed., Pacific Grove, CA: Brooks/Cole.

Gilmore, S. (1973). *The Counselor-in-Training,* Englewood Cliffs, NJ: Prentice-Hall.

Gladding, S.T. (1988). The theory and practice of individual counseling: Affective approaches. In *Counseling: A Comprehensive Profession,* Columbus, OH: Merrill, Chapter 4.

Gladstein, G. (1983). Understanding empathy: Integrating counseling, development and social psychology perspectives, *Journal of Counseling Psychology, 30,* 467–482.

Glasser, W. (1965). *Reality Therapy,* New York: Harper & Row.

Glasser, W. (1972). *The Identity Society,* New York: Harper & Row.

Glasser, W. (1985). *Positive Addiction,* New York: Harper & Row.

Glasser, W. and Zunin, L.M. (1979). Reality therapy, in R.J. Corsini, Ed., *Current Psychotherapies,* 2d Ed., Itasca, IL: F.E. Peacock, pp. 287–316.

Goldfried, M.R. and Davison, G.C. (1976). *Clinical Behavior Therapy,* New York: Holt, Rinehard & Winston.

Goldfried, M.R., DeCenteceo, E.T., and Weinberg, L. (1974). Systematic rational restructuring as a self-control technique, *Behavior Therapy*, *5*, 247–254.

Goldstein, A.P. (1980). Relationship-enhancement methods. In F.H. Kanfer and A.P. Goldstein, Eds., *Helping People Change*. New York: Pergamon Press, pp. 18–57.

Goldstein, A.P. and Huff, C.R. (1993). *The Gang Intervention Handbook*, Champaign, IL: Research Press.

Good, G.E., Gilbert, L.A. and Scher, M. (1990). Gender aware therapy: A synthesis of feminist therapy and knowledge about gender, *Journal of Counseling and Development*, *68*, 376–380.

Goodrich, T.J., Ed. (1991). *Women and Power: Perspectives for Family Therapy*, New York: W.W. Norton.

Goodrich, T.J., Rampage, C., Ellman, B., and Halstead, K. (1988). *Feminist Family Therapy*, New York: W.W. Norton.

Goodyear, R.K. (1981). Termination as a loss experience for the counselor, *Personnel and Guidance Journal*, *59*, 347–350.

Gordon, R.L. (1969). *Interviewing Strategy, Techniques, and Tactics*, Homewood, IL: Dorsey.

Gottman J. (1991). Predicting the longitudinal course of marriages, *Journal of Marital and Family Therapy*, *17*, 3–7.

Gottman, J. (1993). A theory of marital dissolution and stability, *Journal of Family Psychology*, *7*, 57–75.

Gottman, J.M. and Leiblum, S.R. (1974). *How to Do Psychotherapy and How to Evaluate It*, New York: Holt, Rinehart, Winston.

Gottman, J.M., Notarius, C., Gonso, J., and Markman, H. (1976). *A Couple's Guide to Communication*, Champaign, IL: Research Press.

Greenberg, L.S. (1979). Resolving splits: Use of the two-chair technique, *Psychotherapy: Theory, Research and Practice*, *16*, 316–324.

Gudykunst, W.B. and Ting-Toomey, S. (1988). *Culture and Interpersonal Communication*, Newbury Park, CA: Sage.

Hackney, H. (1978). The evolution of empathy, *The Personnel and Guidance Journal*, *55*, 35–39.

Hackney, H. and Cormier, S. (1994). *Counseling Strategies and Interventions*, 4th Ed., Boston, MA: Allyn & Bacon, Chapter 9, Conceptualizing problems and setting goals.

Haley, J. (1963). *Strategies of Psychotherapy*, New York: Grune & Stratton.

Haley, J. (1973). *Uncommon Therapy*, New York: W.W. Norton.

Haley, J. (1976). *Problem-solving Therapy*, New York: McGraw-Hill.

Haley, J. (1980). *Leaving Home*, New York: McGraw-Hill.

Hall, W.S., Cross, W.E., and Freedle, R. (1972). Stages in the development of Black awareness: An exploratory investigation. In R.L. Jones, Ed., *Black Psychology*. New York: Harper & Row.

Halstead, R.W., Brooks, D.K., Goldberg, A., and Fish, L.S. (1990). Counselor and client perceptions of the working alliance, *Journal of Mental Health Counseling, 12*, 208–221.

Hamilton, S.A. and Fremouw, W.J. (1985). Cognitive-behavioral training for college basketball foul-shooting performance, *Cognitive Therapy and Research, 9*, 479–484.

Hansen, J.C., Himes, B.S., and Meier, S. (1990). *Consultation: Concepts and Practices*, Englewood Cliffs, NJ: Prentice Hall.

Hansen, J.C., Rossberg, R.H., and Cramer, S.H. (1994). *Counseling Theory and Process*, 5th Ed., Chapter 13, Stages in the counseling process.

Hardy, R. (1991). *Gestalt Psychotherapy*, Springfield, IL: Charles C. Thomas.

Haynes, S.N., Jensen, B.M., Wise, E., and Sherman, D. (1981). The marital intake interview: A multimethod criterion validity instrument, *Journal of Consulting and Clinical Psychology, 49*, 379–387.

Helms, J.E. (1990). *Black and White Racial Identity*, Westport, CT: Praeger.

Helms, J.E. (1994). Racial identity and career assessment, *Journal of Career Assessment, 2*, 199–209.

Herr, E.L. (1991). Ecological challenges to counseling in a world of cultural and racial diversity. In E.L. Herr and J.A. McFadden, Eds., *Challenges of Cultural and Racial Diversity to Counseling*, Alexandria, VA: ACA Press, pp. 9–20.

Hill, C.E. and Corbett, M. (1993). A perspective on the history of process and outcome research in counseling psychology, *Journal of Counseling Psychology, 40*, 3–24.

Hill, C.E., Siegelman, L., Gronsky, B.R., Sturniolo, F., and Fretz, B.R. (1981). Nonverbal communication and counseling outcome, *Journal of Counseling Psychology, 28*, 203–212.

Hoffman, L. (1981). *Foundations of Family Therapy*, Cambridge, MA: Harvard University Press.

Holdstock, T.L. and Rogers, C.R. (1977). Person-centered theory. In R.J. Corsini, Ed., *Current Personality Theories*, Itasca, IL: F.E. Peacock, Chapter 5, pp. 125–151.

Homme, L., Csanyi, A., Gonzales, M., and Rechs, J. (1969). *How to Use Contingency Contracting in the Classroom*, Champaign, IL: Research Press.

Hosford, R. and deVisser, L. (1974). *Behavioral Approaches to Counseling: An Introduction*, Washington, D.C.: American Personnel and Guidance Association Press.

Hosford, R., Moss, C., and Morrill, G. (1976). The self-as-a-model technique: Helping prison inmates change. In J.D. Krumboltz and C.E. Thoresen, Eds., *Counseling Methods*, New York: Holt, Rinehart & Winston.

Hulnick, M.R. and Hulnick, H.R. (1989). Life's challenges: Curse or opportunity? Counseling families of persons with disabilities, *Journal of Counseling and Development, 68,* 166–170.

Hutchins, D.E. (1979). Systematic counseling: The T-F-A model for counselor intervention, *Personnel and Guidance Journal, 57,* 529–531.

Hutchins, D.E. (1982). Ranking major counseling strategies with the T-F-A matrix system, *Personnel and Guidance Journal, 60,* 427–431.

Hutchins, D.E. (1984). Improving the counseling relationship, *Personnel and Guidance Journal, 62,* 572–575.

Iberg, J.R. (1981). Focusing. In R.J. Corsini, Ed., *Handbook of Innovative Psychotherapy,* New York: Wiley.

Ibraham, F.A. (1991). Contribution of cultural worldview to generic counseling and development, *Journal of Counseling and Development, 70,* 13–19.

Ivey, A.E. (1994). *Intentional Interviewing and Counseling,* 3d Ed., Pacific Grove, CA: Brooks/Cole.

Ivey, A.E. and Gluckstern, N. (1976). *Basic Influencing Skills: Participant Manual,* Amherst, MA: Microtraining Associates.

Ivey, A.E., Ivey, M.B., and Simek-Morgan, L. (1993). *Counseling and Psychotherapy: A Multicultural Perspective,* 3d Ed., Boston, MA: Allyn & Bacon.

Jackson, B. (1975). Black identity development, *Journal of Education Diversity, 2,* 19–25.

Jackson, D.D. and Weakland, J.H. (1961). Conjoint family therapy: Some consideration of theory, technique and results, *Psychiatry, 24,* 30–45.

Jackson, D.D. (1961). Interactional psychotherapy. In M.T. Stein, Ed., *Contemporary Psychotherapies,* New York: Free Press.

Jackson, D.D. and Weakland, J.H. (1961). Conjoint family therapy: Some consideration of theory, technique and results, *Psychiatry, 24,* 30–45.

Jackson, D.N. and Hayes, D.H. (1993). Multicultural issues in consultation, *Journal of Counseling and Development, 72,* 144–147.

Jacobs, E. (1992). *Creative Counseling Techniques,* Odessa, FL: Psychological Assessment Resources.

Jacobson, E. (1939). Variation of blood pressure with skeletal muscle tension and relaxation, *Annual of Internal Medicine, 2,* 152.

Jessop, A.L. (1979). *Nurse-Patient Communication: A Skills Approach,* North Amherst, MA: Microtraining Associates.

Jevne, R. (1981). Counselor competencies and selected issues in a Canadian counselor education program, *Canadian Counselor, 15,* 57–63.

Johnson, D.W. (1993). *Reaching Out: Interpersonal Effectiveness and Self-actualization,* 3d Ed., Boston, MA: Allyn & Bacon.

Johnson, D.W. and Johnson, R.T. (1994). Constructive conflict in the schools, *Journal of Social Issues, 50,* 117–138.

Josselson, R. (1992). *The Space Between Us: Exploring the Dimensions of Human Relationships.* San Francisco: Jossey-Bass.

Kanfer, F.H. (1980). Self-management methods. In F.H. Kanfer and A.P. Goldstein, Eds., *Helping People Change*, 4th Ed., New York: Pergamon, pp. 309–355.

Kanfer, F.H. and Gaelick-Buys, L. (1991). Self-management methods. In F.H. Kanfer and A.P. Goldstein, Eds., *Helping People Change*, 4th Ed., New York: Pergamon, pp. 305–360.

Kantrowitz, R. and Ballou, M. (1992). A feminist critique of cognitive-behavioral therapy, *Personality and Psychopathology: Feminist Reappraisals*, New York: Guilford, pp. 70–87.

Karoly, P. (1982). Perspectives on self-management and behavior change, in P. Karoly & F.H. Kanfer, Eds., *Self-management and Behavior Change*, New York: Pergamon, pp. 3–31.

Karoly, P. and Kanfer, F.A., Eds. (1982). *Self-management and Behavior Change*, New York: Pergamon Press.

Kasdin, A.E. (1973). Covert modeling and the reduction of avoidance behavior, *Journal of Abnormal Psychology*, *81*, 89–95.

Keen, S. (1991). *Fire in the Belly*, New York: Bantam Books.

Kelley, C.R. (1979). Freeing blocked anger, *The Radix Journal*, *1*, 19–33.

Kelly, G. (1955). *The Psychology of Personal Constructs*, Vols. I and II, New York: W.W. Norton.

Kepner, J. (1993). *Body Process: Working with the Body in Psychotherapy*, San Francisco: Jossey-Bass.

Kim, S.C., Lee, S.U., Chu, K.H., and Cho, K.J. (1989). Korean Americans and mental health: Clinical experiences of Korean American mental health services, *Asian American Psychological Association Journal*, *13*, 18–27.

Kleinke, C.L. (1994). *Common Principles of Psychotherapy*, Pacific Grove, CA: Brooks/Cole.

Knapp, M. (1978). *Nonverbal Communication in Human Interaction*, 2d Ed., New York: Holt, Rinehart and Winston.

Knudson-Martin, C. (1994). The female voice: Applications to Bowen's family systems theory, *Journal of Marital and Famly Therapy*, *20*, 35–46.

Kottler, J. (1994). *Beyond Blame: A New Way of Resolving Conflicts in Relationships*, San Francisco: Jossey Bass.

Kottler, J.A. and Brown, R.W. (1992). *Introduction to Therapeutic Counseling*, 2d Ed., Pacific Grove, CA: Brooks/Cole.

Krumboltz, J.D. (1966). Behavioral goals for counseling, *Journal of Counseling Psychology*, *13*, 133–159.

Krumboltz, J.D. and Thoresen, C.E. (1969). *Behavioral Counseling: Cases and Techniques*, New York: Holt, Rinehart and Winston.

Kurpius, D.J. (1978). Consultation theory and process: An integrated model, *Personnel and Guidance Journal*, *56*, 335–338.

L'Abate, L. (1981). Toward a systematic classification of counseling and therapy theorists, methods, processes, and goals. The E-R-A model, *Personnel and Guidance Journal*, *59*, 263–266.

Laidlaw, T., Malmo, C., and Associates (1990). *Healing Voices: Feminist Approaches to Therapy with Women*, San Francisco: Jossey-Bass.

Laing. J. (1988). Self-report: Can it be of value as an assessment technique? *Journal of Counseling and Development, 67,* 60–61.

Lanning, W. and Carey, J. (1987). Systematic termination in counseling, *Counselor Education and Supervision, 26,* 168–173.

Larson, P.C. (1982). Counseling special populations, *Professional Psychology, 13,* 843–858.

Lazarus, A.A. (1966). Behavioral rehearsal vs. non-directive therapy vs. advice in effecting behavior change, *Behavior Research and Therapy, 4,* 209–212.

Lazarus, A.A. (1971). *Behavior Therapy and Beyond*, New York: McGraw Hill.

Lazarus, A.A. (1989). *The Practice of Multimodal Therapy*, Baltimore: Johns Hopkins University Press.

Lee, C.C. (1991). Cultural dynamics: Their importance in multicultural counseling. Chapter 2 in C.C. Lee & B.L. Richardson (Eds.), *Multicultural Issues in Counseling: New Approaches to Diversity,* Alexandria, VA: ACA Press.

Lee, C.C. and Richardson, B.L. (1991). *Multicultural Issues in Counseling: New Approaches to Diversity*, Alexandria, VA: ACA Press.

Lehrer, P.M. and Woolfolk, R.L. (1982). Self-report assessment of anxiety: Somatic, cognitive, and behavioral modalities, *Behavioral Assessment, 4,* 167–177.

Levin, P. (1988). *Cycles of Power*, Deerfield Beach, FL: Health Communications.

Lewis, R., Walker, B.A., and Mehr, M. (1990) Counseling with adolescent suicidal clients and their families. In Roberts, A.R. (1990), *Crisis Intervention Handbook: Assessment, Treatment, and Research,* Belmont, CA: Wadsworth.

Lin, J.C.H. (1994). How long do Chinese Americans stay in psychotherapy? *Journal of Counseling Psychology, 41,* 288–291.

Lloyd, M.E. (1983). Selecting systems to measure client outcome in human service agencies, *Behavioral Assessment, 4,* 55–70.

Loesch, L.C., Crane, B.B., and Tucker, B.B. (1978). Counselor trainee effectiveness: More puzzle pieces, *Counselor Education and Supervision, 17,* 195–204.

Lombana, J.H. (1989). Counseling persons with disabilities: Summary and projections, *Journal of Counseling and Development, 68,* 177–179.

Lorand, S. (1982). *Techniques of Psychoanalytic Therapy*, New York: St. Martin's Press.

Lore, R.K. and Schultz, L.A. (1993). Control of human aggression, *American Psychologist, 48,* 16–25.

Lowen, A. (1974). *The Language of the Body*, New York: Collier.

Lyons, L. and Woods, P. (1991). The efficacy of rational-emotive therapy: A quantitative review of the outcome literature, *Clinical Psychology Review, 11*, 357–369.

Madanes, C. (1981). *Strategic Family Therapy*, San Francisco: Jossey-Bass.

Mahoney, M.J., Mauara, N., and Wade, T. (1973). The relative efficacy of self-reward, self-punishment, and self-monitoring techniques for weight loss, *Journal of Consulting and Clinical Psychology, 40*, 404–407.

Malmo, C. (1990). Recreating equality: A feminist approach to ego-state therapy. In T. Laidlaw and C. Malmo, Eds., *Healing Voices: Feminist Approaches to Therapy with Women*, San Francisco: Jossey-Bass, pp. 288–319.

Mann, J. (1973). *Time-limited Psychotherapy*, Cambridge, MA: Harvard University Press.

Marquis, N.J., Morgan, W.G., and Piaget, G. (1973). *A Guidebook for Systematic Desensitization*, 3d Ed., Palo Alto, CA: Veteran's Workshop.

Marx, J.A. and Gelso, C.J. (1987). Termination of individual counseling in a university counseling center, *Journal of Counseling Psychology, 34*, 3–9.

Matson, J.L. (1989). *Treating Depression in Children and Adolescents*, New York: Pergamon.

Mattick, R.P. and Peters (1988). Treatment of severe social phobia: Effects of guided exposure with and without cognitive restructuring, *Journal of Consulting and Clinical Psychology, 56*, 251–260.

Maultsby, M.C. (1984). *Rational Behavior Therapy*, Englewood Cliffs, NJ: Prentice-Hall.

Maurer, R.E. and Tindall, J.H. (1983). Effect of postural congruence on the client's perception of counselor empathy, *Journal of Counseling Psychology, 30*, 158–163.

McCordick, S.M., Kaplan, R.M., Smith, S., and Finn, M.E. (1981). Variations in cognitive behavior modifications for test anxiety, *Psychotherapy: Theory, Research, and Practice, 18*, 170–178.

McFall, R.M. and Twentyman, C. (1973). Four experiments on the relative contributions of rehearsal, modeling, and coaching to assertion training, *Journal of Abnormal Psychology, 81*, 199–218.

McGoldrick, M., Anderson, C., and Walsh, F., Eds. (1989) *Women in Families: A Framework for Family Therapy*, New York: W.W. Norton.

McGoldrick, M., Pearce, J.K., and Giordano, J., Eds. (1982). *Ethnicity and Family Therapy*, New York: Guilford Press.

McKeachie, W.J. (1976). Psychology in America's bicentennial year. *American Psychologist, 31*, 819–833.

McLean, P.D. (1976). Therapeutic decision-making in the behavioral treatment of depression. In P.O. Davidson, Ed., *Behavioral Management of Anxiety, Depression, and Pain*, New York: Brunner/Mazel, pp. 54–90.

McMullin, R.E. and Giles, T.R. (1981). *Cognitive-Behavior Therapy: A Restructuring Approach.*, New York: Grune & Stratton.

Meador, B.D. and Rogers, C.R. (1984). Person-centered therapy. In R.J. Corsini, Ed., *Current Psychotherapies*, 3d Ed., pp. 142–195.

Meichenbaum, D.H. (1971). Examination of model characteristics in reducing avoidance behavior, *Journal of Personality and Social Psychology*, *17*, 298–307.

Meichenbaum, D. (1972). Cognitive modification of test anxious college students, *Journal of Consulting and Clinical Psychology*, *39*, 370–380.

Meichenbaum, D. (1977). *Cognitive-Behavior Modification: An Integrative Approach*, New York: Plenum.

Meichenbaum, D. (1991). Evolution of cognitive-behavioral therapy. In J. Zeig, Ed., *The Evolution of Psychotherapy*, New York: Brunner/Mazel.

Miller, M.J. (1990). The power of the "OCEAN": Another way to diagnose clients, *Counselor Education and Supervision*, *29*, 283–290.

Miller, S., Wackman, D.B., Nunnally, E.W., and Miller, P. (1989). *Connecting.* Minneapolis: Interpersonal Communication Programs.

Mintz, L.B. and O'Neil, J.M. (1990). Gender roles, sex, and the process of psychotherapy: Many questions and few answers, *Journal of Counseling and Development*, *68*, 381–387.

Minuchin, S. (1974). *Families and Family Therapy*, Cambridge, MA: Harvard University Press.

Minuchin, S. and Fishman, H.C. (1981). *Family Therapy Techniques*, Cambridge, MA: Harvard University Press.

Mitchell, L.K. and Krumboltz, J.D. (1987). The effects of cognitive restructuring and decision-making training on career indecision, *Journal of Counseling and Development*, *66*, 171–174.

Moore, T. (1992). *Care of the Soul*, New York: Harper Collins.

Moreno, J.L. (1946). *Psychodrama*, Vol. 1, New York: Beacon House.

Morris, R.J. (1980). Fear reduction methods. In F.H. Kanfer and A.P. Goldstein, Eds., *Helping People Change*, New York: Pergamon, pp. 248–293.

Morse, C.L. and Bockoven, J. (1989). Improving the efficacy of DUSO-R through the use of a Children's Intake Interview, *Elementary School Guidance and Counseling*, *24*, 102–111.

Moursund, J. (1985). *The Process of Counseling and Psychotherapy*, Englewood Cliffs, NJ: Prentice-Hall.

Nelson, M.L. (1993). A current perspective on gender differences: Implications for research in counseling, *Journal of Counseling Psychology*, *40*, 2, 200–209.

Nelson, R.O., Hayes, S.C., Spong, R.T., Jarrett, R.B., and McKnight, D.L. (1983). Self-reinforcement, *Behavior Research and Therapy*, *19*, 187–192.

Nichols, M.P. and Schwartz, R.C. (1994). *Family Therapy: Concepts and Methods*, 3d Ed., Boston: Allyn & Bacon.

Noesjirwan, J. (1978). A rule-based analysis of cultural differences in social behavior: Indonesia and Australia. *International Journal of Psychology, 13*, 305–316.

Notarius, C. and Markman, H. (1993). *We Can Work It Out*, New York: Putnam.

Nugent, F.A. (1990). *An Introduction to the Profession of Counseling*, Columbus, OH: Merrill.

Nwachuku, U. (1989). *Culture-specific counseling: The Igbo case.* Unpublished doctoral dissertation, University of Massachusetts, Amherst.

Nwachuku, U. (1990, July). *Translating multicultural theory into direct action: Culture-specific counseling.* Paper presented at the International Roundtable for the Advancement of Counseling, Helsinki, Finland.

Nwachuku, U. and Ivey, A.E. (1991). Culture specific counseling: An alternative approach. *Journal of Counseling and Development, 70*, 106–111.

Osberg, T.M. (1989). Self-report reconsidered: A further look at its advantages as an assessment technique, *Journal of Counseling and Development, 68*, 111–113.

Öst, L.G., Jerremalm, A., and Johannson, J. (1981). Individual response patterns and the effects of different behavioral methods in the treatment of social phobia, *Behavior Research and Therapy, 19*, 1–16.

Öst, L.G., Westling, B.E., and Hellström, I. (1993). Applied relaxation, exposure *in vivo* and cognitive methods in the treatment of panic disorder with agraphobia, *Behaviour Research and Therapy, 31*, 383–394.

Ottens, A.J. and Fisher-McCanne, L. (1990). Crisis intervention at the college campus counseling center. In Roberts, A.R. (1990), *Crisis Intervention Handbook: Assessment, Treatment, and Research*, Belmont, CA: Wadsworth.

Ozer, E.M. and Bandura, A. (1990). Mechanisms governing empowerment effects: A self-efficacy analysis, *Journal of Personality and Social Psychology, 88*, 472–486.

Pace, T.M. and Dixon, D.N. (1993). Changes in depressive self-schemata and depressive symptoms following cognitive therapy, *Journal of Counseling Psychology, 40*, 288–294.

Palazzoli, M., Cecchin, G., Prata, G., and Boscolo, L. (1978). *Paradox and Counterparadox*, New York: Jason Aronson.

Papp, P. (1976). Family choreography. In P.J. Guerin, Ed., *Family Therapy: Theory and Practice*, New York: Jason Aronson.

Papp, P. (1980). The Greek chorus and other techniques of paradoxical therapy, *Family Process, 19*, 45–57.

Pate, R.H. (1982). Termination: End or beginning? In W.H. Van Hoose and M.R. Worth, Eds., *Counseling Adults: A Developmental Approach*, Pacific Grove, CA: Brooks/Cole.

Patterson, L.E. and Eisenberg, S. (1994), *The Counseling Process*, 4th Ed., Boston: Houghton Mifflin.

Pederson, P.B. (1977). The triad model of cross-cultural counselor training, *The Personnel and Guidance Journal, 56*, 94–100.

Pederson, P.B. (1991). Multiculturalism as a generic approach to counseling, *Journal of Counseling and Development, 70*, 6–12.

Perry, M.A. and Furukawa, M.J. (1980). Modeling methods. In F.H. Kanfer and A.P. Goldstein, Eds., *Helping People Change*, New York: Pergamon, pp. 131–171.

Pierrakos, J. (1990). *Core Energetics*, 2d Ed., Mendocino, CA: Life Rhythm.

Pietrofesa, J.J., Hoffman, A., Splete, H.H., and Pinto, D.V. (1984). *Counseling: An Introduction*, 2d Ed., Boston: Houghton Mifflin.

Pinkerton, R.S. and Rockwell, W.J.K. (1990). Termination in brief psychotherapy: The case for an eclectic approach, *Psychotherapy, 27*, 362–384.

Pope, A.W., McHale, S.M., and Craighead, N.E. (1988). *Self-Esteem Enhancement with Children and Adolescents*, New York: Pergamon.

Preli, R. and Bernard, J.M. (1993). Making multiculturalism relevant for majority culture graduate students, *Journal of Marital and Family Therapy, 19*, 5–16.

Priest, R. (1991). Racism and prejudice as negative impacts on African-American clients in therapy, *Journal of Counseling and Development, 70*, 213–215.

Prochaska, J.O., DiClemente, C.C., and Norcross, J.C. (1992). In search of how people change: Applications to addictive behaviors, *American Psychologist, 47*, 1102–1114.

Prochaska, J.O. and Norcross, J.C. (1994). *Systems of Psychotherapy: A Transtheoretical Analysis*, 3d Ed., Pacific Grove, CA: Brooks/Cole.

Quintana, S.M. (1993). Expanded and updated conceptualization of termination: Implications for short-term individual psychotherapy, *Professional Psychology, 24*, 426–432.

Quintana, S.M. and Holahan, W. (1992). Termination in short-term counseling: Comparison of successful and unsuccessful cases, *Journal of Counseling Psychology, 39*, 299–305.

Ramirez, M. (1991). *Psychotherapy and Counseling with Minorities: A Cognitive Approach to Individual and Cultural Differences*, New York: Pergamon.

Raskin, N.J. and Rogers, C.R. (1989). Person-centered therapy. In R.J. Corsini and D. Wedding, Eds., *Current Psychotherapies*, 4th Ed., Itasca, IL: F.E. Peacock, pp. 155–194.

Remley, T.P., Jr., (1993). Consultation contracts, *Journal of Counseling and Development, 72*, 157–158.

Richardson, B.L. (1991). Utilizing the resources of the African American church: Strategies for counseling professionals. In C.C. Lee and B.L. Richardson, Eds., *Multicultural Issues in Counseling: New Approaches to Diversity*, Alexandria, VA: ACA Press, Chapter 6.

Ridley, C.R., Mendoza, D.W., and Kanitz, B.E. (1994). Multicultural training: reexamination, operationalization, and integration, *The Counseling Psychologist, 22*, 227–289.

Rigazio-Digilio, S. (1993). Family counseling and therapy. In A. Ivey, M.B. Ivey, and Simek-Morgan, L., Eds., *Counseling and Psychotherapy: A Multicultural Perspective*, 3d Ed., Boston, MA: Allyn & Bacon.

Rimm, D.C. and Masters, J.C. (1979). *Behavior Therapy: Techniques and Empirical Findings*, 2d Ed., New York: Academic Press.

Roberts, A.R. (1990). *Crisis Intervention Handbook: Assessment, Treatment, and Research*, Belmont, CA: Wadsworth.

Roberts, A.R. and Roberts, B.S. (1990). A comprehensive model for crisis intervention with battered women and their children. In Roberts, A.R. (1990), *Crisis Intervention Handbook: Assessment, Treatment, and Research*, Belmont, CA: Wadsworth.

Rogers, C.R. (1957). The necessary and sufficient conditions of therapeutic personality change, *Journal of Consulting Psychology, 21*, 95–103.

Rogers, C.R. and Rablen, R.A. (1958). A scale of process in psychotherapy. Unpublished manuscript, University of Wisconsin. (Available in mimeo from Center for Studies of the Person, La Jolla, CA.)

Rosenthal, T. and Steffek, B. (1991). Modeling methods. In F.H.Kanfer and A.P. Goldstein, Eds., *Helping People Change*, 4th Ed., New York: Pergamon, 70–121.

Rowe, W., Murphy, H.B., and DeCsipkes, R.A. (1975). The relationship of counseling characteristics and counseling effectiveness, *Review of Educational Research, 45*, 231–246.

Rychlak, J.F. (1973). *Introduction to Personality and Psychotherapy*, Boston: Houghton Mifflin.

Sage, G.P. (1991). Counseling American Indian Adults. In C.C. Lee and B.L. Richardson, Eds., *Multicultural Issues in Counseling: New Approaches to Diversity*, Alexandria, VA: ACA Press.

Salter, A. (1949). *Conditioned Reflex Therapy*, New York: Farrar, Straus and Giroux.

Schein, E.H. (1978). The role of the consultant: Content expert or process facilitator? *Personnel and Guidance Journal, 56*, 339–343.

Schulman, N.M. (1990). Crisis intervention in a high school: Lessons from the Concord High School experiences. In Roberts, A.R. (1990), *Crisis Intervention Handbook: Assessment, Treatment, and Research*, Belmont, CA: Wadsworth.

Sexton, T.L. and Whiston, S.C. (1994). The status of the counseling relationship: An empirical review, theoretical implications, and research directions, *The Counseling Psychologist, 22*, 6–78.

Shainberg, D. (1993). *Healing in Psychotherapy*, 2d Ed., Y–Parc, Switzerland: Gordon & Breach.

Shapairo, F. (1989). Eye movement desensitization: A new treatment for post-traumatic stress disorder, *Journal of Behavior Therapy and Experimental Psychiatry, 20*, 211.

Sherman, R. and Fredman, N. (1986). *Handbook of Structured Techniques in Marriage and Family Therapy*, New York: Brunner/Mazel.

Shertzer, B.E. and Stone, S.C. (1980). *Fundamentals of Counseling*, 3d Ed., Boston: Houghton Mifflin.

Sluzko, C.E. (1978). Marital therapy from a systems theory perspective. In Thomas J. Paolino, Jr. and Barbara S. McCrady, Eds., *Marriage and Marital Therapy*, New York: Brunner/Mazel, Chapter 7.

Smith, K.L., Subich, L.M., and Kalodner, C. (1995). The transtheoretical model's stages and processes of change and their relation to premature termination, *Journal of Counseling Psychology, 42*, 34–39.

Smith, M.L. and Glass, G.V. (1977). Meta-analysis of psychotherapy outcome studies, *American Psychologist, 32*, 752–760.

Snygg, D. and Combs, A. (1949). *Individual Behavior*, New York: Harper & Row.

Speight, S.L., Myers, L.J., Cox, C.I., and Highlen, P.S. (1991). A redefinition of multicultural counseling, *Journal of Counseling and Development, 70*, 29–36.

Spooner, S.E. and Stone, S. (1977). Maintenance of specific counseling skills over time, *Journal of Counseling Psychology, 24*, 66–71.

Steenbarger, B.N. (1993). A multicontextual model of counseling: Bridging brevity and diversity, *Journal of Counseling and Development, 72*, 8–15.

Stevenson, H.C. and Renard, G. (1993). Trusting ole' wise owls: Therapeutic use of cultural strengths in African-American families, *Professional Psychology: Research and Practice, 24*, 433–442.

Stone, H. and Winkelman, S. (1989). *Embracing Ourselves: The Voice Dialogue Manual*, Sherman Oaks, CA: Delos, Inc.

Strong, S. (1968). Counseling: An interpersonal influence process, *Journal of Counseling Psychology, 15*, 215–224.

Strong, S. and Claiborn, C. (1982). *Change Through Interaction: Social Psychology Processes of Counseling and Psychotherapy*, New York: Wiley-Interscience.

Strong, S. and Schmidt, L. (1970). Expertness and influence in counseling, *Journal of Counseling Psychology, 17*, 81–88.

Sue, D.W. (1992). Derald Wing Sue on multicultural issues: An interview, *Microtraining Newsletter*, North Amherst, MA, p. 6.

Sue, D. W. and Sue, D. (1990). *Counseling the Culturally Different, Theory and Practice*, 2d Ed., New York: Wiley.

Szapocznik, J. and Kurtines, W.M. (1993). Family psychology and cultural diversity: Opportunities for theory, research and application, *American Psychologist, 48*, pp. 400–407.

Szapocznik, J., Santisteban, D., Kurtines, W.M., Perez–Vidal, A., and Hervis, O. (1984). Bicultural effectiveness training: A treatment intervention for enhancing adjustment in Cuban American Families, *Hispanic Journal of Behavioral Sciences, 6*, 317–344.

Tata, S.P. and Leong, F.T.L. (1994). Individualism-collectivism, social-network orientation, and acculturation as predictors of attitudes toward seeking professional psychological help among Chinese Americans, *Journal of Counseling Psychology, 41*, 280–287.

Taussig, I.M. (1987). Comparative responses of Mexican-Americans and Anglo-Americans to early goal-setting in public mental health clinics, *Journal of Counseling Psychology, 34*, 214–217.

Teyber, E. (1992). *Interpersonal Process in Psychotherapy*, 2d Ed., Pacific Grove, CA: Brooks/Cole.

Thompson, C.L. and Rudolph, L.B. (1992). *Counseling Children*, 3d Ed., Pacific Grove, CA: Brooks/Cole.

Thorne, B., Kramarae, C., and Henley, N., Eds. (1983). *Language, Gender, and Society*, Cambridge, MA: Newbury House.

Tomine, S.I. (1991). Counseling Japanese Americans: From internment to reparation. In C.C. Lee and B.L. Richardson, Eds., *Multicultural Issues in Counseling: New Approaches to Diversity*, Alexandria, VA: ACA Press.

Turner, W.T. (1993). Identifying African-American family strengths, *Family Therapy News, 24*, 9, 14.

Turock, A. (1980). Immediacy in counseling: Recognizing clients' unspoken messages, *Personnel and Guidance Journal, 59*, 168–172.

Tran, N.C. (1981). Counseling Vietnamese women in transition, *Helping Indochinese Families in Transition Conference*, [Compiled proceedings]. University of Nebraska, Lincoln, May 11–12.

Usher, C.H. (1989). Recognizing cultural bias in counseling theory and practice: The case of Rogers, *Journal of Multicultural Counseling and Development, 17*, 63–71.

Vásquez, J.M. (1991). Puerto Ricans in the counseling process: The dynamics of ethnicity and its societal context. In C.C. Lee and B.L. Richardson, Eds., *Multicultural Issues in Counseling: New Approaches to Diversity*, Alexandria, VA: ACA Press.

Visher, E. and Visher, J. (1988). *Old Loyalties, New Ties: Therapeutic Strategies with Stepfamilies*, New York: Brunner/Mazel.

Vontress, C.E. (1985). Existentialism as a cross-cultural counseling modality. In P. Pederson, Ed., *Handbook of Cross-Cultural Counseling and Therapy*, Westport, CT: Greenwood, pp. 207–212.

Vontress, C.E. (1988). Social class influences on counseling. In R. Hayes and R. Aubrey, Eds., *New Directions for Counseling and Human Development*, Denver, CO: Love, pp. 346–364.

Waehler, C.A. and Lenox, R.A. (1994). A concurrent (vs. stage) model for conceptualizing and representing the counseling process, *Journal of Counseling and Development* (In press).

Walen, S., DiGuiseppe, R., and Dryden, W. (1992). *A Practitioner's Guide to Rational-Emotive Therapy*, 2nd Ed., San Francisco: Jossey/Bass.

Ward, D.E. (1984). Termination of individual counseling: Concepts and strategies, *Journal of Counseling and Development, 63*, 21–25.

Warren, R., McLellarn, R., and Ponzoha, C. (1988). Rational-emotive therapy vs. general cognitive behavior therapy in the treatment of low self-esteem and related emotional disturbances, *Cognitive Therapy and Research, 12*, 21–38.

Watson, D.L. and Tharp, R.G. (1993). *Self-directed Change: Self-Modification for Personal Adjustment*, 6th Ed., Pacific Grove, CA: Brooks/Cole.

Watzlawick, P., Weakland, J., and Fisch, R. (1974). *Change: Principles of Problem Formation and Problem Resolution*, New York: W.W. Norton.

Weakland, J. Fisch, R., Watzlawick, P., and Bodin, A. (1974). Brief therapy: Focused problem resolution, *Family Process, 13*, 141–168.

Wegscheider, S. (1981). *Another Chance*, Palo Alto, CA: Science & Behavior Books.

Wegscheider-Cruse, S., Cruse, J., and Bougher, G. (1990). *Experiential Therapy for Co-dependency*. Palo Alto, CA: Science and Behavior Books.

Weiss, L. (1986). *Dream Analysis in Psychotherapy*, New York: Pergamon.

West, J.D. (1988). Marriage and family therapy assessment, *Counselor Education and Supervision, 28*, 169–180.

West, J.F. and Idol, L. (1993). The counselor as consultant in the collaborative school, *Journal of Counseling and Development, 71*, 678–683.

Westbrook, F.D., Kandell, J.J., Kirkland, S.E., Phillips, P.E., Regan, A.M., Medvene, A., and Oslin, Y.D. (1993). University campus consultation: Opportunities and limitations, *Journal of Counseling and Development, 71*, 684–688.

White, P.E. and Franzoni, J.B. (1990). A multidimensional analysis of the mental health of graduate counselors in training, *Counselor Education and Supervision, 29*, 258–267.

Whitman, J. and Verrone, T. (1992). *Things That Make You Go Hmmm*. Unpublished manuscript, West Virginia University, Morgantown, WV.

Wilson, G.T. and Agras, W.S. (1992). The future of behavior therapy, *Psychotherapy, 29*, 39–43.

Wilson, G.T., Rossiter, E., Kleifield, E.I., and Lindholm, L. (1986). Cognitive behavioral treatment of bulimia nervosa: A controlled evaluation, *Behavior Research & Therapy, 24*, 277–288.

Wolpe, J. (1958). *Psychotherapy by Reciprocal Inhibition*, Stanford, CA: Stanford University Press.

Wolpe, J. (1982). *The Practice of Behavior Therapy*, 3rd ed., New York: Pergamon.

Wolpe, J. and Lazarus, A.A. (1966). *Behavior Therapy Techniques*, New York: Pergamon.

Wolpe, J. (1990). *The Practice of Behavior Therapy*, 4th Ed., New York: Pergamon.

Wrenn, C.G. (1962). The culturally encapsulated counselor, *Harvard Educational Review, 32*, 444–449.

Wrenn, C.G. (1985). Afterward: The culturally encapsulated counselor revisited. In P. Pederson, Ed., *Handbook of Cross-cultural Counseling and Therapy* (pp. 323–329). Westport, CT: Greenwood.

Yost, E.B., Beutler, L.E., Corbishley, M.A., and Allender, J.R. (1986). *Group Cognitive Therapy: A Treatment Method for Depression in Older Adults*, New York: Pergamon.

Zajonc, R.B. (1980). Feeling and thinking: Preferences need no inferences, *American Psychologist, 35*, 151–175.

Zuk, G. (1975). *Process and Practice in Family Therapy*, Haverford, PA: Psychiatry and Behavioral Science Books.

TO THE OWNER OF THIS BOOK:

We hope that you have found *The Professional Counselor* useful. So that this book can be improved in a future edition, would you take the time to complete this sheet and return it? Thank you.

School and address: _____

Department: _____

Instructor's name: _____

1. What I like most about this book is: _____

_____

2. What I like least about this book is: _____

_____

3. My general reaction to this book is: _____

_____

4. The name of the course in which I used this book is: _____

_____

5. Were all of the chapters of the book assigned for you to read? ___

    If not, which ones weren't? _____

6. In the space below, or on a separate sheet of paper, please write specific suggestions for improving this book and anything else you'd care to share about your experience in using the book.

_____

_____

Optional:

Your name: _____     Date: _____

Please mail to:
    Allyn and Bacon Publishing Co.
    160 Gould St.
    Needham Heights, MA 02194
    Att: Ray Short

# Index